Licensing Intellectual Property

Intellectual Property Series

How to License Technology by Robert C. Megantz

Intellectual Property Infringement Damages: A Litigation Support Handbook by Russell L. Parr

Intellectual Property: Licensing and Joint Venture Profit Strategies by Gordon V. Smith and Russell L. Parr

Law and the Information Superhighway: Privacy, Access, Intellectual Property, Commerce, Liability by Henry H. Perritt, Jr.

Licensing Intellectual Property: Legal, Business, and Market Dynamics by John W. Schlicher

Managing Intellectual Property Rights by Lewis C. Lee and J. Scott Davidson

Multimedia Legal Handbook: A Guide From the Software Publisher's Association by Thomas J. Smedinghoff

The New Role of Intellectual Property in Commercial Transactions by Melvin Simensky and Lanning G. Bryer

Protecting Trade Dress by Robert C. Dorr and Christopher H. Munch

Protecting Trade Secrets, Patents, Copyrights, and Trademarks by Robert C. Dorr and Christopher H. Munch

Software Industry Accounting by Joseph M. Morris

Software Patents by Gregory A. Stobbs

Technology Licensing Strategies by Russell L. Parr and Patrick H. Sullivan

Valuation of Intellectual Property and Intangible Assets, Second Edition by Gordon V. Smith and Russell L. Parr

Licensing Intellectual Property: Legal, Business, and Market Dynamics

John W. Schlicher

John Wiley & Sons, Inc.
New York • Chichester • Toronto • Brisbane • Singapore

This text is printed on acid-free paper.

Copyright © 1996 by John Wiley & Sons, Inc.

All rights reserved. Published simultaneously in Canada.

Reproduction or translation of any part of this work beyond
that permitted by Section 107 or 108 of the 1976 United States
Copyright Act without the permission of the copyright
owner is unlawful. Requests for permission or further
information should be addressed to the Permissions Department,
John Wiley & Sons, Inc., 605 Third Avenue, New York, NY
10158-0012.

This publication is designed to provide accurate and
authoritative information in regard to the subject
matter covered. It is sold with the understanding that
the publisher is not engaged in rendering legal, accounting,
or other professional services. If legal advice or other
expert assistance is required, the services of a competent
professional person should be sought.

Library of Congress Cataloging in Publication Data:
Schlicher, John W.
    Licensing intellectual property: legal, business, and market
    dynamics / John W. Schlicher.
      p. cm. — (Intellectual property library)
    Includes bibliographical references.
    ISBN 0-471-15312-5 (cloth : alk. paper)
    1. Patent licenses—United States. 2. License agreements—United
States. 3. Intellectual property—United States. I. Title.
II. Series: Intellectual property library (John Wiley & Sons)
KF3145.S35 1996
346.7304'8—dc20
[347.30648]   96-33703

Printed in the United States of America

10 9 8 7 6 5 4 3 2 1

SUBSCRIPTION NOTICE

This Wiley product is updated on a periodic basis with supplements to reflect important changes in the subject matter. If you purchased this product directly from John Wiley & Sons, Inc., we have already recorded your subscription for this update service.

If, however, you purchased this product from a bookstore and wish to receive (1) the current update at no additional charge, and (2) future updates and revised or related volumes billed separately with a 30-day examination review, please send your name, company name (if applicable), address, and the title of the product to:

>Supplement Department
>John Wiley & Sons, Inc.
>One Wiley Drive
>Somerset, NJ 08875
>1-800-225-5945

For customers outside the United States, please contact the Wiley office nearest you:

Professional & Reference Division
John Wiley & Sons Canada, Ltd.
22 Worcester Road
Rexdale, Ontario M9W 1L1
CANADA
(416) 675-3580
1-800-567-4797
FAX (416) 675-6599

John Wiley & Sons, Ltd.
Baffins Lane
Chichester
West Sussex, PO19 1UD
UNITED KINGDOM
(44) (243) 779777

Jacaranda Wiley Ltd.
PRT Division
P.O. Box 174
North Ryde, NSW 2113
AUSTRALIA
(02) 805-1100
FAX (02) 805-1597

John Wiley & Sons (SEA) Pte. Ltd.
37 Jalan Pemimpin
Block B # 05-04
Union Industrial Building
SINGAPORE 2057
(65) 258-1157

This book is dedicated to my lovely and gracious wife and advisor Susan and our children Heather, William, and Kate, whose academic accomplishments make writing this book look simple.

About the Author

John W. Schlicher practices law with Fish & Neave in its Palo Alto, California office. His patent prosecution, counseling, and licensing work relates to the biotechnology, pharmaceutical, diagnostic, medical device, and chemical industries. His counseling and licensing work has also involved the computer, software, electronics, and semiconductor industries. He was formerly Associate General Counsel of Genentech, Inc. and worked as a scientist at Stanford University and Syntex Corporation. He is also a Lecturer in Law at Stanford Law School teaching a course on patent law (including licensing). He is listed in *Who's Who in American Law*.

For many years, Mr. Schlicher has served as the chair of committees on patents and licensing of the American Intellectual Property Law Association, the American Bar Association (ABA) Patent Section, and the ABA Antitrust Section. He has spoken frequently at national conferences on intellectual property or licensing, including the Antitrust program sponsored by the Conference Board and the Technology Licensing program sponsored by the Practising Law Institute. In 1986, he organized the licensing program for a national meeting of the American Intellectual Property Law Association.

He has testified before the Patent and Trademark Office on biotechnology patents, and before the Senate Judiciary Committee on intellectual property and licensing. He has advised the Department of Justice on antitrust and intellectual property, and the Office of Technology Assessment on its report on commercial biotechnology. He took an active role in numerous legislative proposals on licensing, such as the National Productivity and Innovation Act of 1983, the Intellectual Property Rights Improvement Act of 1986, the Omnibus Trade Bill of 1987, and the Patent Licensing Reform Act of 1988. He has also testified as an expert witness on licensing. He was appointed to the National Panel of Patent Arbitrators of the American Arbitration Association.

ABOUT THE AUTHOR

Mr. Schlicher is the author of the treatise "Patent Law: Legal and Economic Principles" (Clark, Boardman, Callaghan 1992). This book has been relied on by the Court of Appeals for the Federal Circuit. He also wrote the original draft of Chapter VIII, "Antitrust Issues Involving Intellectual Property: Patents, Copyrights, Trademarks and Trade Secrets," of the ABA—Antitrust Section's authoritative book on antitrust law, *Antitrust Law Developments* (2d ed. 1984). He also contributed the chapter "An Introduction to the Antitrust and Misuse Limits on Commercial Exploitation of a Patent" to an early book on biotechnology, *Banbury Report 10: Patenting of Life Forms* (1982).

He has published many articles on patent and licensing topics, including:

"Tying Arrangements Involving a Patent License," *Current Trends in Domestic and International Licensing of Technology,* Practising Law Institute (No. 112, 1979)

"The Patent Arbitration Law: A New Procedure for Resolving Patent Infringement Disputes," *The Arbitration Journal,* American Arbitration Association (1985)

"Judicial Regulation of Patent Licensing, Litigation and Settlement Under Judicial Policies Created in *Lear v. Adkins,*" American Intellectual Property Law Association, Selected Legal Papers (1985)

"Some Thoughts on the Law and Economics of Government Regulation of Licensing Patent and Related Intellectual Property Rights in the United States, the EEC and Japan," American Intellectual Property Law Association, Continuing Legal Education Institute (February 3–5, 1986)

"Some Thoughts on the Law and Economics of Licensing Biotechnology Patent and Related Property Rights in the United States," *Technology Licensing 1987,* Practising Law Institute (1987), pages 333–385, and *Journal of the Patent and Trademark Office Society* **69,** 263 (1987)

"Comments on Reverse Engineering and Patents," in *Reverse Engineering: Legal and Business Strategies* (Prentice Hall, 1992)

"If Economic Welfare Is the Goal, Will Economic Analysis Redefine Patent Law?" in *Journal of Proprietary Rights* **4,** 12 (Prentice Hall, 1992)

ABOUT THE AUTHOR

"Department of Justice Antitrust Policy, Economic Growth, and Intellectual Property Licensing," *Intellectual Property/Antitrust 1993*, Practising Law Institute (1993)

"Biotechnology, Patent Law and Economics," in *The Patent Office at Stanford* (Stanford Law School 1994).

Mr. Schlicher graduated with highest distinction from Northwestern University, majoring in chemistry, and received his law degree from Stanford University. He is a member of the national honorary societies for liberal arts (Phi Beta Kappa), chemistry (Phi Lambda Upsilon), and science (Sigma Xi).

Contents

Preface   **xxv**

1 The Business of Licensing Intellectual Property Rights   **1**

    1.1 Technology, Licensing, and Law   3
    1.2 The Commercial Value, Cost, and Risk of Technology   5
    1.3 A Market Perspective on Intellectual Property Rights to Technology   9
        (a) Self-Help   11
        (b) Contracts   12
        (c) Trade Secrets   13
        (d) Patents   15
        (e) Copyrights   16
        (f) Licensing   18
    1.4 The Commercial Value of Intellectual Property Rights   18
        (a) Demand for Rights Depends on Demand for Tangible Products and Processes Embodying the Rights   18
        (b) Demand for Rights Depends on Future Costs of Producing and Selling (or Using) Tangible Embodiments, Not Sunk Costs   19
    1.5 An Example of the Demand for Intellectual Property Rights   20
    1.6 The Business Decision to Exploit Rights by Vertical Integration or by Licensing   23

	(a)	Where Vertical Integration and Licensing Are Equally Efficient and Profitable	24
	(b)	Where Vertical Integration and Licensing Are Not Equally Efficient and Profitable	27
1.7	Factors that Influence the Profitability of Licensing		30
	(a)	The Time Horizon for Profit-Maximizing Business Decisions	30
	(b)	Product Pricing (and Royalties) May Affect the Long Run Industry Output and Price	31
	(c)	Royalty Rates and Structure Will Affect Industry Output, Price, and Licensing Profits	32
	(d)	Royalty Rates and the Licensee Profits— What Profits Matter and Is There a Universally Ideal Relationship?	33
	(e)	The Royalty Base—Unit Sales	35
	(f)	The Royalty Base—Sales Revenue	35
	(g)	The Royalty Base—Profits	36
	(h)	The Royalty Base—Lump Sum Payments	37
	(i)	The Royalty Base—A License under Licensee's Rights	38
1.8	Licensing Negotiations in View of Bargaining Problems, Licensee Alternatives, Transaction Costs, Intellectual Property Litigation, and Risk		39
	(a)	The Expected Value and Cost of the License	39
	(b)	Payments and Small Number Bargaining Problems	41
	(c)	Payments and the Substitute Technologies Available to the Potential Licensees	42
	(d)	An Example of the Effect of Substitute Technologies Available to the Potential Licensees	43
	(e)	The Transaction Costs of Licensing	47
	(f)	The Expected Value and Cost of Litigation Rather than Licensing	48
	(g)	The Risk of Licensing and Litigation	53
1.9	An Overview of Licensing Strategy		57

	(a)	Provisions to Maximize and Capture Demand	57
	(b)	Provisions to Decrease Transaction Costs	61
	(c)	Provisions to Decrease Uncertainty and Risk	61
	(d)	Provisions to Reduce the Licensee's Ability to Substitute Other Rights	62
1.10		Licensing Strategy, Terms, and Profits	63
	(a)	Controlling the Supply and Price of Licenses under the Rights	63
	(b)	Using Different Terms for Licensees with Different Demands	64
	(c)	Terms to Induce Licensee Investments	69
	(d)	Licensing to Increase Asset-Specific Investment by Product Customers	72
	(e)	Terms to Induce Licensee Investments and Limit Licensee Output Restriction	74
	(f)	The Impact of Monospsony (Negotiating with a Single Potential Licensee)	77
	(g)	Adjusting the Terms to Provide the Proper Scale of Production by Licensees	78
	(h)	Terms to Induce Licensees to Use Inputs in the Right (Low-Cost) Proportions	82
	(i)	Increasing Demand for the Rights by Increasing the Supply of Complementary Products	83
	(j)	Increasing Demand for the Rights by Increasing the Supply of Complementary Technology	84
	(k)	Practices that Reduce the Transaction Costs	86
	(l)	Terms to Reduce the Costs of Uncertainty and Litigation about Rights	87
	(m)	Controlling Rivalry from Substitute Rights Produced and Owned by Others	88
1.11		An Overview of How the Law Limits Licensing Practices	89

2 The Law of Licensing Intellectual Property Rights   93

2.1   The Legal Limits on Licensing   95
2.2   An Introduction to Intellectual Property Law   95
    (a)   Patent Law   95
    (b)   Copyright Law   97
    (c)   Trade Secret Law   97
2.3   The Legal Theories of Intellectual Property Rights to Technology   99
    (a)   Property Rights   100
    (b)   Monopoly Rights   102
    (c)   Regulated Natural Monopoly Rights   109
    (d)   A "Public" Contract   110
2.4   Fundamental Legal Concepts of Licensing   112
2.5   The Limits on Licensing under Antitrust, Misuse, and Public Policy Doctrines   114
2.6   Antitrust Standards   116
2.7   Misuse Standards   124
    (a)   The Supreme Court Creates the Misuse Defense—*Morton Salt*   125
    (b)   The Misuse Defense Beyond Practices Categorically Condemned by the Supreme Court—*Windsurfing, USM,* and *Mallinckrodt*   132
    (c)   The Patent Act and the Judicial Standards   141
2.8   The Public Policy Standard   146
2.9   A Brief History of the Legal Limits on Licensing   147
    (a)   Legislation   147
    (b)   Judicial Decisions   149
    (c)   Tying   149
    (d)   Exclusive Dealing   151
    (e)   Package Licensing   151
    (f)   Royalties   152
    (g)   Resale Restrictions on Field of Use   152
2.10   The Economic Principles Underlying Legal Limits on Licensing Patent and Related Rights   153
    (a)   Markets and Competition   153

	(b)	An Illustration of the Effects of Anticompetitive Agreements and Conduct	155
	(c)	Markets, Competition, and Technical Information	157
	(d)	Markets, Competition, and Intellectual Property Law	157
	(e)	An Illustration of the Effects of Intellectual Property Law	158
	(f)	Intellectual Property as Monopoly in Legal Doctrine	160
2.11	The Basic Options of Intellectual Property Owners		164
	(a)	Capture the Commercial Value of the Rights Other than by Limiting Rivalry with Substitute Rights	165
	(b)	Increase the Profitability of Supplying Rights or Products by Limiting Rivalry with the Cooperation of Suppliers of Substitute Rights or Substitute Products	165
	(c)	Increase the Profitability of Supplying Rights or Products by Limiting Rivalry without the Cooperation of Suppliers of Substitutes	166
2.12	The Law and the Basic Options of Intellectual Property Owners		166
	(a)	Licenses that Primarily Limit Rivalry among Suppliers of Substitute Products	167
	(b)	Licenses that Primarily Limit Rivalry among Suppliers of Substitute Rights	168
	(c)	Licenses that Limit Rivalry in Markets beyond the Scope of the Rights by "Foreclosing" Other Suppliers of "Unprotected" Products	170
	(d)	Evaluating the Potential Effects of Licensing in Markets for Products beyond the Reach of the Rights	172
	(e)	The Time Horizon for Judging Anticompetitive Effects	173

3 The Decision to License and Payments for Licenses — 175

- 3.1 Acquiring Rights — 177
- 3.2 Refusing to Use or License — 178
- 3.3 The Amount of Royalty Payments — 181
- 3.4 The Relation of Royalty Payments to the Scope of the Patent — 185
  - (a) The *Zenith* Rule on Royalty Payments — 185
  - (b) The Competitive Effects — 186
  - (c) Procompetitive Reasons for Basing Royalties on Patented and Unpatented Products — 190
  - (d) An Alternative Interpretation of the *Zenith* Rule — 191
- 3.5 The Relation of Royalty Payments to the Patent Term — 192
  - (a) The *Brulotte* Rule on Royalty Payments — 192
  - (b) The Competitive Effects — 193
  - (c) Procompetitive Reasons for Basing Royalties on a Term Extending Beyond the Rights — 196
  - (d) Other Implications of *Brulotte* — 197
- 3.6 The Relation of Royalty Payments to the Value of Rights in Different Uses or to Different Users—Discriminatory Royalties — 200
  - (a) The Shrimp Peeler Rule on Royalty Payments — 200
  - (b) The *USM* Rule on Royalty Payments — 202
  - (c) The Competitive Effects — 202
  - (d) Procompetitive Reasons for Discriminatory Royalties — 204
  - (e) Baxter's Parable Illustrating the Market Effects of Discriminatory Royalties — 204
- 3.7 The Relation of Royalty Payments to the Value of Rights to Different Users—Royalties Proportional to Use of a Patented Machine — 211
- 3.8 The Relation of Royalty Payments to the Value of Rights to Different Users—

		Royalties Payable by Licensed Sellers and Licensed Buyers of a Single Product	213
	3.9	Sharing Royalties with Licensees	215
	3.10	Licensing in Exchange for Rights—Grantbacks	216
		(a) The *Transparent-Wrap* Rule	216
		(b) The Applications of *Transparent-Wrap*	221
		(c) The Competitive Effects	224

4 The Nature of Products and Rights Supplied Together—Tying and Package Licensing — 227

	4.1	Supplying Tangible Products with a License—Tying Arrangements	229
	4.2	The Law Applied to Tying Arrangements	229
	4.3	The Theory of Tying—Acquiring a "Limited Monopoly" beyond the Scope of the Rights	239
	4.4	The Competitive Effects of Tying Arrangements	239
		(a) Supply All Complements—Full Vertical Integration	240
		(b) Supply the Protected Product—Partial Vertical Integration	240
		(c) Supply the Protected Product with an Express Royalty-Bearing License—Partial Integration with Economic Discrimination	241
		(d) Supply the Protected Product at Price Proportional to Intensity of Use—Partial Integration with Economic Discrimination	241
		(e) Supply the Protected Product and a Complementary Product to Meter Intensity of Use—Partial Integration with Economic Discrimination	242
		(f) Supply the Protected Product and a Complementary Product that Would Be Supplied by a Single Seller—	

		Reducing the Harm from Monopoly Supply of a Complement	243
	(g)	Supply the Protected Product and a Complementary Product at Prices that Encourage Use in Low-Cost Proportions	243
	(h)	Supply the Protected Product and a Complementary Product to Assure Compatibility and Quality	244
	(i)	Supply a Complementary Product to Reduce the Transaction Costs of Express Licensing	244
	(j)	Supply the Protected Product and a Complementary Product to Acquire Market Power in Supply of the Complement	246
4.5	The Leading Decisions and Statutes on Extending the Rights		247
	(a)	*Heaton-Peninsular Button-Fastener*	247
	(b)	*Henry v. A.B. Dick*	250
	(c)	*Motion Picture Patents*	251
	(d)	*Carbice*	258
	(e)	*Leitch*	262
	(f)	*Morton Salt* and *B.B. Chemical*	264
	(g)	The *Mercoid* Cases	265
	(h)	*Special Equipment*	272
	(i)	The 1952 Amendment to the Patent Act	273
	(j)	*Dawson*	274
	(k)	The 1988 Amendment to the Patent Act	278
4.6	Licensing More than One Patent or Copyright in a Single Agreement—Package Licensing		279
	(a)	The Law	279
	(b)	The Theory of the Law on Package Licensing	287
	(c)	Royalties and Package Licensing	287
	(d)	The Competitive Effects	289

CONTENTS

5 The Nature and Scope of Licensed Rights—Exclusivity, Field of Use, Price, Quantity, Territory, Customer, and Cross-Licensing — **291**

- 5.1 Assigning the Rights to Others — 293
- 5.2 Granting an Exclusive License — 295
- 5.3 Exclusive Dealing—Restrictions Against a Licensee Dealing in Substitute Products — 297
- 5.4 Field of Use Restrictions — 299
  - (a) The *General Talking Pictures* Rule on Limited Fields of Use — 300
  - (b) The Competitive Effects — 303
  - (c) The *General Talking Pictures* Rule on Field of Use Limits on Purchasers from a Licensee — 304
  - (d) The Application of the Rule on Field of Use Limits on Purchasers from a Licensee — 304
  - (e) The Application of the Rule on Field of Use Limits to Products Made by a Patented Process — 306
- 5.5 Price Restrictions — 307
  - (a) The Competitive Effects — 308
  - (b) The *General Electric* Rule — 309
  - (c) Price Limits under Cross-Licensed Patents—*Line Material* — 311
  - (d) Price Limits on Resale—*Bauer* — 312
  - (e) Resale Price Limits—*Univis Lens* and *Ethyl Gasoline* — 313
  - (f) Price Limits in Licenses used for Cartel Administration — 314
- 5.6 Quantity Restrictions — 314
  - (a) The Law — 315
  - (b) The Competitive Effects — 318
- 5.7 Territorial Limitations — 319
- 5.8 Customer Limitations — 322
- 5.9 Cross-Licensing and Limitations on the Grant of Licenses — 322

CONTENTS

6	Licenses Deemed to Arise From Sale of a Product—Implied Licenses and Exhaustion of Rights	337
	6.1 Licenses Arising from the Sale of a Product	339
	6.2 A License May Be Express or Implied	340
	6.3 The Circumstances that Imply a License	341
	6.4 The Legal Theory of Exhaustion	348
	6.5 The Origins of the Exhaustion Doctrine—*Bloomer*	351
	6.6 Exhaustion Applies Only to Authorized, Unconditional Sales—*Mitchell*	354
	6.7 Some Early Applications of Exhaustion—*Adams, Hobbie, Keeler*	357
	6.8 The Development of Antitrust and Misuse Limits to Exhaustion—*Henry, Bauer, Motion Picture Patents*	363
	6.9 The Modern Exhaustion Doctrine	366
	(a) *Univis Lens*	366
	(b) *General Talking Pictures*	367
	(c) *Mallinckrodt*	372

7	The Limits on Licensing Under the Doctrine of Federal Preemption	375
	7.1 Federal Preemption and the State Law of Licensing	377
	7.2 Patent Invalidity as a Defense to Royalty Obligations	378
	7.3 A Licensee May Show Patent Invalidity if Part of an Antitrust Defense to Royalty Obligations	379
	7.4 A Licensee May Defend an Action for Royalties by Proving on Patent Invalidity—*Lear*	383
	(a) The Doctrinal Basis for *Lear*	383
	(b) The Decision on Licensee Estoppel	385
	(c) The "Decision" on the Enforceability of Payment Terms of Patent Licenses	387
	(d) The Effects of Licensee Estoppel and a Licensee's Agreement to Pay Regardless of Validity	388
	(e) When Do Royalty Obligations End under *Lear?*	393

	(f)	The Enforceability of a Licensee's Express Agreement Not to Challenge Validity	397
	(g)	Antitrust and Misuse Implications of Agreements Not to Assert Invalidity	401
	(h)	The Enforceability of Termination Provisions	402
7.5		The Enforceability of Trade Secret and Know-how Licenses—*Kewanee*	403
7.6		The Enforceability of Royalty Obligations in Patent and Know-how Licenses—*Aronson*	407
7.7		The Enforceability of Royalty Obligations in Licenses Made in the Context of Litigation—Consent Judgments and Settlement Agreements	410
7.8		The Enforcement of Patents Against Parties to Assignments and Exclusive Licenses	413

Index **417**

Preface

The business and legal environment for licensing has changed over the past fifteen to twenty years. This book is designed to help people understand and take advantage of the new situation.

During this period, R&D opportunities expanded in many important industries—health care, electronics, computers, telecommunications, and others. The number of companies and organizations seeking to pursue and exploit those R&D opportunities exploded. Many of these entities had the talent and resources for R&D, and not for production and marketing. Organizations with little or no chance of vertical integration strove to develop and acquire important intellectual property rights. Licensing expanded as intellectual property rights owners and integrated producers strove to sort out the situation to their mutual advantage.

Licensing also expanded for fully integrated companies as scale economies (in research, production, and consumption), the frequent need for customers to make technology-specific investments, and other factors increased the opportunities for solutions involving partial integration through contracts. Research and development (R&D) and licensing deals even acquired some fancier-sounding names—corporate partnering and strategic alliances.

The legal environment for licensing also changed dramatically during this period. However, the driving forces did not directly involve the business community. During the 1980s, the intellectual property rights owners' traditional enemy, the Antitrust Division of the Justice Department, became their most effective ally. Under Bill Baxter's leadership, the Division threw out an enforcement policy that for years had effectively bullied intellectual property rights owners into avoiding many potentially useful license practices. The Division also tried to increase licensing freedom as part of a major legislative initiative.

The formal legal constraints on licensing also changed. During the late 1970s and 1980s, several thoughtful federal court judges changed the way antitrust and misuse laws limited licensing options. They insisted that the law should interfere with a voluntary license only if someone showed that the transaction would harm the process of competitive rivalry. They said it was no longer enough to simply offer some farfetched theory about how harm might result.

Perhaps to avoid missing out entirely on these efforts to improve the country's economic productivity, Congress also joined the movement with amendments to the antitrust and patent laws.

These legal changes were aided from another—and some would say—unlikely source, the nation's law schools and economics departments. Several law and economics professors developed a better understanding of industrial organization, contracts, and business behavior. They vigorously criticized the existing legal constraints on business deals and activities. Their analysis laid the conceptual basis for the judicial and legislative action.

This new legal environment has expanded the range of licensing options. Due to these changes, lawyers and business professionals operating within the confines of the old law are missing valuable opportunities. As you have probably detected, I prefer the expanded freedom. Many of the old legal restraints on conducting business were counterproductive for the people and businesses of the country.

APPROACH

How does one go about understanding and profiting from the new situation? The most direct approach is to learn and apply the concepts and methods that lead to the legal changes. The new methods do not treat law and business behavior as separate subjects. These methods integrate issues of law and business organization. That is the approach of this book. There are several benefits to understanding both the contractual incentives and the law of licensing.

First, it is impossible to plan, write, or negotiate the best license

PREFACE

without some business model. How does one select a sensible pricing rate and structure without some way of measuring the value of the rights to the potential licensee and predicting the impact of the deal on the licensee and the market? Is the price too high, too low, or just about right? How does one choose among alternative contract terms without understanding the incentives those terms create for the licensee or licensees?

Second, the United States is a free-market economy, but that does not mean executives in technology companies are free to do whatever they want. The government regulates licensing with an astonishing array of legal devices:

> Antitrust law (a federal system in this context),
>
> Misuse law (a subset of some intellectual property laws),
>
> Public policy doctrine (a rule that appeared out of nowhere in particular), and
>
> Preemption doctrine (a constitutional doctrine to protect the federal government's laws from interference by a state government's law).

The penalties for crossing the legal boundaries are severe. These laws can nullify or modify the parties' agreement, render the underlying rights unenforceable, require the owner to grant licenses on terms it may not unilaterally set, and subject the parties to monetary and criminal liability. Since the 1980s, the legality of most licensing strategies and agreements depends on the likely effects of the license on industry structure and performance. Hence, in order to predict the legal consequences of a proposed practice, one must analyze the likely economic effects, and know what types of effects the law deems harmful.

Third, since the early 1980s, the antitrust enforcement policy of the U.S. government also has been based predominantly on economic analysis. Government antitrust enforcement policy is important because the federal government sometimes singles out technology producers for special antitrust attention. Economic success often attracts attention in Washington as well as on Wall Street. Today, those equipped with the best economic arguments are better able to deal with antitrust enforcers.

Fourth, the law sometimes judges agreements by legal standards different from those existing at the time the agreement was made. If the law changes, the courts sometimes apply the standards existing at the time of later litigation. This requires business people and lawyers to predict the future of the law. Crystal-ball gazing is, oddly, mandatory. The most powerful predictive tool of the direction of the law is an understanding of economic effects. The recent changes have been most strongly influenced by economic analysis, and there is no reason to expect that trend to change.

In sum, licensing executives and their lawyers are not able to predict the legality or profitability of licensing unless they understand the likely marketplace effects of alternative licensing strategies and terms. Those shooting blindfolded will occasionally hit the profit bull's-eye. In industries undergoing rapid technical change, luck is often as important as skill. Nonetheless, those shooting at a specific target will hit it much more often (and do far less unintended damage).

Of course, two traditional sources of business and legal decisions also have value. They are past industry practices and the thousands of judicial decisions that describe and rule on specific situations. These sources are the stuff of most books on licensing. In all endeavors, history is a powerful tool. An executive's working knowledge of past practices in an industry is very helpful, but it is not sufficient. There is always room for creativity in business as well as technology. And past practices may be misleading in a changing environment. If industry practices have not adapted quickly to the new situation (and it would seem they have not), many opportunities may be missed.

A lawyer's working knowledge of the facts and results in the reported cases is also no longer enough for business or legal decisions. Very few prior judicial decisions provide useful information about the marketplace effects of license practices and terms. Why? The law, at the time, did not determine legality based on those effects. Hence, the lawyers did not present them and the courts did not discuss them.

ORGANIZATION

This book is designed for business people as well as their professional advisors (lawyers, consultants, and accountants). It provides business professionals with a consistent framework for making decisions to license, for defining specific licensing objectives, and for accomplishing

PREFACE

those objectives at minimum legal risk. This book also provides lawyers with the modern law, an explanation of why the law is what it is and how to apply the law to develop better approaches to licensing, whether in a planning, deal-making, or litigation context.

The first long chapter of this book sets out the analytical framework for business decisions. It summarizes intellectual property rights from the perspective of a technology producer. It describes how the value of intellectual property rights is derived from the demand and costs facing commercial producers. It outlines the decision between vertical integration and licensing. It shows how royalty rates and structure will affect industry output, price, and profits. It tries to take some of the mystery out of the relationship between the licensee's profits and royalty rates. It sets out the incentives created by various rate bases for royalties. It describes a model, using a specific real-world example, of how license negotiations are influenced by

- Bargaining problems,
- Alternative technologies available to a potential licensee,
- The transaction costs of licensing,
- The realities of potential infringement litigation, and
- The many sources of risk.

Finally, this first part provides an overview of licensing strategy and lists the factors that most strongly influence essential terms, including

- Implementing economic discrimination,
- Inducing licensee and customer investments in asset-specific resources,
- Controlling licensee incentives to limit output,
- Limiting the licensee's incentives to substitute against a licensed component or material,
- Creating incentives for the development of improved technology,
- Reducing transaction costs,
- Reducing litigation and other sources of uncertainty, and
- Constraining the supply of substitute rights and products.

PREFACE

Again, the book illustrates the importance of these concepts with specific examples. It also describes the types of provisions often used to address those issues and identifies the corresponding legal issues.

Chapter 2 describes the legal framework. It also explains intellectual property rights from a legal perspective, and the antitrust, misuse, and "public policy" doctrines that courts apply to licensing practices. It provides a brief history of the development of the legal constraints to help the reader understand where the law has come from and where it is going. It then describes the basic strategic options of intellectual property owners and how the law limits those options. This chapter also discusses the legal concepts of markets, competition, monopoly, and the competitive effects of agreements.

The remaining chapters are devoted to particular license terms or situations. Chapter 3 discusses the decision to license and the payments and other forms of consideration by licensees. Chapter 4 covers when the intellectual property rights and tangible products should and may be supplied together. This involves the grandfather of all rules—the limits on tying arrangements—and its nephew—the rule against package licensing. Chapter 5 addresses the nature and scope of licensed rights. When should a licensee be granted exclusive rights and when should the licensee agree to deal exclusively in the licensed rights? When should the owner limit the licensee's field of operations, product price, quantity, customers, and territory? When is cross-licensing wise and lawful? Chapter 6 is devoted to two rules that create licenses the owner may not have intended to create—the implied license rule and the exhaustion doctrine. Chapter 7 explains the influence of federal preemption on payment terms and agreements about litigation.

DEBTS

I have been fortunate to have had the opportunity to learn and think about licensing from a variety of perspectives: planning, drafting, negotiating, and advising about agreements; studying the legal, business, and economic literature; litigating; speaking and writing to business and lawyer groups; working on legislation and government policy; working with

PREFACE

committees of lawyer organizations; and teaching law students at Stanford Law School. During these activities, I have learned from the comments and experience of many people. I will not attempt to name everyone who has contributed to my thinking on this subject.

But there is one large debt I must acknowledge. I am forever grateful to William F. Baxter of Stanford Law School, who taught me so much about intellectual property, antitrust, economics, and the way the world works. In the 1970s, Baxter introduced me to the sad state of legal regulation of licensing and the importance of the technology for the growth of the American economy. In the wonderful early 1980s, Baxter (as chief of the Antitrust Division of the United States Justice Department) led the effort to improve the legal climate for technological innovation. Tad Lipsky once called me a *Baxterian,* a title I try (but rarely succeed) to live up to.

I also wish to thank Norman E. Rosen, senior vice president and general counsel of General Electric subsidiary, GE and RCA Licensing Management Operation, and a licensing expert in every conceivable sense, for reviewing and providing valuable comments on a draft.

Finally, I wish to thank my publisher, John Wiley & Sons, and my editor, Marla Bobowick.

In all respects, the views expressed in this book are mine alone.

John W. Schlicher
January 1996

Licensing Intellectual Property

1

The Business of Licensing Intellectual Property Rights

1.1	Technology, Licensing, and Law	3
1.2	The Commercial Value, Cost, and Risk of Technology	5
1.3	A Market Perspective on Intellectual Property Rights to Technology	9
1.4	The Commercial Value of Intellectual Property Rights	18
1.5	An Example of the Demand for Intellectual Property Rights	20
1.6	The Business Decision to Exploit Rights by Vertical Integration or by Licensing	23
1.7	Factors that Influence the Profitability of Licensing	30
1.8	Licensing Negotiations in View of Bargaining Problems, Licensee Alternatives, Transaction Costs, Intellectual Property Litigation, and Risk	39
1.9	An Overview of Licensing Strategy	57
1.10	Licensing Strategy, Terms, and Profits	63
1.11	An Overview of How the Law Limits Licensing Practices	89

1.1 TECHNOLOGY, LICENSING, AND LAW

Technology is commercially important.[1] Technology is a key element of business strategy.[2] The growth of industries and companies depends primarily on their success or failure at producing, protecting, and commercializing better technology. Investments in technological improvements are driven by the quest for profits. Intellectual property rights often improve the rate of return to investments in technical change. These rights may permit technology producers to capture a larger part of the commercial value of the technology. The U.S. patent, copyright, and trade secret laws have existed throughout the technology-rich history of this country. Virtually every technology producer relies on intellectual property laws to preserve some advantage over others for some time.

Technology producers also decide how to exploit that technology by evaluating profit potential. There are two basic strategies: (1) full vertical integration into the business using the technology and (2) "partial vertical integration" by contract with technology users. The value of technology may be captured by integrating the technology into the producer's business. A technology producer may incorporate the technology into its products and production processes. However, full vertical integration into all uses and all markets is rarely the most profitable strategy. Partial vertical integration by contract is often preferable. These contracts almost always involve a written or unwritten license under intellectual property rights.

Contracts licensing intellectual property rights to technological information are limited by the usual market forces.[3] However, the price and

---

[1] Analysis of the value, cost, and risk of technology is summarized in the following section 1.2.
[2] For example, Michael E. Porter, *Competitive Strategy: Techniques for Analyzing Industries and Competitors* 1980 (The Free Press, New York).
[3] See generally, Edwin Mansfield, *Microeconomics, Theory and Applications* 1979 (Norton, New York) ("Mansfield"); George J. Stigler, *The Theory of Price* 1966

terms of licenses are not determined in a simple way by markets for rights. Technology owners and technology users cannot easily determine the price or terms for a license by identifying "going market" prices and terms. Most intellectual property transactions are not simple spot market sales. There are no national exchanges in which rights are traded.

One reason is that each bundle of licensed rights is unique. Therefore, each license is unique. If there is no uniqueness to the rights, there are very probably no rights the law will recognize and enforce, and nothing of value to license. Most users will not agree to pay for a license without evaluating the expected value of the particular rights to their business. Hence, there is no public market in licenses that provides price or other information pertinent to any particular license. The parties must generate this information.

More importantly, the price and other terms of a license will have important effects on the long-run demand and supply of products made and sold under the license. The price and terms of the license will affect the profits that "trickle up" to the owner or "trickle to" the licensee(s). This happens because the price and terms influence the incentives of the licensee(s). The behavior of the licensee(s) will influence the supply and demand for products incorporating the rights. The supply and demand for those products will determine the revenue and profits from operating under the license. The revenue and profits from licensed operations will determine the revenue and profits available to the owner.

For that reason, sophisticated owners and users of intellectual property rights try to understand and take advantage of the incentives the license creates. For that reason, this book discusses the contract incentives and market forces that determine how owners of rights take maximum advantage of the rights. The problem is essentially one of business organization by contract. How does an owner create, monitor, and enforce an agreement so that its licensee or licensees behave in the manner the owner would have ordained had they been part of the same company?[4]

(Macmillan, London) ("Stigler"). See very generally, Adam Smith, *The Wealth of Nations* 1776 (The Modern Library, New York).
[4] For an explanation of the best thinking on this general subject, see Paul Milgrom and John Roberts, *Economics: Organization and Management,* 1992 (Prentice Hall, Englewood Cliffs, N.J.) ("Milgrom and Roberts").

1.2 THE COMMERCIAL VALUE, COST, AND RISK OF TECHNOLOGY

This is the 1990s, not the 1890s when there were basically no legal constraints on licensing. Today, owners and users must know more than the business of licensing. Owners and users do not have unfettered control of the price and terms of their licenses. The law regulates their licenses with rules (and remedies) that compel attention. Owners and users of rights must adapt to a bewildering array of legal constraints to successfully maximize profits. The government as antitrust enforcer also from time to time looks over their shoulders.

1.2 THE COMMERCIAL VALUE, COST, AND RISK OF TECHNOLOGY

Technology is commercially valuable because technology is critical to industrial growth.[5] Technology is also critical to the growth and survival of individual companies.[6] A company with better technology may have an important competitive advantage. Technology may permit a company to provide customers with better and cheaper products. A technology advantage is often a key to long-run profitability.

Economic growth means that consumers and producers are sharing a larger and larger pie as time passes. *Business Week* recently reported that Robert Barro of Harvard calculated one measure of the impact of growth.[7] Real per-capita gross domestic product (GDP) of the United States grew by 1.75 percent per year from 1870 to 1990 to the world's highest level—from $2,224 to $18,258 (in 1985 dollars). Had the U.S. growth rate been 1 percent less (or 0.75 percent a year), then real U.S.

---

[5]There has been an enormous amount of empirical and theoretical work on the commercial dynamics and importance of research and development. Valuable sources are: F.M. Scherer, *Innovation and Growth,* 1984 (MIT Press, Cambridge); Zvi Griliches (ed.), *R&D, Patents, and Productivity,* 1984 (University of Chicago Press, Chicago); William D. Nordhaus, *Invention, Growth, and Welfare,* 1969 (MIT Press, Cambridge); Edwin Mansfield, *Industrial Research and Technological Innovation,* 1968 (Norton, New York); Jacob Schmookler, *Invention and Economic Growth,* 1966 (Harvard Press, Cambridge); Joseph A. Shumpeter, *Capitalism, Socialism, and Democracy, 1942 (Harper, New York).*

[6]*Business Week,* "How R&D Spending Pays Off," in *Innovation in America,* 1989 (special issue) at 177.

[7]*Business Week,* "Productivity to the Rescue," October 9, 1995, 134–146.

per-capita GDP in 1990 would have been $5,519. This means that the total value of goods and services produced in the United States in 1990 adjusted for inflation and divided by the U.S. population would have been about the same as Mexico and $1,000 less than Portugal. While GDP per capita is larger than personal consumption per capita, the implication of this calculation is clear enough to anyone who has visited Mexico.

There have been many efforts to measure the contribution of technology to economic growth. Michael Boskin and Laurence Lau recently estimated that nearly 70 percent of the growth in United States industrial output from 1948 to 1985 was due to the combined effects of technical progress and capital growth.[8] Technology alone accounted for about 50 percent of the growth in total output. Over that period, output grew at an average annual rate of 3.1 percent. Boskin and Lau also assessed the relative contributions of capital, labor, and technical progress in France, West Germany, Japan, the U.K., and the United States over the period roughly 1957 to 1985. Their analysis showed that over this period "technical progress is by far the most important source of economic growth, accounting for half or more (three-quarters for the European countries). . . ."[9]

Another way to think about technology is to imagine what you would have to do without if technology had not changed since 1948. You would travel long distances by train or propeller-driven airplane (not by jet); drive a car with manual transmission and steering (not an automatic transmission and power steering); cook with gas or electric coils (not with a microwave oven); calculate with pencil and paper, slide rule, or mechanical adding machine (not with pocket calculator or spreadsheet software); process numbers and other information with paper and mechanical machines (not by pocket calculator or personal computer); send letters by mail (not by fax); prepare documents with a typewriter (not with a computer and word processing software); copy documents with

---

[8]Michael J. Boskin and Laurence J. Lau, *Capital, Technology, and Economic Growth*, in N. Rosenberg, R. Landau, and D.C. Mowery, eds., *Technology and the Wealth of Nations*, 1992 (Stanford University Press, Stanford California). They measure industrial output by the Gross Domestic Product, the value of goods and services produced in the United States. They also summarize the results of other studies trying to measure the contribution of technology progress on economic growth.
[9]Id. at 46–49.

1.2 THE COMMERCIAL VALUE, COST, AND RISK OF TECHNOLOGY

carbon paper or ditto machine (not with an office copier); listen to records (not CDs or tapes); watch movies at theaters (not on your VCR); play board games (not video games); and record family events with a still camera (not with a video camera).

Consider health care over a longer period, 1920 to the present. According to a report by the Boston Consulting Group, in 1920, some of the leading causes of death in the United States were tuberculosis, syphilis, diphtheria, whooping cough and measles.[10] Death rates from those causes fell over 90 percent after the introduction of related vaccines and antibiotics. According to that report, between 1960 and 1991, new drugs reduced the death rate from cardiovascular disease by over 20 percent, early infant disease by over 80 percent, peptic ulcers by over 60 percent, kidney infections by well over 80 percent, and influenza by over 90 percent. As a result of these and other health improvements, the average life expectancy of people in the United States increased from 54 years in 1920 to 75 years for those born in 1990. While this dramatic change in life expectancy may cause great difficulty for government planners trying to run health care and retirement subsidy programs, it is a wonderful development for the rest of us.

Technology is valuable. Technology is also expensive to produce. New technology, like lunch, is not freely produced. In the period 1953 to 1984, total annual U.S. research and development (R&D) investment has been estimated as between 1.40 to 2.66 percent of gross national product (GNP), increasing over time from $8.7 to $42.9 billion stated in 1972 dollars.[11] In 1985, total U.S. nondefense R&D expenditures were about $74 billion (or 1.8 percent of GNP).[12]

Private investors directly provide the bulk of R&D investment. In 1984, private (that is, nongovernment) R&D investment in the United States was about 54 percent of that total R&D (1.44 percent of GNP).[13] In 1987, U.S. companies invested $91 billion in R&D (2.4 percent of

---

[10] The Boston Consulting Group, Report on "Sustaining Innovation in U.S. Pharmaceuticals," (January 1996). This report was sponsored by several major pharmaceutical companies in relation to proposed changes to the Patent Act.
[11] David C. Mowrey and Nathan Rosenberg, *Technology and the Pursuit of Economic Growth,* 1989 (Cambridge University Press, Cambridge) at 125–127.
[12] Id. at 207–209.
[13] Id. at 129.

business sector GNP), constituting 64 percent of total R&D.[14] In 1990, the private sector directly provided about 66 percent of total worldwide R&D investment of $138 billion.[15] In many industries, the direct private share of total R&D costs is much higher. In 1990, privately financed expenditures in the chemical, food and beverage, and petroleum products industries exceeded 98 percent of the total.[16] Those investments speak volumes about the commercial importance of technology. "Private sector" companies and individuals also paid the "government" share of those R&D investments through tax payments. The fact that the money flowed through the government does change its source.

Many companies reinvest 6 to 10 percent of their current revenue in research and development. According to government data, in 1977, the pharmaceutical industry reinvested 10.8 percent of its sales revenue in R&D.[17] The computer industry reinvested 8.9 percent of sales. The semiconductor industry reinvested 6.1 percent of sales. Companies in the pharmaceutical industry invest between 12 percent and 19 percent of revenue in R&D.[18] As Mike Scherer, a leader in analyzing the dynamics and economics of R&D, has said, "Company-financed R&D is without doubt a profit-seeking activity."[19] Thousands of small privately funded startup companies invest in R&D amounts that are several hundred percent greater than their revenue. For all these companies, these investments make sense only if they pay off and, for this latter group of companies, pay off an amount several times larger than the investment.

Investing in technology is also risky. Unlike most other available investments (that is, investments other than hunting for sunken Spanish sailing ships full of gold and trading commodity futures), investing in an R&D project has an unusually low probability of a positive payoff.

---

[14] F.M. Scherer and David Ross, *Industrial Market Structure and Economic Performance,* 1990 (Houghton Mifflin, Boston) ("Scherer and Ross") at 615.
[15] Ralph Landau and Nathan Rosenberg, "Successful Commercialization in the Chemical Process Industries," in N. Rosenberg, R. Landau, and D.C. Mowery, eds., Technology and the Wealth of Nations, 1992 (Stanford University Press, Stanford California).
[16] Id. at 73–74.
[17] Scherer and Ross at 615–616.
[18] The Boston Consulting Group, Report on "Sustaining Innovation in U.S. Pharmaceuticals," (January 1996).
[19] F.M. Scherer, *Innovation and Growth,* 1984 (MIT Press, Cambridge) at 286.

1.3 A MARKET PERSPECTIVE

Mike Scherer guestimated the riskiness of R&D.[20] He used studies by Edwin Mansfield (another giant in the study of the commercial importance of R&D) on the probability of commercially successful R&D projects, and a variety of other data suggesting the actual cost of successful R&D projects in the mid-1970s and the annual R&D budgets of large manufacturing (Fortune 500) companies. For a prototypical company about the size of the two hundred fiftieth largest U.S. company, Scherer divined that each year the firm would have 48 projects underway, each with a $2.5 million cost over three years. Each year, only four of the 48 current projects would deliver a return greater than the firm's opportunity cost of capital. The probability of success is less than 10 percent.

In some industries, the likelihood of success is much lower. According to one report, only about 1 in 6000 compounds tested in pharmaceutical industry R&D projects becomes a commercial product.[21] This report also said that the average investment in R&D and in obtaining government permission to sell each new drug was $500 million, and that investment was made over an average period of 12 to 15 years before the first sale. Risk is important because private investors demand a higher return for investments in uncertain activities.

Technology provides great benefits to American companies and consumers, and requires large investments in expensive and risky research and development. Long ago, these characteristics of technology attracted the attention of law makers.

1.3 A MARKET PERSPECTIVE ON INTELLECTUAL PROPERTY RIGHTS TO TECHNOLOGY

I use *intellectual property* to refer to any law that creates privately owned rights protecting technological information from unauthorized use. U.S. companies produce antibiotics instead of snake oil, personal computers instead of typewriters, telephones instead of telegraphs, and airlines instead of trains and buses. They do so because of the information they

---

[20] Scherer and Ross at 620.
[21] The Boston Consulting Group, Report on "Sustaining Innovation in U.S. Pharmaceuticals," (January 1996).

possess about therapeutics, data processing, communications, and transportation.

For the last two hundred years, the United States has had patent, copyright, and trade secret laws to create private rights to technological information. Owners may agree not to assert those rights against certain people. These agreements are often licenses. For about the last one hundred years, the law has also regulated licensing the rights.

Intellectual property laws can appear to be complex, detailed, and sometimes arbitrary sets of rules. This perception is partially deserved. However, intellectual property law has one unifying concept that helps explain the nature of the rights and the legal limits on licensing. Those uninterested in the economic or legal ideas underlying intellectual property law may wish to skip this section. The essentials of intellectual property laws are described in Chapter 2.

Intellectual property rights prohibit certain uses of technical information about the nature and characteristics of physical products and processes. The information is intangible. The best and simplest way to understand intellectual property laws is to view those laws as attempts to increase investment of resources in producing information (patents and trade secrets) or in disseminating information (copyrights).[22] Why should the law be concerned?

A market may misdirect resources if private producers do not take into account the effects of their activities on the welfare of other people who have not agreed to be affected in that way. These effects may be harmful or beneficial to others. Those harms or benefits are sometimes called *externalities*.[23] In the absence of corrective rules, producers of information are likely to provide external benefits for others.

---

[22]This book is directed primarily to technology licensing. Little will be said about trademarks and trademark licensing. Trademarks are generally treated as a branch of intellectual property law. Trademark law is best understood as a rule to increase investment in activities that reduce the searching or shopping costs of consumers. One form of such an investment is the cost of maintaining a predictable level of product quality over time. For an explanation of trademarks, see J. Thomas McCarthy, *Trademarks and Unfair Competition* (Clark Boardman Callagan, New York).

[23]George J. Stigler, *The Citizen and the State: Essays on Regulation,* 1975 (University of Chicago Press, Chicago) at 104–105 ("An external effect of an economic decision is an effect, whether beneficial or harmful, upon a person who is not a party to the decision. If my neighbor's carelessness in storing gasoline causes my house to burn, and he does not compensate me, this is an externality of his decision. If the

1.3 A MARKET PERSPECTIVE

Since a producer's use of technical information in producing goods and services may require disclosure to competitors and users, others may benefit from the technology without being required to pay. There are many ways a producer of technology may lose exclusive possession of it. Rivals may learn the information by studying products incorporating it. Former employees may carry the information to rivals. Suppliers and customers who need the information may disclose it to rivals.

In these and other ways, information may become available to users who contributed nothing to the producer. A portion of the total demand for the information is satisfied without dealing with the producer. The commercial value the information producer expects to capture is lower than the actual value of the information. Information producers who anticipate being unable to capture all of that value will invest too few resources producing information.

Technical information has another characteristic. To use Kenneth Arrow's term, information is *indivisible*.[24] Information is indivisible in the sense that its production costs are fixed. Once the information has been produced, no additional (or marginal) information-producing costs need be incurred to make the first and all following uses of the information. One person's use of information does not interfere with use by anyone else. Arrow characterized the externality problem by saying information is *inappropriable*. Products having those two characteristics are sometimes called public goods.

(a) Self-Help

This problem does not mean that, absent law, profit-oriented people would produce no commercially valuable technical information. Even if

---

parties to a decision do not reckon in the costs that will fall on others, they may undertake activities which are harmful from the viewpoint of society as a whole. If the parties to a decision do not reckon in benefits which accrue to others, they may spurn activities which would be socially advantageous. Private decisions will not lead to a maximum of satisfaction unless externalities are negligible; or, to use essentially equivalent language, resources are not used with maximum efficiency unless all the results, good and bad, of an investment (that is, its marginal social product) accrue to the person making the investment.").

[24] Kenneth J. Arrow, "Economic Welfare and the Allocation of Resources for Invention," in *The Rate and Direction of Inventive Activity,* 1962 (Princeton University Press, Princeton) at 619–625.

contracts relating to information were not enforced, trade secret law never prohibited acquiring information from rivals, and patents and copyrights did not exist, producers would still try to deal with this problem.

Producers would exploit their product or process designs in their own operations and take security precautions to avoid disclosure to others. They would run companies with locked files, numbered documents, need-to-know rules, guards, small staffs (preferably members of the producer's family), compartmentalized research and production, devices to conceal key design features of products and so on. Self-help measures are likely to be expensive, inefficient, and only partially successful. For example, self-help measures are frequently impossible for product designs. New product designs may become available to competitors and users by mere observation or reverse engineering.

(b) Contracts

If the law enforces contracts, profit-oriented producers and users will also try to use contracts to increase production of commercially valuable technical information. Technical information produced and supplied under contracts is frequently called know-how. Producers and users of information will think about agreeing that a producer will produce a new product or process design, supply it to the users, and the users will pay an agreed fee for that service. Producers and users will try to use contracts to reduce the harmful incentives of information externalities. If business people could solve this problem themselves, the law need merely enforce the agreements and then get out of the way.[25]

The law will enforce contracts dealing with production and use of information. However, contracts will not alone solve the externality problem for all designs, because transaction costs and strategic bargaining problems are enormous. Transaction costs are the costs of gathering information about contract opportunities, preparing and negotiating terms, monitoring performance, and enforcing agreements. It is plainly too costly to expect a market to arise in which the potential ben-

---

[25]Ronald H. Coase, "The Problem of Social Cost," *Journal of Law and Economics* **3**, 1 (1960); Guido Calabresi, "Transaction Costs, Resource Allocation and Liability Risks—A Comment," *Journal of Law and Economics* **11**, 67 (1968) and Harold Demsetz, When Does the Rule of Liability Matter?, *Journal of Legal Studies* **1**, 13 (1972).

1.3 A MARKET PERSPECTIVE

eficiaries of all technical innovations always make prior agreements with potential suppliers when that will produce mutual benefits.

Even if the information, negotiation, and enforcement costs could be overcome, there are two major bargaining problems. First, the producer cannot guarantee that only users who are parties to the agreement will have access to the information. The information may become available to nonparties. Each potential user may believe that enough other people will cooperate to produce it without his or her help. Some users may decide not to contribute and hope to enjoy the information for free. They will hold out and hope to free-ride on the contribution of others. This *free-rider* problem makes such agreements difficult.

Second, the parties have very different information about the value of the rights, and incentives to misstate their true evaluations for strategic reasons. Under the contract and trade secret regimes, the rights are not known to both parties prior to entering into an agreement. The supplier has little incentive to make the information available to the user until that user has agreed to pay. The user has difficulty agreeing to pay without knowing what it is paying for. This information gap between producer and user prevents the price from accurately reflecting the real value of the information to them.

Certain technologies are more amenable to the contract solution than others. In general, contracts are likely to be most profitable where the number of potential producers is small, the number of potential users is small, the information about the cost of production and value in use is certain and inexpensive to obtain, and the prospects for a free-rider to benefit from the invention without paying are small because self-help measures are not costly (for example, the technology may be exploited by use in a well-guarded plant and known only to a small number of very well paid personnel).

(c) Trade Secrets

In order to create better incentives for information production, the law intervened with trade secret law. Lawyers and judicial decisions talk about trade secret law as a doctrine of contact law, tort law, property law, and "commercial morality" law. A better view is that trade secret law simply attempts to reduce the transaction costs of contracts and the costs of self-help measures.

THE BUSINESS OF LICENSING INTELLECTUAL PROPERTY RIGHTS

Trade secret law gives certain rights to a producer of information that is not generally available to potential users and that is potentially valuable in production of goods or services. The law gives the right to preclude use of trade secrets by two types of people. First, the law permits the producer to preclude use by those who acquired the information from it as part of a voluntary transaction in which the acquirer "agreed" implicitly to use the information only for the benefit of the producer and then used it in other ways. Second, the law permits the producer to preclude use by those who acquired the information by an activity that overcame reasonable self-help measures and that produced no other benefits, such as by theft of documents from the possessor's plant or flying over a facility under construction. Trade secret law prohibits external benefits in these circumstances.

Trade secret law supplements the contract system. Trade secret doctrines close the divergence between real and private value of information by reducing the costs of making contracts and self-help measures. Contracting costs are reduced, because trade secret law provides confidentiality provisions for a variety of consensual relationships even though the parties do not incur the costs of negotiating about restrictions on disclosure and use. The law provides a confidentiality "provision" where the efficiency of the transaction would be improved by the provision. The parties need not expressly provide this term. This reduces the transaction costs of preproduction and postproduction information transactions between producers and users.

In most states, the law will imply obligations of nondisclosure and nonuse only if the information qualifies as a trade secret. This means the information must not have been generally available to the public. If there was an easily accessible public source of the information, the law will not impose these obligations even though the person receiving the information under some type of contract did not know it. A person without the information may be perfectly happy to pay for it even though there are other ways he or she might have acquired it. People pay small fortunes to universities to (they hope) dispense information that is widely known and cheaply accessible in libraries and book stores. People who need technical information also are willing to pay for the knowledge that the law will not protect as a trade secret. However, the parties to this exchange must expressly provide the obligations of the recipient.

1.3 A MARKET PERSPECTIVE

Trade secret law also reduces the costs of self-protective measures, such as document security systems and giant tents over construction sites. Trade secret rules impose liability on users who obtain information by activities that overcome self-help security measures and that have no productive value other than permitting someone to acquire the information. Permitting a user to acquire information in that way only forces producers to waste money on better self-help security measures.

(d) Patents

The law did not stop with contracts and trade secrets. The third legal device for dealing with the externality issue is to create exclusive rights in certain information about products and processes called inventions. Patent law is the property law for intangible technical information. Patent law gives the first producer rights to exclude in the same manner as personal and real property laws give rights to exclude to the owner of tangible things and land.[26]

However, the rights protected by these legal devices are different and work in a somewhat different way. Property law for a tangible machine gives the owner exclusive rights to possess, use, dispose of or transfer the thing owned. The owner of U.S. patent rights to the same machine does not also become the owner of all machines covered by the patent. The owner of the patent rights has the right to exclude others from making covered machines and to exclude the owners of covered machines from using or selling them in the United States.

However, the owner of a machine may also exclude the patent owner from possessing, using and transferring his or her machines. While the courts have sometimes had a difficult time understanding the difference, patent rights are entirely separate from so-called personal property rights, and may be exchanged separately. This allocation of rights sets the stage for some people to specialize in designing machines and others to specialize in making and selling them. These people can

---

[26] For an explanation of patent law, see John W. Schlicher, *Patent Law: Legal and Economic Principles,* 1992 (Clark Boardman Callagan, New York); Herbert F. Schwartz, *Patent Law and Practice,* 1988 (Federal Judicial Center, Washington, D.C.).

exchange their rights in a way that permits production and sale of products incorporating the contributions of both.

There is a similar allocation of rights among owners of different patents. The owner of U.S. patent rights to one invention embodied in a machine has the right to exclude others from making and selling machines using that invention. However, the patent does not give the patent owner the right to make and sell the machine. If the machine also embodies an invention patented by someone else, the owner of this patent may exclude the other patent owner from using its invention. This allocation of rights also sets the stage for mutually beneficial cooperation between people specializing in different parts of a technological puzzle embodied in any product or process.

Patent law assigns to the *first creator* (the first inventor) the right to obtain a patent. The patent gives the owner the right to exclude others from using certain product and process information in the production or sale of goods or services. For the limited term, all such users and sellers are excluded, whether they reverse engineered the design or independently developed it. Patent law increases the private value of producing information without preproduction agreements or self-help measures. Patent law makes preproduction agreements with users unnecessary. The users will be excluded, unless they agree to pay. Self-help is unnecessary because the rights do not depend on preserving secrecy or on how a user acquired the information.

In general, patents are granted on inventions that were not cheaply available by searching for and reading a particular item of the prior art or by assembling several items of prior art and combining them with a relatively low-cost, low-risk effort in adding to them to obtain the invention. In other words, patents are granted for inventions for which the cost of producing the invention from the prior art is significant in terms of resources, time, and risk. If an invention is found in an item of prior art or could be produced from the prior art at very low cost, the system declines to grant rights to it on the assumption that it will be produced in any event at about the same time.

(e) Copyrights

The fourth legal device is copyrights for those who author original "works" in some tangible medium from which the "work" may be per-

1.3 A MARKET PERSPECTIVE

ceived, reproduced, or otherwise communicated.[27] Copyright protects original expressions of information embodied in tangible objects that people could use to learn the information. Copyright may protect one description of the technology useful in producing goods and services. Copyright does not protect the information actually embodied in a good or service; patents do.

Viewed in this way, copyright is directed to avoiding externalities that result from the creation of, for example, the written description of a product and the publishing of copies of that description. Copyright does not seek to prevent externalities that arise from creation of design of the product and selling the product itself. Copyright prevents others from making and distributing copies of a written description of a product to increase the incentives to write and publish product descriptions. Copyright grants no general right to prevent all use of the copyrighted description of a good. Copyright gives no right to prevent others from reading the copy in which the description is embodied and building the product described.

The purpose of copyright is to increase incentives to make descriptions of goods available for people to refer to and to learn about goods. Building a product based on a copyrighted description is not prohibited, because the product design itself is not protected. A product itself is an "invention" that is protectible only by the patent rights. Any use of a product description that does not decrease incentives to make descriptions of goods available for people to learn about goods is not prohibited. The basic activity prohibited by copyright is the making and distribution of copies of a description made by copying from the copyright owner (that is, by actually free-riding on information he or she produced). Those activities appropriate the protectible parts of the description.

The law sometimes has a difficult time deciding whether certain types of activities are more appropriately treated under the patent regime or the copyright regime. Piano rolls describe music and also permit player pianos to produce music. Accounting ledgers describe an accounting system and also permit people to use the system. Computer software describes various operations to perform on data and also permits computers to carry out those operations. The law often struggles with

---

[27]For an explanation of copyright law, see Paul Goldstein, *Copyright* (Little Brown, Boston).

such dual use products. The issue is not as difficult as the legal developments in the software area make it appear. However, that subject is beyond the realm of this book.

(f) Licensing

A license authorizes a person, usually called a *licensee,* to do things that would violate one or more of the rights.[28] The rights are violated by certain activities of people or companies. A license provides the owner's authority for the licensee to act in ways that would otherwise be infringement.

1.4 THE COMMERCIAL VALUE OF INTELLECTUAL PROPERTY RIGHTS

(a) Demand for Rights Depends on Demand for Tangible Products and Processes Embodying the Rights

Intellectual property rights prohibit certain uses of technical information about the nature and characteristics of physical products and processes. The information is intangible. However, intellectual property rights generally prohibit acts involving tangible things that embody the information. For example, patent rights preclude making, selling, or using products that incorporate the protected invention. Patent rights do not preclude others from drawing the product on a piece of paper or describing it in a document. Copyrights preclude others from reproducing or distributing material objects that contain the protected work and from which the work may be perceived or communicated.

The rights are generally designed to permit the owner to capture the value of tangible things that incorporate the protected information. The rights are violated when the information is combined with tangible

---

[28]*General Talking Pictures Co. v. Western Electric Co.,* 304 U.S. 175, 181 (1931) ("The Transformer Company . . . was a mere licensee under a non-exclusive license, amounting to no more than 'a mere waiver of the right to sue'."), on rehearing, 305 U.S. 124 (1938).

1.4 THE COMMERCIAL VALUE

resources and put into practice. The rights seek to protect the profits available from the sale and use of tangible embodiments.

The value of proprietary rights to intangible ideas is derived from the actual or expected market value of their physical embodiments. The amount people will pay for any intellectual property right is derived from the amount people will pay for the physical products (or processes) that may not be sold to (or used by) them without the permission of the owner of that right. However, the value of the rights is not the same as the market value of a product embodying the rights. Consumers usually buy a license bundled with a product. The license is generally not transferred to consumers and priced separately from the product. When the rights are licensed separately, it becomes clear that the value of the rights is different from the value of the product.

For simplicity, assume the license is being negotiated after the rights owner has produced the protected information and secured the rights and before the buyer has commenced production or use. Whether the rights are sold to a producer or consumer, the buyer must obtain and pay for the tangible resources and processes needed to make the product. The rights are merely one thing that the buyer needs to obtain a product. The buyer must pay for other things needed to make a tangible product—further research and development, a manufacturing facility, raw materials, labor, marketing, distribution, other necessary rights and so on. The owner may negotiate only for what is left over after the buyer has recovered those costs. This game is worth the effort because the leftovers can be huge.

(b) Demand for Rights Depends on Future Costs of Producing and Selling (or Using) Tangible Embodiments, Not Sunk Costs

For purposes of this discussion, it is assumed the owner of intellectual property rights is negotiating a license to rights already developed. The owner's costs of producing the information are sunk. It is also assumed a potential licensee's costs of using the information are not sunk. In this situation, a potential licensee has the alternative of rejecting the license and not incurring R&D, production, and marketing costs. Accordingly, a potential licensee will pay no more than the difference between the value it may capture from exploiting the rights and the average total cost of doing so, including some return to the licensee's investment in fixed assets. The owner may negotiate only for what is likely to be left over after the licensee has recovered those costs plus some return on invested capital.

This sunk cost problem does not always work against the owner. If the potential licensee ventured into production and sale without a license, and the "licensee" already incurred some significant, specialized fixed costs for plant, equipment, and marketing, the price for the license will be higher than it would have been if negotiated before those investments. If an infringing company cannot sell the specialized fixed assets, it will accept a license and continue production if the amount left over after payment is sufficient to cover variable costs for materials, labor, and the like.

Similarly, if a license is negotiating for rights before the protected information is produced and the rights secured, the price for the license may increase because the prospective owner's production costs are future costs. The prospective owner can threaten not to incur those costs. While there are important factors that work in the other direction in pre-production licenses, such as the "licensee's" possible cost-sharing, risk-taking, and ability to create the rights independently, the sunk cost problem also helps the "owner" in that situation.

The important point is that the price for the license will depend on the time of the negotiation and on which party will bear future costs. The price for the license will not depend on the amount of past (that is, sunk) costs.

1.5 AN EXAMPLE OF THE DEMAND FOR INTELLECTUAL PROPERTY RIGHTS

The value of a license cannot exceed the difference between consumers' demand for products or processes that embody the rights and the licensee's average future costs of producing those products or processes. The nature of this derived demand for intellectual property rights is illustrated in Figure 1.1. The vertical axis is the price or cost of buying or

1.5 AN EXAMPLE OF THE DEMAND

(a)
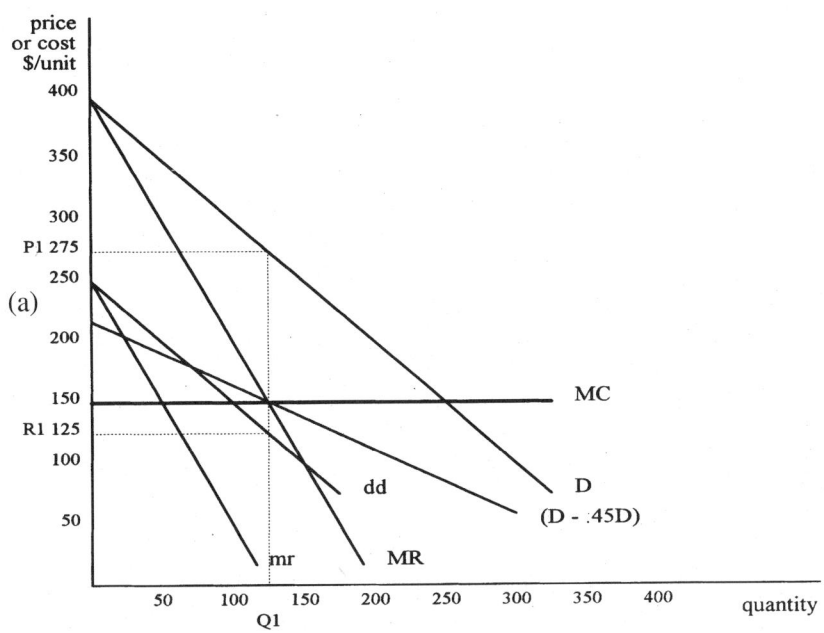

The Demand for Intellectual Property Rights

(b)
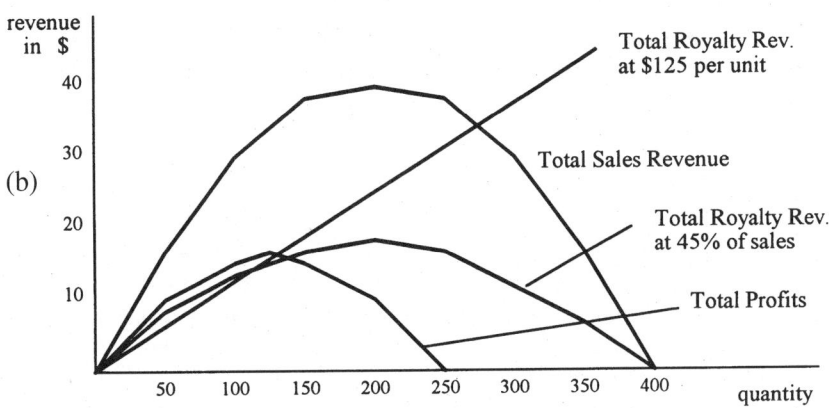

Revenue and Profits from Product Sales and Licensing

Figure 1.1

producing a product in dollars. The horizontal axis is the number of units of a product supplied or demanded at various prices.

The curve D is the annual demand for a patented product over the term of the license.[29] For simplicity of illustration, assume that demand does not change over time, and that this year's price will not affect total market product demand over time. There are no network externalities or other demand-side scale economies. The curve D shows the quantity consumers will buy at the prices shown on the vertical axis. This curve shows the average per unit revenue earned each year at each level of output. The availability and price of substitute products limit the price that consumers will pay for the patented product. The only lawful way to capture any part of the value of the product reflected in this demand curve, D, is to use the rights.

Assume the average annual total cost per unit of producing and selling the product over the period of the license is $150 per unit. I include as part of this "cost" a sufficient return to the producer's capital investment in plant, equipment, and other fixed costs to induce those investments in this situation. As with demand, assume that unit costs do not change over time. There are no cost reductions from learning by doing. Assume here that the average total cost of producing and selling each unit is the same regardless of the quantity produced. That means that there are also no scale economies in production or distribution, and that total quantity will be provided by many optimally sized and operated facilities. Given that assumption, the long-run cost of producing the last unit, the marginal cost, will be constant and will be the same as the average total cost of producing each unit. The curve MC shows this average and marginal per-unit cost of producing the product. MC shows the quantity that suppliers will produce given the price of the product.

---

[29]For an explanation of the basics of demand and supply analysis, see Scherer and Ross, ch. 2; Mansfield, ch. 2, 5, and 7–9; Stigler, ch. 4, 6, 10, 11. For a shorter explanation geared to licensing and antitrust, see W.F. Baxter, "Legal Restrictions on Exploitation of the Patent Monopoly," *Yale Law Review* **76**, 267 (1966) (appendix). For an explantion generally geared to antitrust, see Richard A. Posner, *Antitrust Law: An Economic Perspective,* 1976 (University of Chicago Press, Chicago) (appendix).

1.6 THE BUSINESS DECISION TO EXPLOIT RIGHTS

The maximum value of rights to an owner, its "derived demand," is equal to product demand of consumers, D, minus the licensee's production costs, MC. For any quantity of product, the maximum that licensees will pay for the rights is the market price for that quantity, shown by D, minus the production cost of a licensee supplying that quantity, shown by MC. If we subtract unit cost from price at each output level, we obtain an amount per unit shown by the curve dd. The derived demand for the rights is shown by the curve dd. The maximum amount a licensee will pay is the area between that product demand and the cost of producing that product at each output level.

Assume that one person sells the product at a single price to all consumers. There are no opportunities to charge different prices to customers who value the product differently. If the product is sold by a single seller at a single price, the additional or "marginal revenue" received by selling each additional unit is shown as MR. The marginal revenue from an additional sale is lower than the price for that level of sales because a lower price is now charged for the last unit and the units that could have been sold at a higher price. If a single per-unit royalty is charged for all sales, the marginal revenue from licensing is shown as the curve mr.

Rights owners and potential licensees will typically not know the demand and supply schedules shown in Figure 1.1 with the precision implied in that figure. Typically, they will negotiate the license based on less certain information about expected prices and costs at different outputs. However, those negotiations will be based on each party's information or assumptions about expected price, cost, quantity, and profit. This uncertainty about the future is not important to the concepts illustrated in this section. Uncertainty will become important later in this chapter.

1.6 THE BUSINESS DECISION TO EXPLOIT RIGHTS BY VERTICAL INTEGRATION OR BY LICENSING

How can an owner go about making a decision to vertically integrate or license? This decision is complex, because business is complex. If business were not complex, there would be no company presidents paid over a million dollars a year, and no business schools. If licensing were not complex, there would also be no vice presidents for licensing (or business development), no licensing groups in law firms, and (most unfortunately) no books on licensing. One way to deal with complexity is to simplify the problem, deal with the simple form, and then deal with (or ignore) more complex versions.

(a) Where Vertical Integration and Licensing Are Equally Efficient and Profitable

In order to simplify this discussion, some basic assumptions need to be made. This is not a exhaustive list, but it is a useful start.

1. Assume that the nature of the product designed and sold, the consumers' demand for the product, and the cost of producing it do not depend on who designed, made, or sold it. The rights owner and all potential licensees could and would produce exactly the same product at the same cost and sell it with the same effectiveness.

2. An important feature of the first assumption is that the value of the product sold to consumers does not depend on licensees making investments that could provide benefits to other licensees who do not make similar investments. There could be "price competition" among several licensees with no penalty from inadequate incentives for licensee investments in product or process improvements (that is, technology) or in distribution or marketing activities specific to the licensed product.

3. Assume also that long-run demand will not depend on the number of product suppliers. The reason for licensing is not that a vertically integrated owner needs to induce customers to make investments that depend on assurances of future supply and safeguards against future price increases. Second sourcing is not necessary.

4. Assume that long-run demand will also not depend on the current price. The price charged in one year will not affect the total demand

1.6 THE BUSINESS DECISION TO EXPLOIT RIGHTS

in later years. There are no network externalities or other demand-side scale economies.

5. Assume also that the market for the product is sufficiently large that many licensees could produce and sell at an efficient scale. In other words, there could be competition among several licensees in selling the product to consumers with no penalty for production on an inefficiently small scale or scope.

6. Assume also that licensing involves no additional costs. There are no transaction costs in gathering information about licensing opportunities, negotiating and granting licenses, administering performance, monitoring compliance by the other party, and enforcing license rights.

7. Assume also that enforcing the rights against infringement is costless, immediate, and certain to be successful.

These assumptions make it possible to think about a situation in which the value of the rights is independent of the terms of the license. In addition to the foregoing, assume that (1) the rights do not relate to a material, component, or part of the product that could be used in the product in varying proportions to other materials, components, or parts, (2) all other inputs needed to make and sell the product are supplied under competitive conditions, and (3) there are no laws or regulations mandating inefficiency that are overcome by licensing.

The basic assumption is that the rights owner and all potential licensees could and would produce exactly the same product at the same cost and sell it with the same effectiveness. In order to maximize profits in that context, the rights owner may pursue two equally profitable courses.

It may produce and sell the most profitable quantity of product and refuse to grant any licenses. There are no benefits from licensing. Assume a single price will be charged to all consumers. Using the example of Figure 1.1, the owner could produce at the most profitable quantity, 125 units or Q1, and sell at price, $275 per unit or P1. That is the quantity at which the cost of producing and selling one additional unit, MC ($150), equals the marginal revenue from that sale, MR (also $150). The owner could earn profits of (P1 − MC)Q1, here (275 − 150)125. Profits would be $15,625 per year. For readers familiar with the concept of demand elasticity, the producer may achieve this result by setting its price − cost margin (that is, P − MC/MC) equal to the inverse of its price elasticity of demand (that is, 1/e).[30] The "Total Profits" curve in Figure 1.1 shows how quantity (and price) changes affect profits.

Alternatively, the owner could grant nonexclusive licenses to many companies at a royalty per unit, $125 or R1. Assuming a single royalty rate to all licensees, the profit-maximizing rate is that at which the marginal revenue from licensing, mr, equals the marginal cost of licensing, zero, given the assumption of no transaction costs. Because there will be competition among licensees, the price to consumers, again $275 or P1, will be equal to the royalty charged by the owner, $125 or R1, plus the marginal cost of producing and selling, $150 or MC.

The competing licensees will earn a competitive rate of return at their selling price, P1. This price would be equal to their production and selling costs, MC, plus royalty payment, R1. The quantity supplied will again be 125 or Q1 units. The owner profits from licensing will be (R1)Q1 or ($125)125. Profits will again be $15,625. Recall that the owner's profits as a product seller were (P1 − MC)Q1. Since R1 is equal to P1 − MC, the owner's profits from licensing will be the same as its profits from selling.

Under the assumptions listed above (and some others), there is no profit incentive for an owner to license, if the demand for products using the rights and the costs of making and selling the product are the same for the owner and potential licensees. An owner's *opportunity cost* of supplying licenses is the profits it could have made by producing and selling the product protected by the rights rather than licensing others.

---

[30] Scherer and Ross, at 35. Demand elasticity is the percentage change in quantity divided by the corresponding percentage change in price. Elasticity of demand is a concept describing the relationship of the amount of a good consumers will buy at different prices in terms independent of the absolute prices or quantities involved. See Stigler at 326–336. This permits people to make meaningful comparative statements about the markets for apples and oranges. The concept is not helpful to describe demand for an intangible product, such as an idea, which lacks quantity.

There are an infinite number of units of any idea. One person's use does not preclude another's. The same difficulty arises in discussing the supply of ideas. William F. Baxter, "Legal Restrictions on Exploitation of the Patent Monopoly: An Economic Analysis," *Yale Law Review* **76**, 267 (1966) ("Baxter"). If elasticity of demand or supply is used to describe the demand or supply of proprietary rights, one arbitrarily adopts the quantities of their physical embodiments on which royalties are based.

1.6 THE BUSINESS DECISION TO EXPLOIT RIGHTS

The usual owner will refuse to license unless the licensees will pay more than the profits the owner could have captured from producing and selling the product protected by the rights.

(b) Where Vertical Integration and Licensing Are Not Equally Efficient and Profitable

The most fundamental reason for licensing is that the profits earned from use by licensees will exceed the profits available from use by the owner. The owner has an incentive to license only if the derived demand for the rights is greater when the rights are used by licensees than when used by the owner.

There are two basic reasons why that may occur. First, the licensees may be able to design, produce, and sell a product that is more valuable to users than the product the owner could produce. Second, the licensees could produce at lower cost. The profit incentive to license is illustrated in Figures 1.2 and 1.3. The rights owner and potential licensees are likely to be able to make, sell, and distribute different products for different markets and to do so at different costs. This changes the basic assumption that the rights owner and all potential licensees could and would produce exactly the same product at the same cost and sell it with the same effectiveness.

Consider the impact of cost differences on relative profits. Figure 1.2 shows the $150 average (and marginal) production costs of a rights owner ("RO") by the curve MC RO. Assume there are three groups of potential licensees ("Lees") for the rights. Lee1 in group 1 are as efficient as the owner. Lee1-type producers' production costs are also $150 per unit. The second group, Lee2, is 33 percent less efficient than the owner and have costs of $200 per unit or MC 2. A third group, Lee3, are 50 percent more efficient with costs of $75 per unit or MC3.

Since the Lee1 group is no more efficient than the rights owner, the maximum value of the invention in the rights owner's or Lee1s' hands is the same. If the rights owner elects to produce and sell, it will produce 125 or Q1 units, sell them at price $275 or P1, and earn profits of $15,625. The licensed value of the invention is the difference between D and MC RO shown by the curve dd1. As shown earlier, $125 or R1 is the rate of

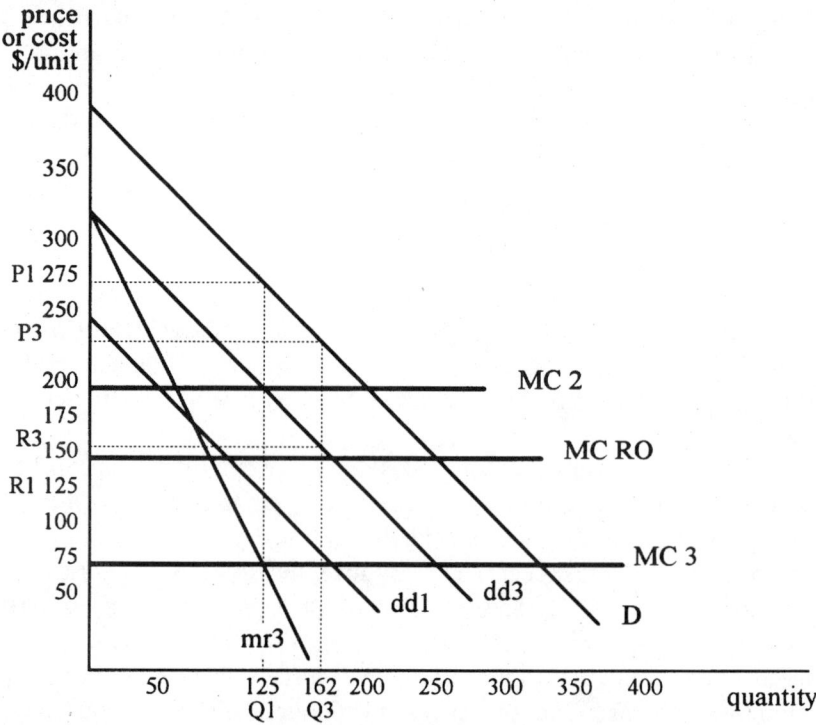

Figure 1.2. The Incentives to License—Lower Costs

profit per unit that maximizes profits under the derived demand curve for the invention, dd1. $125 per unit would also be the profit-maximizing royalty rate the owner would charge to the Lee1 group. The owner has nothing to gain from granting those licenses.

Similarly, suppose that the less efficient Lee2 group exists. The value of the invention to the Lee2 group will be less than its value in the hands of the rights owner, because of Lee2's higher costs. Licensing the Lee2 group would decrease the value of the invention. After the $125 royalty, their costs would be $325 per unit.

The Lee3 group is more efficient than the owner. The invention is more valuable in the hands of the Lee3 group than in the hands of the owner or the Lee1 or Lee2 groups. If the Lee3 group is licensed, the de-

1.6 THE BUSINESS DECISION TO EXPLOIT RIGHTS

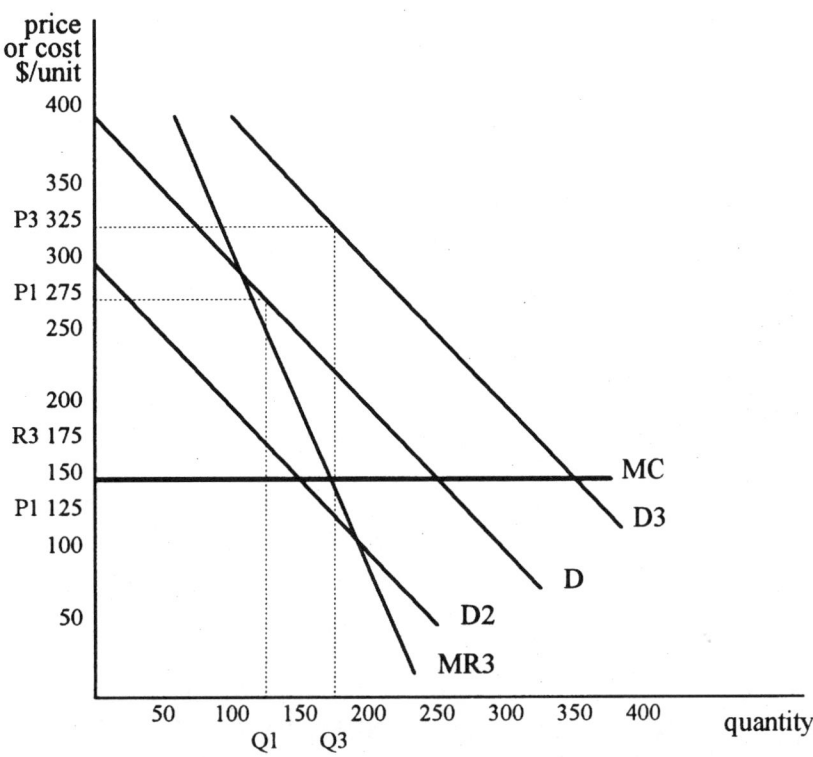

Figure 1.3. The Incentives to License—Higher Demand

rived demand is shown by dd3. The profit-maximizing royalty to this group is $162.5 or R3 per unit. Lee3 licensees will treat the royalty as a cost. If there are a sufficient number of producers licensed at $162.5 per unit to create competition, output will increase to 162.5 or Q3 units and owner profits will increase from $15,625 to $26,406 (R3(Q3) or $162.5 times 162.5).

Changes in the product have the same consequences. Assume there is a product protected by the rights. The demand for any product varies with its utility to users, the income of users, the price of complements, the price of substitutes, and the degree of competition among suppliers. Assume that different producers could make products having different features or qualities. This could occur because different users have access to different complementary information, have different abilities to predict customer taste, or have different product designing skills, or for other reasons.

Figure 1.3 shows the demand conditions based on three different products: D, the demand for a product that the rights owner and Lee1 would have produced; D 3, the demand for a more valuable product produced by Lee3; and D 2, the demand for a less valuable product produced by Lee2.

Since the product produced by Lee1 is identical to that produced by the rights owner, the owner again has no incentive to license. The owner can earn profits of $15,625 (P1 − MC)Q1 by selling and cannot earn greater profits by licensing Lee1. Lee2 would produce a less valuable product and is out of the game. Lee3 could supply the best product, whose demand would be D3. The profits available under the derived demand curve for D3, dd3, exceed the profits available under the curve D, if supplied by the rights owner. Again assuming competition among many licensees like Lee3, the owner may increase profits to $30,625 ($175(175) or R3(Q3)) by licensing.

1.7 FACTORS THAT INFLUENCE THE PROFITABILITY OF LICENSING

(a) The Time Horizon for Profit-Maximizing Business Decisions

One of the original assumptions listed above was that current pricing decision will not affect long-run demand. There are several reasons this may not be true. Before mentioning why, there is a more fundamental issue.

Over what time period is the owner trying to maximize profits? If the time period is the next two or three years, licensing strategy tries to maximize advantage without too much change. If the period is the next ten or twenty years, a very different approach applies—one in which almost anything can change. If the owner is taking a long-run view, then what is the most important change to focus on and try to influence?

If technology development and growth will increase demand for rights more than short-run productive efficiency, then a strategy would

1.7 FACTORS THAT INFLUENCE THE PROFITABILITY OF LICENSING

focus on long-run technology incentives. Short-run efficiency is much less important, though one must always discount future profits at a sensible rate. If the owner's discount rate lets it think five, ten, or twenty years out, then the licensee(s) R&D and innovation incentives are more important. A licensee's current lack of any experience in production and marketing may be far less important than its R&D and innovation prowess.

Many "short-run" issues will be discussed in what follows because the short run (indeed next week) usually matters and sometimes matters critically. However, one should never lose focus on the fact that small positive shifts in demand and small cost reductions over time will swamp short-run efficiency—who can produce the best product at lowest cost tomorrow.

Short-run issues also need to be discussed with full appreciation of the time value of money and compound interest tables. Future money is worth less than current money and with compounding disappears rapidly.

(b) Product Pricing (and Royalties) May Affect the Long-Run Industry Output and Price

Contrary to the simple model described so far, short-run pricing decisions may change the rate of growth of long-run demand. A single seller may initially sell at a lower price than the short-run optimum (say P1 in Figure 1.1) to maximize its advantage (and profits) over a longer period. The seller may engage in some form of *limit pricing* to deter entry or expansion by fringe firms.[31] The seller may charge lower prices than optimum in early years, because the long-run viability of the product may depend on the rate at which consumers buy the product. There may be powerful network externalities or similar demand-side scale economies that swamp short-run results.[32]

---

[31] Scherer and Ross at ch. 10.
[32] Paul A. David, "Some New Standards for the Economics of Standardization in the Information Age," Technological Innovation Project, Working Paper No. 11, 1986 (Center for Economic Policy Research Stanford University); Michael L. Katz and Carl Shapiro, "Network Externalities, Competition, and Compatibility," *American Economic Review,* vol. 75 (1985) at 424; and many others.

These pricing strategies make the royalty strategies more complex, because the per-unit royalty rate must be consistent with the optimal pricing strategy. Royalties and pricing need to be viewed interactively. A licensing policy may be vastly profitable in the long-run if it captures only a small percentage of licensees' relevant profits in the short-run and that induces many competing licensees to supply large quantities at correspondingly "low" prices. This is likely to be true when products become more valuable to all users as the number of users of that product increase (such as telephones and computers).

The initial expansion of a regional telephone company may have seemed silly when few people have phones, but may look very wise if it leads to a company with the only national network. The decision by a computer company with marvelous production and sales ability to license its most efficient potential competitors may have seemed silly when few people have computers, but may look very wise if it leads to a computer with vast supplies of trained users and compatible software. IBM may have used this strategy to its advantage in the personal computer industry. Apple may have decided against such a policy to its "long-run" detriment.

However, this possibility does not change the basic point. If limit pricing is the best product pricing strategy, then limit pricing is the best license royalty strategy. The same conclusion applies to other pricing strategies that sacrifice some short-run profits to obtain greater long-run profits.

(c) Royalty Rates and Structure Will Affect Industry Output, Price, and Licensing Profits

Few people are likely to question that the reason for licensing is that the profits earned from use by licensees will exceed the profits available from use by the owner. It is also simple to understand that this is usually possible only if licensees are able to produce and sell a more valued product or produce at lower cost. Finding the most efficient potential licensee(s) is important. It is also important to structure royalties to give the licensee(s) incentives that maximize the owner's licensing profits.

The royalty rate and terms will have an impact on the licensees' output (and price) and on industry profits. The owner will fail to maximize profits if it fails to take into account that royalties will affect in-

1.7 FACTORS THAT INFLUENCE THE PROFITABILITY OF LICENSING

dustry output, price, and profits. Assuming single pricing, the rights owner should try to charge royalties (and create other conditions) so that its licensees produce at a price and quantity equal to the price and quantity that would be produced by a monopolist of the product having the same costs. This quantity and price will generate maximum returns to the rights owner.

If the owner in our example in Figure 1.1 had charged an amount equal to two-fifths (or 40 percent) of per-unit profits at the most profitable output, or $50 per unit, the licensees would add that amount to their costs and expand output to 200 units. At that level, total royalty revenue would decrease by 36 percent, from $15,625 to $10,000. Royalties at 20 percent of the optimum rate, $25 per unit, would yield total revenue of $5,625 (a 64 percent decline) on total output of 225 units.

The same revenue losses occur if royalties are too high. Higher prices are not always the most profitable prices. Royalties at 140 percent of the optimum rate, $175 per unit, would yield total revenue of $13,125 on total output of 75 units. Royalties at 160 percent of the optimum rate, $200 per unit, would yield total revenue of $10,000 on total output of 50 units. Hence, even if the owner could convince a licensee to accept that rate, it will have hurt itself. These effects are illustrated in Figure 1.1 with total revenue and total profits curves.

This example assumed single pricing by licensees and a single royalty rate by the owner. There is nothing inevitable about charging all consumers or licensees the same price. If a single seller could figure out a way to charge a consumer its full demand for the product, the seller could in this example earn profits twice the single pricing amount. With perfect price discrimination, output would expand to 250 units and the price for each unit would be that shown by the demand schedule, D. Profits could be $31,250 rather than $15,625. A rights owner could achieve the same result if it could induce the licensees to price in this fashion and capture that increased revenue.

(d) Royalty Rates and the Licensee Profits—What Profits Matter and Is There a Universally Ideal Relationship?

In the example in Figure 1.1, the profit-maximizing per-unit rate was about 45.5 percent of sales and 100 percent of licensee profits in excess of the "profits" needed to justify the licensee's capital investment. As shown earlier, if the per-unit royalty was 20 percent of that rate, royalty revenue would decline by 64 percent.

Some people say that as a "rule of thumb"—invoking the language of carpenters before the invention of the ruler—the most profitable royalty rate in any industry and for any patent rights is 25 percent or some other percent of expected licensee profits. I am not aware of any studies that support this view in the licensing context.[33] While there is strong evidence that groups often develop customs and informal norms to reduce disputes and encourage mutually advantageous behavior, it does not seem possible that any generally followed norm could exist due to the sheer number of participants in the general technology creating–licensing business and the changing conditions that confront them.

Rather, it seems clear that a better rule is to identify and negotiate a royalty rate and structure that induces licensees (or a licensee) to produce in the long run at the most profitable output (and price). This means that the owner should not take the licensees' expected profit rate as a given and negotiate for a rate that is some share of those profits. This also means that the profit-maximizing rate may vary over a wide range relative to licensees' expected profits. While there are significant barriers to obtaining royalties that drive the industry (and the rights owner) to the maximum profit position previously described, there is no reason to believe that these rules of thumb always or even often prove reliable.

We must also be clear about what expected licensee "profits" we are discussing.[34] In Figure 1.1, some "profit" is included as part of the licensees' average annual total cost of producing and selling the product. Part of the annual $150 per-unit manufacturing cost is a sufficient return to the producer's capital investment in R&D, plant, equipment, and other fixed costs to induce those investments, given their riskiness. That return is included as part of the licensees' costs because no licensee will accept a license unless it expects to earn that return.

If capital investments are very small relative to the variable costs and relative to licensee expected volume, and risk is low, then the per-

---

[33] Businesses use a variety of pricing formulas for a variety of reasons. Scherer and Ross at 261–265.
[34] For a more detailed explanation and some interesting empirical data, see Gordon S. Smith and Russell L. Parr, *Intellectual Property: Licensing and Joint Venture Profit Strategies,* 1993 (John Wiley & Sons, New York).

1.7 FACTORS THAT INFLUENCE THE PROFITABILITY OF LICENSING

unit "profit" charge may be a small percentage of licensee average cost. If the opposite holds true, it may be large. In any event, this expected return may vary over a wide range from industry to industry, company to company, and even product to product. There seems to be no reason to assume this return is likely to be 75 percent of sales revenue, so that only 25 percent is left over for royalties. Nor is there anything inevitable about any other percentage. Hence, these rules of thumb seem counterproductive, except, of course, in situations where there are repeat transactions among the same companies, and industry conventions significantly reduce transaction costs and uncertainty.

While a "25 percent" rule may be odd, there are several reasons why a rights owner will rarely be wise or able to negotiate a royalty that captures 100 percent of the licensees' profits after a reasonable return to capital. These have to do with creating incentives for future licensee investments in improving the product and lowering its production costs rather than investing in potential substitutes, creating incentives for long-run growth of demand, the legal uncertainty of the rights, the information and transaction cost barriers to creating a perfect auction for licenses, and so forth (sections 1.9 and 1.10).

(e) The Royalty Base—Unit Sales

I have described a set of licenses basing on a fixed dollar amount per unit. A more common base for royalties is some stated percentage of licensee sales revenue. Hence, some might doubt the usefulness of this approach. For purposes of illustrating how to determine the rate that will generate maximum revenue, that understandable skepticism is easily answered.

(f) The Royalty Base—Sales Revenue

In the example in Figure 1.1, the owner could have achieved precisely the same incentives by setting royalties as 45.5 percent of sales. Licensees would treat their effective revenue from sales as the price minus 45.5 percent. This effective demand is shown by the curve "D − .45D." Licensees would again sell up to the point where effective revenue from sales equals cost, 125 units, and charge customers the same price, $275 per unit. Royalty revenue would be the same. There are often good reasons to base royalties on sales revenue rather than a fixed per-unit fee. However, use of that royalty base does not change the basic analysis.

Why do owners often base royalties on sales revenue rather than unit sales? Product sellers rarely base prices on buyer revenue. Why do license "sellers" so often price differently?

First, a license commonly seeks to grant rights at a specified price over a many-year term. Even if the parties know current demand and cost conditions, the future is highly uncertain. A fixed charge per unit places all the risk of declining demand on the licensee and all the risk of increasing demand on the licensor. A fixed charge per unit also places all the risk of increasing costs on the licensee and all the risk of decreasing cost on the licensor. A fixed charge per unit places all the risk of inflation on the licensor and the risk of deflation on the licensee. A charge based on a percentage of revenue permits risk-sharing arising from unpredictable market shifts. This reduces the rate discount that must be applied to "pay" each party to bear risk.

Second, a rate based on a percentage of product revenue is more likely to better measure derived demand of each licensee in the short and long runs than numbers of units sold. In the short run, total revenue is more likely to relate directly to licensee profits than total units times a fixed dollar amount. Royalties based on a fixed fee per unit increase in direct proportion to unit sales. This is illustrated in Figure 1.1 by the case "Total Royalty Rev. at $125 per unit." However, total revenue (and total profits) from sales are unlikely to increase proportionally. Given some supply and demand conditions, product revenue increases as unit sales increase over some range and then decreases. A percentage of revenue fee more closely matches those changes. In the long run, total revenue monitors demand changes more closely than unit sales. For example, a percentage of revenue permits the owner to receive a share of the profits resulting from later improvements that expand demand or receive the same real return if inflation artificially increases demand.

(g) The Royalty Base—Profits

A royalty based on a percentage of licensee profits measures derived demand even more closely. However, basing royalties on licensee profits

1.7 FACTORS THAT INFLUENCE THE PROFITABILITY OF LICENSING

requires a more detailed agreement because "profits" is not a sufficient definition. This measure would increase bargaining and monitoring costs for the owner. It would also increase risk because the temptation for cheating by the licensee (in the form of accounting cost allocations) would increase. Another way to attempt to match license payments more closely to licensee profits is to receive all or part payment in the form of licensee's stock.

(h) The Royalty Base—Lump Sum Payments

There is a third royalty base—a fixed lump sum fee. The owner could charge a fee for a license for a specified period equal to the discounted present value of the profit stream that would be generated by a licensee operating in the most profitable manner. In Figure 1.1, the most profitable quantity per year was 125 units sold at $275 per unit. That is the quantity at which the cost of producing and selling one additional unit, MC ($150), equals the marginal revenue from that sale, MR (also $150). The per-unit royalty was $125 and annual profits were $15,625 per year. The owner could license for a lump sum fee equal to the present value of that profit stream. Assuming no uncertainty (about the future of technology, government policy, inflation or other factors), no risk aversion, and constant costs, that rate base would produce the same licensing profits. It would change licensee behavior.

If an owner collects all or part of the future profit stream as a one-time lump sum fee, licensee(s) will treat that payment as a sunk cost. Licensee(s) will ignore that payment for output decisions. The lump sum does not change marginal cost. If there are several competing licensees, the licensees may expand unit sales beyond 125 units and sell at prices below $275 per unit. If the entire payment was a lump sum and the licensees treated the payment as a sunk cost, output may expand to 250 units and price fall to $150 per unit. This is the optimal result for the economy as a whole, as long-run incentives to produce technology and short-run incentives to use the existing supply are achieved.

However, prospective licensees will recognize that the fee changes their fixed (and average) costs. This may limit the number of licensees who will accept the license. If average production costs per unit were constant before the fee, average costs will be declining after the fee. Average costs decline as the fee is spread over more units. Declining average costs are inconsistent with many competing licensees. A lump sum fee may require a single or small number of licensees for each market, because several licensees vigorously competing may not be able to pay the fee and sell at a price greater than each licensee's average cost.

There is another potential effect. If average production costs decline over some range and then increase before the fee, they will shift up after the fee. Under these conditions, there may be multiple licensees. Total industry output will limited by increased average costs. In this situation, the lump sum fee creates an artificial scale economy, and may induce each licensee to invest in too large a scale of operations or to expand its production beyond the most efficient rate for a given "plant" size.[35]

Lump sum payments also may be desirable for other reasons. For example, the owner may discount future payments at a higher discount rate or be more risk averse than the licensee(s). Lump sums permit allocation of risk to the best risk bearer. Lump sum payments also minimize the risk of litigation about the agreement or the underlying rights.

(i)   The Royalty Base—A License under Licensee's Rights

There is another "royalty base"—a license from the potential licensee under the licensee's intellectual property rights. There are situations where the total value from use of rights is maximized by royalty-free cross-licensing. Each owner may gain more from having the royalty-free right to use the "licensee's" rights than it loses from forgone royalty payments and lower prices on its sales (due to the absence of a royalty). This may occur because the parties as producers gain from the increased output that follows from the absence of the addition of royalties to average costs.

There is one incentive for a licensor to receive back nonmonetary consideration in exchange for the grant that has nothing to do with efficiency. It is to evade legal regulation. The Supreme Court's rules limiting the royalty obligations have not been applied to other types of consideration. Therefore, nonmonetary consideration becomes more profitable than monetary consideration. However, it is impossible to

---

[35]Roger D. Blair and David L. Kaserman, *Law and Economics of Vertical Integration and Control,* 1983 (Academic Press, New York) at 69–77.

1.8 LICENSING NEGOTIATIONS

evaluate technology and rights before they are developed. Therefore, it is impossible to trade off with any precision royalties and the value of future rights developed by the licensee. Escaping legal regulation comes at a price—higher risk.

Section 1.8 describes how the basic licensing process is influenced by transaction costs, the uncertainty and cost of intellectual property litigation, and the risk of licensing and litigation.

1.8 LICENSING NEGOTIATIONS IN VIEW OF BARGAINING PROBLEMS, LICENSEE ALTERNATIVES, TRANSACTION COSTS, INTELLECTUAL PROPERTY LITIGATION, AND RISK

Licensing is potentially more profitable than vertical integration only if the expected value of a license to some potential licensee (ignoring the payments to the owner) exceeds the expected value of rights to the owner if it vertically integrates the rights into its company.

Licensing is actually more profitable only if there is a negotiation, an agreement, and performance. It was assumed earlier that the licensing process involves no costs for the rights owner or licensee. It was assumed there are no transaction costs for the owner in gathering information about licensing opportunities, negotiating and granting licenses, monitoring compliance by licensees, and enforcing licenses. It was assumed there are no transaction costs for the licensee in gathering information about licensing opportunities, negotiating and receiving licenses, administering the license, and enforcing its rights under the license. It was also assumed that enforcing the rights against infringement is costless, immediate, and certain to be successful. Those assumptions are rarely true in practice. How does this change the process?

(a) The Expected Value and Cost of the License

For purposes of developing a shorthand notation, let the owner's expected value of using the rights rather than licensing be *EVnl,owner*. Assume for simplicity that the total expected profits from licensing to the owner are the payments it receives from the licensee. The owner will license only if the expected payments it receives from licensing exceed the expected value of using the rights (and not licensing). Let the expected payments the owner receives from licensing be *EP*. These "payments" may involve things the owner values other than money.

Assume also that the total expected cost of the license for the potential licensee is the expected payments to the owner. The potential licensee will accept a license only if the cost of licensing, by assumption also *EP*, is less than its expected profits made possible by a license, *EVl,licee*.

If we ignore the transaction costs and risk of licensing, the first essential condition for licensing is:

$$EVnl, owner < EP < EVl, licee \qquad (1)$$

Unless the rights are more valuable when used by the licensee than when used by the owner, this condition cannot be satisfied and licensing is not possible.

Consider an example. Figure 1.2 shows the demand for a patented product, D. The Patent Owner Company, PO, owns a patent on a product that it may make and sell for a profit of $125.00 per unit if it does not license and enforces the patent. The per-unit value of the patent to PO is $125.00 per unit. This was shown in Figure 1.1.

One Potential Licensee Company, Lee1, is no more or less efficient than PO and its use of the invention under a license would also yield that $125 per unit. Under those facts, there is no benefit to PO and Lee1 from cooperating with each other by entering a license. Moving the right to use the invention from PO to Lee1 produces no benefits. Because no value is created by granting a license, there is no value for the parties to share by entering an agreement.

Said differently, if the parties do not cooperate by entering a license, PO may sell the product and earn $125.00 per unit. If there is no license, L may earn nothing. If the parties do not cooperate, the payoff for PO is $125.00 per unit and nothing to L for a total value of $125.00 per unit. If the parties cooperate by nonexclusive licensing, PO will earn $125.00 per unit on the part of the market it supplies and L will earn

1.8 LICENSING NEGOTIATIONS

$125.00 per unit on the part it captures. The total profits, however, will be the same as those PO would have earned had it not licensed. Therefore, the value of cooperation is $125.00 per unit on the same quantity of sales.

Another group of Potential Licensee Companies, Lee3, are more efficient than PO. Their lower production cost, $75 per unit, is shown by MC3. Granting a license to the Lee3 group would permit production at lower cost. There is now some benefit from cooperation. The value of the patent in Lee3s' hands would be $162.50 per unit.

In that situation, PO would threaten not to license, and sell the product and earn the $125.00 per unit. The value from cooperating would be $162.50 per unit (the value available under licensing) minus $125.00 per unit (the value of the invention in the absence of a license). The potential surplus from cooperation is $37.50 per unit.

Because the value of the rights to the licensees greatly exceeds their value to the owner, there may be a range of potential payments that will permit an agreement. This range could be shown by a diagram in which increasing dollar amounts are shown along a line.

$$EVnl, owner < \quad EP \quad < EVl, licee$$

```
———————————-//////////////////-———————————
$0              125            162.5
```

(b) Payments and Small Number Bargaining Problems

If there are many Lee3-type companies that could pay the $162.50 per unit and make a profit, and they compete for licenses, the owner may be able to achieve that royalty rate. With many licensees, price will decrease and output increase to 162.5 units.

If there are very few companies able to produce profitably at $162.50 per unit, or the costs of negotiating with many companies are large, the owner may not be able to employ competition for licenses to bid the price for licenses to that level. Assume there is only one company in the position of Lee3. One solution to reaching a bargain in that situation is for the parties to equally divide the surplus. A possible solution would be a royalty of $143.75 per unit. One possible solution to a bargaining problem in which a surplus is created is for each party to receive the value it would capture by not cooperating plus 50 percent of the surplus from cooperation, $18.75. In this case, PO would receive $143.75 (that is $125 plus $18.75) per unit and Lee3 $18.75 per unit (plus, of course, the competitive profit on capital included as an item of cost).

(c) Payments and the Substitute Technologies Available to the Potential Licensees

The owner is not the only person with an alternative not involving the license. The potential licensees also have the alternative of rejecting the license and producing an alternative product or process not protected by the owner's rights. A licensee's *opportunity cost* of producing products under the license is the value of the next-most-profitable alternative product that it could have produced if it refused the license.

The usual licensee will pay no more for a license than the difference between the profits it might capture from exploiting the rights and the profits it could have captured by producing the next-most-profitable product that could be made without the rights. The owner may negotiate only for the difference. The demand for a license cannot exceed the difference between the profits available from products or processes that embody the rights and the profits available from producing the next-most-profitable alternative products or processes. Such an alternative product may be one free of intellectual property rights, one protected by the licensee's rights, or one licensed from a third party.

If the license is for the period of the next year, the alternative must be available during that period. If the license exists for a multiyear term, the licensee will take into account alternatives that the licensee could produce over the term. Actual long-run royalty payments may be enhanced if the per-unit royalty is limited to reduce the licensee's incentives to produce substitute technology. This is a form of so-called limit pricing.

Given the long term of many licenses, the ability of the licensee or someone else to develop an alternative may have an important downward effect on royalty rates, especially when those rates are compared with short-run licensee profits. Business people often regard intellectual property protection as deterring entry of competing products by only several years and raising imitation costs in a limited way.[36] Those perceptions

---

[36]Scherer briefly describes some of these surveys. Scherer and Ross at 627–629.

1.8 LICENSING NEGOTIATIONS

will have an important effect on payments. In extreme form, royalty payments may not exceed the cost of developing a noninfringing alternative product.

The alternatives (and negotiating threats) that define the bargaining range are more complex. The owner may threaten to use the rights (and not license) or to license someone other than the person with whom it is negotiating. A patent owner's threat value (namely the amount it would have made by not entering a license) would be equal to the greater of

1. The royalties it would have received from use by another licensee or other licensees (whether existing or potential), or
2. The amount of profits it would have made from its own use.

A potential licensee's threat value is the greater of

1. The profits it would make from not accepting a license and not selling the product (which is always zero), or
2. The profits it would make from not accepting the license and selling the next-most-profitable alternative product.

If there is a surplus created by granting a license, we should expect many bargains in which the patent owner and the licensee would receive its threat value plus some share of the surplus.

If we include this factor in equation (1), and use $dEVl,licee$ to indicate the difference between the profits the licensee could make using the rights and the profits it could make producing the next-most-profitable product, the first essential condition for licensing becomes:

$$EVnl, owner < EP < dEVl, licee < EVl, licee \qquad (1')$$

(d) An Example of the Effect of Substitute Technologies Available to the Potential Licensees

This is illustrated in Figures 1.4, 1.5 and 1.6. Figure 1.4 shows the derived demand for a patented process given an alternative inferior process. D shows the demand for some unprotected product. There is a patent on a process that would permit production at $250 per unit, shown as MC1.

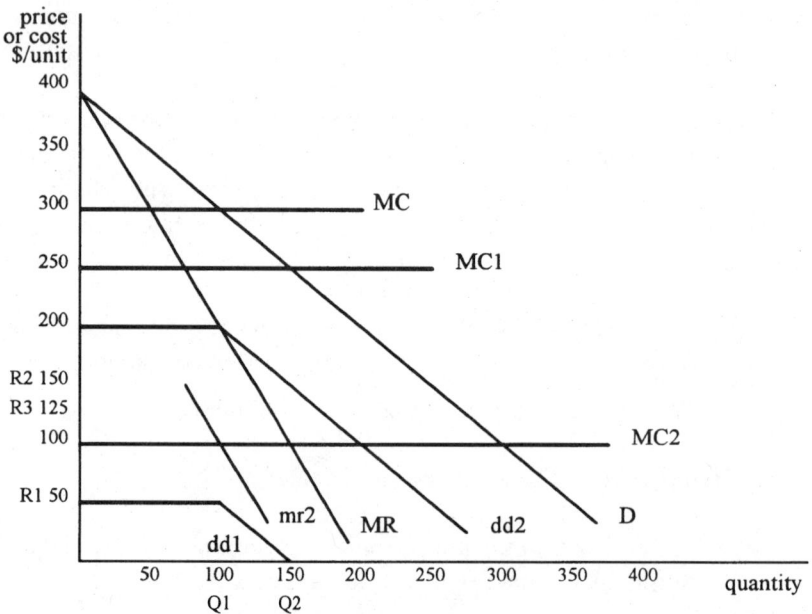

Figure 1.4. The Demand for a Patent on a Process of Making a Product with Demand Less Sensitive to Price Changes

There is also an unpatented old process that would involve higher costs of $300 per unit, MC. The derived demand is no longer the difference between demand for the product and the cost of production using the rights. If competing sellers use (or could easily switch to using) the old process, no one will be able to sell at prices above $300. The curve MC defines the product demand (and the derived demand for rights, dd1) at outputs up to 100 units. Above that output, the product demand becomes effective because producers using the old process cannot profitably sell for less than $300. If licensing is costless and the rights certain, the most profitable royalty rate is $50 per unit, the full cost savings per unit.

Notice that if the new and protected process dramatically reduced cost, the most profitable royalty rate would be something less than the total per-unit cost savings. Suppose a patented process would permit production at $100 per unit, shown as MC2. The old process involved costs of $300 per unit, MC. Cost savings are $200 per unit. The derived de-

1.8 LICENSING NEGOTIATIONS

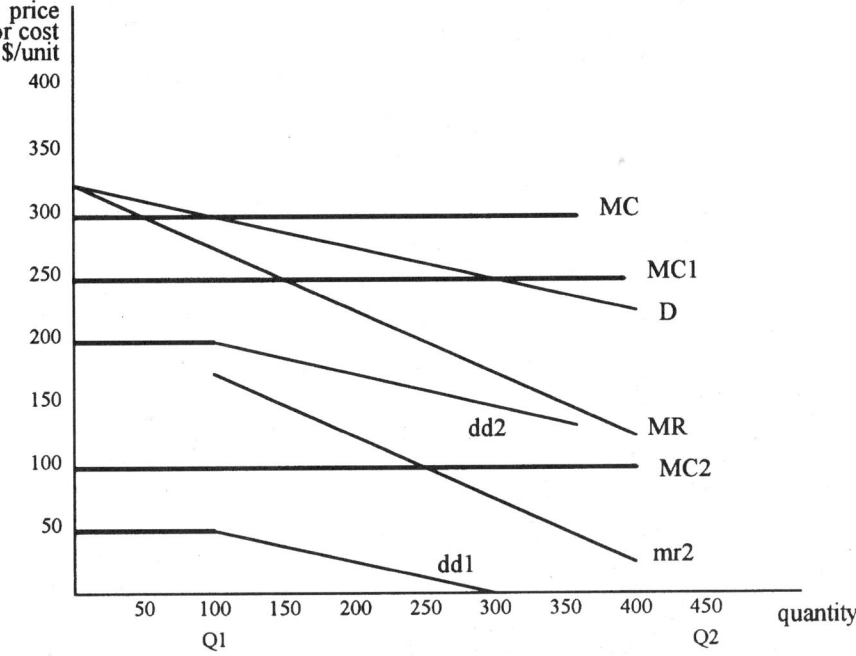

Figure 1.5. The Demand for a Patent on a Process of Making a Product with Demand More Sensitive to Price Changes

mand is now shown by dd2. Again, if licensing is costless and the rights certain, the most profitable royalty rate is $150 per unit, less than the full cost savings. The reason is that the owner now wants output to expand, from 100 to 150 units. If the owner charged $200 per unit, royalty revenue would be $20,000. At the lower $150 rate, revenue will increase to $22,505. If we assumed that the marginal revenue curve, MR, was the demand, D, it could be shown that the most profitable rate falls to $125 per unit (or about 60 percent of the cost savings).

Figure 1.5 shows the derived demand for the same patented processes, MC1 and MC2, where demand for the product is much more sensitive to price changes. D shows the demand for this different unprotected product. Original output is again 100 units. For the process that would permit production at $100 per unit, shown as MC2, the derived demand is now shown by dd2. The royalty rate is $112.50 per unit. Out-

THE BUSINESS OF LICENSING INTELLECTUAL PROPERTY RIGHTS

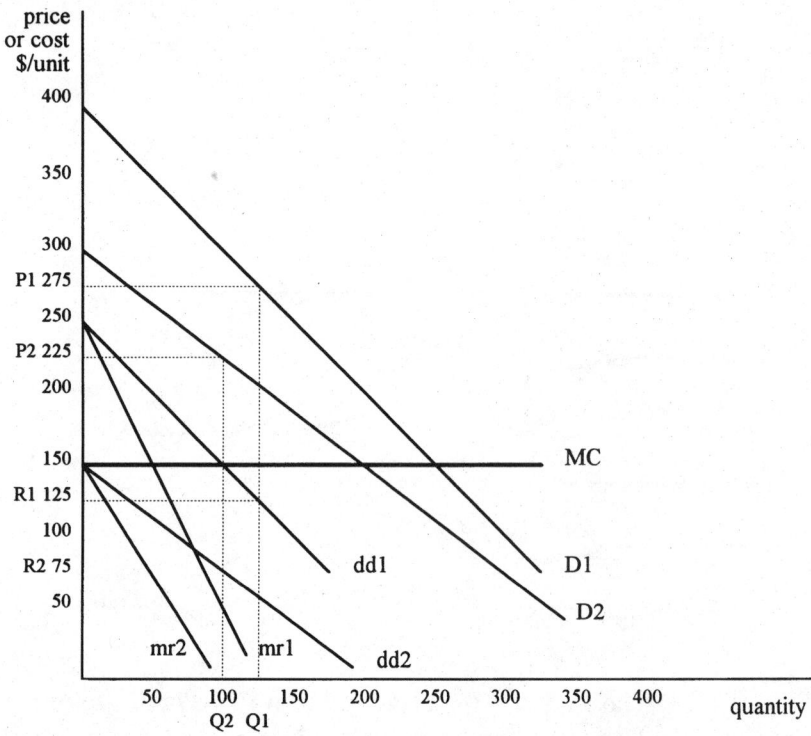

Figure 1.6. The Demand for a Patent on a Product

put would expand more significantly, from 100 to 450 units. Royalty revenue increase to about $50,000.

While more difficult to illustrate, the same analysis applies to patents and other intellectual property rights to products. Figure 1.6 shows the derived demand for a patented product given an alternative inferior substitute product. D1 shows the demand for the patented product prior to the availability of the inferior alternative. Production costs are $150 per unit, shown as MC. Derived demand is determined in the usual way, leading to the usual $125 per-unit royalty and $275 price. Assume an unpatented alternative now becomes available. The alternative product is less valuable to consumers. But given its price, demand for

1.8 LICENSING NEGOTIATIONS

the patented product decreases by 25 percent. The derived demand is now smaller, dd2, the optimal royalty lower, $75, and price lower, $225. If the owner insists that licensees continue to pay the $125 rate, only about 33 units will be sold, and royalty revenue will fall by about 70 percent.

(e) The Transaction Costs of Licensing

It is assumed that the owner and potential licensee incur no costs in the process of licensing. Licensing is typically a costly process. Potential licensees must search for valuable information and for the owner of any rights to that information. Rights owners must search for potential licensees. Rights owners and potential licensees must study the nature of the information and the legal rights. They must negotiate and reach an agreement. They must comply with the agreement and monitor compliance by the other party. They must negotiate and litigate about disagreements about compliance.

The transaction costs will depend on the nature of the rights. Transaction costs of agreements between producers and users are likely to be lower under a patent system than a contract and trade secret system. The cost of searching for information about the existence of and rights to use technical information are likely to be significantly lower for patented information than unpatented information. Searching costs are reduced because there is a recording system that permits anyone at any time to consult a central repository of the information and a record of rights. The costs of ascertaining the nature of rights and reaching a bargain for those rights are also reduced, because the rights are known to both parties prior to entering into an agreement. That is typically not possible under the contract and trade secret regime. Under that system, there are likely to be more significant differences in private information about the value of the rights. This information gap between producer and user prevents the price from accurately reflecting the value of the information.

Transaction costs, like taxes, are a wedge between what the owner would be willing to receive and the potential licensee would be willing to pay. If these anticipated transaction costs by both owner and potential licensee exceed the value of the license, there will be no license. Licensing will occur only if

1. The owner's expected value of not licensing, *EVnl,owner*, plus its transaction costs of licensing, *TC*, is less than the expected payments from licensing, *EP*, and
2. The potential licensee's expected cost of licensing, by assumption also *EP*, is less than its expected profits from a license, *EVl,licee*, minus its transaction costs of licensing, *TC*.

Transaction costs shrink the potential range of payment for a bargain. The second essential condition for licensing becomes:

$$EVnl,owner + TC < EP < EVl,licee - TC \qquad (2)$$

If in the example of Figure 1.1 the owner and licensee each anticipate transaction costs averaging $10 per unit, the bargaining range shrinks by $20. The potential surplus from a license shrinks from $37.50 per unit to $17.50.

```
───────────────·////////·───────────────
$0           125 135    152.5 162.5
```

(f) The Expected Value and Cost of Litigation Rather than Licensing

There is another feature of licensing that is different from most transactions in tangible products. In markets for tangible products, the buyer may not obtain the seller's product without first paying or agreeing to pay a price. Unless there is a bargain, theft is the only "option." The expected value of a tangible product to a person who does not pay is zero. In intellectual property contexts, this is commonly not the case.

A potential licensee of intellectual property rights may be able to learn the invention, work, or other information and use it without agreeing to pay. The potential licensee's choice is not simply to accept or reject the license. The options are to use the rights under a license, to not use the rights (and avoid any need for a license), or to use the rights without a license and litigate any infringement claim. In many situations, the validity or scope of the rights may be unclear. Licenses are always negotiated in the shadow of the law and the possible infringement litiga-

1.8 LICENSING NEGOTIATIONS

tion. Licenses are often best viewed as settlements of potential future litigation. As such, the analysis of litigation settlement applies.[37] If the potential licensee has commenced using the rights without a license, then the negotiation will involve settlement of the owners's claim for past infringement. For purposes of the following discussion, assume the negotiation involves only a license for the future.

A potential licensee having the option of commencing use without a license will evaluate the expected likelihood and cost of losing infringement litigation. A potential licensee possessing the "protected" information will accept a license only if the cost of licensing, EP, is less than the expected cost to it of the remedies from litigation, $EClit,licee$. For the same reason, the owner will license such a person only if the expected payments from licensing, EP, exceed its expected value of litigating, $EVlit,owner$.

If we ignore direct litigation costs such as attorneys' fees, the third necessary condition for licensing is:

$$EVlit,owner < EP < EClit,licee \qquad (3)$$

Now, include direct litigation costs, LC. Recall that transaction costs narrowed the possibilities for a potential agreement. Transaction costs are a wedge that separates the parties. Notice that litigation costs work in the opposite direction. They are a "reverse wedge" that drives them together. Litigation costs lower the value of litigation to the owner and increase the cost of litigation to the potential licensee. With litigation costs, the third condition for licensing becomes:

$$EVlit,owner - LC < EP < EClit,licee + LC \qquad (4)$$

In the example in Figure 1.1, the owner and licensee as a business proposition had a payment range (given transaction costs) between $135 and $152.50 per unit within which a license would be mutually advantageous.

---

[37] One of the earliest rigorous explanations of the settlement decision-making process was William F. Baxter, *The Political Economy of Antitrust,* 1980 (Lexington Books, Lexington, Mass.), at 11–26, 78–80.

THE BUSINESS OF LICENSING INTELLECTUAL PROPERTY RIGHTS

The litigation prospect imposes a second condition that is not directly connected to their evaluations of expected market and business conditions. Assume the owner and potential licensee each expect that litigation is certain if there is no agreement. Assume also that the remedies for successful owners permit the potential licensee to capture and not repay a large part of the value of the information. Assume litigation is inexpensive.

Under those conditions, the litigation option may reduce the payments for a license. Suppose the owner expects the value of litigation to be $50 per unit and litigation costs to be $10 per unit. Suppose the potential licensee also expects the cost (i.e., remedies) of litigation to be $50 per unit and its litigation costs to be $10 per unit. The bargaining range shrinks by $20. The potential surplus from a license shrinks from $37.50 per unit to $17.50.

$EVnl, owner + TC < \quad EP \quad < EVl, licee - TC$

```
————————————//////////——————————
$0                    135     152.5
```

$EVlit, owner - LC < EP < EClit, licee + LC$

```
——————————————— . //// . ————————————————
$0                  40    60     135      152.5
```

There is a potential for a license, but at a per unit price between $40 (the minimum the owner will accept) and $60 (the maximum the potential licensee will pay). The business range becomes irrelevant, given the litigation option.

The numbers could, of course, work out exactly the opposite. If any litigation range always exceeds the business range, the litigation option will become irrelevant, except for a potential licensee who did not know about the rights. Potential licensees who know of that prospect will not infringe the rights. As to the potential licensees who seek a license before infringing, the litigation option becomes irrelevant. The most important point is that both conditions operate to limit the licensing option.

What are the expected value of litigating to the owner, *EVlit, owner*, and the expected cost of the remedies from litigation, *EClit, licee*? These

1.8 LICENSING NEGOTIATIONS

will depend on the law of remedies for each type of right. However, certain factors will be common to all rights. At first approximation, the expected value of an action to the rights owner is its estimate of the probability that it will win times the value of the judgment minus the cost of litigation. The expected cost of an action to the potential licensee is its assessment of the probability that it will lose times the cost of a judgment plus the cost of litigation. Each party will multiply (and reduce) its own estimate of probability of success times the value or cost to it of that outcome.

If the parties are risk neutral, licensing will occur only if there is some licensing amount, EP, that

1. Is greater than the owner's estimate of the probability it will win, Pw, times the value of winning, Vw, minus the rights owner's cost of litigation, LC, and
2. Is less than the potential licensee's estimate of the probability it will lose, Pl, times the cost of losing, Cl, plus the potential licensee's cost of litigation, LC.

The third essential condition for licensing becomes:

$$Pw \times Vw - LC < EP < Pl \times Cl + LC \tag{5}$$

The parties' evaluation of expected litigation outcomes and remedies can have important impact on the price of a license. If intellectual property law provided monetary awards that were always small fractions of the economic value of the rights, and only rarely awarded injunctions against infringement, the price for intellectual property licenses would be reduced to the same fraction of economic value. If the probability of winning an intellectual property infringement action is always very low, the price for licenses would also be reduced in direct proportion. Hence, the substance of intellectual property law and litigation can have a very important effect on the price of a license.

We could add a further element. I have assumed that the each party believes the other will litigate if there is no license. The potential licensee may further discount the expected cost of litigation if it believes that there is some chance the owner will look the other way and not sue even if the negotiation fails. The potential licensee may escape liability regardless of the merits of the claim. Similarly, the owner may discount the expected value of the litigation if it believes the potential licensee will abandon the infringement without the need for litigation. The price of a license will be influenced by each party's evaluation of the other's actual intentions.

We could also add the sunk cost problem to the analysis. If the potential licensee is already in the business and has invested in assets whose value depends entirely on the continuation of the business, it is in a difficult position. This potential licensee may no longer make a credible threat to switch to an alternative, and an injunction against use of the committed assets may destroy their value. This potential licensee may pay much more for a license than one with other options. This potential licensee may pay an amount that minimizes future losses.

Notice also the importance of expected litigation costs on licensing. If both parties evaluate the expected litigation in the same way (that is, each evaluates the probabilities and remedies in the same way), there should always be "settlement" with respect to past conduct, because this will save litigation costs. Any license for future acts will depend on the business factors.

There is likely in most intellectual property situations to be an added component to the expected value of one action to the rights owner. Intellectual property litigation can affect the behavior and rights of companies that are not parties to a particular litigation. This adds a further level of complexity. At least in the patent context, if an owner loses an action against one company, that loss may prevent its action against others and permit others to avoid previously agreed-on royalty payments. In the more general context, any one loss may induce others to use the rights without a license, and so the expected value of an action is reduced. Hence, any particular action is worth

1. The value of an injunction and damages against the potential licensee if the rights owner is successful, minus
2. The costs to the rights owner if an unsuccessful action against the potential licensee induces third parties to act in ways harmful to the rights owner.

1.8 LICENSING NEGOTIATIONS

The expected value, V, of the action to the rights owner is its probability of winning, Pw, times the sum of the value of an injunction against the potential licensee, $Vinj$, plus the value of damages against the potential licensee, $Vdam$, minus the probability of losing, Pl, times the harm from increased competition from others induced by the result of the action, $Cinc.comp$. Symbolically,

$$V = Pw(Vinj + Vdam) - Pl(Cinc.comp.) \qquad (6)$$

To add further complexity, there are rules, again in the patent context, that make the probability of winning any particular litigation dependent on previous licensing decisions. If the rights have been widely licensed and the information widely adopted, the law says this increases the probability of success in future litigation. Hence, lowering the price for a license increases the likelihood of litigation success, which increases the expected payments from litigation settlement. The business economics and litigation economics decisions can become interdependent, at least for intellectual property owners fond of trying to emulate strategies recommended by von Clausewitz.[38]

It is important to understand that licensing and litigation are not mutually exclusive options at least in the patent context. This problem issue is discussed in Chapter 7. Since about 1969, patent owners have been faced with the prospect of "licensing" in exchange for a reduced payment that made sense if they had avoided litigation, and then being required to litigate about the validity of the rights to collect the payment. This rule makes equation (4) incomplete.

(g) The Risk of Licensing and Litigation

There is another major factor in the licensing decision. It is risk and uncertainty. Intellectual property licensing and litigation involve uncertainty about expected value and costs.

First, licenses are often directed to products and processes that have not been sold or used commercially. Hence, there is often little or no market experience from which to project future prices, quantities, or costs.

---

[38] Carl von Clausewitz, *On War*, 1984 ed. (Princeton University Press, Princeton).

Second, the fact that licensing often involves new technology implies a dynamic situation. The short-run supply of complementary and substitute technology is often difficult to evaluate and, even if known, may change rapidly. The long-run supply of complementary and substitute technology is almost unknowable.

Third, technology rights also typically exist for long periods, from a few years to decades. Licenses often provide rights and payments for long periods. The long time periods increase risk because the variability of possible outcomes increases.

Fourth, intellectual property rights also are subject to legal uncertainty. There may be a significant risk about the validity, scope, and enforceability of the rights. The outcomes of litigation about intellectual property rights may be highly unpredictable.

For these and other reasons, licensing involves more than normal market levels of risk for the owner and potential licensee. What does it mean to say a person or company is risk averse?[39] Said simply, they are like most of us. They do not go rock climbing or drive race cars for fun. They also require a higher return on more risky investments. Said with more rigor, a risk-averse person or company would prefer a certainty of receiving a given amount of money to an uncertain chance of obtaining a larger amount even though both options have the same expected value. For example, suppose an owner has a 70 percent chance of winning $1,000 by litigating an infringement claim. The expected value of an action is $700 (the 70% chance of winning $1,000 and a 30% chance of having nothing). A risk-averse owner may prefer to settle that claim and receive a certain payment of $400. The owner prefers receiving a certain $400 payment even though the expected value of that action is $700.

A risk-averse person or company would also prefer to make a certain payment over an uncertain prospect of making another payment, even though the cost of the certain payment is greater than the expected cost of the uncertain payment. For example, a potential licensee may prefer to pay $850 to avoid litigation in which it has a 70 percent chance of paying $1,000 and a 30 percent chance of paying nothing (an ex-

---

[39] Jack Hirshleifer and John C. Riley, *The Analytics of Uncertainty and Information*, 1992 (Cambridge University Press, Cambridge), part I; A. Mitchell Polinsky, *An Introduction to Law and Economics*, 1983 (Little, Brown, Boston), ch. 7–10; Milgrom and Roberts at 460–467; Scherer and Ross at 128–129.

1.8 LICENSING NEGOTIATIONS

pected cost to it of $700). The greater the uncertainty about the expected judgment, the more likely risk-averse parties are to license.

If the rights owner and the potential licensee are risk averse (and the evidence is most people and companies are), their perceived value of rights is less than their expected value of those rights.[40] The perceived value of an uncertain future benefit (or cost) is sometimes called its *utility*. The utility of an uncertain benefit to a risk-averse person is less than its expected value. With uncertainty, the utility of the rights to the owner with no licensing, $Unl,owner$, is less than the actual expected value of those profits, $EVnl,owner$. The utility of the rights to the potential licensee, $Ul,licee$, is less than their expected value, $EVl,licee$.

If both parties are risk averse, the payment range for a bargain is reduced. Risk reduces the payment below the actual expected value of the rights. If both parties are risk averse, licensing is possible only if

1. The utility of the rights to the owner without licensing, $Unl,owner$ (which is less than their actual expected value) is less than the payment, EP, and
2. The payment EP is less than the utility of the rights to the potential licensee, $Ul,licee$ (which is less than the expected value).

Stated symbolically and leaving out transaction costs,

$$Uowner < EVnl,owner < EP < Ul,licee < EVl,licee \tag{7}$$

In the example of Figure 1.1, the owner and licensee as a business proposition had a payment range (given transaction costs) between $135 and $152.50 per unit within which a license would be mutually advantageous. Assuming risk aversion, uncertainty about the economic value of the rights lowers the range at both ends to, for example, $110 and $130.

---

[40] The insurance industry is a monument to risk aversion. Las Vegas is a monument to the fact that some people prefer risk. There is no reason to think that intellectual property owners and potential licensees have any different risk preferences than average people or companies.

$$Unl,owner + TC < EP < Ul,licee - TC$$

```
─────────────────·//////////·──────────────────────
$0                100  130 135                152.5
```

Similarly, the perceived value of litigation to a risk-averse owner is less than its expected value. The utility of an uncertain claim to the rights owner, $Uowner$, is less than its actual expected value, $EVlit,owner$. The perceived cost (or *disutility*) of an uncertain judgment to a risk-averse potential licensee exceeds the expected cost of that action. The disutility of the judgment to a potential licensee, $DU\ licee$, is greater than the action's expected cost, $EClit,licee$. Viewed from the litigation perspective, if both parties are risk averse, licensing is possible if

1. The utility of an action to the rights owner, $Uowner$ (which is less than its expected value), is less than the payment EP, and
2. EP is less than the disutility of the uncertain judgment to the potential licensee, $DU\ licee$ (which is greater than the expected cost).

Stated symbolically and leaving out litigation costs,

$$Uowner < EVlit,owner < EP < EClit,licee < DU\ licee \qquad (8)$$

In the example of Figure 1.1, the owner and licensee as a litigation settlement proposition had a payment range (given litigation costs) between $40 and $60 per unit within which a license would be mutually advantageous. Assuming risk aversion, uncertainty broadens the range at both ends to, for example, $20 and $90.

$$Uowner - LC < EP < DUlicee + LC$$

```
─────────────────·//////////·──────────────────────
$0                20 40 60 90   135           152.5
```

Risk affects licensing strategy in many other ways. Payment structures are typically designed to reduce the sources of risk, share risk, and allocate risk to the best risk-bearer.[41]

---

[41] Reducing risk is something of great value and something that licensors and licensees alike sensibly pursue. One of the great risks of licensing is that a licensee will commence an action to destroy the licensed property. This is regarded as crim-

1.9 AN OVERVIEW OF LICENSING STRATEGY

If the profits from licensing are likely to exceed the opportunity cost of licensing, the owner's goal is to design a licensing strategy that maximizes the demand for the rights and captures as large a part of that demand as possible while minimizing transaction costs and risk. A strategy should also minimize the legal risks of destroying the rights or creating other liability. As the following section discusses in more detail, the owner will do so by, among other things:

1. Increasing the demand for the products made using the rights,
2. Decreasing production cost,
3. Controlling the licensee's power to restrict production, and
4. Minimizing transaction and risk costs.

In theory, the licensor may also attempt to decrease the licensee's ability to substitute other rights for the licensed rights or to use the rights to administer a cartel.

(a) Provisions to Maximize and Capture Demand

Many intellectual property rights will cover end products such as pharmaceuticals and computers. Others will relate to processes of making end products or to raw materials or parts used in those processes. The owners of each of those rights have a common goal—to increase the demand for the final product using or made using the rights. Increasing final product demand increases the demand for the rights.

Maximizing demand for the rights is profitable only to the extent the licensor captures that demand. Economic discrimination is fundamental to capturing that value (section 1.10(b)). It is highly likely that any particular set of intellectual property patents and know-how will be applicable to users or uses with different demand *elasticities* for the

---

inal for lessees of houses or automobiles, but is encouraged when one leases a different variety of personal property, namely, a patent. One can lease a car and ask the lessee to agree not to destroy it. One can rent a house and have the renter agree to return it in as good a condition as when he or she is given possession of it. But when one leases a patent, one cannot today ask the licensee to agree not to try to have it held invalid. See Chapter 7.

rights. A licensor must evaluate separately and maximize the demands for each of those uses. It is a colossal mistake to set the terms or the royalty rates for any intellectual property rights without considering the potential for economic discrimination. There are many different provisions used to accomplish economic discrimination. One problem arises regardless of the method chosen to accomplish discrimination. It is the need to prevent the "low" royalty products from being resold in the "high" royalty segments. Difficult legal issues arise from the current confusion regarding license provisions that seek to limit resale of a product.

The demand for the product depends upon the specific features of the product, the services that support it, and the marketing effort to sell it. It may be unnecessary to agree to provisions that compel the licensee to produce a product of a certain quality, support it with related services, or engage in certain marketing efforts. A licensee's and licensor's incentives to maximize final product demand are the same, unless there are free-riding or asset specificity problems.

Free-riding will arise in many intellectual property licenses (section 1.10(c)). It is common for intellectual property licenses to be granted long before the product or process has been developed and the product approved for sale. There will typically be substantial additional fixed costs to be incurred. Those additional activities will probably be conducted most efficiently by the licensee. A proper level of investment in those activities will increase demand for the final product.

A licensee's incentives to do so will be less than the owner would desire, if those investments give rise to benefits of a technical or marketing nature, accruing to other licensees or to unlicensed sellers of the same or substitute products. No exclusivity is called for simply because a large further investment is required by the licensee. Exclusivity is called for only where that investment has some likelihood of benefiting sellers of competing products who do not make the same investment.

The licensee's incentives will also depend on who owns the assets those investments create (section 1.10(d)). Normally, the licensee will own the assets that are useful only with the rights and the owner will not be permitted to change the royalty rate after the licensee invested in creating those assets. Asset specificity can create a hold-up problem that can deter licensee investment.[42] If the license had a

---

[42] Milgrom and Roberts at 307–308.

1.9 AN OVERVIEW OF LICENSING STRATEGY

short term or provided that the royalty could be changed, the licensee would fear that the owner would increase the rate after these assets had been created. The licensee would not invest or would invest too little in such assets.

Proprietary rights may be used to prevent the external benefits. The most common method is to grant the licensee some exclusive position for a period of time. Exclusivity is designed to preclude free-riding. Where exclusivity is appropriate, the dilemma for the licensor is that, during the term of exclusivity, the licensee may exercise market power to limit production. Preventing the free-rider problem gives rise to the successive monopoly problem (section 1.10(e)).

A licensee with market power will produce up to the point at which marginal cost (including royalties) equals marginal revenue. This level of production will be below the royalty-maximizing level at which licensee marginal cost equals selling price. In the extreme case, the licensee may exercise market power to limit production under the license to zero, in favor of exploiting substitute rights it owns or hopes to acquire in the future. This is a devastating result for the licensor. Licensors may seek to prevent such restrictions on output by a contract with diligence requirements, minimum quantity requirements, increased minimum royalty rates if production is too low, or maximum product prices. Again, antitrust and misuse rules have sometimes been said to prohibit some of these terms.

A second critical issue is licensee efficiency. A licensor, like a seller of any product, benefits if its licensee is efficient and suffers if it is not. Licensee efficiency is vital. In many intellectual property situations, there will be scale, scope or *learning-curve* economies in production (section 1.10(g)). The licensee must make significant investments in further development, testing, complying with government rules and regulations, building a plant suitable for production, and establishing a marketing organization.

Where there are scale economies in some or all of these activities relative to the size of the market, minimum production cost will be achieved if a single manufacturer or a small number of manufacturers supply the market. Such markets will exhibit the characteristics of natural monopolies. One or a small number of producers will ultimately survive in a competitive environment. In such situations, the licensor may choose to grant only one or a small number of licenses. Declining costs may require assurances to licensees that there will be one or a small number of licenses. Creating more competition than the market can tolerate will increase risk and decrease the licensee's incentives to invest. Granting one or a limited number of licenses may again give the licensee discretion over price and lead to restriction in output.

Another demand-side concern for rights owners arises from input substitution. (section 1.10(h)). When the rights relate to a tangible input, the demand for the input is derived from the demand for the end product. The elasticity of derived demand for the input will increase as the demand for the end product becomes more elastic, the elasticity of substitution increases, and the elasticity of supply of other inputs increases.[43] The issues and devices to increase final product demand are the same. However, the input rights owner must also think about ways to reduce substitution of other inputs for the protected one.

There are many potential responses. As noted years ago, the most common is to base royalties on end product output or sales, rather than on input use or sales.[44] This reduces the licensee's incentives to make inefficient decisions to substitute other inputs for the one to which the rights relate. This approach is useful whether the licensor or licensee produces the input. Therefore, if other factors favor production and sale by the licensor, an end product royalty structure remains useful. In theory, lump sum payments may perform the same function.

Another mechanism to increase demand for the rights is to increase the supply of complementary products and rights (sections 1.10(i) and (j)). Just as existing rights become more valuable to the extent substitutes are not available, existing rights become more valuable to the extent that complementary technology is developed and is cheaply available to the licensee. There are several sources of complementary products and rights whose incentives the owner may seek to influence—third parties, the licensee(s), and the owner itself.

---

[43] Patent licensors with rights to an input used in variable proportions can probably learn a thing or two from the labor unions. Tom Campbell has written an interesting paper on how labor unions maximize derived demand for their lawful market power over labor. Thomas J. Campbell, "Labor Law And Economics," *Stanford Law Review* **38**, 991 (1986).

[44] Baxter, at 302–303.

1.9 AN OVERVIEW OF LICENSING STRATEGY

(b) Provisions to Decrease Transaction Costs

Licensors and licensees have a common interest in reducing transaction costs (section 1.10(k)). Negotiating, performing, detecting violations, and enforcing license agreements can be expensive. Any provision that reduces those costs leaves more for the parties to share.

(c) Provisions to Decrease Uncertainty and Risk

Uncertainty is ubiquitous in licensing. Almost every provision is touched by uncertainty. Because of uncertainty and the general need to make the term of the agreement long enough to justify a licensee's fixed investments, risk costs are high. Properly allocating and reducing uncertainty is always desirable.

A typical feature of licensing is that the agreement has a very long term. This is not inevitable. However, if the licensee is going to make substantial investments the profitability of which depends upon the continued existence of the license, the term of the license must be appropriately long. The demand for the rights over a long period is highly uncertain. Neither licensor nor licensee can predict with very much certainty the nature of that demand function over the entire term of the license. Rather than thinking of a "demand" for the licensed rights, it is more accurate to think about a set of expected "demands" with a large variance. The potential in the long run for legal, technical, or market obsolescence of intellectual property rights increases the variation in those potential demands. For this reason, many major patent licenses, particularly international portfolio licenses, have a relatively short term, such as five years, to permit periodic review of changes in the rights and the markets, and allow renegotiation to reflect more current conditions.

Payment provisions will be influenced by risk. The parties may also attempt to reduce the risk of legal obsolescence (by a licensee's agreement not to challenge validity or, less efficiently, to pay regardless of validity). Legal issues abound when a licensor attempts to reduce risk. Antitrust and preemption issues arise whenever owners and their licensees seek to reduce the risk and cost of litigation (section 1.10(l)).

(d) Provisions to Reduce the Licensee's Ability to Substitute Other Rights

The demand for any particular intellectual property rights decreases as it becomes easier for the licensee to substitute other rights for the license. The extent to which a licensee may substitute other rights for the licensed rights will vary greatly from situation to situation. In intellectual property, the supply of substitute rights commonly changes rapidly and is highly unclear at the time of the license.

A first response to decreasing substitution is to patent innovations to the maximum extent possible. Only a patent prohibits the use of independently developed techniques. Second, it is very common that a number of organizations do research on similar problems. The supply of substitute rights may be high. There will be incentives in many areas of intellectual property for a company possessing rights to acquire competing rights or to otherwise eliminate competition in their supply by cross-licensing or other types of pooling arrangements. Considerable legal issues are, and ought to be, raised by such agreements.[45] (section 5.9).

A licensor may also attempt to limit a licensee's incentive to substitute other rights for the licensed rights. Terms to that end include an agreement by a licensee (1) not to use substitute rights, (2) to pay the licensor whether or not the licensed rights or substitute rights are used, and (3) to diligently exploit diligently the licensed rights (a poor substitute for number 1), and (4) to grant to the licensor rights developed by the licensee (section 1.10(m)). In most situations, it will not be profitable for a intellectual property licensor to forgo the present income necessary to induce the licensee to agree not to do competing research or sell competing products. The potential producers of the substitute rights are too numerous to make this profitable. A licensor with broad or generic rights may wish to use grantbacks, since he or she may be able to license a sufficiently large percentage of sources of substitute developments to make it worthwhile. Again, antitrust and misuse issues arise. (section 3.10).

---

[45]Roger B. Andewelt, "Analysis of Patent Pools under the Antitrust Laws," *Antitrust Law Journal* **53**, 611 (1984); John S. McGee, "Patent Exploitation: Some Economic and Legal Problems," *Journal of Law and Economics* **9**, 135 (1966).

1.10 LICENSING STRATEGY, TERMS, AND PROFITS

This section addresses some of the most important features of license strategy and terms that assist to maximize long-run profits. Frequently, this involves dealing with a world in which the earlier assumptions (section 1.8) are not true.

(a) Controlling the Supply and Price of Licenses under the Rights

For tangible products, the marginal cost of producing the product and supplying it for any particular use is positive. For tangibles, there will be no supply unless the price equals at least the marginal cost of producing the input. Assuming a price that exceeds those costs, suppliers of tangible products will sell them for a particular use only if the price paid exceeds their price if sold for the next-most-valuable use.

An owner of existing intellectual property rights typically faces similar choices. However, an owner's marginal production costs are often zero. The technology has typically been produced and the rights procured. The transaction costs of granting, monitoring, and enforcing a license may be very small. Hence, if there are several uncoordinated suppliers of licenses under the same rights, the price for licenses will tend toward zero.

Consider the example shown in Figure 1.1. However, assume that the owner is not capable of producing and selling. The owner must license to earn any profits. If there is only one supplier of licenses, the owner will license and charge $125 per unit. Given the assumptions, licensees will supply 125 units at price $275, the quantity and price that maximizes profits for the owner. Profits from licensing will be $15,625. The supplier will refuse to grant licenses for a royalty of less than $125 per unit. If the owner licensed at a lower rate, licensees would supply more than 125 units at a price below $275 and reduce total profits to the owner.

Imagine that there were five co-owners each having the right to supply licenses without the consent of the others and without any obligation to share royalty revenue. Imagine that each tried to capture the largest share of licensing revenue, and ignored the effects of doing so on total profits. Competition among those co-owners in granting licenses will reduce the royalty below $125, and may reduce the royalty to close to zero.

For this reason, the first priority of an owner of any intellectual property right is to preserve a situation in which there is effectively only one supplier of licenses under the rights. This seemingly modest goal is sometimes easier said than done. The law sometimes creates obstacles. The antitrust and misuse rules are sometimes said to forbid an owner from agreeing with its licensees that no additional licenses will be granted without everyone's consent (sections 5.2 and 5.9). The antitrust and misuse rules also call into question an owner's ability to grant an exclusive license and not also grant the licensee the unfettered right to grant additional licenses (section 5.9). The antitrust and misuse rules have also called into question an owner's ability to grant a license for one use and prevent the products made by the licensee from being used for a use the owner wished to license on different terms or to different licensees (sections 5.4 and 6.10).

(b) Using Different Terms for Licensees with Different Demands

Assuming there is only one supplier of licenses for any right, the licensor will grant licenses on terms that maximize the derived demand for the rights and capture the maximum part of that value for the licensor. Typically, the licensor will recognize that the rights have different values to different users or in different uses. The licensor will attempt to apply different prices and other terms to different users and to different uses. The licensor will try to engage in economic discrimination. Whether called market segmentation or price discrimination, this strategy is absolutely fundamental to any licensing program.[46]

The benefits (and difficulties) of economic discrimination are illustrated in Figures 1.7 and 1.8. As always, the vertical axis is dollars. The horizontal axis is the number of units of a product supplied or demanded at various prices.

---

[46]For an explanation of the financial principles, see Scherer and Ross at ch. 13. For the earliest analysis in the licensing context, see W.F. Baxter, "Legal Restrictions on Exploitation of the Patent Monopoly," *Yale Law Review* **76**, 267 (1966). Also Hausman and Mackie-Mason, "Price Discrimination and Patent Policy," *Rand Journal of Economics* **19**, 253 (1988).

1.10 LICENSING STRATEGY, TERMS, AND PROFITS

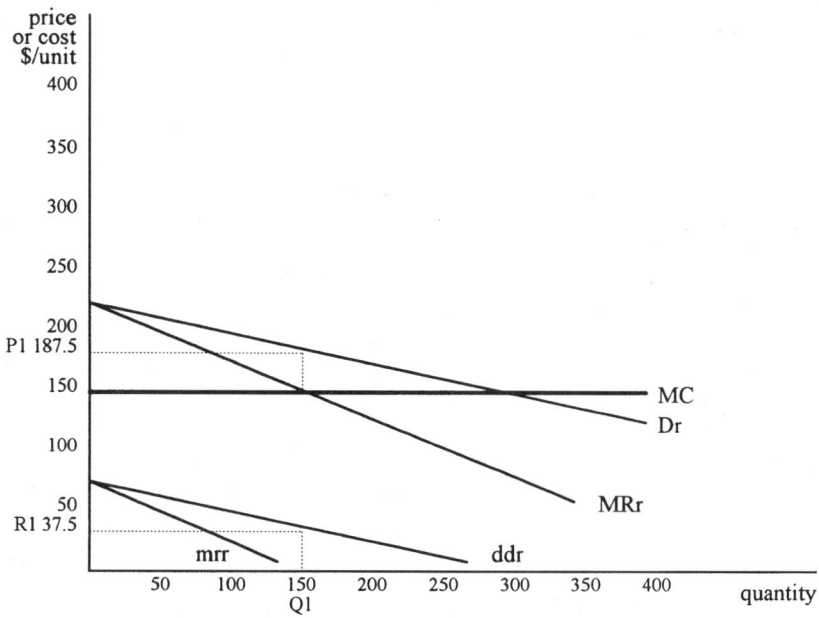

Figure 1.7. Economic Discrimination—Lower-Value Product

Assume the rights are patents and the technology is an invention. The invention relates to a component of an electronic device for producing sound that amplifies a signal. The component is called an amplifier. Amplifiers improve the quality of sounds produced by electronic devices. Amplifiers are useful in many different products.

In Figure 1.7, Dr is the demand of radio users for radios having the patented amplifier. The radio market is very large. There are a hundred radio manufactures. The amplifier improves radio performance very little. Radios without an amplifier are close substitutes for radios with an amplifier. Hence, the demand for the patented radios is relatively *elastic*. As the price of radios with amplifiers changes, there are large changes in the quantity people want to buy.

Figure 1.8 shows the demand for large, high-performance sound equipment used in theaters, D. In theaters, equipment with the patented amplifier performs vastly better (from a theater patron perspective) than

THE BUSINESS OF LICENSING INTELLECTUAL PROPERTY RIGHTS

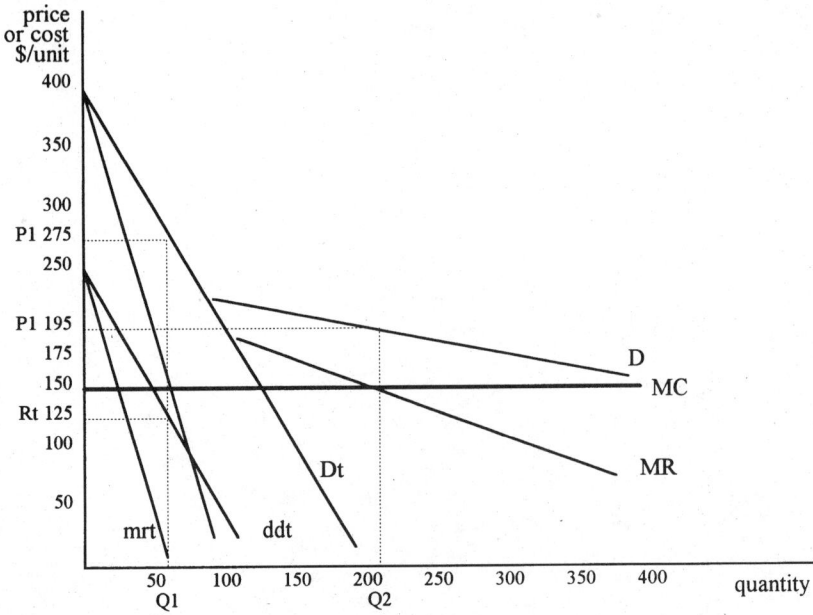

Figure 1.8. Economic Discrimination—Higher-Value Product

other available equipment. Demand for theater equipment is relatively more *inelastic*. As the price of equipment sold to theaters changes, there is a smaller effect on the quantity sold. The market for theater equipment is smaller and may be supplied by a single producer.

Assume that the average and marginal costs of producing and selling radios and theater equipment are constant and the same, $150 or MC. The maximum value of the rights to radio licensees is Dr minus production costs, MC (Figure 1.7). The derived demand for the rights for that use is the curve ddr. Assuming single pricing among radio makers, marginal licensing revenue is mrr. The profit-maximizing royalty to radio licensees is $37.50 or Rr. This means that radio licensees must be confined to selling radios to radio users and radio buyers must be prevented from reselling amplifiers to theater equipment makers. If this can be accomplished, radio licensees will produce 150 units (Q1) and sell them for radio use at $187.50 (P1). The maximum value of the rights to

1.10 LICENSING STRATEGY, TERMS, AND PROFITS

theater licensees is D minus production costs, MC. The derived demand for the rights for theater use is ddt, and marginal revenue mrt. The profit maximizing royalty of theater licensees, $125 or Rt, is much higher than the profits maximizing radio royalty, $37.50. The most profitable quantity of theater equipment is 62 units (Q1) at price $275 (P1). Total licensing revenue will be about $13,375.

Economic discrimination requires preventing arbitrage. In this situation, radio licensees must be confined to selling radios to radio users and radio buyers must be prevented from reselling to theater equipment makers. In the actual situation that provided this example, the owner tried to accomplish this by granting the higher-priced theater license to a wholly owned subsidiary, thereby giving it some control over that licensee's temptation to purchase amplifiers from the radio licensees. The owner used infringement litigation to control sales by radio licensees to theater owners.

If the law compels the owner to license for all uses at a single rate, licensing becomes much less profitable. If economic discrimination is not lawful or practical, the licensor will attempt to supply fewer licenses at a price that may preclude some users or uses, but that maximizes revenue from those with higher values.

For example, if economic discrimination is not possible, the owner may maximize revenue by licensing only the theater equipment makers at $125 (Rt) and forgoing the radio use. Or the owner may license all uses at some intermediate rate higher than Rr and lower than Rt, such as $45, which it generates by summing the demands previously treated separately to arrive at demand D. The higher rate will reduce use of the amplifier by the radio manufactures and increase use by theaters. However, licensing revenue will fall from $13,375 to about $9225, a 31 percent decline.

In this illustration of economic discrimination there are two readily identifiable groups of consumers having different values for the rights. However, there is no limit to the number of users or uses that the owner may seek to license at different rates or on different terms.

Economic discrimination may involve licensing each end product user at a different "rate." This could be illustrated by use of Figure 1.1. Assume the rights relate to a farming implement that reduces the cost of harvesting a crop by $.01 per bushel. The implement is valuable to different farmers in direct proportion to their scale of operations. The owner may maximize revenue by making and supplying the implement to farmers and licensing use at $.01 per bushel. That practice requires farmers who used the implement more extensively to pay higher royalties on a per-machine basis than those who used it less extensively. The effect of the license is to charge each user at a rate proportional to the value of the implement (and the rights) to it. The owner charges each licensee what the market would bear on a licensee-by-licensee basis.

Assume there are generally four groups of farms. Each group has 50 farms of roughly equal size. Group 1 farms are the largest and would be willing to pay $200 per year for a license. Group 2 farms are the next largest and would pay $150. Groups 3 and 4 would pay $100 and $50. If the owner licensed by a single royalty on a per-farm basis, the rate would be $125, and profits $15,625. Farms 3 and 4 would not accept a license at that rate. If the farms were licensed on a per-bushel basis, the effective rates per farm would be different. Licensing profits would increase to $200(50) + $150(50) + $100(50) + $50(50), or $25,000. Group 1 and 2 farms would pay more than under the single rate. Groups 3 and 4 now would be able to accept the license and use the implement. Use of the implement would double on a per-farm basis, and increase somewhat less on a per-bushel basis.

Notice that the owner accomplished this different treatment by charging each farm the same rate per bushel. The number of bushels metered the intensity of use. Of course, this rate requires farmers to keep records and make reports they do not want to bother with. This rate is also difficult for the owner to monitor. How does it show that a farmer is not telling the truth when it says it harvested by hand last year? For these and other reasons (such as decreasing the farmer's incentive to substitute hand picking or other options for part of its acreage in order to reduce royalty payments), the owner and farmers may prefer licenses at different rates on a per-farm basis. This may attract the attention of the law.

Again, the antitrust and misuse rules raise concerns (sections 3.6, 4.4, 4.6, 5.4, 6.10). The antitrust and misuse rules have been said to limit an owner's ability to charge different royalties to different licensees. The antitrust and misuse rules limit tying arrangements that may be useful to collect "royalties" based on intensity of use. They limit use of package licensing that may be used for discrimination. The antitrust and misuse rules have been asserted to prohibit an owner from seeking to prevent a buyer of a product from a low-value licensee from reselling to a

1.10 LICENSING STRATEGY, TERMS, AND PROFITS

high value user, and even from limiting the types of products a licensee may sell.

(c) Terms to Induce Licensee Investments

An owner of rights increases the demand for the rights by licensing strategies that increase their value. The demand increases for rights as the demand increases for tangible products and processes employing the rights. The licensor will adopt a licensing strategy that seeks to induce the licensees to produce the most valuable product at the lowest cost. Long-run licensing profits will depend on future growth in demand and reduction in cost. The incentives the license creates for licensees to increase demand and reduce cost may have a far greater impact on long-run license revenue than the most well-informed and -designed royalty rate and structure. This may require creating and protecting licensee profit margins, a goal that seems folly in the short run.

The owner may not always be able to rely on the users' incentives to produce the most valuable product or the most valuable bundle of marketing, product, and service.[47]

One common reason is that licensee investments may yield external benefits for other licensees. For example, if one licensee's investments in additional R&D, advertising and marketing, or customer services will produce benefits for competing licensees who do not pay for those benefits, too few of those other activities will take place. Those other investments may be in additional research and development that yields unprotectible information. They may be advertising and promotional investments that expand demand for all suppliers. They may be

---

[47]There is vast business, economic, and legal literature on this issue, most of it in the context of tangible goods rather than rights. The reasons for coordination and control in the sale or distribution of physical products are the same that arise in licensing. Hence, that learning is directly applicable to licensing. See Milgrom and Roberts, ch. 3–9, 16; Scherer and Ross, ch. 15; Jean Tirole, *The Theory of Industrial Organization,* 1988 (MIT Press, Cambridge) ch. 4; Roger D. Blair and David L. Kaserman, *Law and Economics of Vertical Integration and Control,* 1983 (Academic Press, New York); Robert H. Bork, *The Antitrust Paradox,* 1978 (Basic Books, New York) ch. 14–20; Richard A. Posner, *Antitrust Law, An Economic Perspective,* 1976 (University of Chicago Press, Chicago) ch. 8–9; William F. Baxter, "The Viability of Vertical Restraints Doctrine," *California Law Review* **75**, 933 (1988).

investments in customer services such as training, quality-assurance, and repairs that may be used by other suppliers' customers. Free-riding may reduce the incentives to make these investments, thereby reducing the demand for the product made using the rights and the derived demand for the rights.

The licensor may grant a license that is exclusive to one licensee to the extent needed to prevent others from benefiting from that licensee's investments. The licensee may be granted exclusive rights to sell particular products, in particular territories, to particular customers, or to all of the owner's rights.

This effect of exclusive licensing may be illustrated by Figure 1.9. Assume that the owner of the rights to a product cannot use the rights

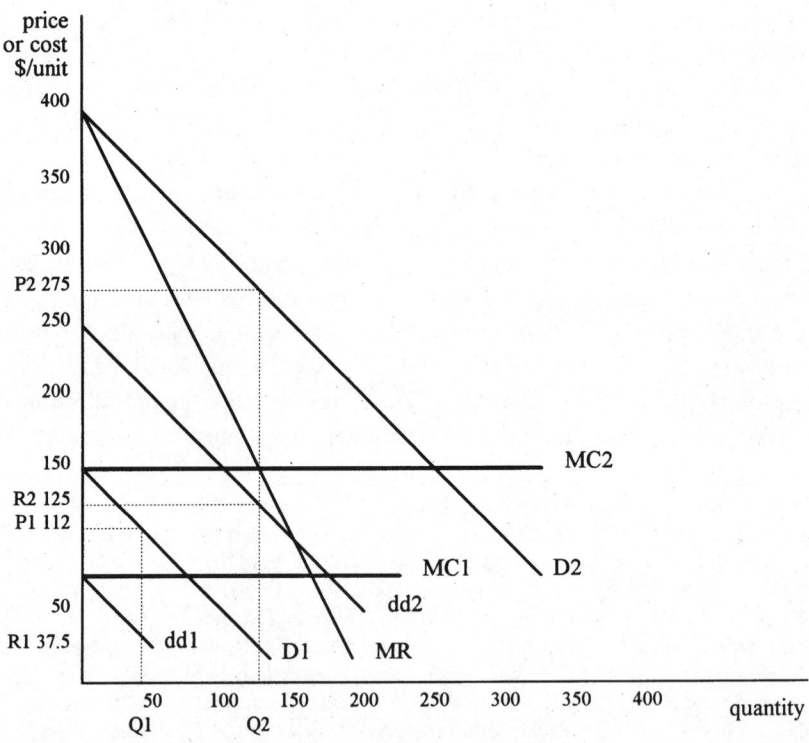

Figure 1.9. The Effect of Exclusive Licensing

1.10 LICENSING STRATEGY, TERMS, AND PROFITS

and must license. Assume that further investments in research, development, and promotion would greatly increase the value of the product. However, many of those investments by any one licensee would produce external benefits for other producers of the product. If such rights are licensed nonexclusively, each licensee may fail to invest sufficiently in further research, development, and promotion that might benefit other licensees, who make no similar investments.

Assume the rights relate to a new pharmaceutical that has been tested, approved by the government for use in treating itchy scalp, and accepted by the medical community and the public for that use. The demand for the product is D1. The average and marginal production and selling costs are $75, MC1. The demand for the rights is dd1. Potential licensing profits are $1,406, R1(Q1). The product is also highly likely to be useful in treating certain cancers. However, large investments in testing, regulatory approval, and marketing need to be done before the product may be sold for that use. If successful, the demand for the product would increase to D2. The average and marginal production and selling costs would increase to $150, MC2. However, the added value more than offsets the cost increase. If those investments are made, derived demand for the rights would increase to dd2. Potential licensing profits would increase to $15,625, R2(Q2).

By granting an exclusive license, the owner seeks to provide incentives for licensees to make investments that enhance the value of the rights. Those investments may increase the value of the product and the rights beyond that which nonexclusive licensing could achieve. The effect of the exclusive license is to increase the level of investment to a level, such as MC2, at which the value of the invention increases, such as to dd2. Accordingly, exclusive licenses may lead to greater profits and production than nonexclusive licensing.

It can be assumed that the licensee will own the assets that enhance the value of the rights and that the owner cannot change the royalty rate after the licensee invested in creating those assets. Asset specificity can create a hold-up problem that deters licensee investment.[48] The future investments by the licensee would be valuable only if used with the rights. The R&D and promotion create assets that are specific to the rights. If the

---
[48] Milgrom and Roberts, at 307–308.

license had a short term or provided that the royalty could be changed from time to time, the licensee would fear that the owner would increase the rate after these assets had been created and the value of the product increased. The licensee would not invest or would invest too little in such assets.

Again, the antitrust and misuse rules raise legal concerns. The antitrust rules impose some constraints on granting an exclusive license. The antitrust and misuse rules have been asserted to prohibit an owner from seeking to prevent a buyer of a product from a low-investment, nonexclusive licensee from reselling to a user in a high-investment, exclusive market.

There are other contract devices for protecting the value of licensee investments. The licensor might grant several licenses and provide that each licensee sell at no less than prices specified from time to time by the licensor. The law has severely limited the availability of that device (section 5.5).

An owner is unlikely to be willing to grant an exclusive license and rely on the licensee's incentives to produce and sell at royalty-maximizing levels (see section 1.10(e)). But the asset specificity problem may arise in another context.

(d) Licensing to Increase Asset-Specific Investment by Product Customers

Licensing is not always designed simply to maximize royalty revenue. The owner may vertically integrate into production and also license companies that are no more efficient than the owner. The "demand for the rights" may be increased even though the licensee produces precisely the same product as the owner at the same cost. Consumer demand may depend on the number of actual or potential product suppliers. The reason for licensing may be that a vertically integrated owner needs to induce customers to make investments that depend on assurances of future supply and safeguards against future price increases. The owner may license to assure potential customers that there will be a second source.

This may occur if customers must make investments the value of which depends on the availability and price of the product. Suppose the protected product is a component of another product, such as a semiconductor device for use in a computer. Customers may have to design

1.10 LICENSING STRATEGY, TERMS, AND PROFITS

and engineer their final products so that they are compatible with the protected product. Customers may have to invest in equipment to produce the final product and in long-term supply arrangements with suppliers of other necessary components. Those investments are *asset specific*. They are valuable only if used with the rights.

Asset specificity can create another form of the hold-up problem that will deter customer investments and limit product demand.[49] The license increases derived demand by increasing product demand even though the licensee is no more efficient than the owner. Indeed, the owner may want to license a second source that will produce precisely the same product as the owner. The rights owner grants its own customers a license to supply the customer's needs if the owner is unable or unwilling to supply the product at agreed prices in the future.

A similar problem arises when value of a product to a user increases as the amount of its use increases or as the total number of users increases. The product may become more valuable because the user has invested time and effort in leaning to use it. It may become more valuable because there is a larger supply of other people trained to use it or repair it for the owner. The product may be more valuable because others have invested in supplying different, compatible products that enhance its usefulness. All of these examples are demand-side scale economy effects. These situations are sometimes called network externalities or industry standards.

In these situations, the rights owner may license other suppliers so that the number of users of its product grows at a more rapid rate than for other competing products. Inducing investments by customers and others may again depend on assurance of continued supply from multiple sources. These situations raise difficult issues. The owner may wish to authorize these licensees to make products that have the features needed to achieve the gains from large scale use, while precluding their use of certain distinctive characteristics for its particular version of the product. There is an incentive for users to cooperate with each other in deciding what product to adopt. There is also an incentive for suppliers of potentially competing products to try to control the rates of growth of their products or to select and share in the benefits of the one product

---

[49] Milgrom and Roberts, at 307–308.

likely to survive. Cooperation among alternative suppliers of course, involves the risk that the suppliers' agreement will not be one to develop the market most quickly and efficiently, but to slow down the growth rate.

(e) Terms to Induce Licensee Investments and Limit Licensee Output Restriction

The value of licensing to the owner will depend on the degree of competition among licensees of the rights. Assume that there are no free-rider problems of the type discussed earlier. Competition among authorized users of rights will not affect the value of the product, D, or the costs of producing and selling, MC.

Competition among licensees will affect the output of the products using the rights, the total revenue from sales, and total royalty revenue. This is illustrated in Figure 1.10. This figure is based on the same assumptions as Figure 1.1, save that it is value maximizing to have many licensees. Assume that the owner must license to earn any profits. The maximum licensing profits will result from licensees as a group supplying 125 units. At that level of output, the market clearing price will be $275. That is the output that a single supplier of the licensed products would choose to maximize profits. At this output, the marginal revenue from supplying the last unit equals the marginal cost of making and selling it. This is also the output at which marginal revenue from licensing equals the marginal cost of licensing, assumed to be zero. The profit-maximizing royalty rate is $125 per unit. Licensees will view the royalty like any other cost. If there is competition among licensees, licensees as a group will supply additional units until the price equals marginal cost plus royalty. This yields maximum profits for the owner. Profits from licensing will be $15,625.

If licensees are not competing on price to make additional sales, quantity will fall below 125 units and licensing profits will be reduced. If a licensee has market power in selling the product, its incentive will be to restrict production below the level that maximizes profits for the licensor. This problem for the licensor is one of *successive monopoly*.[50] Assume that there is a single licensee with market power in supplying

---

[50] Scherer and Ross at ch.14; Mansfield at 241–242; Stigler at 207–208.

1.10 LICENSING STRATEGY, TERMS, AND PROFITS

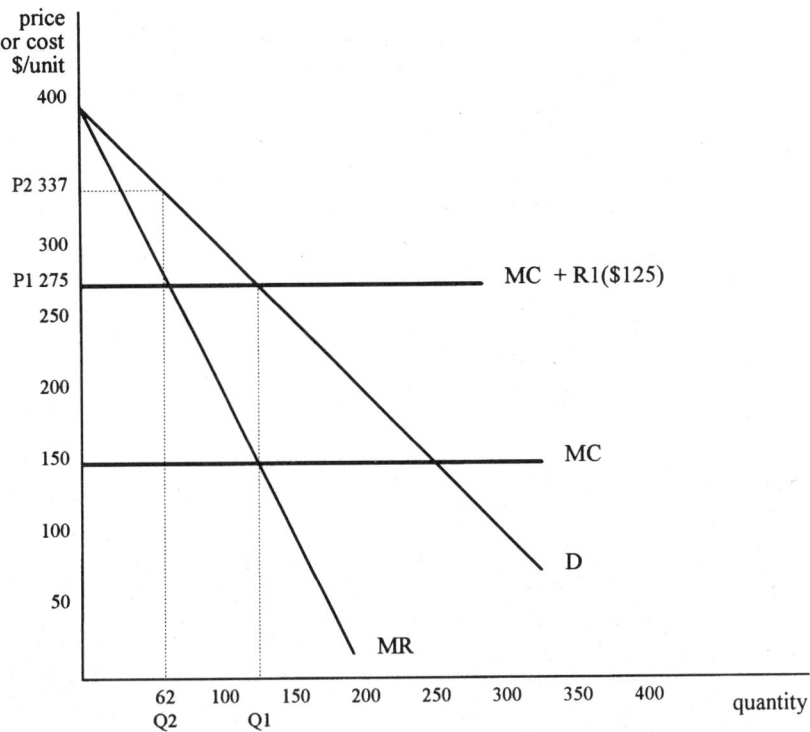

Figure 1.10. The Effect of Royalties and Licensee Market Power on Output and Owner Profits

the product. This may result from an exclusive license from the owner. The licensee will treat the royalty as a cost.

However, the licensee has some discretion as to the quantity supplied. The licensee will determine its marginal revenue, MR, from product sales and supply until that revenue equals marginal cost plus royalty. The licensee will restrict quantity from 125 units to about 62 units and sell at a higher price $337.50. The owner loses licensing profits by that additional restriction on output. In this example, the owner loses half its profits. The licensee captures a part of the value of the rights, but less than the owner lost. Overall value has been reduced.

In the extreme case, the licensee may exercise market power to limit production under the license to zero, in favor of exploiting substitute rights it owns or hopes to develop in the future. This is a devastating result for the owner.

Granting a licensee some exclusivity may be necessary to avoid a free-riding problem. The solution may create a successive monopoly problem. The owner faces a difficult decision. Can the owner limit the exclusive licensee's independent exploitation of any market power beyond the level necessary to induce to the desired investments?

Some contract devices to deter the licensee from exercising market power are:

1. To require that the licensee not deal in substitute products (to reduce the incentive to restrict exploitation of the licensed rights to zero and to compel it to devote its further investments to the owner's rights),
2. To require the licensee to *diligently* exploit the rights (a second-best response to the legal problems created by number 1),
3. To set quotas or performance standards for minimum further investments, production, and sales (a task sometimes requiring unrealistic omniscience on both sides or risk-taking on one side),
4. To increase minimum royalty rates if production or sales are too low,
5. To set the maximum price for licensee sales, or
6. To reward the licensee with additional rewards if set goals are achieved.

The first, third, and the fifth raise issues under U.S. law (sections 5.3, 5.5, 5.6). The alternative is for the owner to chose between the value of correct investment or the value of correct output and pricing.

Negotiating and creating incentives for the licensee to abide by such restriction may be aided by sharing some portion of the profits from cooperation with the licensee. The parties have a mutual interest in avoiding the problem. Total profits will be greater without individual, uncoordinated maximizing. However, obtaining and assuring the licensee's

1.10 LICENSING STRATEGY, TERMS, AND PROFITS

cooperation requires that the licensee receive part of the resulting benefit. This translates into a lower per-unit royalty and increased licensee profits. Those increased profits will also help to reduce the licensee's incentives to cheat, because termination will become more costly.

The successive monopoly problem may arise in another situation. There may be only one potential licensee, an existing company with market power in the market where the rights are useful. The potential licensee's position as the sole potential user of the rights may result from complementary rights it owns that are also necessary to produce or sell the licensed product. The potential licensee may own a *dominant* right. The source of this potential licensee's position may lie elsewhere. Whatever the reason, the owner faces the same dilemma. The *downstream* monopoly may decrease the profits from use of the rights. Again, the parties will advance their mutual profits by coordinating (reducing) royalties and price.

(f) The Impact of Monospsony (Negotiating with a Single Potential Licensee)

There is an added dilemma when a single owner faces a single potential licensee. A single product seller decides how much to produce by taking into account the effect of its output on the market price. A single seller limits production. A single buyer will do the same thing. It will decide how much to buy by taking into account the effect of its purchases on the market price. If additional purchases cause price to rise (because per-unit costs increase for suppliers), a single buyer may purchase less than several buyers would. Where competing sellers face a single buyer, this situation is called *monopsony*. In a monopsony situation, any seller is unlikely to obtain a price as high as would have prevailed had there been competition on the buyers' side.[51] If a single seller faces a single buyer (called *bilateral monopoly*), the outcome for price and output (and total profits) is uncertain.[52]

Where there is a single potential licensee, the owner cannot use competitive bidding to extract the full value of the rights. In Figure 1.1, the owner is unlikely to be able to negotiate the $125 rate. If the owner

---
[51] Mansfield at 332–340; Stigler at 87, 205–207.
[52] Scherer and Ross at ch. 14.

is incapable of producing, the bargaining range is between zero and $125. The outcome will depend more on bargaining ability than business facts. Where transaction costs are large relative to anticipated licensing revenue, the owner may not be able to negotiate with more than a few potential licensees. Those licensees may recognize the opportunity and seek to negotiate as a single buyer.

The owner may attempt to increase its bargaining position by negotiating licenses in a context in which it has a viable option not to license. A licensor engages in a waiting and wishing game (which it will ultimately lose) if it negotiates without the ability to make a credible threat that it will decline to license unless the prospective licensee agrees to its terms. A licensor not able to use the technology may maximize revenue by selling or exclusively licensing the patent to a person or firm better placed to engage in those negotiations. The owner may abandon direct licensing in favor of outright sale of the rights to the potential licensee or licensing indirectly through a licensee.

If there is a single licensee, and the payment rate per unit increases for all units as licensee output increases, licensing revenue will also be limited by the licensee's limiting its "purchases" of licenses. At a constant per-unit rate, this will not occur.

(g) Adjusting the Terms to Provide the Proper Scale of Production by Licensees

License terms may seek to decrease the cost of producing the physical goods from which demand is derived. The licensor increases demand for rights by license terms designed to minimize average total production cost. The licensor increases derived demand for rights by license terms that provide incentives for the most efficient scale and number of licensees.[53]

If the nature of the licensee's costs are such that there are economies of scale relative to the size of the market, a licensor's goal of minimizing production costs may require limiting the number of producers.[54] Production economies can result from scale or scope of production.

---

[53] Mansfield at 318–319; Stigler at 247–253.
[54] Scherer and Ross at 97–141; Mansfield at 183–184, 213–214; Stigler at 184–187.

1.10 LICENSING STRATEGY, TERMS, AND PROFITS

Economies may result from experience or learning by doing. These economies may have dramatic impact on unit costs over time.

Costs are of two types, fixed and variable. Fixed costs, such as a manufacturing facility, are those that may not be altered in response to short-run changes in demand. Variable costs, such as raw materials, may be increased or decreased in response to short-run changes in demand. The sum of fixed and variable costs at each quantity is the total cost of production. Average total costs is the number of units produced divided by the total cost of producing that number of units. The rate of change of total costs from increasing production by one unit is referred to as *marginal cost.*

It is important for an owner to consider the most efficient, that is, low-cost, scale for licensee production. Assume that the demand is such that the market may be supplied at lowest cost by a single firm. Average costs of a single firm continue to decline over the range of optimum market output. This is shown in Figure 1.11. The market value of the rights is greatest if used at the most efficient scale. Under these conditions, the most efficient and profitable level of output is level Q1. The value of the rights at that level is the difference between P1 and average total cost, AC1, which is also equal to marginal cost, MC1, assuming the one producer is operating at the correct scale.

Suppose that the owner licenses more than one producer. If the licensees enter at the efficient scale, their production will occur at an inefficiently small level. Licensee production then occurs at a point at which both average total cost and average variable cost exceed minimum costs. Inefficient production causes costs to rise and sales to fall below Q1, such as to Q2. A licensee anticipating producing at a level below Q1 will enter with an inefficiently small facility or will not enter at all. Any licensee having a nonexclusive license may recognize that at least one other licensee may enter with a large-scale, efficient plant. That licensee will be able to reduce its per-unit costs by expanding output. Any licensee that enters with a small plant might fail as price falls below its minimum cost.

If more than one licensee enters at the efficient scale, they may recognize that only one licensee is likely to survive. In any event, part of the value of the invention is wasted, because the licenses induce production at an improperly small scale or lead to wasteful competition by multiple licensees entering at the proper scale. As in the case of the free-

THE BUSINESS OF LICENSING INTELLECTUAL PROPERTY RIGHTS

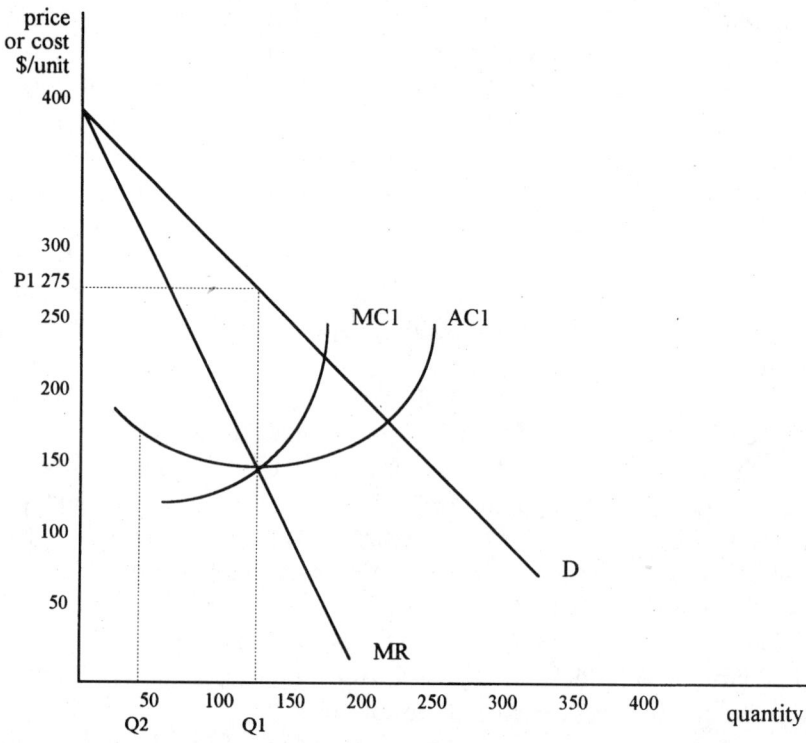

Figure 1.11. The Effects of Scale on Licensee Costs

riding problem, economies of scale relative to the size of a market lead to the successive monopoly problem.

Suppose average costs of a single firm continue to decline over all possible ranges of market output. This is shown in Figure 1.12. The owner now faces a particularly difficult problem. Fixed costs can be such a large percentage of total costs that average and marginal costs decline over all potential outputs. An example would be average total cost, AC2, and marginal cost, MC2. There is no output at which the price can equal both average and marginal costs. This cost situation is incompatible with long-run competition among licensees. If licensees continue to compete for expanded sales, there is no stable situation where multiple licensees can sell at a price that will cover average cost. There will ultimately be

1.10 LICENSING STRATEGY, TERMS, AND PROFITS

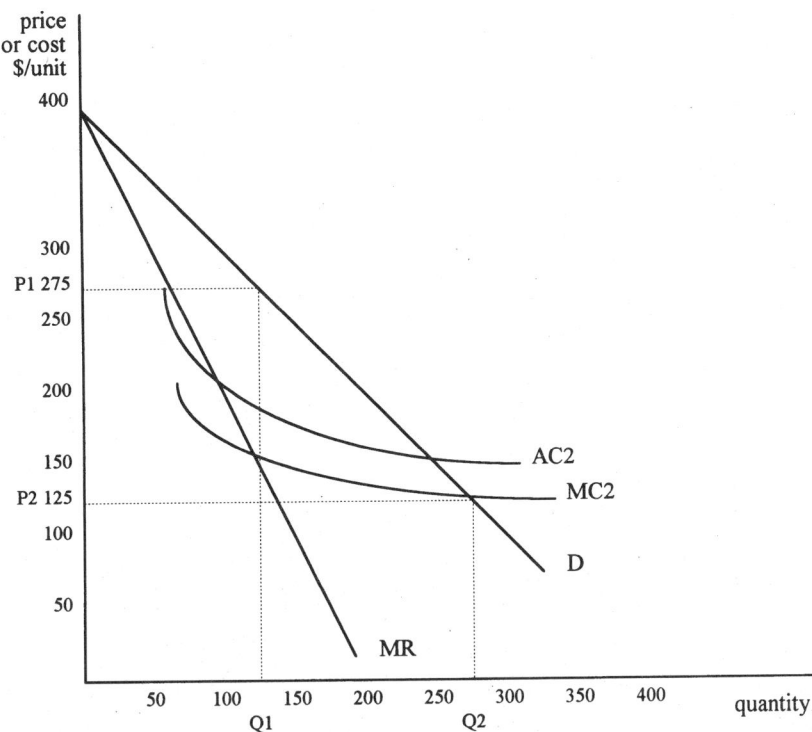

Figure 1.12. The Effect of Declining Costs

one survivor, which may then have the ability to reduce output. The owner must make a trade-off between cost reduction and licensee competition.[55]

This declining cost problem may also call for adaptation of royalty structure. A royalty structure that encouraged price discrimination in product sales may permit achieving low-cost production and recovery of average costs.[56] For example, the owner might charge higher royalties for

---

[55] An example of how to make that trade-off is William F. Baxter, Paul H. Cootner, and Kenneth E. Scott, *Retail Banking in the Electronic Age,* 1977 (Allanfeld, Osmun, Montclair) ch. 5–6.

[56] F.M. Scherer and David Ross, *Industrial Market Structure and Economic Performance,* 1990 (Houghton Mifflin, Boston) at 496–502.

sales to customers whose demand is zero to Q1, and lower for customers from Q1 to Q2. This would seek to encourage pricing of $275 for the high-value customers and slightly above $125 (marginal cost) to lower-value customers.

(h) Terms to Induce Licensees to Use Inputs in the Right (Low-Cost) Proportions

If the rights relate to one physical component used in variable proportions with other components to make a final product, an owner may seek to limit the incentives of the licensees to substitute other components for the protected one. This is a complex decision. There are four factors, each of which will determine the demand for a component useful in variable proportions to other components.[57]

The owner may benefit because the licensee will use the components in a proportion that lowers final product cost. The owner may wish to supply both the protected component and other components in the most profitable ratio. The owner may wish to supply (or license others to supply) the protected component at marginal cost and license final product

---

[57] Scherer and Ross at 521–535, 565–569; Mansfield at 309–310; Stigler at 242–244, 346–347.

First, the elasticity of demand for the end product is directly related to the elasticity of derived demand for the input. If the quantity of the end product sold decreases very little in response to a price increase, an increase in the price of an input will lead to a small decrease in the amount used.

Second, the elasticity of derived demand for an input will increase as the elasticity of substituting other inputs for it increases. Elasticity of substitution measures the extent to which physical inputs, such as capital and labor, may be substituted for each other as their relative prices change.

Third, the elasticity of derived demand depends directly upon the elasticity of supply of complementary inputs. An increase in the price paid to any input will be acceptable only if the price paid by buyers of the final product increases or the prices paid to suppliers of other inputs decrease. If a small decrease in the price paid to other inputs will lead to a large decrease in the quantity available, then the elasticity of demand for the other input will increase.

Fourth, in some circumstances, the derived demand for an input increases as the share of the total cost of the product of which it is a part increases. In other words, the elasticity of demand for an input will be lower if it constitutes a smaller share of total cost. However, this relationship does not always hold.

1.10 LICENSING STRATEGY, TERMS, AND PROFITS

sellers with royalties based on final product sales. Or the owner may simply license a final product seller at royalties based on final product sales. These devices will avoid the inefficient substitution incentives. Again, the law may impose restraints (sections 3.4, 4.3, 4.4).

(i) Increasing Demand for the Rights by Increasing the Supply of Complementary Products

The demand for a product embodying certain rights often depends on the supply and price of other products and services used with the product. Conversely, the demand for these other products and services often depends on the supply and price of the product embodying the rights.

Suppose that an inventor devises an improved home movie camera. The improved movie camera will increase the demand for movie screens, film, and various camera replacement parts. When the demand for a product increases as the price of another product goes down, that product is said to be *complementary* to the one whose price changed. Complements are typically products that are used together to satisfy some need. Bacon and eggs are consumed together. If the price of eggs went down significantly, the demand for bacon might increase. Rather than consuming less bacon as eggs become more cheaply available, people would consume more.

Protected products, like all others, are likely to have many complements. Rights owners and licensees are likely to sell protected products and unprotected complements. The demand for any right increases as the availability of complementary products and services increases. The demand for any particular right decreases as the cost of complementary products and services increases.

The law has had an enormously difficult time dealing with a rights owner that improves the value of (or lowers the cost of making) a protected product and increases the value of (and demand for) complementary unprotected products. The owner of a patent on an improved button-fastening machine increases the demand for such machines and the demand for buttons used with machines. The owner of an improved salt-depositing machine increases the demand for machines and the demand for salt used with machines. The inventor of a process of making concrete roads increases the demand for use of that process and demand for bituminous emulsion used to make those roads.

Where patent owners have gone into the business of supplying the patented product with the unpatented complement or licensing the process with unpatented materials or supplies, the law has frequently viewed those activities as suspicious and even harmful. In this century, the courts created rules to preclude patent owners who devised improved machines and processes from making agreements under which the users of their patented machines and processes agreed to purchase the patented complements from the patent owner (Chapter 4).

If patent owners attempted to supply the patented product or the patented process with the supply of its complementary products, the courts frequently declared the patent unenforceable in order to "protect" the market for the complementary goods from the patent owner. Because the complementary products were not patented, an effort by the patent owner to supply them was deemed to be the equivalent of an effort to monopolize their supply. While this fear in many cases was not logical, the courts pursued it with a vengeance.

(j) Increasing Demand for the Rights by Increasing the Supply of Complementary Technology

Another device to increase demand for the rights is to increase the supply of complementary rights. Just as existing rights become more valuable if substitutes are not available, existing rights become more valuable to the extent that complementary technology is developed and is cheaply available to the licensee. There are three sources of complementary rights.

The first source is third parties. If there are third parties' rights that dominate practice of the license rights or that make that practice more valuable, then the royalty a licensee would be willing to pay for the rights cannot be determined without knowing the price for the complementary rights. It is in the interest of all owners of complementary rights to pool and jointly license those rights, since individual maximization by separate owners will lead to higher royalties and lower total revenue for all owners than joint maximization. Many profitable opportunities will arise for cross-licensing arrangements, which permit complementary rights to be made available at a known price for the package. The courts frequently

1.10 LICENSING STRATEGY, TERMS, AND PROFITS

miss the importance of the distinction between competing and complementary rights.

The second source of complementary rights is the licensee. I discussed earlier the general free-rider problem. This problem may cause an owner to try to protect a licensee's profit margins to induce it to develop complementary rights, which would have a substantial likelihood of benefiting other licensees. It is never sensible for a licensor to discourage a licensee from developing improvements that the licensor will not develop. Such improvements only increase the demand for the licensor's rights by increasing demand for the final product or reducing production costs.

Even if there is no need for special provisions to induce licensee R&D, licensee(s) may be important future sources of complementary technology. If the owner is also a producer or has more than one licensee, the owner may wish to forgo royalty revenue in exchange for a *grantback* of a licensee's rights that complement the licensed rights. The law regulates that agreement (section 3.10).

A licensor's interest in that regard is exactly the opposite of its interest with respect to the licensee's development of substitutes. The goal is to encourage the development of complementary, but not substitute, rights and obtain for the licensor and its other licensees the right to use them in a manner that does not deter their development. There is no single best answer on how to do that.

The distinction between complementary and substitute rights is not easy to draw prospectively. For example, if a licensor owns rights to a particular product, rights directed to new uses for the product are complementary to those rights and should be encouraged for that reason. However, if the licensor also owns or hopes to develop rights to new uses, a licensee's new use rights may be substitutes or potential substitutes for the licensor's rights.

The owner is the third source of complementary future technology. The same considerations that guide the terms of an agreement with respect to the licensee's further development apply to the licensor. Not surprisingly, the law treats them very differently. The law is generally indifferent to a grant that includes rights developed in the future by the licensor.

(k) Practices that Reduce the Transaction Costs

Licensing can involve high transaction costs.[58] Transaction costs, like taxes,[59] are a wedge between the amount licensees would be willing to pay and licensors would be willing to receive. The primary transaction costs are

1. The information costs of identifying buyers and sellers, and informing buyers of the rights for sale, and
2. The costs of negotiating agreements, performing under them, and detecting and stopping violations.

A technology owner may seek to patent technology, rather than rely on secrecy, to reduce information costs. For rights applicable to hundreds of potential licensees, the cost of negotiations alone may be daunting. Detecting violations may be difficult. There may be little public information permitting violations to be detected. A rate base for payments that can be performed without extensive legal analysis and verified based on public information reduces the cost of performing and detecting cheating. The costs of enforcement and defense will be significant. Provisions regarding challenges to validity, arbitration, attorney's fees for enforcement, and interest on late payments should be considered.

One way to reduce licensing costs is do not license. All of these negotiation, violation detecting, and enforcement costs are reduced to the extent that the owner retains both the intellectual and tangible property and merely provides tangible products to the "licensee" for further use.

The antitrust and misuse rules impose limits on the ability of an owner and licensee to limit transaction costs by use of simplified royalty measures that are easy to apply and difficult to cheat, packages licenses that eliminate complex questions, and tying arrangements that make it easy to make payments proportional to the extent of use by the licensee (sections 3.4, 3.5, 4.4, 4.6).

---
[58] Mansfield at 225–226.
[59] Jude Wanniski, *The Way The World Works* 1983 (Simon and Schuster, New York) pp. 71–96.

1.10 LICENSING STRATEGY, TERMS, AND PROFITS

The long-run technical and production-efficiency position of an intellectual property owner in other areas may depend on research and manufacturing experience. The license may permit the licensee to move down a research or production learning curve faster than the licensor. Research by the licensee may generate adversely held rights, which foreclose other fields of research or business for the licensor. The owner may attempt to limit those risks through broad grantbacks, output limits, and other devices.

(l) Terms to Reduce the Costs of Uncertainty and Litigation about Rights

There may be great uncertainty at the time a license is entered regarding future demand and supply conditions and the existence or scope of legal protection. Reducing or allocating uncertainty reduces costs paid to someone to bear the risk.

Transactions in proprietary rights are different from transactions for tangible goods in an important way. The ownership of tangible goods is usually almost perfectly clear. Litigation about title is highly unlikely. If a prospective buyer of a tangible good challenges the title of the prospective seller, the seller has a self-help remedy—do not transfer possession of the product. Most transactions in markets for tangible goods take place at prices that are not discounted by uncertainty about title or by the prospect of litigation to resolve any question of title.

In the context of intellectual property rights, there is often significant uncertainty about the validity or scope of the rights. In addition, a prospective licensee may learn about the protected information, reject the license, disregard the rights, and substitute litigation for permission. To the extent that uncertainty exists and the prospect of litigation increases, the demand for the rights decreases.

Patent rights are subject to the rules designed to make it profitable for a licensee to substitute litigation for the license and more difficult for the parties to reduce risk costs of uncertainty about validity.[60] Since the lower federal courts said an owner and licensee could not agree that the licensee will not challenge the validity of the patent, it has not been pos-

---

[60] *Lear v. Adkins,* 395 U.S. 653 (1969). John W. Schlicher, "A *Lear v. Adkins* Allegory, *Journal of the Patent Office Society* **68**, 427 (1986).

sible for the parties to agree (prior to filing an action) that the licensee would not substitute litigation for the license. After an action is commenced, the rules are reversed and it is lawful for the licensee to agree to forgo the litigation. One option that the law gives to intellectual property licensors is to require that licensees substitute arbitration for litigation of patent disputes arising under the license.[61]

The more important point is that an intellectual property owner should consider the effect of all provisions on incentives for litigation. Patent owners may attempt to do so by making the payment obligations independent of litigation and patent validity. This may be done by requiring lump sum payments. It may also be done by licensing and leasing a bundle of rights and property and basing payments on events independent of the existence or validity of the patents. Difficult legal issues attend such efforts (Chapters 3 and 7).

Allocating uncertainty to the proper party is also desirable. Uncertainty plays a crucial role where the risk preferences of the licensor and the licensee vary. If the licensor and the licensee have the same risk preference, allocating uncertainty to one or the other party is a matter of indifference. However, where the risk preferences to the parties are different, it is very important to allocate the risk to take those preferences into account. If the licensor is risk neutral and the licensees are all risk averse, agreements that leave the licensees to bear risk (such as large lump sum payments or requirements to buy minimum amounts of other inputs) will lead the licensee to produce at a lower level than is in the interest of the licensor.

(m) Controlling Rivalry from Substitute Rights Produced and Owned by Others

Another general issue for a rights owner is whether it should attempt to control the rivalry with competing sellers of rights. The owner of one set of rights must compete with owners of substitute rights. The owner may consider using licensing as a device to limit rivalry between people who would otherwise lawfully engage in that rivalry.

---

[61]35 U.S.C. § 294. See generally, John W. Schlicher, "The Patent Arbitration Law: A New Procedure for Resolving Patent Infringement Disputes," *Arbitration Journal* **40**, 7 (Dec. 1985).

The owner may compete with others in producing technical information, in licensing substitute rights, or in supplying tangible products. The owner needs the cooperation of its rivals to limit these forms of competition. The owner and its rivals may attempt to use licensing to limit such competition. In certain situations, licenses may provide a device for such agreements. One company's rights may be "licensed" to competing product sellers and provide mutually beneficial "limits" on some parameter of their rivalry (such as, R&D, price, quantity, territory, or customer). A company possessing certain rights may acquire competing rights or otherwise eliminate competition in their supply by cross-licensing or other types of pooling arrangements.

An owner may also consider trying to limit rivalry from others without their cooperation. The owner may attempt to buy their cooperation by granting licenses that forgo some royalty revenue and try to limit the rivalry. A licensor may try to buy a licensee's agreement not to develop substitute rights or accept a license from others under substitute rights. In most situations, it will not be profitable for an intellectual property owner to forgo the royalty income necessary to induce the licensee to agree not to do competing research or sell competing products. The potential producers of the substitute rights are likely to be too numerous to make this profitable.

1.11 AN OVERVIEW OF HOW THE LAW LIMITS LICENSING PRACTICES

The profitability of licensing depends on two sets of laws: (1) the intellectual property laws that provide rights and (2) the laws regulating how those rights may be exploited. The most dangerous legal limits on licensing new technology are the antitrust and misuse laws. If licensing intellectual property rights always violates the antitrust or misuse laws, the rights become liabilities, not assets. The antitrust and misuse laws have the potential for nullifying much of the economic benefit of intellectual property rights. This is a tragic result because the dynamic benefits of technological change easily swamp the static benefits of allocative efficiency that is so often the primary concern of antitrust law.[62]

---

[62] Scherer and Ross, at 32, 613; William F. Baxter, "Antitrust Law and Technological Innovation," in *Issues in Science and Technology,* Winter 1985 (Nat. Academy

A rational owner of information protected by intellectual property laws will try to do one of three things with the rights.

First, the owner may attempt to capture the largest part of the value flowing from the use of the rights. It may develop the technology or induce others to develop it further. It may put the invention to actual use to produce goods and services at the lowest cost. If others are able to produce better goods or the same goods at lower cost, the owner may market the rights to others and seek to induce them to make the best goods at lowest cost.

Second, the owner may use the rights as a device to limit production or otherwise decrease rivalry between people who could otherwise lawfully compete. The owner may compete with others in producing technical information or supplying tangible products. The owner and its rivals may attempt to use a license as a device to limit that competition.

Third, the owner may attempt to agree with potential users of the rights to waive the rights in exchange for the user's agreement not to compete with it or to impair the ability of someone else to compete with it in a manner that it could not control simply by enforcing the rights.

If these are the owner's only options, we should expect the law to try to discourage the second and third kinds of behavior and encourage the first kind. In general, that is what the courts have said the law attempts to do. However, the law has not accomplished its objectives. This has resulted from a difficulty in distinguishing between the first and third types of conduct. When was the owner's conduct designed to exploit the rights? When was the owner's conduct designed to limit competition by exchanging the rights for the licensee's agreement to do things that were against the licensee's interest, and limit competition in some way that the rights themselves did not permit the owner to control?

Many limits on licensing options were developed to identify and punish intellectual property owners, especially patent owners, who were deemed to be pursuing the third option—"extending the scope" of the right's effects. Beginning in the early part of this century, the Supreme Court created rules to prevent *extensions of the patent monopoly.* Throughout this century, the courts have frequently concluded that li-

---

of Sciences) at 80; Frank W. Easterbrook, "Intellectual Property Is Still Property," *Harvard Journal of Law & Public Policy* **13**, 108 (1990).

censors were licensing the rights, especially patents, to acquire market power that did not inherently exist by virtue of those rights.[63] The courts, particularly the Supreme Court, condemned various provisions that theoretically might be used to achieve this purpose.

The Court first declared such provisions unenforceable. Licensees coerced into accepting undesired terms could simply capitulate, then ignore them. Even though unenforceable terms cannot hurt the economy, the Court later created a rule under which patent property rights are temporarily forfeited if a patent owner tries the impossible. The Court never has revealed the trick by which a patent owner coerces a licensee into complying with an unenforceable obligation.

In fact, the conditions under which an extension strategy would be profitable are unlikely to occur in many markets for rights. A owner must forgo current revenue to induce a licensee to forgo more profitable options and, thereby, to acquire market power the rights did not provide. That market power must be exploited to earn a profitable rate of return on the "costs" incurred to acquire it. Often, this market power is unlikely to last long enough to permit sufficient returns to be captured. Nonetheless, the Supreme Court from 1917 to 1969 found that patent owners frequently employ this extension strategy.[64]

The most significant practical problem in licensing is that provisions useful to pursue the first goal are unavailable or risky, because the law mistakes them for devises to pursue the extension-of-rights goal. Even if the owner of rights is not employing the extension-of-rights strategy, the courts may find that it is. There are many license provisions

---

[63]For example, *Zenith Radio Corp. v. Hazeltine Research, Inc.*, 395 U.S. 100, 136 (1969); *Brulotte v. Thys Co.*, 379 U.S. 29, 32–33 (1964); *United States v. Line Material Co.*, 333 U.S. 287, 308 (1948); *Morton Salt Co. v. G.S. Suppiger Co.*, 314 U.S. 488 (1942); *B.B. Chem. Corp. v. Ellis*, 314 U.S. 495, 496–497 (1942); *Ethyl Gasoline Corp. v. United States*, 209 U.S. 346, 456 (1939); cf., *Jefferson Parish Hosp. Dist. No. 2 v. Hyde*, 466 U.S. 2, 16–17 (1984) (dicta); *Blonder-Tongue Laboratories, Inc. v. Univ. of Illinois Foundation*, 402 U.S. 313, 343 (1971) (dicta).

[64]Ward S. Bowman, Jr., *Patent and Antitrust Law* (1973); Testimony of John W. Schlicher, Hearings on S.1841 and S.1535, pp. 177–198 (S. Hrg. 98–1008, 98th Cong., 2nd Sess. April 3, 1984); William F. Baxter, Remarks to the National Association of Manufacturers on May 10, 1983, CCH Trade Reg. Rep. § 50,447 (1983); Abbott B. Lipsky, Jr., Remarks to the ABA Antitrust Section, November 5, 1981, CCH Trade Reg. Rep. § 50,434 (1981).

that the courts have said are useful to "extend the monopoly." Often, those provisions may contribute to solving one or more of the problems identified above. None of the provisions—save agreements to deter development or independent licensing of substitute technology—depend for their success on decreasing competition not inherently the result of the existence of the rights.

The next chapter discusses important changes in the legal environment in the last fifteen years. These changes are creating important new opportunities.

2

The Law of Licensing Intellectual Property Rights

2.1	The Legal Limits on Licensing	95
2.2	An Introduction to Intellectual Property Law	95
2.3	The Legal Theories of Intellectual Property Rights to Technology	99
2.4	Fundamental Legal Concepts of Licensing	112
2.5	The Limits on Licensing under Antitrust, Misuse, and Public Policy Doctrines	114
2.6	Antitrust Standards	116
2.7	Misuse Standards	124
2.8	The Public Policy Standard	146
2.9	A Brief History of the Legal Limits on Licensing	147
2.10	The Economic Principles Underlying Legal Limits on Licensing Patent and Related Rights	153
2.11	The Basic Options of Intellectual Property Owners	164
2.12	The Law and the Basic Options of Intellectual Property Owners	166

2.1 THE LEGAL LIMITS ON LICENSING

The law constrains the licensing business. Antitrust, misuse, contract, and intellectual property laws limit licensing options. This chapter introduces the basic doctrines. Later chapters describe their application to particular contract devices. Licenses presume the existence of intellectual property rights.

2.2 AN INTRODUCTION TO INTELLECTUAL PROPERTY LAW

(a) Patent Law

Article I of the U.S. Constitution gives Congress certain "limited" powers.[1] One of those powers is to grant patents to inventors and copyrights to authors. Article I, Section 8, Clause 8 of the Constitution states:

> The Congress shall have Power . . . To promote the progress of Science and useful Arts, by securing for limited Times to Authors and Inventors the exclusive Right to their respective Writings and Discoveries.

In 1790, Congress enacted the patent laws.[2] Patents grant property rights to technical information about the nature of tangible products and processes. Patent law calls this information an "invention." The Supreme Court has declared that the purpose of patent law is to improve incen-

---

[1] The reality is that Congress can enact almost any law it wants regardless of the constitutional powers. This may be changing.
[2] *Patent Act,* 1 Stat. 109 (1790).

tives for people to engage in the research and development that produces technical information.³

The Patent Act provides that an inventor of any new and useful process, machine, article, or composition of matter, and any improvement of them, may obtain a patent.⁴ A patent grants to the inventor the right to exclude others from making, using, or selling products and processes embodying the invention throughout the United States for the term of the patent (for most patents, seventeen years after the patent issues).⁵ When the patent term ends, the owner's patent rights cease. During the term, others may not make, use, or sell products and processes using the invention without violating those rights.⁶

In addition, the owner has rights against others who did not make, use, or sell a patented product. The owner has rights against those who actively induce others to infringe the patent.⁷ In some circumstances, others may also not sell unpatented components of a patented product or sell materials or apparatus useful in carrying out a patented process.⁸ In

---

³ *Kewanee Oil Co.* v. *Bicron Corp.,* 416 U.S. 470, 477–478, 480, 481 (1974) ("The patent laws promote this progress by offering a right of exclusion for a limited period as an incentive to inventors to risk the often enormous costs in terms of time, research, and development. The productive effort thereby fostered will have a positive effect on society through the introduction of new products and processes of manufacture into the economy, and the emanations by way of increased employment and better lives for our citizens."); *Sears, Roebuck & Co. v. Stiffel Co.,* 376 U.S. 225, 229–230 (1964) ("Patents are not given as favors, as was the case of monopolies given by the Tudor Monarchs, see *The Case of Monopolies (Darcy v. Allein),* 11 Co. Rep. 84b, 77 Eng. Rep. 1260 (K.B. 1602), but are meant to encourage invention by rewarding the inventor with the right, limited to a term of years fixed by the patent, to exclude others from the use of his invention."); *Dr. Miles Medical Co. v. Park & Sons Co.,* 220 U.S. 373, 401 (1911) ("The purpose of the patent law is to stimulate invention."); *Grant v. Raymond,* 31 U.S. 218, 241–242 (1832)("[I]t cannot be doubted, that the settled purpose of the United States has ever been, and continues to be, to confer on the authors of useful inventions an exclusive right in their inventions, for the time mentioned in their patent. It is the reward stipulated for the advantages derived by the public for the exertions of the individual, and is intended as a stimulus to those exertions.").
⁴ 35 U.S.C. § 101 (1976).
⁵ 35 U.S.C. §§ 154, 271 (1976).
⁶ 35 U.S.C. §§ 112, 154 (1976); *Special Equipment Co. v. Coe,* 324 U.S. 370, 378 (1945).
⁷ 35 U.S.C. § 271(b).
⁸ 35 U.S.C. § 271(c).

2.2 AN INTRODUCTION TO INTELLECTUAL PROPERTY LAW

some circumstances, others may also not supply unpatented components of a patented product intending that the product be made outside the United States.[9] In some circumstances, others may not import, sell, or use a product made by using a patented process.[10]

(b) Copyright Law

Copyrights seek to improve the incentives for authors to invest the time and effort needed to write original works. Copyright protection also exists only under federal law.[11] A copyright grants to authors for limited times the exclusive right to reproduce copies of the work, to prepare derivative works based on it, to distribute copies of it, and in certain cases, to perform or display the work publicly.[12] A copyright protects only the author's original expression of ideas and does not preclude others from reproducing only the ideas expressed in the work.[13] Unlike a patent, a copyright affords protection only against others who copy the work of the original author. A copyright provides no rights against anyone who independently creates an identical work.[14] Also unlike a patent, a copyright does not grant to its owner the right to exclude others from all uses of the copyrighted work.[15]

(c) Trade Secret Law

Licenses under existing or potential patents frequently include licenses to use unpatented technical information. Indeed, technical information may be licensed when it is not patented and later becomes patented. Also, technical information may be licensed when it is patented and later becomes unpatented.

---

[9] 35 U.S.C. § 271(f).
[10] 35 U.S.C. § 271(g).
[11] 17 U.S.C. §§ 102, 301 (1976).
[12] 17 U.S.C. §§ 106, 302–305 (1976).
[13] 17 U.S.C. §§ 102 (b); *Baker v. Selden,* 101 U.S. 99 (1880).
[14] 35 U.S.C. §§ 102 (1976); *Kewanee Oil Co. v. Bicron Corp.,* 416 U.S. 470, 477–478 (1974).
[15] *Bauer & Cie v. O'Donnell,* 229 U.S. 1, 13–14 (1913).

State law governs the protection afforded unpatented information that is commonly called a *trade secret*. There are two state law definitions of a potentially protectible trade secret.

Prior to the 1980s, the courts generally followed the Restatement of Torts(2d) definition. Under this definition, a trade secret may be any "secret" information that is used or could be used in a business and give that business a competitive advantage over other businesses that do not use or know the information.[16] Any secret technical or business information that could be used to obtain an industrial or commercial advantage may be protected as a trade secret.[17] In the 1980s, many states adopted all or parts of the Uniform Trade Secret Act to define trade secret protection.[18] The Uniform Act provides certain remedies against "misappropriation" of a "trade secret." A trade secret is information that (1) derives independent economic value, actual or potential, from not being generally known to the public or to other persons who can obtain economic value from its disclosure or use; and (2) is the subject of efforts that are reasonable under the circumstances to maintain its secrecy.[19]

Information may be protected as a trade secret even though it could have been patented and was not.[20] Federal patent law does not preclude the state law protection of potentially patentable trade secrets.[21] How-

---

[16] Restatement, Torts § 757, Comment b.

[17] Restatement, Torts § 757, Comment b. The Restatement did not define when information was sufficiently "secret" to constitute a protectible "trade secret." The Restatement said a "trade secret" was defined in some unexplained way by considering six factors. These factors related to the extent to which the information was known outside the business, known inside the business, the measures to guard secrecy, the value to its possessor and competitors, the amount of the money expended to develop it, and the ease or difficulty of properly acquiring or duplicating it.

[18] Civil Code §§ 3426–3426.10 and Code of Civil Procedure § 2036.2.

[19] That definition differs from the Restatement definition primarily in that it makes reasonable self-protective efforts a necessary condition to trade secret status. Under the Restatement view, the reasonableness of efforts to preserve secrecy was simply one of six factors.

[20] *Kewanee Oil Co. v. Bicron Corp.*, 416 U.S. 470, 483 (1974); *Telex Corp. v. I.B.M.*, 510 F.2d 894, 929–930 (10th Cir. 1975).

[21] *Kewanee Oil Corp. v. Bicron Corp.*, 416 U.S. 470 (1974) (state law may grant injunction against use and disclosure of trade secrets by former employees until such time as the information becomes generally available to the public); *Aronson v. Quick Point Pencil Co.*, 440 U.S. 257 (1979) (state law may enforce a trade secret

ever, the Supreme Court has declared that patent law does preempt certain principles of state contract law, and thereby limits certain license terms (see Chapter 7).

Unlike patent law, trade secret law does not prohibit all unauthorized users of a protectible trade secret. Rather the law gives the owner rights against those who obtain the secret from the owner in certain circumstances. Trade secret law prohibits disclosure or use of trade secrets by two types of people. Trade secret law provides rights against people who obtain the information under an expressed or implied obligation to keep it secret or not to use it. Trade secret law also prohibits disclosure or use of trade secrets by others, who obtain the information by improper means. Trade secret law provides no rights against a person who independently develops or properly obtains the information.[22]

As discussed earlier in section 1.3(c), information may be disclosed and licensed when it is not generally to the public, and later become public. Moreover, information, commonly called know-how, may be disclosed and licensed when it is not known the licensee, but is available to the public in some manner. In each of these situations, the parties try to provide limits on use of information beyond those trade secret law would provide.

2.3 THE LEGAL THEORIES OF INTELLECTUAL PROPERTY RIGHTS TO TECHNOLOGY

There are four competing legal models of intellectual property law, discussed in the following. These laws generally developed from the models. It is helpful to some to understand the theories, because the theories largely answer several basic questions: Can I refuse to license? Can I refuse even if I am not using the rights? Can I charge any price I want? Do I have to treat everyone the same?

---

license requiring payment of royalties based upon sales of products occurring after any "trade secret" has been publicly disclosed). See Chapter 7.
[22] *Kewanee Oil Co. v. Bicron Corp.*, 416 U.S. 470, 490 (1974); *Dr. Miles Medical Co. v. Park & Sons Co.*, 220 U.S. 373, 400–402 (1911).

(a) Property Rights

Technical information has the two characteristics of so-called public goods (see Chapter 1).[23] The term *public good* is unfortunate because it implies that, unless the government produces the good, none of it will be produced. Public goods pose a problem for systems where decentralized markets direct business activity—not central planners or agencies administering industrial policy.

A market economy depends on private opportunity and incentives to produce goods and services. In a market system, private incentives to produce public goods may be too low or too slow. For example, an economy without patent laws will invest too little or too slowly in designing new products and processes the law calls "inventions."[24] Investment will be too low or too late, because the private value of an invention to its producer is likely to be much less than the value of the invention to consumers. Because the rate of inventing over time is too slow, supply and demand conditions for goods and services do not improve as quickly as they should. Resources are wasted using processes and making products

---

[23] On the public good problem generally, see Harold Demsetz, "The Private Production of Public Goods," *Journal of Law and Economics* **13**(2), 293 (1970); Armen Alchian and William Allen, *Exchange and Production, Theory in Use,* 1969 (Wadsworth, New York) at 251–253 (later edition, Alchian and Allen, *Exchange and Production: Competition, Coordination, and Control,* 2nd ed., 1977); Ronald Coase, "The Lighthouse in Economics," *Journal of Law and Economics* **17,** 357 (1974).
On the public good problem of technical information, see Kenneth J. Arrow, *Economic Welfare and the Allocation of Resources for Invention, in the Rate and Direction of Inventive Activity,* 1962 (Princeton University Press, Princeton) at 619; and Harold Demsetz, "Information and Efficiency: Another Viewpoint," *Journal of Law and Economics* **12**, 1 (1969).
[24] F.M. Scherer and David Ross, *Industrial Market Structure and Economic Performance,* 1990 (Houghton Mifflin, Boston) ("Scherer and Ross"), ch. 17; John W. Schlicher, *Patent Law: Legal and Economic Principles,* 1992 (Clark Boardman Callaghan, New York), ch. 2; Frank W. Easterbrook, "Intellectual Property Is Still Property," *Harvard Journal of Law & Public Policy* **13**, 108 (1990); William F. Baxter, "Antitrust Law and Technological Innovation," in *Issues in Science and Technology,* Winter 1985 (Nat. Academy of Sciences) at 80; Edmond W. Kitch, "The Nature and Function of the Patent System," *Journal of Law and Economics* **20,** 265 (1977); William D. Nordhaus, *Invention, Growth, and Welfare,* 1969 (MIT Press, Cambridge).

2.3 THE LEGAL THEORIES OF INTELLECTUAL PROPERTY RIGHTS

that are not as valuable as those that would have been used or made with better technology.

There is a legal device that leaves production of public goods to private producers and market incentives—create property rights in technical information. The law reduces the gap between private and total value by giving the owner the right for a time to exclude others from using the protected information. Under this theory, intellectual property laws are simply property rights systems for an intangible good.

Intellectual property rights permit the producer to exclude use by others. Intellectual property law does not require the owner to exercise those rights. Intellectual property rights, like other property rights, may be transferred and waived. Therefore, postproduction markets for the rights may arise. There will again be transaction costs involved in making postproduction agreements. Strategic bargaining problems are eliminated, because free-riders are excluded.

Transfers of rights are vital to the purpose of the system. If the owner may not transfer the rights, the private value of the information to the owner is likely, in many (if not most) cases, to continue to be well below its real value. The owner may be a very efficient producer of information and a very minor or poor user. Granting rights to exclude is not sufficient to permit an information producer to capture the benefits flowing from that information. The owner of the rights must be permitted to waive them.

What legal limits should apply to property transfers? The owner must be permitted to charge as high a price as users will bear, and to refuse to transfer for any reason. If the law compels a transfer, this *off-market* option will reduce the price, and defeat the reason for the grant. If the law compels "equal treatment" of users, the law will again reduce the value of the rights, because users will have different values for the rights. Indeed, compelling equal treatment of users would be folly.

The public good dilemma for a market system is that a single price cannot ration efficiently the existing supply and provide accurate information and incentives *(price signals)* for future production. In many situations, it may be possible for the owner of the rights to sell them to different users at different prices. A single price is not inevitable. Economic discrimination may be possible. If Jones values an invention less than Smith, a price at Smith's value will prevent Jones from using it. However, it is always in the interest of the seller of that product to supply it to Jones and Smith at a price equal to its value to each of them. If it is possible to sell to Smith at a higher price than Jones (and that obviously requires some way to prevent Jones from reselling to Smith), both may use it. Perfect economic discrimination among users and uses permits both long-run signaling and short-run rationing goals to be achieved.

The courts have recognized this property rights theory on and off for many years.[25] However, the courts have never treated it as the only theory.

(b) Monopoly Rights

In the early part of this century, the Supreme Court often abandoned the property rights theory in the patent area. In its place, the Court adopted the view that patent law gave patent owners monopolies. Patent "monopolies," like monopolies produced by horizontal cartels, were thought to be harmful to a market-driven "competitive" economy.

The origins of the U.S. patent system may have contributed to the judicial confusion about whether patents were property rights or monopolies. In the seventeenth and eighteenth centuries in England, private enterprise existed, but it was private enterprise for the few. The system was commonly called mercantilism. Under mercantilism, markets existed but the only people who could transact business in them were those authorized by some king, queen or other unelected official. The government would charter its relatives, political allies, friends, or "financial backers" by granting exclusive rights to engage in various businesses, such as the right to sell tea to the colonies.

---

[25] *Dawson Chem. Co. v. Rohm & Haas,* 448 U.S. 176, 221 (1980); *Kewanee Oil Co. v. Bicron Corp.,* 416 U.S. 470, 480–481, 484 (1974); *Sears, Roebuck & Co. v. Stiffel Co.,* 376 U.S. 225, 229–230 (1964); *Transparent-Wrap Machine Corp. v. Stokes & Smith Co.,* 329 U.S. 637, 643 (1947); *United States v. United Shoe Mach. Co.,* 247 U.S. 32, 57 (1918); *Continental Paper Bag Co. v. Eastern Paper Bag Co.,* 210 U.S. 405, 429 (1908); *Seymore v. Osborne,* 78 U.S. 516, 560 (1871); *Kendall v. Winsor,* 62 U.S. 322 (1859); *Wilson v. Rousseau,* 45 U.S. 646, 674–675 (1846); *Grant v. Raymond,* 31 U.S. 218, 241–243 (1832). On property rights generally, see Demsetz, H., "The Exchange and Enforcement of Property Rights," *Journal of Law and Economics* **7,** 11 (1964), and Demsetz, H., "Toward a Theory of Property Rights," *American Economic Review* **57,** 347 (1967).

2.3 THE LEGAL THEORIES OF INTELLECTUAL PROPERTY RIGHTS

As early as 1602, the English Courts declared that a monopoly granted for importing, manufacturing, and selling playing cards was illegal at common law. In *Darcy v. Alein,* the English Court said a monopoly was illegal at common law, if (1) it prevented a craftsman from carrying on his ordinary trade, (2) it tended to raise the price of a commodity and lower its quality, or (3) the Crown was deceived in granting it intending the grant to be for the public good where, in fact, it was not. The decision apparently made no mention of patents for inventions.

In 1624, Parliament tried to preclude the sovereign from granting those rights without Parliament's consent. Parliament declared in the Statute Of Monopolies that all monopolies, dispensations and grants were void unless valid at common law. Section 6 of the Act said:

> Provided also (and be it declared and enacted) that any declaration before mentioned shall not extend to any letters, patents and grants of privilege for the term of fourteen years or under, hereafter to be made, of the sole working or making of any manner or new manufacturers within this realm, to the true and first inventor and inventors of such manufacturers which others at the time of making such letters and grants shall not use, so as also they be not contrary to the law or mischievous to the state, by raising prices of commodities at home, or hurt of trade, or generally inconvenient.

The act specifically authorized grants for a limited time of exclusive rights to those who created the new technical information. Hence, the patent system traces its conceptual origins to a statute, unfortunately named the "Statue Of Monopolies," that in one stroke eliminated government grants of exclusive rights to supply products and authorized grants of exclusive rights for a limited time to exploit new technical information by supplying new products made possible by the information. In the 1770's, Adam Smith demolished the economic logic of mercantilism, and the colonists declared themselves free of the system. However, they also embraced the idea of patents.

In 1890, Congress enacted the Sherman Act declaring it a misdemeanor to "monopolize . . . any part of the trade or commerce among the States...."[26] The courts had considerable difficulty defining what Congress meant by "monopolizing" part of commerce. However, it was plain that to say a person acquired or held a monopoly was different from saying a person acquired or owned property. Whatever "monopoly" meant, it was something that was sometimes undesirable.

By the early 1900s, the Supreme Court began to use the term with increasing frequency to describe patent rights. In 1923, the Supreme Court said, "[a] patent confers a monopoly."[27] However, the Court sometimes seemed to use the term as a shorthand way of describing the fact that patents gave the right to exclude others from using the invention. Used in that way, the term had no necessary connotation that a patent "monopoly" was necessarily the same as a harmful economic monopoly.[28] In 1933, the Court said in *United States v. Dubilier Condensor Corp.*,[29] "[t]hough often so characterized, a patent is not, accurately speaking, a monopoly, for it is not created by the executive authority at the expense and to the prejudice of all the community except the grantee of the patent." The Court said that, according to *Webster's New International Dictionary,* a monopoly was "... the giving of an exclusive privilege for buying, selling, working or using a thing which the public freely enjoyed prior to the grant." A patent did not fit the bill because "[a]n inventor deprives the public of nothing which it enjoyed before his discovery...."

While that definition of a monopoly is something different from an economist's definition, the idea seemed clear enough that patents did not have the feature that made "monopolies" undesirable.

Beginning perhaps as early as 1917, the Supreme Court used the term *patent monopoly* in a way that implied that patents had the presumably harmful consequences of economic monopolies. In 1917 in *Motion Picture Patents Co. v. Universal Film Mfg. Co.*,[30] the Supreme Court began to equate "patent monopolies" with economic monopolies. A patent owner granted a license to a company to sell a patented motion

---

[26] 15 U.S.C. § 2.
[27] *Crown Co. v. Nye Tool Works,* 261 U.S. 24, 37 (1923).
[28] *United States v. United Shoe Mach. Co.,* 247 U.S. 32, 57–58 (1918).
[29] 289 U.S. 178, 179–180 (1933).
[30] *Motion Picture Patents Co. v. Universal Film Mfg. Co.,* 243 U.S. 501, 510–517 (1917). See section 4.5(c).

2.3 THE LEGAL THEORIES OF INTELLECTUAL PROPERTY RIGHTS

picture projector with a notice that it was licensed only for use with films containing the invention of another patent owned by the patent owner. The Court treated the notice as one permitting use of the machine only with unpatented films obtained from the owner of the projector patent. The film patent had expired. The Court declared the notice ineffective.

The Court said that to enforce the notice would "create a monopoly in the manufacture and use of moving picture films. . . ." This would extend the "power of the owner of the patent to fix the price of the unpatented supplies [, films,] as effectively as he may fix the price on the patented machine." The patent owner may have no "power" to control the price of projectors. It may have had no projector monopoly in an economic sense. However, the Court plainly talked as if it did, and wanted to make sure that the projector monopoly position did not become an undesirable film monopoly.

The monopoly theory reached its heights in the early 1940s. In the 1940s, the Supreme Court came to use the term *patent monopoly* in a way that implied that patent owners always were or, if they wished, could become monopolists in an economic sense.

In 1942, the Supreme Court enunciated a rule limiting a patent owner's options in licensing the rights.[31] The patent owner had leased a machine on the condition that the lessee use the machine only with salt tablets purchased from the patent owner. Congress had enacted a specific antitrust statute to govern that practice. The Supreme Court said we need not concern ourselves with whether the patent owner violated the limits Congress specified. The Court asserted power to condemn conduct that Congress had not because a patent is a monopoly, monopolies are harmful, and the Court had inherent power to regulate use of that monopoly. Hence, conduct that would have been lawful under the standards set by Congress became unlawful under the standards set by the Court.

In a companion case, a patent owner pointed out that unless it was permitted to earn money by selling products used with a patented process, there was no economical way for the owner to earn any returns at all from the invention.[32] Licensing each user was too expensive. The Court

---

[31] *Morton Salt Co. v. G.S. Suppinger Co.*, 314 U.S. 488, 490–494 (1942). See section 4.5(c).
[32] *B.B. Chem. Corp. v. Ellis*, 314 U.S. 495, 498 (1942). See section 4.5(c).

brushed aside that point by saying that it not need concern itself with the effects of its decision. The Court essentially said that, if its decision prevented inventions from being made in the first place because they could not be profitably exploited, the Supreme Court was indifferent to that possibility.

In 1944, in a somewhat similar kind of situation, the patent owner told the Court that the effect of its decision was to eliminate all remedies against people who sold products that could be used only to make the patented product, a remedy that greatly reduced the number of lawsuits a patent owner had to bring to stop infringement.[33] Justice Douglas declared the efficiency of the remedies against infringement to be a matter that he and the Court need not even pause to consider. Patents were monopolies and monopolies must be kept within strict boundaries, even if doing so defeats the whole purpose of the patent system for particular types of inventions.

In 1945, the Supreme Court said the same thing in a different way. The Court declared that patents were an "exception" to the general rule against monopolies and in favor of "free and open" markets.[34] Justice Douglas emphasized the point (though in a dissenting opinion) saying "[i]t is a mistake therefore to conceive of a patent as but another form of private property."[35] Calling patent rights an "exception" to the general rule favoring competitive markets has an important consequence. Whenever the Court was uncertain about whether a patent owner was exercising patent rights in a harmful or beneficial way, the proper result was to protect the general rule and keep the exception as limited as possible.[36] All ties and uncertain cases were to be decided against the patent owners.

In later years, the Supreme Court sometimes recognized that patent rights do not always provide their owners economic monopolies. In 1958, in *Northern Pacific R. Co. v. United States*,[37] the Court said, "[o]f course it is common knowledge that a patent does not confer a monop-

---

[33] *Mercoid Corp. v. Mid-Continent Co.*, 320 U.S. 661, 669 (1944). See section 4.5(d).
[34] *Precision Co. v. Automotive Co.*, 324 U.S. 806, 816 (1945).
[35] *Special Equipment Co. v. Coe*, 324 U.S. 370, 380 (1945).
[36] *Mercoid Corp. v. Mid-Continent Co.*, 320 U.S. 661, 665–666 (1944); *United States v. Masonite Corp.*, 316 U.S. 265, 280 (1942).
[37] 356 U.S. 1, 10 n. 8 (1958).

2.3 THE LEGAL THEORIES OF INTELLECTUAL PROPERTY RIGHTS

oly over a particular commodity." In 1980, the Supreme Court signaled that it was, perhaps, dispensing with the "general rule–exception" dichotomy. The Court declared that the policy of competition and the policy of invention were of equal importance.[38] In 1984, Justice O'Connor and three other members of the Court declared that there was no reason to believe that patents had the characteristics of an economic monopoly.[39]

The monopoly theory has some appeal when viewed in a static sense, that is, by ignoring the beneficial effects the law will have over time due to changes in behavior. Static analysis has been a major obstacle to developing rational law. Ignore that patent law increases the rate of invention production. Assume the number and type of inventions is not influenced by patents. A patent grants one person exclusive rights to use an invention. That person is the sole supplier of it. The owner may have very little discretion in the price the rights command. There may be very close substitutes. However, the patented invention may have sufficient advantages to command a positive price.

From an economic perspective, the problem with monopolies is that, for a time, the price of a product exceeds its marginal production cost, and the market will direct too few resources to producing that product. The costs of making the invention are fixed. The marginal costs of using it are zero. Once created, any particular invention may be used once or a million times at the same additional production cost—zero. A single price set by a single supplier of an invention for all users will exceed marginal production cost. That price seems to have the same problem as a monopoly price.

The conceptual defects of the monopoly theory were the failure to identify the time period over which resource use is to be optimized, to recognize that not all monopolies are undesirable, and to accept that patent law exists to increase the long-run supply of inventions.

The existence at any particular time of an economic monopoly is not cause for concern so long as the competitive process is operating. Economic monopolies may exist for a time because one product supplier produced technical information that permits it to produce more efficiently than others and took the risk of putting that information into practice. This should be a cause for public celebration, not legal jeopardy.

---

[38] *Dawson Chem Co. v. Rohm & Haas,* 448 U.S. 176, 221 (1980).
[39] *Jefferson Parish Hosp. Dist. No. 2 v. Hyde,* 466 U.S. 2, 37 n.7 (1984).

The short-run output restriction due to a positive price will signal others to enter the market with the same or different technology. Their entry will limit any market power that permitted supernormal returns to investment in the industry. By this process, society will have moved from a less productive to a more productive state. Societies that fail to do this for a long enough period are ultimately viewed by those that did as "primitive" and "poverty stricken."

Think about the future difference between an economy growing at 3 percent and one growing at 5 percent.[40] Imagine that U.S. gross national product (GNP) this year is $5 trillion. Under existing government policies, all industries have ten to twenty roughly equal-sized companies competing for business. The economy will grow at 3 percent per year. GNP will grow to $5.8 trillion in five years and $9.1 trillion in twenty.

Assume instead that the government changes existing policy and grants to politically favored companies monopolies in many industries. This policy reduces GNP by $0.5 trillion this year and in every later year due to restrictions on output resulting from the government protected monopolies. The economy could provide an extra $0.5 trillion of current output each year, but does not. The economy endures that $0.5 trillion loss every year. Assume that this change also has the effect of increasing the rate of growth to 5 percent per year starting from the lower $4.5 trillion base because the various monopolists increase the rate of technical change.

When will the policy begin to pay off for consumers? In five years, GNP in the monopoly economy growing at 5 percent will catch up with the competitive 3 percent economy. In later years, the monopoly economy will be larger by increasing amounts each year. After ten years, GNP in the monopoly economy ($7.3 trillion) will exceed the competitive economy ($6.7 trillion) by over $0.5 trillion. If the policy change resulted in an increased growth rate to only 3.5 percent, the GNP would be greater after twenty years.

The exercise of a property right to technical information at any particular time should be no cause for concern. If one focuses on resource use over a period of time rather than a single point in time, apparent present losses from "too high" prices and "too little use" of a nonscarce resource become irrelevant. It is impossible for a single price for use of

---

[40] This example is borrowed from Scherer and Ross at 32, 613.

2.3 THE LEGAL THEORIES OF INTELLECTUAL PROPERTY RIGHTS

technical information to be equal to both long-run and short-run marginal cost of information production.

Over a period of time, those prices are the signals that induce creation of the information in the first place. Those prices are unavoidable if an economy wishes to have the right amount of technical information in the future. Those prices will signal others to enter and compete with substitute technical information. Much of law in this century developed in an unsuccessful effort to deal with static analysis.

(c) Regulated Natural Monopoly Rights

Another model is that technical information has the same problem as so-called "natural monopolies." The costs of producing information for all users and in all uses are declining. Viewed in static terms, average production cost will always exceed marginal cost. Information producing therefore seems to present a natural monopoly problem. The theory becomes that (1) it is desirable to grant rights to induce the investment needed to obtain the information (for without them the producer is a natural failure, not a monopolist), (2) the grant leads to too little use of the information during the term of the patent by restrictions on "output" that monopoly theory explains and (departing here from the property theory), (3) the law should regulate use of the information during the term of the rights to avoid "unnecessary" underuse.

This theory, like the monopoly theory, posits that all rights have the impact on resource use of an economic monopoly. This suggests that intellectual property owners should be regulated by the courts as "public utilities." This *public utility* model would suggest that the courts should limit the rights and remedies to increase use of the information while magically preserving the incentives created by the rights. In public utility regulation, government agencies specify the product to be produced, limit its production to a single company, require that company to supply it on a nondiscriminatory basis, and regulate the price so that the company earns only a reasonable rate of return on investment.

If rights were granted for an infinite term, there might be some theoretical basis for considering rate regulation of protected information. However, the term of patents and copyrights is limited, as required by the Constitution. That limited term reflects the compromise by permitting a "monopoly" price to be charged for use of the invention to attract capital to making it, but limiting that term so that the loss of use resulting from that high price comes to an end and more optimal use is achieved after the term.

Even if the rights were granted for an unlimited term, price regulation would be desirable only if a government agency could fix prices and terms of use and sale at levels which would permit greater use, while inducing the same or higher levels of information production than would appear in an unregulated market for information. There are many reasons to believe that such regulation would fail to accomplish that purpose. The relationship between the nature and amount of resources devoted to producing technical information and achieving successful conclusions is highly uncertain. Moreover, it is difficult to identify the costs of making a particular bit of technical information or to determine what rate of return on those costs would be necessary to induce people to undertake those activities. Because of these problems, it is unlikely that rate regulation could achieve its goal without lowering the level of information production, misdirecting resources to less valuable innovation, and incurring enormous administrative costs.

The public utility theory was rejected by the Supreme Court.[41] In the 1960s to 1970s, isolated lower courts began to impose traditional public utility regulation on patent owners. A few courts said the owner of the patent must make the invention available to users on a nondiscriminatory basis.[42] One district court suggested that a patent owner could not always refuse to grant licenses.[43] However, the idea never caught on.

(d) A "Public" Contract

Another theory appeared in the patent context. It is that patent laws are needed to induce people who know about inventions to disclose them to

---

[41] *Hartford-Empire Co. v. United States,* 323 U.S. 386, 432–433 (1945); *Continental Paper Bag Co. v. Eastern Paper Bag Co.,* 210 U.S. 405, 424–426, 429 (1908); *United States v. Bell Telephone Company,* 167 U.S. 224, 250 (1897).
[42] *LaPeyre v. FTC,* 366 F.2d 117 (5 Cir. 1966); *Peelers Co. v. Wendt,* 260 F. Supp. 193 (W.D. Wash. 1966); *Laitram Corp. v. King Crab, Inc.,* 244 F. Supp. 9, *modified* 245 F.Supp. 1019 (D. Alaska 1965).
[43] *Allied Research Prods., Inc. v. Heatbath Corp.,* 300 F.Supp. 656, 657 (N.D. Ill. 1969).

2.3 THE LEGAL THEORIES OF INTELLECTUAL PROPERTY RIGHTS

others. The public disclosure of the invention in the patent is called the *"quid pro quo"* for the grant.[44] This theory probably arose because the only thing the law requires an inventor to do to obtain a patent is disclose the invention. Therefore, this disclosure must be the benefit that justifies the grant.

Patent law is sometimes viewed as a social "contract" between a person knowing an invention and the government acting as agent for the public. The usual *quid pro quo* theory is that production of goods and services will increase, because some secrets will be revealed *and* will be used freely after the patent expires. Under this theory, government always makes a bad deal for the public. People knowing inventions will attempt to exploit them in secrecy and create additional inventions based on them. The government offers (but does not compel acceptance of) a limited-term right to exclude in exchange for the disclosure. The only people who will accept that offer are those holding inventions they expect will be made public (by them or someone else) in less than the limited term. Hence, the net effect of the patent grant is always to prolong the period of exclusive use, not reduce it. The "contracted for" ability of society to use the invention freely after the term is never more valuable than the ability society would have had to use the invention if the patent not been granted. That theory is inadequate.[45]

---

[44] *Scott Paper Co. v. Marcalus Mfg. Co.*, 326 U.S. 249, 255–256 (1945); *Sinclair Co. v. Interchemical Corp.*, 325 U.S. 327, 330–331 (1945); *Special Equipment Co. v. Coe*, 324 U.S. 370, 378 (1945); *United States v. Dubilier Condenser Corp.*, 289 U.S. 179, 186–187 (1933); *United States v. Bell Telephone Co.*, 167 U.S. 224, 239 (1897).

[45] This model has one other theoretical justification the courts sometimes mention. Because of the disclosure, the information on which to build subsequent inventions will become available more quickly as some secrets are disclosed in exchange for the patent. Economic performance may improve because inventions will be made at a faster rate. The problem is that a person knowing an invention will also take the potential private benefit of "add-on" inventions into account in deciding whether to accept the offer. A person will not forgo the advantage in developing additional inventions unless the value of the term exceeds the expected value of secret exploitation of the patented invention and the additional inventions it could have made quicker or more cheaply than others if it retained the secret. The deal probably remains a bad one for the consumer.

2.4 FUNDAMENTAL LEGAL CONCEPTS OF LICENSING

A license authorizes a person, usually called a "licensee," to do things that would violate one or more of the exclusive rights.[46] In spite of a tendency for the law and lawyers to talk about whether certain rights "cover" certain products, intellectual property rights are not violated by the mere existence of products. The rights are violated only by certain activities of people or companies that involve those products. For example, the Patent Act says a person infringes a patent by acting in certain ways "without authority."[47] A license provides the patent owner's authority for the licensee to act in ways that would otherwise be infringement.

A license insulates a company's authorized acts from infringement liability and remedies. If a licensee acts in a manner not authorized by the license and forbidden by one of the rights, the owner's recourse is an action for infringement.[48] If a licensee infringes a right by acts not authorized by the license, the owner's right to terminate the license depends on the terms of the agreement. A license does not necessarily include the licensee's agreement not to infringe the rights.

Intellectual property law does not compel an owner to license. Intellectual property law permits licensing. The decision to license is left to the owner. Intellectual property law also permits the owner of a particular patent, copyright, or trade secret to license some of the rights and withhold a license to others. Intellectual property rights are divisible.

Patent, copyright, and trade secret rights are divisible by activity. For example, a patent license may authorize a particular licensee to use all or only some of the rights. A person "without authority" infringes a patent by making, using, or selling products embodying the invention.[49]

---

[46] *General Talking Pictures Co. v. Western Electric Co.*, 304 U.S. 175, 181 (1931) ("The Transformer Company . . . was a mere licensee under a non-exclusive license, amounting to no more than 'a mere waiver of the right to sue'."), *on rehearing,* 305 U.S. 124 (1938).

[47] 35 U.S.C. §§ 271 (a) and 282 (1).

[48] There are sometimes important procedural wrinkles. Under the statutory definition of patent infringement, the absence of authority would seem to be a necessary element of a claim for infringement. However, the Patent Act also says and the courts have held that the existence of "authority" from the owner is a defense to an action for infringement; 35 U.S.C. §§ 271 (a) and 282 (1). Hence, the existence of a license is a defense that must be proved by an alleged infringer.

[49] 35 U.S.C. §§ 154, 271 (1976).

2.4 FUNDAMENTAL LEGAL CONCEPTS OF LICENSING

A patent owner may authorize the licensee to make and use a patented product and withhold the right to sell it. A patent owner may also authorize the licensee to make and sell a certain type of product and withhold the right to sell other types.[50] A patent owner may authorize the licensee to sell for a limited time or in a limited area (sections 5.7 and 6.7).

Patent, copyright, and trade secret rights are also divisible by people and companies.[51] The rights under a particular patent or other similar right may be licensed to one person or to many people. Within certain limits, a patent owner may deal exclusively with one licensee or deal nonexclusively with any other number of licensees. By granting an exclusive license, the patent owner gives up the right to use the invention and to grant the same rights to anyone else.[52] The patent owner may also grant an exclusive license and expressly reserve its right to use the invention.[53] By granting one person or company a nonexclusive license, the patent owner retains the right to use the invention and to grant licenses to others. By granting one person or company a license, the owner does not become obligated to license anther company. There is no general "one in, all in" rule.

The authority to use the rights is different from the authority to enforce the rights. A license does not necessarily give the licensee any right to bring an action to enforce the rights against others. In addition, a licensee's right to sue for infringement is not determined entirely by the owner and licensee in the agreement. Patent law limits who has "standing" to enforce a patent. Under the Patent Act, the owner of a patent may sue for infringement of the patent rights.[54] An exclusive licensee under substantially all of the patent owner's rights to exclude may be treated as the owner and have standing to bring an action for infringement.[55] For this purpose, the law treats such an exclusive li-

---

[50] *United States v. General Electric,* 272 U.S. 476, 489–490 (1926); *General Talking Pictures Co. v. Western Electric Co.,* 304 U.S. 175, 179–180, 182 (1938), *on rehearing,* 305 U.S. 124, 127 (1938).
[51] Trademark rights are not necessarily divisible.
[52] *Bement v. National Harrow Co.,* 186 U.S. 70, 94 (1902).
[53] *United States v. Krasnov,* 143 F.Supp. 184, 200–202 (E.D. Pa. 1956), *aff'd per curiam,* 355 U.S. 5 (1957).
[54] 35 U.S.C. § 281 (1976).
[55] *United States v. General Electric Co.,* 272 U.S. 476, 485 (1926); *Waterman v. Mackenzie,* 138 U.S. 252, 255 (1891).

cense as an assignment of the patent. Any other licensee has no standing to bring an action for infringement, even if a license attempts to provide that right to sue.

The authority to use the rights is different from the authority to grant further rights to others. A license also does not necessarily give the licensee any right to grant licenses to others. However, an owner may authorize any licensee to grant licenses to others.[56]

Finally, a license may be granted *expressly* by a written or oral agreement and *impliedly* from other conduct by the owner.[57] (See Chapter 6.) The law may also imply rights to supplement those expressly granted a licensee or to supply rights to people who buy products from the owner or a licensee. In addition, the exhaustion doctrines may insulate others from infringement liability. The implied license and exhaustion doctrines provide a "license" that the owner did not expressly grant and may not have intended to grant. These doctrines may undermine an owner's licensing strategy by effectively creating licenses that the owner and its express licensee may not have wanted or even anticipated.

2.5 THE LIMITS ON LICENSING UNDER ANTITRUST, MISUSE, AND PUBLIC POLICY DOCTRINES

The law regulating licensing is complex. U.S. law contains four sets of rules to regulate licensing. These are the federal antitrust laws, the intellectual property doctrine of misuse, a *public policy* doctrine, and the constitutional rule of federal preemption. These rules have different consequences for intellectual property owners. These rules have different standards for determining violations. There are many types of conduct that the courts have condemned under all rules. However, a court may declare a patent unenforceable without regard to whether there has been an antitrust violation. A court may also refuse to en-

---

[56] *United States v. L.D. Caulk Company,* 126 F.Supp. 693 (D. Del. 1954).
[57] *Waterman v. Mackenzie,* 138 U.S. 252 (1891) (license under certain patents implied from the express grant of licenses under other patents); *Hunt v. Armour & Co.,* 185 F.2d 722, 729 (7th Cir. 1950); *Radio Corporation of America v. Andrea,* 90 F.2d 612, 615 (2d Cir. 1937) (license implied from the patent owner's sale of a patented product, in the absence of any express reservation of rights).

2.5 THE LIMITS ON LICENSING

force a provision of a license without regard to antitrust standards. For these reasons, owners of United States rights must understand all sets of rules.

Preemption analysis is quite different from the others. This is addressed separately in Chapter 7.

The antitrust, misuse, and "public policy" rules each have very different potential effects on an owner that violates those rules.

An agreement or practice violating the antitrust laws creates a private remedy for treble damages by anyone injured in their business or property by the violation.[58] People not injured by a particular violation lack standing to bring an antitrust action. The U.S. Department of Justice may also bring actions against antitrust violations.[59] In antitrust actions, a court may enjoin the violation and order other relief to remedy the effects of the violation.[60]

Unlike the misuse defense, antitrust violations do *not* render the patent unenforceable against infringement. An antitrust violation may limit the owner's rights in two ways. First, a court may enjoin enforcement of all or parts of an agreement involved in the violation. Second, an order to remedy the effects of a violation may require the owner to grant royalty-bearing licenses, if necessary to alleviate the effects of the violation.[61] The Supreme Court has declined to order the owner to grant royalty-free licenses or to dedicate the patents to the public.[62] The only

---

[58] 15 U.S.C. § 15; *Brunswick Corp. v. Pueblo Bowl-O-Mat, Inc.*, 429 U.S. 477, 488–489 (1977); *Zenith Radio Corp. v. Hazeltine Research, Inc.*, 395 U.S. 100, 123–124 (1969).

[59] 15 U.S.C. § 4.

[60] 15 U.S.C. § 21–22.

[61] *United States v. Glaxo Group, Ltd.*, 410 U.S. 52, 64 (1973); *United States v. United States Gypsum Co.*, 340 U.S. 76 (1950); *United States v. Paramount Pictures, Inc.*, 334 U.S. 131 (1948); *Hartford-Empire Co. v. United States*, 323 U.S. 386 (1945); *Ethyl Gasoline Corp. v. United States*, 309 U.S. 436 (1940).

[62] *United States v. National Lead Co.*, 332 U.S. 319, 338 (1947) (the Court declared the issue concerning dedication and royalty-free licensing to be undecided; "Without reaching the question whether royalty-free licensing or a perpetual injunction against the enforcement of a patent is permissible as a matter of law in any case, the present decree [ordering compulsory licenses at a reasonable royalty] represents an exercise of sound judicial discretion."); *Hartford-Empire Co. v. United States*, 323 U.S. 386, 415 and 324 U.S. 570 (1945) (the Court expressly declined to order dedication on the grounds that "a patent is property, protected against appropriation both by individuals and by government.").

diminution in the owner's rights against infringement is the effect of licenses the court may order the owner to grant.

The patent misuse defense operates differently. If a patent owner engages in patent misuse, the patent is unenforceable until the conduct constituting the misuse has stopped and the effects are fully dissipated.[63] Patent misuse renders a patent unenforceable against any infringer even though that infringer was not harmed by the owner's misconduct.[64] Because the effect of misuse is to eliminate all remedies for infringement, conduct constituting patent misuse may be more costly to an owner than conduct violating the antitrust laws. In addition, patent misuse may arise from conduct that does not violate the antitrust laws.[65] For this reason, patent misuse may deter an owner from certain modes of exploitation that are lawful under antitrust law.

The public policy rule also has different effects. Even if there is no antitrust violation or misuse, the Supreme Court has from time to time declared certain types of agreements and practices to be contrary to public policy and unenforceable.[66] Because an offending agreement or practice is not enforced, the other party is permitted to ignore it. If the agreement or practice was designed by the patent owner to limit the scope of a license someone received, that person obtains a license without the limitation. The person's rights are broadened. However, the person is not free to ignore the patent. Nor are others. The patent continues to be fully enforceable.

2.6 ANTITRUST STANDARDS

The Sherman Act is the pertinent antitrust law for most licensing activities. The courts say the Sherman Act rests on the premise that unrestrained competition will yield the best use of scarce economic resources, the lowest prices, the highest quality, and the greatest material progress.[67]

---

[63] See section 2.7.
[64] Id.
[65] Id.
[66] See section 2.8.
[67] *Northern Pacific Railway Co. v. United States,* 356 U.S. 1, 4–5 (1958).

2.6 ANTITRUST STANDARDS

In general, the Sherman Act prohibits certain types of conduct that interferes with the process of competition.[68] The Sherman Act does not prohibit all conduct that "interferes" with the existence of a "competitive" market structure at any point in time.

Section 1 of the Sherman Act declares illegal any contract, combination, or conspiracy that restrains trade or commerce.[69] As interpreted, section 1 makes unlawful agreements between two or more separate enterprises that unreasonably restrain trade.[70] In general, section 1 prohibits agreements between firms that limit some aspect of competition in a market without producing an offsetting economic gain, such as increasing competition in some other respect.[71]

Section 2 of the Sherman Act prohibits an enterprise from monopolizing, attempting to monopolize, or conspiring to monopolize trade or commerce.[72] In general, section 2 forbids a single firm having a particularly significant position in a market (a "dominant" or "monopoly" position) from engaging in conduct that harms competition in a market ("predatory" or "exclusionary" conduct) and serves merely to maintain or enhance that firm's position.[73] Such firms are said to have or seek "monopoly power." For purposes of the Sherman Act, monopoly power is the power to raise prices and exclude competition.[74]

---

[68] *Brunswick Corp. v. Pueblo Bowl-O-Mat, Inc.*, 429 U.S. 477, 488 (1977).
[69] 15 U.S.C. § 1 (1982).
[70] *National Soc'y of Professional Eng'rs v. United States*, 438 U.S. 679, 687–690 (1978); *Continental T.V., Inc. v. GTE Sylvania, Inc.*, 433 U.S. 36, 49 (1977); *Standard Oil Co. v. United States*, 221 U.S. 1, 58 (1911).
[71] *National Soc'y of Professional Eng'rs v. United States*, 438 U.S. 679, 687–690 (1978); *Continental T.V., Inc. v. GTE Sylvania, Inc.*, 433 U.S. 36, 49 (1977); Richard Schmalensee, "Agreements Between Competitors" (at 98), and Frank H. Easterbrook, "Ignorance and Antitrust" (at 119), both in *Antitrust, Innovation and Competitiveness,* 1992 (Jorde and Teece, eds.) (Oxford University Press, New York); Phillip E. Areeda, Antitrust Law, 1991 (Little, Brown, Boston) part three; William F. Baxter, "The Viability of Vertical Restraints Doctrine," *California Law Review* **75,** 933 (1988); Frank H. Easterbrook, "The Limits of Antitrust," *Texas Law Review* **63,** 1 (1984); Robert H. Bork, *The Antitrust Paradox,* 1978 (Basic Books, New York) ch. 7; Richard A. Posner, *Antitrust Law, An Economic Perspective,* 1976 (University of Chicago Press, Chicago) ch. 3.
[72] 15 U.S.C. § 2 (1982).
[73] *United States v. Grinnell Corp.*, 384 U.S. 563, 570–571 (1966).
[74] *United States v. Grinnell Corp.*, 384 U.S. 563, 576 (1966).

The Supreme Court has condemned certain types of licensing practices under section 1 without evaluating the actual effects of the practices on competition in the markets in which they were used. In those cases, the Court applied a so-called *per se rule of illegality*.[75] In all other circumstances, section 1 condemns an agreement only if the agreement's effects on the competitive process are more harmful than beneficial. In these situations, the Court applies the so-called *rule of reason*.[76] Under the rule of reason, the antitrust laws condemn an agreement only if it has likely anticompetitive effects in a market and is, on balance, anticompetitive rather than procompetitive.[77]

In applying rule of reason standards to restrictions in license agreements, the Supreme Court sometimes articulates the test by asking whether the agreement is reasonably related to the owner's effort to exploit the rights.[78] The Court's 1926 decision in *United States v. General Electric* used this basic standard:[79]

> Conveying less than title to the patent, or part of it, the patentee may grant a license to make, use and vend articles under the specification of his patent for any royalty and upon any condition the performance of which is reasonably within the reward which the patentee by the grant of the patent is entitled to secure. . . . The patentee may make and grant a license to another to make and use the patented articles, but withhold its right to sell them. . . . If the patentee goes further, and licenses the selling of the articles, may he limit the selling by limiting the method of sale or price? We think he may do so, provided that the conditions of sale are normally and

---

[75] For example, *United States v. Line Material Co.*, 333 U.S. 287, 308 (1948); *Ethyl Gasoline Corp. v. United States*, 209 U.S. 346, 456 (1939).

[76] *Broadcast Music, Inc. v. Columbia Broadcasting System, Inc.*, 441 U.S. 1, 8–9, 19–20 (1979).

[77] *Jefferson Parish Hosp. Dist. No. 2 v. Hyde*, 466 U.S. 2, 16–17 (1984) (concurring opinion); *Continental T.V. v. GTE Sylvania, Inc.*, 433 U.S. 36, 49–59 (1977); *Rothery Storage & Van Co. v. Atlas Van Lines, Inc.*, 792 F.2d 210 (D.C. Cir. 1886); *USM Corporation v. SPS Technologies, Inc.*, 694 F.2d 505, 513–514 (7 Cir. 1982).

[78] *General Talking Pictures Co. v. Western Electric Co.*, 304 U.S. 175, 179–180, 182 (1938), *on rehearing*, 305 U.S. 124, 127 (1938); *United States v. General Electric*, 272 U.S. 476, 189–190 (1926); *United States v. United Shoe Mach. Co.*, 247 U.S. 32, 57–58 (1917).

[79] *United States v. General Electric*, 272 U.S. 476, 489–490 (1926).

2.6 ANTITRUST STANDARDS

reasonably adapted to secure pecuniary reward for the patentee's monopoly.

In *General Talking Pictures Co. v. Western Electric Co.*, the Court said:[80]

> The question of law requiring decision is whether the restriction in the license is to be given effect. That a restrictive license is legal seems clear. *Mitchell v. Hawley,* 16 Wall. 544. As was said in *United States v. General Electric Co.,* 272 U.S. 476, 489, the patentee may grant a license "upon any condition the performance of which is reasonably within the reward which the patentee by the grant of the patent is entitled to secure."

Under both *per se* and rule of reason approaches, the courts have often noted the need to distinguish the market effects of a licensing agreement and the market effects of the existence of the licensed rights. The effects of the licensed rights on competition are not to be treated as anticompetitive effects. The courts often say that the exploitation of the patent by use and licensing in a manner consistent with the scope of the patent does not violate the antitrust laws.[81] A patent owner may violate the Sherman Act by using the patent to obtain a monopoly beyond the scope of the patent or to unreasonably restrain trade beyond the scope of the patent.[82]

---

[80] *General Talking Pictures Co. v. Western Electric Co.,* 304 U.S. 175, 179–180, 182 (1938), *on rehearing,* 305 U.S. 124, 127 (1938).

[81] *United States v. United Shoe Mach. Co.,* 247 U.S. 32, 57 (1917) ("Of course, there is restraint in a patent. Its strength is in the restraint, the right to exclude others from the use of the invention absolutely or on the terms the patentee chooses to impose. This strength is the compensation which the law imparts for the exercise of invention. Its exertion within the field covered by the patent law is not an offense against the Anti-Trust Act. In other circumstances, it may be. . . ."); *cf., General Talking Pictures Corp. v. Western Electric Co.,* 304 U.S. 175, 181, *aff'd on reh.,* 305 U.S. 124 (1938), *reh. denied,* 305 U.S. 675 (1939).

[82] *Ethyl Gasoline Corp. v. United States,* 309 U.S. 436, 456 (1940) ("The patent law confers on the patentee a limited monopoly, the right to exclude all others from manufacturing, using or selling the invention. The extent of that right is limited by the definition of his invention, as its boundaries are marked by the specification and claims of the patent. He may grant licenses to make, use or vend, restricted in point of space or time, or with any other restriction upon the exercise of the granted privilege, save only that by attaching a condition to his license he may not enlarge his

Hence, a license may be unlawful if the owner uses agreements with others as a means of creating monopoly power or unreasonably restraining trade in selling or using products and processes not protected by the patent.

While these general standards direct attention to effects on competition in markets, they do not describe how to identify anticompetitive and procompetitive effects, or how to balance those effects. They do not tell you how to determine whether an agreement is reasonably adapted to secure a financial reward to the owner. A more specific form of analysis is needed.

The current form of antitrust analysis of patent licensing developed from William F. Baxter's classic 1966 article "Legal Restrictions on Exploitation of the Patent Monopoly: An Economic Analysis" in the *Yale Law Journal*.[83] While Baxter is better known for applying economics to change Department of Justice antitrust enforcement policy in the early 1980s, Baxter also pioneered the economics-based approach to antitrust and licensing.[84]

In the late 1970s and early 1980s, the courts began to employ economic analysis in antitrust actions involving licensing.[85] This development was influenced by the Supreme Court's increasing reliance on economics in antitrust decisions during this period.[86] In particular, the Court declared in 1977 in *Sylvania* that a seller's use of nonprice restraints on distributors of its product are evaluated under the rule of rea-

---

monopoly and thus acquire some other which the statute and the patent together did not give." [citations omitted]); *United States v. Line Material Co.,* 333 U.S. 287, 308 (1948) ("It is equally well settled that the possession of a valid patent or patents does not give the patentee any exemption for the provisions of the Sherman Act beyond the limits of the patent monopoly.").

[83] Baxter, W.F., "Legal Restrictions on Exploitation of the Patent Monopoly: An Economic Analysis," *Yale Law Journal* **76,** 267 (1966).

[84] Several years later, Professor Ward Bowman applied the same approach. W. Bowman, *Patent and Antitrust Law: A Legal and Economic Appraisal* 1973 (University of Chicago Press, Chicago).

[85] *USM Corporation v. SPS Technologies, Inc.,* 694 F.2d 505 (7th Cir. 1982); *United States v. Studiengesellschaft Kohle,* 670 F.2d 1122 (D.C. Cir. 1981); *Mannington Mills v. Congoleum Industries,* 610 F.2d 1059 (3rd Cir. 1979).

[86] *Broadcast Music, Inc. v. CBS,* 441 U.S. 1 (1979); *Continental T.V., Inc. v. GTE Sylvania Inc.,* 433 U.S. 36 (1977); *United States Steel Corp. v. Fortner Enters., Inc.,* 429 U.S. 610 (1977); *Brunswick Corp. v. Pueblo Bowl-O-Mat, Inc.,* 429 U.S. 477 (1977).

2.6 ANTITRUST STANDARDS

son, and the economic effects of the restraint on competition, and output, in the market for that seller's and other sellers' products (called *interbrand* competition) must be considered.[87] Perhaps as important was the Court's declaration in 1979 in *BMI v. CBS* that an agreement among copyright owners and a licensing organization to provide blanket licenses under their copyrights for a price set by the licensing organization was also subject to the rule of reason.[88] In both decisions, the Court refused to apply *per se* rules that would eliminate economic analysis of effects. In 1994, a well-known antitrust lawyer characterized the legal standards this way: "Therefore, after *Sylvania* economic theory matters and matters decisively."[89]

In 1979, the Court of Appeals for the Third Circuit in *Mannington Mills* also looked to the economic analysis of licensing and the Supreme Court's treatment of vertical restrictions to define a rule of reason test for the legality of license restrictions. This test required analysis of economic effects. The alleged violations were that (1) a patent owner offered foreign companies licenses under both patents and know-how, and offered a U.S. company a license only under patents, and (2) the patent owner conspired with foreign licensees to cancel the U.S. company's foreign sales license. The court said:[90]

> Vertical restrictions imposed upon licensees by a patentee, like those imposed by a nonpatentee upon its distributors, may often be useful, and perhaps even essential, to the patentee's efforts to maximize the monopoly income to which the patent grant entitles him. See W. Bowman, *Patent and Antitrust Law: A Legal and Economic Appraisal* 54–57 (1973); Baxter, *Legal Restrictions on Exploitation of the Patent Monopoly: An Economic Analysis,* 76 Yale L.J. 267, 313 (1966).

---

[87] *Continental T.V., Inc. v. GTE Sylvania Inc.,* 433 U.S. 36 (1977).
[88] *Broadcast Music, Inc. v. CBS,* 441 U.S. 1 (1979).
[89] M. Laurence Popofsky and Mark S. Popofsky, "Vertical Restraints in the 1990s: Is There a 'Thermidorian Reaction' to the Post-Sylvania Orthodoxy?" *Antitrust Law Journal* **62,** 729, 738 (1994).
[90] *Mannington Mills v. Congoleum Industries, Inc.,* 610 F.2d 1059, 1070–1071 (3rd Cir. 1979).

* * *

But restrictive licensing practices may also have significant anticompetitive effects.

In 1981, the Court of Appeals for the District of Columbia in *United States v. Studiengesellschaft* followed suit in evaluating an agreement relating to licensing under the rule of reason.[91] The owner of a patent on a process for making an old and valuable catalyst, ATA, granted to one U.S. company an exclusive license to make and sell the catalyst, and to other companies nonexclusive licenses limited to making and using catalysts in their own manufacturing operations. At the time, patent law was that the sale of the product would not infringe the process patent. The government asserted that the licenses were unlawful because "the agreements were designed to expand a legal monopoly of the process into an impermissible monopoly of the unpatented product." The district court "first determined that the restriction imposed was outside the scope of the patent protection, then examined the unprotected restriction to determine if it constituted an attempt to monopolize or an unlawful restrain of trade."[92] The Court of Appeals found no violation and rejected the two-step process as effectively a *per se* rule:[93]

> Such a formalistic, two-step analysis forecloses adequate consideration of the fundamental fact that a patent by definition restrains trade, and in effect makes most exclusive patent licenses *per se* violations of the antitrust laws. But as the Supreme Court noted in *E. Bement & Sons v. National Harrow Co.*, 186 U.S. 70, 91, 22 S.Ct. 747, 755, 46 L.Ed. 1058 (1902), "[t]he very object of [the patent laws] is monopoly. . . . The fact that the conditions in the contract keep up the monopoly does not render them illegal." Thus, as appears more fully below, we conclude that a rule of reason rather than a *per se* rule applies here. Under our analysis, the protection of the patent laws and the coverage of the antitrust laws are

---

[91] *United States v. Studiengesellschaft Kohle, m.b.H.*, 670 F.2d 1122 (D.C. Cir. 1981).
[92] Id. at 1126 and 1128.
[93] Id. at 1128.

2.6 ANTITRUST STANDARDS

not separate issues. Rather, the conduct at issue is illegal if it threatens competition in areas other than those protected by the patent, and is otherwise legal.[9] The patentee is entitled to exact the full value of his invention but is not entitled to endanger competition in other areas by manipulating his patent monopoly. It was thus error to consider the scope of the patent protection irrespective of any competitive effects in the first phase of the case, and then rule separately on the anticompetitive effects of the arrangement without consideration of the protection of the patent.

[9] *See United States v. Griffith,* 334 U.S. 100, 68 S.Ct. 941, 92 L.Ed. 1230 (1948) (use of monopoly power, even if lawfully acquired, to foreclose competition in other markets unlawful); *SMC Corp. v. Xerox Corp.,* 645 F.2d 1195 (2d Cir. 1981) (refusal to license patent is legal where not used to extend patent monopoly); *United States v. Westinghouse Elec. Corp.,* 471 F.Supp. 532 (N.D. Cal. 1978), aff'd 648 F.2d 642 (9th Cir. 1981) (rejecting view that patent licensing contract should, if at all possible, be found illegal). *See generally* L. Sullivan, Handbook of Law of Antitrust § 184c (1977); W. Bowman, Patent and Antitrust Law 53–57 (1973); Adelman & Juenger, *supra,* at 294–96; Baxter, *Legal Restrictions on Exploitation of the Patent Monopoly: An Economic Analysis,* 76 Yale L.J. 267, 275–79, 312–14 (1966); Buxbaum, *Restrictions Inherent in the Patent Monopoly: A Comparative Critique,* 113 U. Pa. L. Rev. 633 (1965).

The court of appeals also noted that the Supreme Court's recent antitrust decisions required analysis of economic effects:[94]

> Even were we otherwise attracted to this purely formalistic distinction between a process patent and a product patent, however, it is clear that such a *per se* approach is no longer acceptable in the wake of the Supreme Court's decision in *Continental TV, Inc. v. GTE Sylvania, Inc.,* 433 U.S. 36, 97 S.Ct. 2549, 53 L.Ed.2d 568 (1977). . . . *Continental TV* is a message to lower courts that antitrust violations should be based upon economic effects rather than upon formal distinctions. As the Supreme Court said:
>
> [W]e do not foreclose the possibility that particular applications of vertical restrictions might justify per se prohibition under *Northern Pac. R. Co.* But we do make clear that departure from the

---
[94] Id. at 1129–1130.

rule-of-reason standard must be based upon demonstrable economic effects rather than—as in *Schwinn*—upon formalistic line drawing. U.S. at 58–59, 97 S.Ct. at 2561–62.

What the district court did below and the government urges here is subject to similar criticism. The government would have us declare that any restraint on products produced by a process patent is outside the protection of the patent laws and illegal per se regardless of the effects of the restraint, on the theory that licensing of the process exhausts the patentee's rights in that process. In the absence of "demonstrable economic effects," however, such a conclusion would be wholly unrelated to any realistic distinction between a process patent and a product patent, and would be just the sort of "formalistic line-drawing" which the Supreme Court condemned.

This conclusion is further supported by the Supreme Court's decision in *Broadcast Music, Inc. v. Columbia Broadcasting System, Inc.,* 441 U.S. 1, 99 S.Ct. 1551, 60 L.Ed.2d 1 (1979). . . . In addition, the Court noted in the related context of copyrights that "we would not expect that any market arrangements reasonably necessary to effectuate the rights that are granted would be deemed a *per se* violation of the Sherman Act." 441 U.S. at 19, 99 S.Ct. at 1562.

While it is possible that some restraints in a patent license, such as tying restrictions, may be illegal per se after *Continental TV* and *Broadcasting Music, Inc.,* it would be necessary at least to show that the restraints involved had no purpose except restraining trade, and had unequivocally anticompetitive effects in the vast majority of cases. . . .

In our view these authorities, along with numerous patent licensing cases discussed below, require that the result turn on a careful analysis of whether the restriction imposed here constituted an unreasonable restraint of trade.

2.7 MISUSE STANDARDS

Patent misuse may arise from the way a patent owner exploits the patent. Misuse often relates to a patent owner's license to someone else to use

2.7 MISUSE STANDARDS

all or some of the patent rights. Misuse may also arise from the patent owner's sale or lease of tangible products.

The Patent Act does not say that patent misuse is a defense to infringement liability. The Patent Act does not say that a patent owner's conduct may create a patent misuse defense. The Act does say that *unenforceability* is a defense that must be pleaded.[95] However, the Act does not say what activities render a patent unenforceable. The reason for this legal oddity is historical.

Congress created the patent laws. Congress did not create the patent misuse defense. The Supreme Court created this defense in 1942. Congress learned about the defense only because someone complained about one decision applying the new defense in 1944. Congress's response was to try to overrule the Court's 1944 decision. Congress did not focus on the larger issue of whether a patent owner's method of exploitation should ever prevent the enforcement. In 1952, Congress implicitly recognized the defense by enacting an exception to it.[96] In section 271(d) of the Patent Act, Congress said that certain types of conduct are not misuse. Strangely, Congress did not say misuse was a defense or say what other types of conduct were misuse.

The test for patent misuse always has two steps. Because Congress has not defined the misuse defense, the judicial standards define the prohibited conduct. If conduct would violate the judicial standards, the Patent Act exclusions must be applied.

(a) The Supreme Court Creates the Misuse Defense—*Morton Salt*

In 1942, the Supreme Court created the misuse defense in a case that involved a tying arrangement—a lease and license conditioned on the requirement that the lessee and licensee buy unpatented products from the patent owner. Prior to 1942, the legal consequences of tying arrange-

---

[95] 35 U.S.C. § 282. This language seems to have been added to the Patent Act in 1952 almost as an afterthought. The language might have simply been a reference to the inequitable conduct defense described in Chapter 10, another judicial creation. In any event, the lower courts have found legislative authority for the misuse defense in section 282.
[96] 35 U.S.C. § 271(d).

ments were that the tying arrangement was not enforced and antitrust liability might exist.[97] The patent continued to be enforceable.

In *Morton Salt,* the Court held that agreements of this type rendered the patent unenforceable.[98] The patent owner leased a patented salt dispensing machine to canners with a license to use the machine on the condition that only the patent owner's salt tablets would be used with the machine. The patent owner brought an action against a seller of infringing machines. The Court did not describe the terms under which the defendant was supplying its machines. The defendant may or may not have been supplying machines with a similar condition about salt. The Court held the patent unenforceable even though the defendant, as machine seller, was directly infringing the patent.

The legal doctrine the Court used to create that new defense was the equitable rule of unclean hands.[99] The misuse doctrine extended the unclean hands rule as it had previously been applied to regulate a patent owner's conduct. Prior to 1942, the unclean hands defense was applied to penalize patentees who obtained perjured testimony or paid witnesses to conceal evidence and attempted to deceive a court into finding the patent valid.[100] The Court struggled somewhat in the *Morton Salt* deci-

---

[97] *International Business Machines Co. v. United States,* 298 U.S. 131 (1936) (applying antitrust law); *Motion Picture Patents Co. v. Universal Film Mfg.,* 243 U.S. 501, 508, 516–518 (1917) (applying the public policy rule to find a "license" limitation unenforceable).

[98] *Morton Salt Co. v. G. S. Suppiger Co.,* 314 U.S. 488, 491–494 (1942).

[99] *Morton Salt Co. v. G. S. Suppiger Co.,* 314 U.S. 488, 492 (1942) ("a party seeking the aid of a court of equity must come into court with clean hands"). Accord, *United States Gypsum Co. v. National Gypsum Co.,* 352 U.S. 457, 465 (1957). The misuse doctrine was different in several respects from the unclean hands doctrine as applied in other areas of law. First, the unclean hands doctrine involved some harmful conduct by the person asserting a claim, and the agreements condemned under the misuse rules were not necessarily harmful. Second, unclean hands rules generally afforded no relief except in favor of a person injured by the conduct, and the misuse doctrine permitted infringement by people not harmed by the patent owner. Third, the unclean hands doctrine generally requires a balancing of the harm done by the plaintiff and the harm done by the defendant. The traditional rule refused to give the plaintiff relief if the injury he caused was more harmful in some sense than the defendant's illegal activity. The misuse doctrine involved no such balancing.

[100] John W. Schlicher, *Patent Law,* ch. 10.

2.7 MISUSE STANDARDS

sion to find a reason to extend this unclean hands doctrine to the context of tying arrangements.[101]

The Court said that granting relief against a seller of an infringing salt dispensing machine would assist the patent owner's efforts to compel people to buy salt from it. To be sure, permitting salt users to purchase and use infringing machines has the effect of making it more difficult for the patent owner to sell its salt. That also makes it more difficult for the patent owner to sell machines. Permitting all forms of infringement prevents the patent owner from obtaining any value from the patent by tying arrangements or in any other way.

In a companion case, *B & B Chemical,* the Court held that misuse rendered the patent unenforceable against any type of infringement.[102] The patent owner sold a material useful in carrying out a patented process. The patent owner's customers received a license to use the purchased material to practice the process. The defendant also supplied materials for use in the process. The owner sued claiming the defendant induced infringement by its customers. The patent owner argued that, because of the large number of users, it was too expensive to grant separate written, royalty-bearing licenses under the patent that would permit use of the process with materials from any supplier. The Court said it was "without significance" that the patent owner's method of doing business was the only practical way of exploiting the invention.[103]

Patent misuse was declared to render the patent unenforceable. The period of unenforceability could end when the patent owner showed that the misuse had been abandoned and that the consequences of the misuse had been fully dissipated.[104] Some courts refer to abandoning the conduct and dissipating its effects as a "purge" of the misuse.[105] The courts

---

[101] 314 U.S. at 492–494.

[102] *B. B. Chemical Co. v. Ellis,* 314 U.S. 495, 496–498 (1942) (process patent).

[103] Id. at 498.

[104] *United States Gypsum Co. v. National Gypsum Co.,* 352 U.S. 457, 465 (1957); *Morton Salt Co. v. G. S. Suppiger Co.,* 314 U.S. 488, 492–494 (1942); *B. B. Chemical Co. v. Ellis,* 314 U.S. 495, 498 (1942).

[105] For example, *United States Gypsum Co. v. National Gypsum Co.,* 352 U.S. 457, 465 (1957).

treat the issue of purge as a question of fact.[106] The courts exercise considerable discretion in determining whether the offending conduct has been abandoned and the effects fully dissipated.[107]

There is one fairly clear limit to the misuse defense. The patent that the patent owner seeks to enforce must have contributed to the conduct which renders its enforcement "inequitable."[108] Most courts have found

---

[106] *United States Gypsum Co. v. National Gypsum Co.*, 352 U.S. 457, 465, 472–473 (1957) (reversing order enjoining continuation of infringement actions based on alleged infringement from 1948–51 where the order was based upon the record in a prior antitrust action holding based on evidence of conduct prior to 1941, that license agreements violated the Sherman Act by fixing prices and the patent owner offered to prove that the price fixing had ceased).

[107] *Performed Line Products Co. v. Fanner Mfg. Co.*, 328 F.2d 265, 278–279 (6th Cir. 1964) (affirming findings that a patentee had abandoned its misuse on January 6, 1960, the date of the district court's opinion and finding of facts, and that the consequences had been dissipated by June 15, 1961, the date of a supplemental hearing on the purge question); *White Cap Co. v. Owens-Illinois Glass Co.*, 203 F.2d 694 (6th Cir. 1953), *cert. denied* 346 U.S. 876 (1953) (affirming a finding of a purge where an objectionable clause in a contract was "canceled" and a showing was made that there were apparently no adverse effects to be dissipated); *Campbell v. Mueller*, 159 F.2d 803, 807 (6th Cir. 1947) (finding no misuse where a minimum price clause included in a contract was never acted upon, was canceled, and due to renegotiation of the contract "at the time of the decision the plaintiff's conduct was blameless in practice and intention."); *Berlenbach v. Anderson and Thompson Ski Co.*, 329 F.2d 782, 785 (9th Cir. 1964) (affirming a grant of summary judgment based on misuse over patentee's assertion that there was a material issue on whether the contract clause in question was ever enforced. "Although we have said that nonenforcement and voluntary relinquishment of an illegal clause will overcome the defense of patent misuse, we know of no case permitting an infringement suit where the clause remains in effect but unenforced."); *Metals Disintegrating Co. v. Reynolds Metals Co.*, 228 F.2d 885, 889 (3rd Cir. 1956) (the significant issue on the purging of an illegal contract provision is a factual one: "When did all performance under this agreement cease? Since the plaintiff did not seek to enforce the bargain after November, 1946, it was not guilty of any misuse with respect to defendant thereafter."); *Westinghouse Elec. Corp. v. Bulldog Electric Prod. Co.*, 179 F.2d 139, 145 (4th Cir. 1950) (reversing a grant of summary judgment upon a finding that the licensor had purged the illegal price maintenance clause "in promptly surrendering all rights under these provisions following the decision in the Line Material case and abandoning all efforts at price control."); *Ansul Co. v. Uniroyal, Inc.*, 448 F.2d 872 (2nd Cir. 1971), *cert. denied*, 404 U.S. 1018 (1972).

[108] *Morton Salt Co. v. G. S. Suppiger Co.*, 314 U.S. 488, 492–493 (1942); *Republic Molding Corporation v. B. W. Photo Utilities*, 319 F.2d 347, 349 (9th Cir. 1963) (". . .[M]isconduct in the abstract, unrelated to the claim to which it is asserted as a

2.7 MISUSE STANDARDS

that the misuse must have involved the patent on which the infringement action is based.[109]

The misuse defense grew out of a theory developed in the Court's earlier patent infringement decisions and in certain antitrust decisions involving tying arrangements.[110] The misuse rule arose out of the Supreme Court's conclusion that tying agreements are always used by patent owners to attempt to obtain a "limited monopoly" in a market for a product that was beyond the reach of the rights. In *Morton Salt,* the Court said misuse arose from the use of the patent to restrain or suppress competition in the sale of an unpatented article and to create a limited monopoly in the sale of that article not granted by the patent:[111]

> It thus appears that respondent is making use of its patent monopoly to restrain competition in the marketing of unpatented articles, salt tablets, for use with the patented machines, and is aiding in the creation of a limited monopoly in the tablets not within that granted by the patent. A patent operates to create and grant to the patentee an exclusive right to make, use and vend the particular device de-

---

defense, does not constitute unclean hands"). Compare, *Ansul Co. v. Uniroyal, Inc.,* 448 F.2d 872, (2d Cir. 1972), *cert. denied,* 404, U.S. 1018 (holding a patent unenforceable based upon resale price fixing in marketing the potential product); *F.C. Russell Co. v. Consumers Insulation Co.,* 226 F.2d 273 (3d Cir. 1955) (holding patent unenforceable based upon restrictions in agreements with distributors of patented windows); *F.C. Russell Co. v. Comfort Equipment Corp.,* 194 F.2d 592 (7th Cir. 1952).

[109] *Kolene Corporation v. Motor City Metal Treating, Inc.,* 440 F.2d 77, 84 (6th Cir. 1961) ("The misuse must be of the patent in suit."); *Carter-Wallace, Inc. v. United States,* 449 F.2d 1374, 1383–1384 (Ct. Cl. 1961) (agreements relating to foreign patents do not render U.S. patents unenforceable); *McCullough Tool Co. v. Well Surveys, Inc.,* 395 F.2d 230, 238–239 (10th Cir. 1968); *Binks Mfg. Co. v. Ransburg Electro-Coating Corp.,* 281 F.2d 252, 259 (7th Cir. 1960); *Sperry Products, Inc. v. Aluminum Company of America,* 171 F.Supp. 901, 904 (N.D. Ohio 1959), *aff'd in pertinent part,* 285 F.2d 911, 925–926 (6th Cir. 1960) (misuse of foreign counterpart patent does not render U.S. patents unenforceable). The general doctrine of unclean hands has been applied by some courts, in the context of improper enforcement, to render unenforceable the patent involved in the inequitable conduct, as well as other related patents on which the infringement action was based. *Keystone Driller Co. v. General Excavator Co.,* 290 U.S. 240, 245 (1933).

[110] See section 4.5.

[111] *Morton Salt Co. v. G. S. Suppiger Co.,* 314 U.S. 488, 491–493 (1942).

> scribed and claimed in the patent. But a patent affords no immunity for a monopoly not within the grant, Interstate Circuit v. United States, 306 US 208, 228, 230, 83 L ed 610, 621, 622, 59 S Ct 467; Ethyl Gasoline Corp. v. United States, 309 US 436, 456, 84 L ed 852, 861, 60 S Ct 618, and the use of it to suppress competition in the sale of an unpatented article may deprive the patentee of the aid of a court of equity to restrain an alleged infringement by one who is a competitor.

The person permitted to infringe the machine patent was not a lessee of the patent owner's machine seeking to use it with other salt suppliers. Nor was the infringer a company selling salt to the patent owner's machine lessees. Permitting such infringement would defeat the owner's supposed plan to acquire a "limited" salt monopoly, yet leave the patent intact. Curiously, the company permitted to infringe was a "competitor" in selling machines. Permitting this infringement eliminates the patent.

The Court also did not say that any specific provision of the Patent Act authorized it to refuse to enforce patents based on the patent owner's method of exploitation. The Court assumed that it had some power to create defenses not defined by the Patent Act. The Court asserted that "public policy" permitted this defense. The Court said that policy was founded in the Constitution and the Patent Act:[112]

> The grant to the inventor of the special privilege of a patent monopoly carries out a public policy adopted by the Constitution and laws of the United States, "to promote the Progress of Science and useful Arts, by securing for limited Times to . . . Inventors the exclusive Right . . . " to their "new and useful" inventions. United States Constitution, Art. I, § 8, cl. 8, 35 USCA § 31. But the public policy which includes inventions within the granted monopoly excludes from it all that is not embraced in the invention. It equally forbids the use of the patent to secure an exclusive right or limited monopoly not granted by the Patent Office and which it is contrary to public policy to grant.

---

[112] Id. at 492.

2.7 MISUSE STANDARDS

The Court did not explain how the owner's practice gave the owner an "exclusive right" not granted by the Patent Office. The Court also did not explain what a "limited monopoly" was.

Whatever the basis, in *Morton Salt,* the Court said misuse arose from the use of the patent to restrain or suppress competition in the sale of an unpatented article and to create an "exclusive right" or "limited monopoly" in the sale of that article not granted by the patent.[113] Tying arrangements require someone to buy an unpatented product from the patent owner. However, the purchase does not mean that the patent owner's purpose is to attempt to acquire a monopoly in sales of the unpatented product or to restrict competition in the sale of the unpatented product in some market. There are many other reasons for a patent owner to employ tying arrangements.[114] This mere purchase also does not mean that there are likely to be any harmful effects. The intensity of the rivalry among sellers of the unpatented product may not be affected by the agreement. Total market quantity may not be reduced, and market price may not be raised.

The Court's expressed concern was about effects on competition and monopoly. Congress had acted to protect competition and to prevent unjustified monopoly by enacting the antitrust laws. Indeed, in 1914, Congress had enacted a specific provision of the antitrust laws, section 3 of the Clayton Act, directed to the patent owner's conduct in *Morton Salt.*[115] The owner's conduct would violate section 3 only if it was proved that the effect of lease and license may be "to substantially lessen competition or tend to create a monopoly in any line of commerce." The Court found the patent unenforceable even though there was no evidence of any injury to competition in the salt industry sufficient to establish a violation of section 3.

The Court said it need not follow the policy of the antitrust laws. The Court said no antitrust violation had to be proved to establish patent misuse.[116] The Court also said that the conduct giving rise to the defense did not have to harm the infringer asserting the defense.[117] The Court did not explain why there should be one standard for patent misuse and a

---
[113] Id. at 491–493.
[114] See section 4.4.
[115] Clayton Act, 38 Stat. 730 (1914) § 3.
[116] *Morton Salt Co. v. G. S. Suppiger Co.,* 314 U.S. 488, 494 (1942). Accord, *Zenith Radio Corp v. Hazeltine Research,* 395 U.S. 100, 140 (1969)
[117] *Morton Salt Co. v. G. S. Suppiger Co.,* 314 U.S. 488, 494 (1942).

different standard for antitrust violations, when both rules allegedly seek to prevent certain kinds of agreements for the same reason, namely because they create unjustified monopolies or restrain competition.[118]

Because there was no clear basis for limiting application of the *Morton Salt* unclean hands rule to tying arrangements, the doctrine was found applicable to other types of restrictions thought to restrain competition outside the scope of the patent. By freeing the misuse doctrine from the main body of antitrust law, *Morton Salt* spawned a body of law that for a time flatly prohibited types of agreements without any evidence of their effects in the market and without any evidence of any procompetitive benefits from them.

(b) The Misuse Defense Beyond Practices Categorically Condemned by the Supreme Court—*Windsurfing, USM,* and *Mallinckrodt*

While *Morton Salt* remains the leading decision, the Courts of Appeal have recently attempted to define the misuse standard more precisely. Those courts have said that, unless the conduct has been categorically condemned by the Supreme Court, there is no misuse unless an antitrust violation is proved under the rule of reason, that is, by proving that the conduct has anticompetitive economic effects.[119]

In 1986, the Court of Appeals for the Federal Circuit decided in *Windsurfing Intn. Inc. v. AMF, Inc.*[120] that a patent owner did not misuse his patent by including in licenses a provision that the licensee acknowledge the validity of certain trademarks of the patent owner and agreed not to use them in any way. The Court said in an opinion by Chief Judge Markey:[121]

> The doctrine of patent misuse is an affirmative defense to a suit for patent infringement, *see Bio-Rad Laboratories, Inc. v. Nicolet In-*

---

[118] Id. at 492–494.
[119] Windsurfing Intn. Inc. v. AMF, Inc., 782 F.2d 995, 1001–1002 (Fed. Cir. 1986); USM Corporation v. SPS Technologies, Inc., 694 F.2d 505, 513–514 (7th Cir. 1982).
[120] *Windsurfing Intn. Inc. v. AMF, Inc.,* 782 F.2d 995 (Fed. Cir. 1986).
[121] Id. at 1001–1002.

strument Corp., 739 F.2d 604, 617, 222 USPQ 654, 664 (Fed. Cir.), *cert. denied,* 105 S. Ct. 516 (1984), and requires that the alleged infringer show that the patentee has impermissibly broadened the "physical or temporal scope" of the patent grant with anticompetitive effect. *Blonder-Tongue Laboratories, Inc. v. University of Illinois Foundation,* 402 U.S. 313, 343, 169 USPQ 513, 525 (1971)....

To sustain a misuse defense involving a licensing arrangement not held to have been per se anticompetitive by the Supreme Court,[9] a factual determination must reveal that the overall effect of the license tends to restrain competition unlawfully in an appropriately defined relevant market.

[9] Recent economic analysis questions the rationale behind holding any licensing practice per se anticompetitive. *See, e.g., USM Corp. v. SPS Technologies, Inc.,* 694 F.2d 504, 510–14, 216 USPQ 959, 963–66 (7th Cir. 1982), *cert. denied,* 462 U.S. 107 (1983); *Competition Policy and the Patent Misuse Doctrine,* Remarks by Roger B. Andewelt, Chief, Intellectual Property Section, Antitrust Division, Department of Justice, Before the Bar Association for the District of Columbia, Patent, Trademark & Copyright J. (BNA) No. 604 at 41, 44–45 (Nov. 11, 1982); *cf. Continental TV, Inc. v. GTE Sylvania, Inc.,* 433 U.S. 36 (1977) (changing the per se prohibition on vertical restrictions to a rule of reason approach).

This test for patent misuse requires that "the alleged infringer show the patentee has impermissibly broadened the 'physical or temporal scope' of the patent grant with anticompetitive effect."[122] The anticompetitive effects element requires that a court evaluate the actual or probable effects in the marketplace and determine that the effects on balance were anticompetitive, not procompetitive.[123] The Court of Appeals made clear that, except in areas where the Supreme Court has required otherwise, the

[122] Id. at 1001–1002.

[123] It is interesting that a few years prior the courts' incorporation of the antitrust rule of reason as the test for patent misuse, legislation was introduced to do the same thing. In 1983, under the guidance of William F. Baxter, the Antitrust Division of the Department of Justice proposed a bill that would have amended the patent laws to make the test for patent misuse congruent with the test for an antitrust violation and would have amended the antitrust laws to require rule of reason analysis of the legality of patent and other intellectual property license agreements. The National Productivity and Innovation Act, S.1841 (1983). The antitrust amendment would also have provided for actual damages, not treble damages, for violations. Congress

actual effects in the market must be evaluated and, on balance, the "overall effect of the license" must "tend to restrain competition unlawfully."

The Court of Appeals cited *Blonder-Tongue* for the proposition that misuse requires proof that "the patentee has impermissibly broadened the physical or temporal scope of the patent grant with anticompetitive effect."[124] In *Blonder- Tongue,* as in the other Supreme Court decisions, the test would have stopped with condemning "attempts to broaden the physical or temporal scope of the patent monopoly."[125] In *Blonder-Tongue,* the Court declared that the misuse rule was based on the idea that a patent owner could use the "monopoly" protected by the patent to create another monopoly the patent did not protect:[126]

> One obvious manifestation of this principle has been the series of decisions in which the Court has condemned attempts to broaden the physical or temporal scope of the patent monopoly. As stated in Mercoid v. Mid-Continent Investment Co. 320 US 661, 666, 88 L Ed 376, 381, 64 S Ct 268 (1944):
>
>> The necessities or convenience of the patentee do not justify any use of the monopoly of the patent to create another monopoly. The fact that the patentee has the power to refuse a license does not enable him to enlarge the monopoly of the patent by the expedient of attaching conditions to its use. United States v. Masonite Corp. [316 US 265,] 277 [86 L Ed 1461, 1474, 62 S Ct 1070] [(1942)]. The method by which the monopoly is sought to be extended is immaterial. United States v. Univis Lens Co. [316 US 241,] 251–252 [86 L Ed 1408, 1418–1419, 62 S Ct 1088] [(1942)]. The patent is a privilege. But it is a privilege which is

---

embraced only a small part of that idea and enacted a bill providing that agreements licensing the results of jointly conducted research were not *per se* unlawful under the Sherman Act, if those cooperating in the research notified the government of their agreements. This was the so-called National Cooperative Research Act. 15 U.S.C. § 4301–4305.
[124] Id. at 1001.
[125] *Blonder-Tongue Laboratories, Inc. v. University of Illinois Foundation,* 402 U.S. 313, 343 (1971). *Blonder-Tongue* related to the doctrine of collateral estoppel, and had nothing to do with patent misuse.
[126] Id. at 343.

2.7 MISUSE STANDARDS

> conditioned by a public purpose. It results from invention and is limited to the invention which it defines." [footnote omitted]

It should have been somewhat awkward for the *Blonder-Tongue* Court in 1977 to rely on its 1944 decision in *Mercoid v. Mid-Continent Investment* for guidance. In 1952, Congress had approved the conduct declared illegal in *Mercoid*.[127] And even though the Court expressly declared in 1980 that Congress rejected *Mercoid*,[128] the Court continues to repeat the same idea. The latest similar *dicta* is found in one opinion in *Jefferson Parrish*:[129]

> Any effort to enlarge the scope of the patent monopoly by using the market power it confers to restrain competition in the market for a second product will undermine competition on the merits in that second market. Thus, the sale or lease of a patented item on the condition that the buyer make all his purchases of a separate tied product from the patentee is unlawful.

The Court of Appeals in *Windsurfing* relied on another important decision defining the misuse defense. In 1982 in *USM Corporation v. SPS Technologies,* Judge Richard A. Posner of the Seventh Circuit Court of Appeals declared that, beyond "the conventional, rather stereotyped boundaries [of the patent-misuse doctrine]," misuse is tested by conventional antitrust principles, in particular the rule of reason.[130]

SPS, the owner of a patent on an industrial fastener, licensed USM to make and sell fasteners. SPS also gave USM the right to grant sublicenses under the SPS patent. SPS had previously granted licenses to four companies. SPS and USM agreed that (1) if USM sublicensed other companies, USM could keep 75 percent of the royalties and pay 25 percent to SPS, and (2) if USM sublicensed an existing SPS licensee (and that company kept its direct license), USM keeps 25 percent and pays SPS 75 percent. In practice, where USM sublicensed new licensees, the rate

---

[127] 35 U.S.C. § 271 (d) (1952).
[128] *Dawson Chemical Co. v. Rohm & Hass Co.,* 448 U.S. 176, 188–193 (1980).
[129] *Jefferson Parish Hosp. Dist. No. 2 v. Hyde,* 466 U.S. 2, 15–16 (1984).
[130] *USM Corporation v. SPS Technologies Inc.,* 694 F.2d 505, 513–514 (7th Cir. 1982).

was usually 4 percent, of which USM kept 3 percent and paid SPS 1 percent. If USM sublicensed an existing licensee, the rate was 5 percent, of which USM kept 1 percent and paid SPS 4 percent. (The opinion does not explain why these payments did not precisely follow the 25–75 split.) The agreement also gave existing SPS licensees the right to obtain a sublicense from USM on the same terms as other sublicensees. Presumably, the USM sublicenses also included rights to USM technology.

Judge Posner characterized the state of the law generally as follows:[131]

> The doctrine of patent misuse has been described as an equitable concept designed to prevent a patent owner from using the patent in a manner contrary to public policy. *Morton Salt Co.* . . . This is too vague a formulation to be useful; taken seriously it would put all rights at hazard; and in application the doctrine has been largely confined to a handful of specific practices by which the patentee seemed to be trying to "extend" his patent grant beyond its statutory limits. An early example was fixing the price at which the purchaser of the patented item could resell it. *See Bower & Cie v. O'Donnell,* 229 U.S. 1 (1913). The courts reasoned (in a rather circular fashion, one must admit) that once the patent owner had given up title to the patented item his patent rights were at an end, and any further restriction on the purchaser would extend the patent beyond its statutory bounds. Similar thinking lies behind the most common application of the doctrine, which is to prevent the patent owner from requiring his licensees to buy an unpatented staple item used with the patented device—for example, ink with a mimeograph machine. See generally *Dawson Chemical Co. v. Rohm & Hass Co.,* 448 U.S. 176, 188–93 (1980).
>
> Both examples—resale price maintenance and tying—suggest an overlap between misuse and antitrust principles. But although resale price maintenance by patentees was condemned as misuse shortly after *Dr. Miles Medical Co. v. John D. Park & Sons Co.,* 220 U.S. 373 (1911), held that the Sherman Act forbade resale price maintenance in nonpatent cases, see, *Bower & Cie v. O'Donell, supra,* and patent tie-ins were condemned as misuse

---

[131] Id. at 510.

2.7 MISUSE STANDARDS

shortly after the enactment of the tying provision (section 3) of the Clayton Act, 15 U.S.C. § 14 in 1914, see, *Motion Picture Patents Co. v. Universal Film Mfg. Co.,* 243 U.S. 502, 517–18 (1917), in both instances, the condemnation of the patentee's conduct was based on the doctrine of patent misuse rather than on antitrust law. More recently, the doctrine has been used to forbid the patentee to require his licensees to pay royalties beyond the expiration of the patent, *Brulotte v. Thys,* 379 U.S. 29 (1964), or to measure royalties by the sales of unpatented end products containing the patented item, *Zenith Radio Corp. v. Hazeltine Research, Inc.,* 395 U.S. 100, 133–40 (1969), or to require licensees not to make any items competing with the patented item. *Stewart v. Mo-Trim, Inc.,* 192 U.S.P.Q. 410 (S.D.Ohio 1975).

This description correctly identifies the conceptual origins of the misuse doctrine. However, I would place the creation of the misuse defense a bit later in history. That summary suggests that the patent misuse doctrine was developed as early as 1913 and 1917. However, *Bower & Cie* and *Motion Picture Patents* did not constitute the truly expansive part of the rule, namely that the conduct provides a defense to an infringment action against anyone, regardless of how they were impacted by the restriction. In *Bower & Cie* and *Motion Picture Patents,* the Court simply refused to enforce the restriction that would have placed the licensees' (and other infringment defendants') conduct outside the protection of the owner's authority. The Court declared the attempted restriction a nullity, leaving the licensees' (and others) within the immunity caused by the patent owner's license and sales. However, the attempted restriction did not prevent the patent from being enforced against others.

The unenforceability of the provisions destroyed their utility to patent owners, but they did not destroy the patent. That did not occur until 1942 in *Morton Salt.*

After reviewing the particular practices historically found to be misuse, Judge Posner declared that, beyond those practices, misuse is tested by antitrust principles:[132]

---

[132] Id. at 511–512.

But whether decided rightly or wrongly these are all cases where the license purports to enlarge the licensee's obligations beyond the limits of the patent grant. There is nothing of that sort here. But we must also consider whether the patent-misuse doctrine goes beyond these specific practices and constitutes a general code of patent licensing distinct from antitrust law.

The doctrine arose before there was any significant body of federal antitrust law, and reached maturity long before that law (a product very largely of free interpretation of unclear statutory language) attained its present broad scope. Since the antitrust laws as currently interpreted reach every practice that would impair competition substantially, it is not easy to define a separate role for a doctrine also designed to prevent an anticompetitive practice—the abuse of a patent monopoly. . . .

But probably cases like *Duplan*—which was, like *Motion Picture Patents Co., supra,* a tie-in case—are best understood simply as applications of the patent-misuse doctrine within its conventional, rather stereotyped boundaries. Outside those boundaries there is increasingly convergence of patent-misuse analysis with standard antitrust analysis. . . .

If misuse claims are not tested by conventional antitrust principles, but what principles shall they be tested? Our law is not rich in alternative concepts of monopolistic abuse; and it is rather late in the day to try to develop one without in the process subjecting the rights of patent holders to debilitating uncertainty. *Cf. Hensley Equipment Co. v. Esco Corp.,* 383 F.2d 252, 261–62 n.19, amended, 386 F.2d 442 (5th Cir. 1967).

We come at last to the particulars of USM's charge of patent misuse, which the district court dismissed on summary judgment and which for the reasons just explained we think must be evaluated under antitrust principles. [citations omitted]

In applying antitrust standards, the court looked for evidence of an actual or probable anticompetitive effect in a relevant market.[133]

---

[133] Id. at 513.

2.7 MISUSE STANDARDS

In any event, USM made no effort to present evidence of actual or probable anticompetitive effect in a relevant market, as is required in every Rule of Reason antitrust case in the Seventh Circuit. *Dos Santos v. Columbus-Cuneo-Cabrini Medical Center,* 684 F.2d 1346, 1352 (7th Cir. 1982). There is no argument that the royalty differential is unlawful per se. Patent licensing agreements between competitors are sometimes struck down under antitrust law, of course, but only upon proof of an anticompetitive effect beyond that implicit in the grant of the patent. See Priest, *Cartels and Patent License Arrangements,* 20 J. Law & Econ. 309 (1977).

In 1992, the Court of Appeals for the Federal Circuit in *Mallinckrodt v. Medipart* confirmed the rule announced in *Windsurfing*.[134] Unless the Supreme Court has declared a particular licensing arrangement to be *per se* anticompetitive, there is no misuse unless the "overall effect of the license tends to restrain competition unlawfully in an appropriately defined relevant market."

Mallinckrodt owned patents on a device for delivering chemicals to the lungs of a patient. Mallinckrodt made kits and sold them to hospitals. The kit had the parts of the device and the chemicals. Certain parts came in contact with the patient during use. Some parts were marked with patent numbers and the inscription "Single Use Only." The package insert accompanying the kit said that each unit was "For Single Patient Use Only" and instructed the user that the entire kit should be disposed of after one use. Some hospitals did not dispose of the device after using it for one patient. Rather, they shipped certain parts of the device to the Medipart company. Medipart sterilized those parts, checked them for damage, assembled them with new parts and shipped the "reconditioned" kits back to the hospital. The kits returned to the hospitals continue to bear the inscription "Single Use Only." Mallinckrodt asserted that Medipart infringed the patent by making the reconditioned kits and induced infringement by hospitals by assisting them in making more than a single use of one kit.

The district court dismissed both claims. The court said there could be no claim because the exhaustion doctrine rendered ineffective

---

[134] *Mallinckrodt, Inc. v. Medipart, Inc.,* 976 F.2d 700, 706 (Fed. Cir. 1992).

all restrictions or conditions on use by a purchaser of a patented product from a patent owner. The Court of Appeals for the Federal Circuit reversed. The hospitals infringed the patent when they used the product in violation of a lawful restriction or condition on use. The Court of Appeals applied the misuse doctrine to determine the lawfulness of the restriction.

Judge Newman also made clear that misuse requires application of the rule of reason as applied to vertical agreements:[135]

> Restrictions on use are judged in terms of their relation to the patentee's right to exclude from all or part of the patent grant, *see, e.g.,* W.F. Baxter, *The Viability of the Vertical Restraints Doctrine,* 75 Calif.L.Rev. 933, 935 (1987) ('Historically, legal prohibition began with [resale price control and tie-in agreements] and, with rare exceptions, now continues only with those devices.'); and where an anticompetitive affect is asserted, the rule of reason is the basis of determining the legality of the provision. In *Windsurfing International, Inc. v. AMF, Inc.,* 782 F.2d 995 (Fed. Cir.), *cert. denied* 477 U.S. 905 (1986), this court stated:
>
> > To sustain a misuse defense involving a license arrangement not held to have been *per se* anticompetitive by the Supreme Court, a factual determination must reveal that the overall effect of the license tends to restrain competition unlawfully in an appropriately defined relevant market.

Judge Newman noted that a license may have anticompetitive effects only to the extent it precludes competition by the licensee that the licensee would have been free to pursue without the license. That is, the license must restrain conduct that would not have been infringement of the licensed patent. Judge Newman's opinion said that even if there were effects extending beyond the patentee's right to exclude, those effects would not "automatically impeach the restriction." "Rather, those effects would be judged in accordance with the rule of reason of antitrust law."[136]

---

[135] Id. at 706.
[136] Id. at 708–709.

2.7 MISUSE STANDARDS

(c) The Patent Act and the Judicial Standards

The judicial decisions led to the following standard for misuse. Unless the Supreme Court has condemned conduct without proof of anticompetitive effects, the Courts of Appeals require economic analysis of anticompetitive effects in determining patent misuse. The overall effect of the license must tend to restrain competition unlawfully in an appropriately defined relevant market. That analysis requires a determination of whether an agreement is, on balance, anticompetitive, rather than procompetitive.[137] Unless the Supreme Court has required otherwise, misuse may not be proved by any remotely plausible theory of "extending" or "enlarging" the "patent monopoly" or using the "patent monopoly to create another monopoly." Harmful economic effects must be proved beyond those created by the mere existence of the patent.

If misuse would exist under this approach, the conduct must be evaluated further to determine whether section 271(d) of the Patent Act prohibits a finding of misuse. That section provides:[138]

> (d) No patent owner otherwise entitled to relief for infringement or contributory infringement of a patent shall be denied relief or deemed guilty of misuse or illegal extension of the patent right by reason of his having done one or more of the following: (1) derived revenue from acts which if performed by another without his consent would constitute contributory infringement of the patent; (2) licensed or authorized another to perform acts which if performed without his consent would constitute contributory infringement of the patent; (3) sought to enforce his patent rights against infringement or contributory infringement; (4) refused to license or use any rights to the patent; or (5) conditioned the license of any rights to the patent or the sale of the patented product on the acquisition of a license to rights in another patent or purchase of a separate product, unless, in view of the circumstances, the patent owner has mar-

---

[137] *Jefferson Parish Hosp. Dist. No. 2 v. Hyde*, 466 U.S. 2, 16–17 (1984) (concurring opinion); *Continental T.V. v. GTE Sylvania, Inc.*, 433 U.S. 36, 49–59 (1977) (which the Court of Appeals cited); *USM Corporation v. SPS Technologies, Inc.*, 694 F.2d 505, 513–514 (7 Cir. 1982).
[138] 35 U.S.C. § 271(d).

ket power in the relevant market for the patent or patented product on which the license or sale is conditioned.

Under that section, certain types of tying arrangements may not be misuse under subsections 1 through 4. In addition, all tying arrangements and package licenses may not be misuse without proof of the owner's market power in the relevant market for the patent or the patented product on which the license or sale is conditioned. Under both the *per se* and rule of reason approaches, section 271(d) may also preclude finding an antitrust violation based on certain types of tying arrangements.[139]

The history of the 1988 amendments suggest even broader implications. In 1988, Congress amended section 271(d) by adding subsections 4 and 5. Subsection 5 says that a patent owner is not guilty of misuse or "illegal extension of the patent right" because it engaged in certain tying arrangements "unless, in view of the circumstances, the patent owner has market power in the relevant market for the patent or patented product on which the license or sale is conditioned."

That amendment was the result of numerous suggested changes to patent misuse and antitrust law between 1983 and 1988. The most comprehensive proposal was the National Productivity and Innovation Act of 1983 that originated in the Baxter Antitrust Division.[140] The pertinent parts of that bill would have changed the antitrust law to require application of the rule of reason to determine the legality of all methods of exploiting and other intellectual property. *Per se* rules would have been forbidden for antitrust purposes. The patent and copyright acts would have been amended to require that there could be no finding of misuse unless the patent or copyright owner's conduct, in view of the circumstances, would constitute a violation of the antitrust laws.

Between 1983 and 1988 there were numerous bills to accomplish selected pieces of what the National Productivity and Innovation Act would have accomplished. Some were never voted on, some were passed in one house and not the other, and some never left their committee. In March, 1988, H.R.4086 was introduced to make individualized changes

---

[139] 35 U.S.C. § 271(d); *Dawson Chem. Co. v. Rohm & Haas,* 448 U.S. 176 (1980). *But see, Grid Systems Corp. v. Texas Instruments,* 771 F.Supp. 1033 (N.D.Cal. 1991).
[140] S.1841 (1984).

2.7 MISUSE STANDARDS

to various types of agreements subject to the misuse rule. The bill said a patent owner is not "considered to have engaged in conduct constituting misuse or illegal extension, because the owner did one of six things." One type of permitted conduct was that a patent owner "refuses to license or use any rights to the patent."

The bill also included a list of activities which were sometimes misuse. The list of conduct that was sometimes prohibited or always prohibited related to tying arrangements, agreements not to deal in "competing goods," package licensing, postexpiration royalties, agreements relating to price, and certain grantback provisions. The prohibition relating to tying arrangements defined misuse as "tying the sale of a patented product to an unpatented staple or the production of an unpatented product to the use of a patented process, except to the extent that the patent owner does not have market power." "Tying" was not defined; however, presumably it referred to an agreement under which a patent owner sold a patented product on condition that the buyer purchase an unpatented product or licensed a patent only on that condition.

In some ways, the definition of the bill seemed to make it easier to prove misuse. In others, it seemed to make it more difficult. However, the prohibition on tying in that bill would be a step in the right direction, if it meant that there was no reason to worry about economic harm unless the patent owner had market power in the sale of the patented product or in the licensing of patents in some market for rights.

However, even if it did have that market power, there are many situations in which there should be no prohibition. Other prerequisites to illegality would be that (1) the patent owner has a reasonable prospect of acquiring market power in the market for the unpatented product for uses other than with the patented product, (2) there is a sensible reason for treating (a) the patented product and unpatented product or (b) the license and the "unpatented" products as separate products, and (3) there is no justification for the agreement (such as being the low-cost method of insuring that the buyer or licensee uses the correct quality of product or pays in proportion to use).

Another type of conduct listed as sometimes prohibited was "unreasonably imposing the condition of granting a license under one patent that the licensee accept another license under a different patent."

In late 1988, the Senate attached to the bill for funding the Patent and Trademark Office a bill separately introduced as S.438 that provided that in an antitrust action an intellectual property right "shall not be presumed to define a market or to establish market power, including economic power and product uniqueness or distinctiveness, or market power" and provided that patent misuse could not be found unless the challenged "practices or actions or inactions, in view of the circumstances in which such practices or actions or inactions are employed, violate the antitrust laws."

Without further hearings or reports, Section 271(d) of the Act was amended to change the law on tying arrangements and package licensing. That bill seemed, like H.R.4086, simply to limit the prohibition on tying arrangements in one respect: The patent owner must have market power before other separate markets are likely to be adversely affected.

However, statements by members of Congress accompanying the change suggested a much broader interpretation. Congressional comments said that the bill did not merely require that market power be determined in view of the circumstances, but that the entire agreement be evaluated in view of the circumstances. Representative Kastenmeier said:

> The use of the term in view of the circumstances, is again designed to give the courts the requisite flexibility to exercise their equitable powers. *See* 35 U.S.C. § 283. This phrase is designed, in part, to allow the courts to assess the potentially competitive or anticompetitive effects of the tie-in practice. In making this assessment the courts may wish to look at whether the tied product is a staple or a non-staple. In the case of tying a product to a non-staple the net effect of such an arrangement may serve to expand the economic rights of the patent owner. This result, however, is generally appropriate because in most situations involving high technology the market for the non-staple product would not exist but for the existence of the patented product.
>
> On the other hand, courts that apply a rule of reason analysis to the tie-in of a patented product involving a staple may evaluate it in a slightly different manner. The ability of a party with a patented product to require that the purchaser or licensee of that product use a particular staple could have an anticompetitive effect. Thus, for cases involving the tie-in of staple products, the courts should be sensitive to the potential anticompetitive burden on commerce such a practice may have if the maker of a compet-

2.7 MISUSE STANDARDS

ing staple has its market substantially diminished as a result of the tie-in.

It is also our intention to avoid the use of inflexible rules once a court has found that market power exists. There may be circumstances in which there is market power and a tie-in, for where a finding of misuse would be inappropriate. One example would be where the patent owner has a business justification for the licensing practice . . . in real world situations where the only practical way to meter output is tie the sale of a patented product to the sale of another separate product then such a practice would be legitimate, unless such a practice—on balance—has a generally anticompetitive effect.

Two Senators echoed the sentiment that a misuse finding did not automatically follow from a finding of market power.[141] One Senator said the courts were "never automatically to conclude that a tie-in constitutes misuse, even where market power is present, unless the court has considered and assessed all the circumstances surrounding, the justifications for, and the impact of the tie-in in the marketplace."

The result of this change in late 1988 may be a revolution in patent misuse history. At least some members of Congress involved seemed to think that they had abolished the "stereotyped" prohibition of tying arrangements and packaged licensing of patents. If the courts read the language to mean what those members said it meant, and the amendment to the Patent Act is deemed to control antitrust litigation, the judicial decisions that articulated and spawned most of the misuse law in this century have been overridden. If one is to believe these people, the courts must always consider all the circumstances. The courts may no longer simply condemn all tying arrangements and cannot, as they did in 1942, close their ears to procompetitive explanations for the agreements.

If that legislation so radically changed the treatment of tie-ins and package licensing, one is left with a curious situation in which the stereotyped wooden rules may continue with respect to agreements such as an agreement by a licensee not to deal in unpatented competing products, a licensee's agreement to pay royalties on unpatented products (after the patent owner has insisted on that provision), and perhaps a variety of re-

---

[141] 134 Cong. Rec. S17, 148–49 (October 21, 1988).

strictions on use of a product purchased from a patent owner or his or her licensee.

However, all of the law that led the courts, with one exception, to create those rules was the Supreme Court's analysis of tie-in cases. If Congress has declared that the Supreme Court was wrong in the rule it laid down for the tie-in cases, it seems very hard to justify continuing the arbitrary rules with respect to all other restrictions. The one possibly surviving exception would be the rules relating to resale price fixing. One might argue (erroneously) that the Courts condemned resale price fixing of patented products before they condemned tying arrangements.

2.8 THE PUBLIC POLICY STANDARD

The courts typically define violations of public policy by tests virtually identical to the patent misuse tests. The Court has declared that license restrictions or other limitations are unenforceable if they attempt to create a "monopoly" beyond the scope of the patent.

The Court's earliest expression of this rule occurred in 1917.[142] In *Motion Picture Patents,* a patent owner licensed a company to make and sell motion picture projectors having a patented film feeding part. The licensee agreed to sell projectors only with the restriction and condition that they be used with motion picture films containing a film invention of a different patent and leased from a licensed film company. The seller put a notice on the projector that the purchase gives the right to use it only with films leased from a film licensee. The Court held that the "restriction" in the notice on the projector was ineffective, because its effect would be to "extend the scope of its patent monopoly." The Court added:

> [The] restriction is invalid because such a film is obviously not any part of the invention of the patent-in-suit; because it is an attempt, without statutory warrant, to continue the patent monopoly on this particular character of film after it [the film patent] has expired, and because to enforce it would be to create a monopoly in the manu-

---

[142] *Motion Picture Patents Co. v. Universal Film Mfg. Co.,* 243 U.S. 501, 508, 516–518 (1917).

facture and use of moving picture films, wholly outside of the patent-in-suit [, the machine patent,] and the patent law as we have interpreted it.

Presumably, section 271(d) of the Patent Act applies to the public policy rule.

2.9 A BRIEF HISTORY OF THE LEGAL LIMITS ON LICENSING

(a) Legislation

Throughout most of the nineteenth century, and its Industrial Revolution, there were no significant limits on exploiting patents or other intellectual property rights. In 1890, about one hundred years after the first Patent Act, Congress enacted the Sherman Act.[143] Section 1 of the Sherman Act generally prohibits every contract or conspiracy between two or more separate enterprises which unreasonably restrains trade. Section 2 prohibits monopolization or attempts to monopolize by a single enterprise. Section 2 prohibits a firm from obtaining or attempting to obtain monopoly power in a market by certain types of conduct. The Sherman Act contains no reference to patents or the Patent Act.

In 1914, Congress enacted the Clayton Act.[144] Prior to 1984, section 3 of the Clayton Act is the only antitrust statute to refer to patents or copyrights. Section 3 prohibits sales of products "whether patented or unpatented" on certain conditions. Section 3 declares it unlawful to lease, sell, or contract to sell "goods, wares, merchandise, machinery, supplies, or other commodities, whether patented or unpatented, . . . on the condition, agreement or understanding that the lessee or purchaser thereof shall not deal in the good, wares, merchandise, machinery, supplies, or other commodities of a competitor or competitors of the lessee or seller, where the effect of such lease, sale, or contract or such condition, agreement, or understanding may be to substantially lessen competition or tend to create a monopoly in any line of com-

---

[143] 15 U.S.C. §§ 1–7.
[144] 15 U.S.C. §§ 12–27.

merce."[145] That section does not apply to other means of exploiting a patent, such as by granting licenses. Likewise, the Robinson Patman Act does not apply to licensing patents or copyrights and contains no reference to them.[146]

In 1952 and 1988, Congress has provided some limited direction on the methods a patent owner may use to exploit the rights.

In 1952, Congress enacted Sections 271(c) and 271(d) of the Patent Act to make clear that patent misuse and antitrust laws do not eliminate the rule of contributory infringement and that it was not unlawful for a patent owner to sell products that would contributorily infringe a patent if sold by another, to license others to do so, or to sue others for such infringement.[147]

In 1988, Congress amended the Patent Act to revise the misuse rules.[148] In 1988, Congress specifically provided that a patent owner may not be denied relief or deemed guilty of misuse or "illegal extension of the patent right" because he or she "refused to license or use any rights to the patent."[149] Congress also declared that certain tying arrangements were no longer unlawful unless there was proof that the patent owner had market power in certain markets.[150]

With those exceptions, Congress has remained silent on the relationship between patent, antitrust, and misuse law. There have been several other legislative proposals relating to patent misuse. In September 1983, a bill was introduced to attempt to change the misuse doctrine.[151] This bill originated in the Antitrust Division of the Department of Justice, then led by William F. Baxter.

This bill would have amended the patent, copyright, and antitrust laws. The bill would have amended the Clayton Act to provide that agreements conveying rights to use patented inventions, copyrights, trade secrets, or other intellectual property are not illegal *per se* in actions under the antitrust laws and that a person injured by such a viola-

---

[145] 15 U.S.C. §§ 14.
[146] 15 U.S.C. § 13–13(f).
[147] 35 U.S.C. § 271(c) and (d) (1952).
[148] 35 U.S.C. § 271(d)(4)–(5) (1988).
[149] 35 U.S.C. § 271(d)(4) (1988).
[150] 35 U.S.C. § 271(d)(4) (1988).
[151] H.R.3878 and S.1841 (1983).

2.9 A BRIEF HISTORY OF THE LEGAL LIMITS ON LICENSING

tion may recover only actual damages plus interest rather than treble damages. The bill would have amended the Patent Act to provide that any use of a patent allegedly to suppress competition does not constitute patent misuse unless such conduct, in view of the circumstances in which it is employed, violates the antitrust laws. A similar amendment was proposed to the Copyright Act. Congress held hearings on the bill, but did not vote on it.

An outgrowth of this bill was an amendment to the antitrust laws to provide rule of reason analysis and actual damage remedies for inventions resulting from a joint research project, but only if the project was disclosed to the government.[152]

(b) Judicial Decisions

The courts have largely defined the methods by which intellectual property rights could be profitably exploited. A brief survey of the courts' decisions shows the difficulty the subject has presented.

(c) Tying

The earliest decisions involved exploitation of patents on machines. The patent owner would sell or lease the machines and separately license their use with supplies also sold by the patent owner, agreements now called tying arrangements. In 1912, the Supreme Court approved such agreements.[153] The Court said that a patent owner could sell a patented machine and limit the purchaser's license to use it to uses only with unpatented supplies also sold by the patent owner. Because the limitation was enforceable, it constituted infringement for others to sell certain types of supplies to that purchaser for use with the patented machine.

Five years later in 1917, the Supreme Court said that such a limitation on a machine purchaser was always unenforceable.[154] Use of supplies purchased from others and sale of those supplies did not constitute infringement. In 1931, the Court said that, if a patent owner sold a

---

[152] 15 U.S.C. § 4300 *et seq.*
[153] *Henry v. A.B. Dick,* 224 U.S. 1, 23–24 (1912).
[154] *Picture Patents Co. v. Universal Film Mfg. Co.,* 243 U.S. 501, 502 (1917).

patented product and separately sold one of the components of the product, another company did not infringe by selling the component to the patent owner's customers.[155]

In 1936, the Supreme Court found that the lease of a patented machine with the agreement to use it only with supplies from the patent owner violated the antitrust laws, even though those supplies were patented.[156] In 1938, the Court said that, if a patent owner sold a product useful in practicing a patented process, the owner could not enforce the patent against other sellers of the product.[157]

Prior to 1942, the legal consequences of tying arrangements were that the tying arrangement was not enforced and antitrust liability might exist. Because the agreement was unenforceable, "restricted" licensees were free to purchase the unpatented supplies or components from whomever they wanted. Those who sold unpatented supplies or components to "restrained" licensees were not guilty of infringement. In 1942, the Supreme Court repeated the rule that tying agreements were unenforceable, and also found that a patent owner who made any such agreement rendered the patent unenforceable against any infringers, whether or not those infringers were harmed by the agreement.[158] The Court said that this newly created defense existed whether or not such agreements violated the antitrust laws.

Curiously, three years later in 1945, the Supreme Court found that, even though a patent owner used a patent in a manner illegal under the antitrust laws, it was inappropriate to require the patent owner to grant royalty-free licenses to others or dedicate the patent to the public.[159]

In 1944, the Supreme Court said that an agreement licensing a patent covering an apparatus only to those who purchased one part of the apparatus from the patent owner or an authorized supplier, consti-

---

[155] *Carbice Corp. v. American Patents Devel. Corp.,* 283 U.S. 27, 31–35 (1931) (patented combination).
[156] *International Business Machines Co. v. United States,* 298 U.S. 131 (1936) (Clayton Act, §3).
[157] *Leitch Mfg. Co. v. Barber Co.,* 302 U.S. 458 (1938) (process patent).
[158] *Morton Salt Co. v. G. S. Suppinger Co.,* 314 U.S. 488, 491–494 (1942).
[159] *Hartford-Empire Co. v. United States,* 323 U.S. 386, 415 (1945).

2.9 A BRIEF HISTORY OF THE LEGAL LIMITS ON LICENSING

tuted patent misuse, even though that part had no use other than in making the apparatus covered by the patent.[160]

(d) Exclusive Dealing

These decisions about tying arrangements led the courts to condemn other types of agreements. A licensee's agreement to deal exclusively in the patented product was condemned shortly after the Supreme Court's 1942 decision. In 1943, a Court of Appeals found that it was always patent misuse for a licensee to agree not to sell products which compete with the product sold under the license and without respect to whether that agreement violated the antitrust laws.[161]

(e) Package Licensing

The tying arrangement decisions also led the Court to prohibit package licensing of two or more patents or copyrights. In 1950, the Supreme Court said there was nothing wrong with an agreement licensing a number of patents, but an owner could not condition the granting of a license under one patent upon the acceptance of a different license.[162] In 1962, the Supreme Court held that an owner of a number of copyrights violated the antitrust laws by leasing those copyrights only as a package.[163] In the 1960s, numerous Courts of Appeals found that it was similarly constituted patent misuse to license a number of patents only as a package, at least where the inventions covered by the patents could be used separately.[164]

---

[160] *Mercoid Corp. v. Mid-Continent Co.*, 302 U.S. 661, 664–665, 667 (1944); *Mercoid Corp. v. Minneapolis-Honeywell Reg. Co.*, 320 U.S. 680, 682–684 (1944). This rule was foreshadowed, if not adopted, earlier by the lower courts. *B.B. Chemical Co. v. Ellis*, 117 F.2d 829, 834–836 (1st Cir. 1941), *aff'd*, 314 U.S. 495 (1942); *Philad Co. v. Lechler Laboratories*, 107 F.2d 747, 748 (2nd Cir. 1939).

[161] *National Lockwasher Co. v. George K. Garrett Co.*, 137 F.2d 255 (3rd Cir. 1943).

[162] *Automatic Radio Mfg. Co. v. Hazeltine Research*, 339 U.S. 827 (1950).

[163] *United States v. Loew's, Inc.*, 371 U.S. 38 (1962).

[164] *Beckman Instruments, Inc. v. Technical Development Corp.*, 433 F.2d 55, (7th Cir. 1970); *Compton v. Metal Products, Inc.*, 353 F.2d 38, (4th Cir. 1971); *Shea v. Blaw-Knox Co.*, 388 F.2d 761, (7th Cir. 1968); *Hazeltine Research v. the Zenith Radio Corp.*, 388 F.2d 25, (7th Cir. 1967), *aff'd in part, rev'd on other grounds*, 395 U.S. 100 (1969).

(f) Royalties

In 1931, the Supreme Court said that a patent owner could license a patent for any royalty it could obtain.[165] In the 1960s, the Supreme Court limited the permissible types of agreements regarding royalty payments. In 1964, that Court held that an agreement requiring royalties to be paid based on use of a patented machine after all the patents expired was to that extent unenforceable.[166] In 1969, the Supreme Court held that a patent owner misused his patent by compelling his licensee to pay royalties on products that were not made or sold under any of the licensed patents.[167]

In 1931, the Supreme Court said that a patent owner had the right to determine who could use the invention.[168] In the 1960s, the lower courts created antitrust and misuse consequences from charging different licensees different royalty rates. In 1964, a few lower courts held that it constituted an antitrust violation and patent misuse for a patent owner, who used the patent, to grant licenses to one group of licensees at one rate per unit of output and another group of licensees at a higher rate, where the effect was to restrict competition between those two groups of licensees.[169] A more limited version of this rule survives. (section 3.6).

(g) Resale Restrictions on Field of Use

In 1938, the Supreme Court found enforceable restrictions on the type of use made by a purchaser of equipment from a licensee authorized to sell the equipment only for certain purposes, and found the customer's use for other purposes constituted infringement.[170] In the 1960s, a number of courts held that it violated the antitrust laws for a patent owner to

---

[165] *Automatic Radio Mfg. v. Hazeltine Research, Inc.,* 339 U.S. 827, 830–833 (1950).
[166] *Brulotte v. Thys Co.,* 379 U.S. 29, 30, 33 (1964).
[167] *Zenith Radio Corp. v. Hazeltine Research, Inc.,* 395 U.S. 100, 135–140 (1969).
[168] *Standard Oil Co. v. United States,* 283 U.S. 163, 179 (1931). *Also, United States v. E.I. du Pont de Nemours & Co.,* 113 F.Supp. 41, 224 (D. Del. 1953).
[169] *LaPeyre v. F.T.C.,* 366 F.2d 117 (5th Cir. 1966), *aff'ing sub nom Grand Caillou Packing Co. Inc.,* CCH Trade Reg. Rep., FTC Complaints, Orders, Stipulations; 16, 927 (F.T.C. 1964); *Peelers Co. v. Wendt,* 260 F.Supp. 193 (W.D. Wash. 1966); *Laitram Corp. v. King Crab,* 244 F.Supp. 193 (W.D. Wash. 1966); *Laitram Corp. v. King Crab, Inc.,* 244 F.Supp. 9, *mod.,* 245 F.Supp. 1019 (D. Alaska 1965).
[170] *General Talking Pictures Corp. v. Western Electric Co.,* 34 U.S. 175 (1937), *rehearing granted* 304 U.S. 87, *aff'd on rehearing* 305 U.S. 124 (1938).

2.10 THE ECONOMIC PRINCIPLES UNDERLYING LEGAL LIMITS

sell a patented product and restrict the uses to which the purchaser could put it.[171] At least one court during this period declined to find misuse in this circumstance.[172] Later decisions modify and limit the influence of the 1960's antitrust decisions. (sections 5.4(c), (d) and Chapter 6).

2.10 THE ECONOMIC PRINCIPLES UNDERLYING LEGAL LIMITS ON LICENSING PATENT AND RELATED RIGHTS

(a) Markets and Competition

According to the courts, the legal limits on licensing seek to forbid acts that interfere with competition in a market. Competition may be understood in two very different ways.

Competition may be used to describe the existing structure of a market. A market for some product may be said to have "competition" or be "competitive." A market with "competition" is one having a number of suppliers and having no one seller with a sufficient advantage over other suppliers that it is able to raise its prices significantly without losing a significant quantity of sales to others. A supplier that makes a large share of the sales in the total market, such as 60 percent, is more likely to have this discretion over its prices. A seller with such discretion may

---

[171] *Hensley Equipment Co. v. Esco Corp.*, 383 F.2d 252, 262–264 (5th Cir.), *modified* 386 F.2d 442 (5th Cir. 1967) (license provision restricting use and sale of patented parts purchased from licensor to original installation on equipment made and sold by the licensee and to use as replacement parts on such equipment constituted *per se* violation of the Sherman Act and a defense to an action for infringement); *Ansul Company v. Uniroyal, Inc.*, 306 F. Supp. 541, 556–559 (S.D.N.Y. 1969), *aff'd in pertinent part* 448 F.2d 872 (2d Cir. 1971) (a patent owner's sale of the patented chemical to distributors subject to resale price maintenance—through suggested, but "required" resale prices—and to limited territories, as a *per se* violation under *U.S. v. Schwinn*, and therefore patent misuse); *United States v. Ciba-Geigy Corp.*, 508 F. Supp. 1118, 1126–1147 (D. N.J. 1976) (supply agreement restricting purchasers of drug in bulk form from reselling in finished dosage form unless in combination approved by the seller violated the Sherman Act), *final judgment*, 1980–81 Trade Cas. (CCH) ¶ 63,813 (D. N.J. 1981).

[172] *Chemagro Corp. v. Universal Chem. Co.*, 244 F.Supp. 486, 489–490 (E.D. Tex. 1965) (sale of chemical restricted to reformulation for commercial market; reformulation for home market prohibited).

be said to have a "monopoly" position. A market is "competitive" in structure where no one seller may noticeably influence the price of the product by changing the quantity it sells.

The term "competition" may also be used to describe how individual firms or groups of firms behave. Firms may be said to be engaged in "competition" where each is striving to enhance its position and its profits at the expense of other suppliers. A firm is said to be engaged in "competition" when it lowers its price or improves its product to attract additional sales. This type of conduct may occur in markets that are not "competitive" in structure. This type of conduct is sometimes called "rivalry" in order to avoid this semantic problem. In this sense, "competition" is the process that takes place in a market over a period of time as firms seek to enhance their profits sometimes at the expense of other firms.

The process of competition may produce a market that is not "competitive" in structure at least for a time. A firm may become the only supplier in a market through innovation and continue to engage in rivalry or "competition." Similarly, a market that is not "competitive" in structure may be one in which a firm or firms are engaging in "competition." A firm may be the only supplier in a market and engage in rivalry or "competition." The firm may change its product to make it even more valuable to consumers. It may change the way it makes the product to lower its costs, permitting it to lower the price it charges and increase its sales and profits. These activities may enhance the firm's position relative to other potential suppliers that might enter the market in the future.

In general, the Sherman Act prohibits two types of conduct that may interfere with the process of competition. The Sherman Act does not prohibit all conduct that may "interfere" with a "competitive" market structure at any point in time. Conduct that interferes with or suppresses the process of competition is sometimes labeled "anticompetitive."

Section 1 of the Sherman Act prohibits agreements between separate enterprises that unreasonably restrain competition. Agreements between actual or potential competitors to limit their rivalry will prevent markets from operating to the maximum advantage of consumers. That is so whether they are rivals in producing inventions or rivals in producing tangible goods. The incentives created by markets for tangible or intangible products depend on the process of competition among ac-

2.10 THE ECONOMIC PRINCIPLES UNDERLYING LEGAL LIMITS

tual and potential suppliers in that market, each independently seeking to maximize its own profits.

Section 2 of the Sherman Act, and Section 7 of the Clayton Act seek to prevent a single firm (or a cooperating group of firms) from acquiring or maintaining monopoly power in a market by activities that interfere with the competition process. Again, those activities are harmful whether they interfere with rivalry in producing inventions or producing tangible goods.

Anticompetitive agreements and monopolies arising from anticompetitive conduct harm consumers by their effects on output and price for a product in a market. Assume some demand for a product and some supply. Assume for simplicity that production costs for all actual and potential suppliers are constant at all levels of output, so that average per-unit cost equals marginal per-unit cost. Under market forces operating free of anticompetitive agreements (and monopolies arising from anticompetitive conduct), the supply of products will increase until price equals average (and marginal) cost. A monopolist (or competitors successfully emulating a monopolist by an agreement) charging the same price to all customers will attempt to restrict output to the point where marginal revenue from additional sales is equal to marginal cost. Under those conditions, output will decrease and price will increase.

Resource waste exists because the value of the goods that would have been produced (but were not) is greater than the cost of producing them. The monopoly price is greater than the cost of producing the goods. This causes those resources to flow to markets (and consumers) where they have less valuable uses, assuming the markets they flow to are operating free of similar restrictions. Hence, resources are wasted (and consumers harmed) as a result of the single-firm monopoly from anticompetitive conduct or the multiple-firm "monopoly" implemented by anticompetitive agreements.

(b) An Illustration of the Effects of Anticompetitive Agreements and Conduct

Figure 2.1(a) is a typical illustration of the losses for consumers arising from anticompetitive agreements and monopolies arising from anticompetitive conduct. This illustration shows output and price in a market under competitive conditions and under monopolistic supply or sup-

THE LAW OF LICENSING INTELLECTUAL PROPERTY RIGHTS

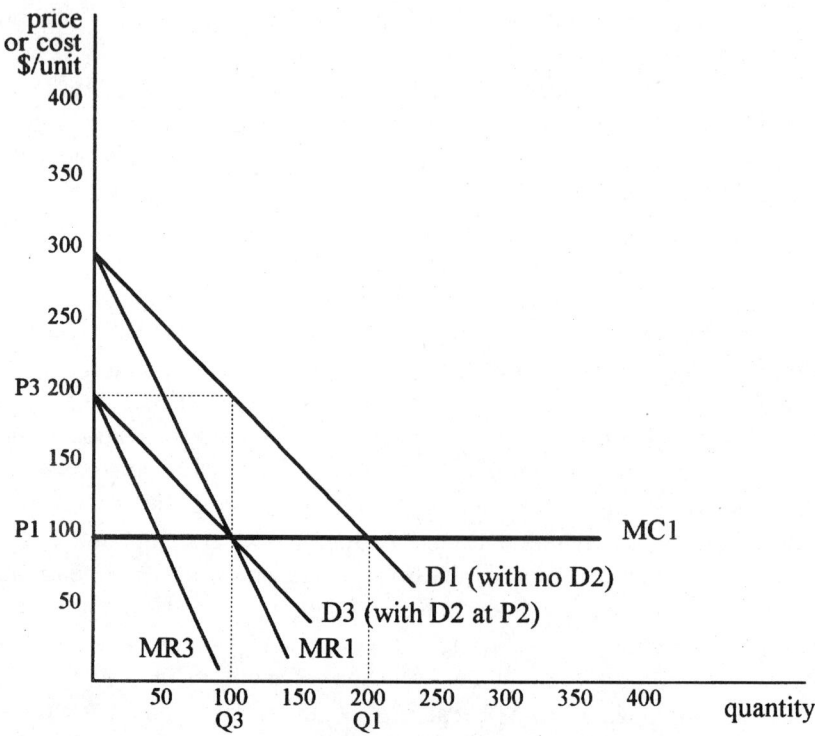

Figure 2.1(a). The Effects of Rights on Sales of Old Products

ply subject to agreements effectively preventing all forms of competition.[173] Assume for simplicity that production costs are constant at all levels of output, so that average per-unit cost equals marginal per-unit cost. Assuming some demand for a product, D1, a supply curve, MC1, and competitive conditions, the supply of products will increase until price equals average cost. In the diagram, output will be at level Q1 (200 units) and price will be P1 ($100 per unit).

A monopolist (or competitors successfully emulating a monopolist by an agreement) will restrict output to the point where marginal revenue from additional sales, MR, is equal to marginal cost, MC1. Under

---

[173] Those lacking familiarity with basic economics may acquire it in the sources identified in Chapter 1.

2.10 THE ECONOMIC PRINCIPLES UNDERLYING LEGAL LIMITS

those conditions, output will be restricted to Q3 (100 units) and price will be P3 ($200). As is clear from the diagram, the value of the goods between quantities Q3 and Q1 is greater than the cost of producing them. The monopoly price is greater than the cost of producing the goods. This causes resources to flow to markets where they have less valuable use, assuming the markets they flow to are competitively operating. Hence, resources were wasted as a result of the single-firm monopoly from anticompetitive conduct or the multiple-firm monopoly from anticompetitive agreements.

(c) Markets, Competition, and Technical Information

A firm may seek to become the only supplier in a market by producing technical information. This is one way of engaging in rivalry or "competition." The firm may conduct a research and development program to make a product more valuable to consumers than existing products. The firm may do R&D to try to find a way to make existing products at lower costs, thereby permitting it to lower the price it charges and increase its sales and profits. If successful, these activities enhance the firm's position relative to other existing or potential suppliers. If consumers judge the innovating firm's products to be much preferable, the suppliers of other products may vanish until they develop an even better product.

This form of "competition" is one important feature of the "competitive" process that takes place in a market over a period of time as firms seek to enhance their profits, sometimes at the expense of other firms. This type of competition may produce a market structure that is not "competitively" structured, at least for a time.

(d) Markets, Competition, and Intellectual Property Law

In a market-driven economy relying on profit incentives to induce the production of technical information, an externality problem may cause too few resources to be used to produce that information.[174]

The patent (and other intellectual property) laws are designed to solve that problem. Patent laws grant to the producers of technical in-

---

[174] John W. Schlicher, *Patent Law: Legal and Economic Principles* (Clark, Boardman, Callahan, 1992).

formation the temporary rights to exclude others from making, using, or selling products embodying the information. Those rights permit their owner to prevent external benefits. Patent laws give to the producers of intangible information the right to exclude that property law gives to the owner of physical property. However, that right is given for a limited period of time. During the term of a patent, the patent owner is permitted to exclude all others and charge a price for use of the invention based upon the market's determination of its value.

The Patent Act rests on the premise that the free use of technical information by all firms will not yield the best use of resources, the lowest prices, the highest quality, and the greatest material progress. In particular, the unrestrained, free use of inventions by all firms will cause too few resources to be used in making inventions and too little long-run economic progress as too few inventions are made and used. Patent law leads to lower prices and higher quality as products employing an increased stream of inventions replace earlier, more expensive, lower-quality products.

The granting of patents does not result in the resource losses caused by unjustified monopolies and anticompetitive agreements. To determine the consequences of the patent law for resource use, we must compare the market as it existed before the invention with the market or markets which exist after the invention is made. To do otherwise ignores the fact that the postinvention market effects are necessary to induce the invention to be made.

It is also necessary to recognize that patents are granted only for processes and products which are new and nonobvious in the sense that they differ technically from those which were used or known before the invention. A patent does not preclude use of any existing, publicly available technology.

(e) An Illustration of the Effects of Intellectual Property Law

This is a simple illustration of these market effects. Assume Figure 2.1(a) shows the market demand, D1, and supply, MC1, for an old product produced under competitive conditions. Quantity Q1, 200 units, is produced at price P1, $100.

A new product is invented and patented, which is superior to the old product for certain uses. Given the prevailing $100 price for the old

2.10 THE ECONOMIC PRINCIPLES UNDERLYING LEGAL LIMITS

product, the demand for the new product is shown by the curve D2 in Figure 2.1(b). For some users of the old product, the new product is more valuable to them, even if sold by a single supplier. These old product users will switch to the new product. The demand curve D1 for the old product shifts to the left to D3, but not to zero. Since the new product is subject to a patent, its seller may exclude others from selling it. The seller will produce a quantity where the marginal revenue equals marginal cost. This will result in the supply of 125 units (Q2) at price $275 (P2). Others may continue to sell the old product and supply 100 (Q3) units at the old $100 price (P1).

No resource loss is involved with respect to the old product because the consumers who switch are better off or they would not have done so.

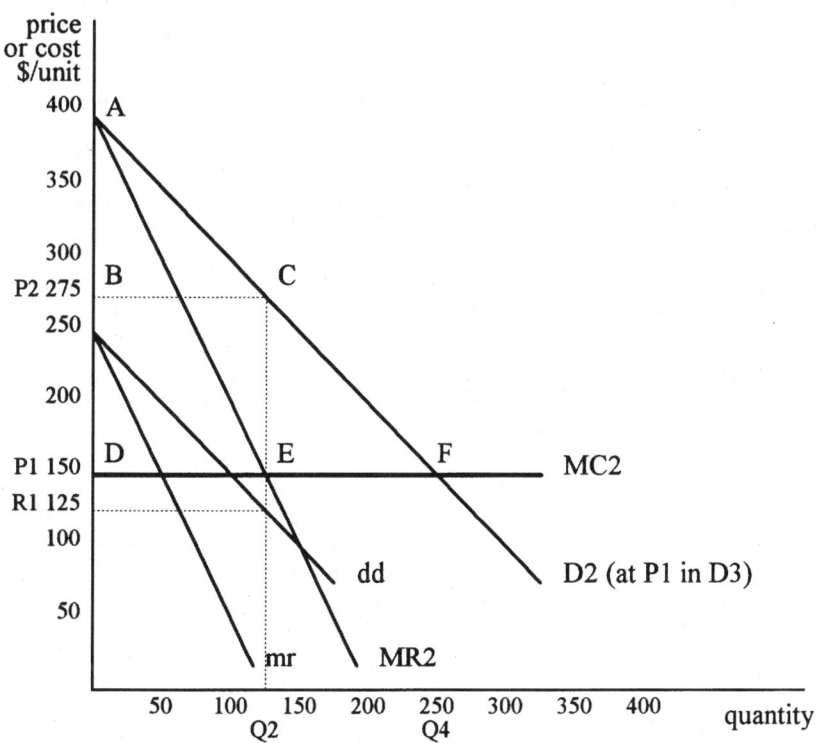

2.1(b). The Effects of Rights on Sales of New Products

THE LAW OF LICENSING INTELLECTUAL PROPERTY RIGHTS

The portion of the demand for the new product not supplied because of lack of competition due to the patent is also not a resource allocation loss, as in the case of an unjustified monopoly or an anticompetitive agreement of the kind of concern to antitrust laws.

The patent took away no production alternatives existing prior to the invention. The demand for the old product is still supplied under "competitive" structural constraints. The new product did not exist and could not have been supplied without the invention. The government grants the rights to induce the invention of the new product. Assuming the invention would not have been available except for the rights, the rights and resulting invention improved the welfare of the consumers.

Without the patent, and the invention it prompted, there would be no product that consumers value by the amounts shown by the demand, D2, and from which to identify a "consumer welfare" or so-called "deadweight" loss, CEF. During the term of the patent, some of the benefits of the new product (in excess of production costs) will be realized by consumers, the area ADEC. They also receive benefits that exceed their payments, the area ABC.

The fact that some purchasers switch from the old product to the new product indicates that they are better off, even during the period the new product is sold at "monopoly" prices. Those who do not switch are no worse off. Resource use has improved. The restriction of output from Q4, 250 units, to Q2, 125 units, is not a loss. The restriction on use of the invention was necessary to induce the invention, and without it that new product would not exist. Once the patent expires, that "loss" will cease, and output will expand to 250 units, and consumers will then also receive the benefits shown by the area CEF.

If the new product is inferior to the old product, while new in a technical sense, the market may assign it a zero value. If it is simply as good as but no better than the currently available old product, it may be introduced and sold at a price equal to P1, because no one will pay more than that given the availability of the old product. In either of those cases, the patent will have no economic consequences.

(f) Intellectual Property as Monopoly in Legal Doctrine

The patent grant and its exclusive right to use the invention is consistent with the purpose of the antitrust laws. Antitrust laws do not require that

2.10 THE ECONOMIC PRINCIPLES UNDERLYING LEGAL LIMITS

all inventions be freely available for use by all firms, because that result will lead to too little production of inventions and new products. While there were once discussions about an "inherent conflict" or unavoidable "tension" between patent and antitrust law, those debates are largely over.

The courts have sometimes recognized the lack of any natural conflict between these laws. The courts often say the exclusion of competition from use of a patent invention is the essence of the right conferred by a patent.[175] They note that the object of the patent laws is to give the inventor a "monopoly" of the use of the invention.[176] Hence, they declare that the mere acquisition and enforcement of a patent does not violate the antitrust laws, even where the purpose and effect is to obtain a monopoly position in a market protected by the patent.[177] Also, they declare it lawful to exploit the patent by use and licensing in a manner consistent with the scope of the rights.[178]

On other occasions, the courts seem less comfortable with the relationship between those laws. For example, in 1971 in *Blonder-Tongue,* the Supreme Court in *dicta* said a patent is a monopoly, with the economic consequences of other monopolies.[179] The Court said:

> ... [al]though recognizing the patent system's desirable stimulus to invention, *we have also viewed the patent as a monopoly* which, *although sanctioned by law, has the economic consequences attending other monopolies.* ... [emphasis added]

---

[175] *Dawson Chem. Co. v. Rohm & Haas,* U.S. (1980); *Transparent-Wrap Machine Corp. v. Stokes & Smith Co.,* 329 U.S. 637, 643 (1947); *Continental Paper Bag Co. v. Eastern Paper Bag Co.,* 210 U.S. 405, 429 (1908).

[176] *United States v. Dubilier Condensor Corp.,* 289 U.S. 178, 186 (1932); *Bement v. National Harrow Co.,* 186 U.S. 70, 91 (1902).

[177] *Walker Process Equipment, Inc. v. Food Machinery & Chemical Corp.,* 382 U.S. 172, 177 (1965); *Simpson v. Union Oil Co.,* 377 U.S. 13, 24 (1964).

[178] *General Talking Pictures Corp. v. Western Electric Co.,* 304 U.S. 175, 181, *aff'd on reh.,* 305 U.S. 124 (1938), *reh. denied,* 305 U.S. 675 (1939); *United States v. United Shoe Mach. Co.,* 247 U.S. 32, 57 (1917) ("Of course, there is restraint in a patent. Its strength is in the restraint, the right to exclude others from the use of the invention, absolutely or on the terms the patents chooses to impose. This strength is the compensation which the law imparts for the exercise of invention. Its exertion within the field covered by the patent law is not an offense against the Anti-Trust Act. ... In other circumstances, it may be. ... ").

[179] *Blonder-Tongue Laboratories, Inc. v. University of Illinois Foundation,* 402 U.S. 313, 343 (1971).

This statement makes sense if one assumes that the patent system does not work. Assuming (contrary to the legislature's decision, the statutory criteria, and the empirical evidence) that patent owners always obtain monopoly positions in product markets, and that patent do not increase the level (or rate) of inventing, the economic consequences are the same. If patent law works, the economic consequences are quite different.

Some Justices repeated this idea in 1984 in *Jefferson Parish Hosp. Dist. No. 2 v. Hyde:*[180]

> For example, if the government has granted the seller a patent or similar monopoly over a product, it is fair to presume that the inability to buy the product elsewhere gives the seller market power.

Four Justices disagreed:[181]

> A common misconception has been that a patent or copyright... [suffices] to demonstrate market power.... [A] patent holder has no market power in any relevant sense if there are close substitutes for the patented product.

The Court in *Blonder-Tongue* also repeated from an earlier decision the view that patent rights are in some sense an exception to the economic principles of antitrust law:[182]

> ... [a] patent by its very nature is affected with public interest.... [*It*] *is an exception to the general rule against monopolies* and to the right to access to a free and open market. [emphasis added]

Even if patents always gave rise to product monopolies, there is no general rule in antitrust law or any other law "against monopolies." Monopolies can be good or bad depending on how they arose. If monopo-

---

[180] *Jefferson Parish Hosp. Dist. No. 2 v. Hyde,* 466 U.S. 2, 16 (1984).
[181] Id. at 37 n.7.
[182] *Blonder-Tongue Laboratories, Inc. v. University of Illinois Foundation,* 402 U.S. 313, 343 (1971).

2.10 THE ECONOMIC PRINCIPLES UNDERLYING LEGAL LIMITS

lies arose from producing better technology, antitrust law has usually identified them as good monopolies. In any event, the Supreme Court seemed to repudiate that view in 1980 in *Dawson Chem. Co., Inc. v. Rohm & Haas Co.,* when it said:[183]

> The policy of free competition runs deep in our law. . . . But the policy of stimulating invention that underlies the entire patent system runs no less deep.

When the Court declares that the public policies served by the patent system are at least as important as the policies served by the antitrust laws, there is no reason to call one the "general rule" and the other an "exception." In practice, this "general rule—exception" characterization was important to the development of the law. Where the Court perceived a possible conflict and there was uncertainty as to which policy should prevail, this approach inclined the Court to avoid deciding the issue by saying antitrust policy prevailed to protect the general principle.

The Court of Appeals for the Federal Circuit has criticized the view that patent rights give rise to monopolies in an economic sense. This Court of Appeals also rejected the view that there is an inherent conflict between patent and antitrust law and that patents are an exception to "the general rule against monopolies." In *Schenck A.G. v. Norton Corporation,* the court said patents were simply property rights:[184]

> Norton begins its file wrapper estoppel argument with "Patents are an exception to the general rule against monopolies. . . ." A patent, under the statute, is property. 35 U.S.C. § 261. Nowhere in any statute is a patent described as a monopoly. The patent right is but the right to exclude others, the very definition of "property." That the property right represented by a patent, like other property rights, may be *used* in a scheme violative of antitrust laws creates no "conflict" between laws establishing any of those property rights and the antitrust laws. The antitrust laws, enacted long after the original patent laws, deal with appropriation of what should belong

---

[183] *Dawson Chem. Co., Inc. v. Rohm & Haas Co.,* 448 U.S. 176, 221 (1980).
[184] *Schenck A.G. v. Norton Corporation,* 713 F.2d 782, 786, n.3 (Fed. Cir. 1983).

to others. A valid patent gives the public what it did not earlier have. Patents are valid or invalid under the statute, 35 U.S.C. It is but an obfuscation to refer to a patent as "the patent monopoly" or to describe a patent as an "exception to the general rule against monopolies."

2.11 THE BASIC OPTIONS OF INTELLECTUAL PROPERTY OWNERS

For purposes of this discussion, I will refer to patents. The ideas and, often, the law apply to all intellectual property rights. The patent laws grant the patent owner the right to exclude others from making, using, or selling the patented invention. Like all other property rights systems, patent law permits its owner to make agreements that others may use the property in exchange for something of value to the owner.

The value of any particular patent will depend upon the value of the invention it protects in view of all alternative inventions. In order for the market for inventions to function, the rights to exclude must be transferable by sale or license to others. The courts have long recognized the owner's right to exploit a patent by transferring or licensing it to others.

Moreover, in order to assure that a price will be agreed upon in the market, the patent owner must have the right to refuse to license or sell the patent for less than what it believes the patent is worth. Unless the patent owner has the absolute right to refuse to license or sell, the market simply cannot determine the value of the rights.

License agreements may simply be transactions by which the supplier of one necessary product provides it to another person for a price. Such transactions make both parties better off. They also make consumers better off by increasing the value of inventing and permitting the invention to be used by people who are able to put it to the most valuable use. If that was the only possible effect of licensing, there would be no need for legal limits. Indeed, any legal limits would be harmful to consumers.

However, a rational owner of an invention protected by a patent may think about trying to do the following three things with the rights.

2.11 THE BASIC OPTIONS OF INTELLECTUAL PROPERTY OWNERS

(a) Capture the Commercial Value of the Rights Other than by Limiting Rivalry with Substitute Rights

The first is the purpose already mentioned. The owner may attempt to create and capture the largest part of the value flowing from the use of the rights. It may develop the invention or license others to develop it further. It may put the invention to use in producing the best goods and services at the lowest costs. If others are able to produce better goods or the same goods at lower cost, the owner may market the rights to others and seek to induce them to make the best goods at lowest cost.

Agreements between a patent owner and its licensees involving the patent owner's efforts to earn maximum returns from the licensees' commercial use of the invention are not anticompetitive. The licensee was never a lawful actual or potential competitor of the patent owner in using or licensing the invention. In the common antitrust jargon, this relationship between a patent owner and its licensee is a *vertical* one. In other words, the patent owner and the licensee supply complementary products—not substitutes.[185] The patent owner is the supplier of an invention, one of many resources needed by the licensees to produce a product. The owner may limit the rights granted or seek to restrict the licensees' future activities to maximize the value of the rights.

(b) Increase the Profitability of Supplying Rights or Products by Limiting Rivalry with the Cooperation of Suppliers of Substitute Rights or Substitute Products

Second, the owner may use the rights as a device to limit production or otherwise decrease rivalry between people who would otherwise lawfully engage in that rivalry. The owner may compete with others in producing future technical information, in licensing substitute rights or in supplying tangible products. The owner and its rivals may attempt to use licensing to limit such competition. In certain situations, patent licenses may provide a device for agreements between actual or potential competitors not to compete in certain respects.

---

[185] For an explanation of the substitute–complement distinction in antitrust generally, see William F. Baxter and Daniel P. Kessler, "Toward a Consistent Theory of the Welfare Analysis of Agreements," *Stanford Law Review* **47,** 615 (1995).

(c) Increase the Profitability of Supplying Rights or Products by Limiting Rivalry without the Cooperation of Suppliers of Substitutes

Third, the owner may attempt to agree with potential users of the rights that it will waive the rights in exchange for the user's agreement to impair the ability of a rival to compete with the owner in a market or in a manner that the owner could not control simply by enforcing the rights. In theory, patent owners may make agreements with users which permit the patent owner to acquire a monopoly not granted by the patent and exploit that monopoly to restrict output in markets for products made and used independent of the patent. This possibility is the basis for virtually all patent misuse law and all *per se* prohibitions under antitrust law.

2.12 THE LAW AND THE BASIC OPTIONS OF INTELLECTUAL PROPERTY OWNERS

If these are the owner's only options, we should expect the law to try to discourage the second and third kinds of behavior and encourage the first kind. In general, the courts have said this is what the law attempts to do. However, the law has had difficulty distinguishing between the first and third types of conduct. When was the owner's conduct designed to exploit the rights? When was the owner's conduct designed to limit competition by exchanging the rights for the licensee's agreement to do things that were against the licensee's interest, and limit competition in some way that the rights themselves did not permit the owner to control? This area is not the only one in which antitrust law has difficulty understanding the effects of business conduct.[186]

Under the current *economic effects* tests, an agreement involving exploitation of a patent is treated as a transaction between the supplier of the rights and a potential user. An owner is under no obligation to use the rights or license them to others. An owner is also under no obliga-

---

[186] Frank H. Easterbrook, "Ignorance and Antitrust," in *Antitrust, Innovation and Competitiveness,* 1992 (Jorde and Teece, eds., Oxford University Press, New York) 119; Frank H. Easterbrook, "The Limits of Antitrust," *Texas Law Review* **63**, 1 (1984).

tion to create competition in products that embody the rights. For example, the law does not regard as anticompetitive a limitation that prevents the licensee from competing in ways a patent prevents. Other types of effects may be anticompetitive.[187]

The Supreme Court's decisions identify three somewhat different potentially anticompetitive agreements of concern to antitrust law.

(a) Licenses that Primarily Limit Rivalry among Suppliers of Substitute Products

First, if a license or a series of licenses is merely a cover or vehicle for actual or potential competitors in the market to limit their competition, the courts may condemn the licenses on that basis even though the licenses on their faces are lawful.[188] If the license is merely used as an instrument to implement an unlawful agreement among companies to eliminate competition that would occur without the license, the license is an antitrust violation.

An "owner" and its "licensee" may have agreed to licenses to eliminate an important type of competition between them that each could undertake without regard to the patents of the other. They use the licenses to implement or assist in enforcement of that agreement. Licenses of that type are designed simply to eliminate competition among potential lawful competitors. Such licenses are unlawful if the underlying agreement is unlawful.

In order to determine if this is the purpose of the parties, the courts consider the circumstances surrounding the entry of the agreement, the nature of the agreement, and its operation in its market setting. The courts consider whether any limitations on competitive conduct by the parties operate independently of what the patents cover. They also consider whether any limitations on competitive conduct are unrelated to

---

[187] For an excellent collection of articles directed to antitrust and innovation, see Thomas M. Jorde and David J. Teece, eds., *Antitrust, Innovation and Competitiveness*, 1992 (Oxford University Press, New York).

[188] *Standard Sanitary v. United States,* 226 U.S. 20 (1912); *United States v. United States Gypsum Co.,* 333 U.S. 364, 399–341 (1948). For analysis of the potential for such agreements, see George L. Priest, "Cartels and Patent License Agreements," *Journal of Law and Economics* **20,** 309 (1977).

maximizing the patent owner's advantages arising by virtue of the patents. In this situation, the law may condemn an agreement even though the particular provisions of the agreement are not improper. A license agreement that appears proper may be unlawful if it was entered not for the purpose of exploiting the value of the patent rights, but to limit competition in the ways that the patent rights would not inherently prevent.

(b) Licenses that Primarily Limit Rivalry among Suppliers of Substitute Rights

Second, where the patent owners hold substitute or, perhaps, complementary patents, and a court finds that an agreement between them has the effect of limiting their competition with respect to individually exploiting or licensing those rights, the court may condemn the agreement for that reason.[189] Agreements may have anticompetitive effects if those patents are competing (that is, cover independently exploitable substitute products or processes). Agreements among owners of different patents are unlikely to have anticompetitive effects if those patents are purely complementary (that is, cover products or processes that may be used together). The courts have not always successfully recognized this distinction.

An agreement among owners of separate patents may eliminate (1) competition between them in licensing their separate patents or (2) competition between them in selling products using the rights. The legal analysis of this problem is not a matter of applying a rigorous formula to easily identified facts. The law assigns the courts broad discretion to consider a wide variety of facts and decide whether competition is unreasonably restricted. The reported decisions relating to cooperation among patent owners in licensing frequently do little more than list a number of facts and announce a decision. The basis for the decision is frequently obscure. The courts' analysis of particular cases reveals instances of economically incorrect analysis. Hence, when two patent owners agree to cooperate, rather than compete, in licensing their patents, they venture into an area of considerable legal uncertainty.

For example, assume Company A and Company B each own existing patents that cover potentially competing types of products. Assume

---

[189] *Standard Oil Co. v. United States,* 283 U.S. 163 (1931).

2.12 THE LAW AND THE BASIC OPTIONS

that products using A's patents could be made and sold without violating B's patents. Assume also that products using B's patents could be made and sold without violating A's patents. Assume they cross-license each other under their existing patents, and each agrees not to grant licenses to third parties under its patents without the consent of the other. That agreement not to grant additional licenses decreases competition in licensing the separate patents to others. Such limitations on competition in licensing may be illegal.

For example, owners of patents on competing processes of producing gasoline eliminated royalty rate competition by jointly setting royalties for licenses under the combined patents.[190] The Supreme Court found there was no violation because the patents did not dominate any gasoline market. The Court implied that, if all gasoline had been produced by those processes, the elimination of royalty-rate competition would have been unlawful. It is, of course, entirely lawful for a single patent owner to charge royalties.

In another situation, the owners of patents on television receivers eliminated competition to license the most efficient production by jointly setting the manufacturing location for licensees under the combined patents.[191] The patent owners give the pool administrator exclusive right to grant licenses and agreed that licenses would be granted only to sell products made in the country of the pooled patents. Foreign manufacturers could not obtain licenses to export into the pool country. The Court found a violation without detailed consideration of dominance.

Assume instead that products using B's patents could not be made and sold without violating A's patents. If one company owned a patent that would have blocked the other party or its licensees from selling products, the situation is different. If at least one patent was necessary for any competition by the other party or its licensees in selling any product, it is less likely that a violation exists. In that situation, the courts are more likely to say that cooperation in licensing was necessary to permit licensees to obtain all rights needed to make a product, and that if the restriction on licensing would have been lawful for the owner of the basic patents, they are lawful under the combined patents.

---

[190] *Standard Oil Co. v. United States,* 283 U.S. 163 (1931).
[191] *Zenith Radio Corp. v. Hazeltine Research, Inc.,* 395 U.S. 100, 123–124 (1969).

However, the law does not always treat the distinction between competing and blocking (or complementary) patents in that way. Hence, the existence of basic patents does not necessarily mean that the owners agree to license jointly. For example, owners of complementary electrical inventions licensed each other and agreed to license third parties to sell at prices fixed by one of them.[192] At the time, the law permitted a single patent owner to lawfully set the prices at which its licensees sold. However, the Court said that the owners of separate patents could not do so, even where one patent blocked any use of the other. If that is so, then even though patents are complementary, patent owners who combine them may not necessarily license them in the same manner as a single patent owner.

(c) Licenses that Limit Rivalry in Markets beyond the Scope of the Rights by "Foreclosing" Other Suppliers of "Unprotected" Products

Third, where the parties to the agreement are not lawful suppliers of substitutes (that is, not horizontal competitors) either in a product market or in a market for rights, a court may find an antitrust violation because the license has harmful effects beyond the scope of the patent.[193] As in the misuse cases, the scope of a patent plays a critical role in determining the legality of various restrictions under this third type of analysis. *Bona fide* agreements between the owner of a patent and licensees are likely to have anticompetitive effects only if there are likely harmful effects in markets for products not covered by the licensed patents.

Under an effects test, restrictions on the licensee that may affect competition in markets beyond the scope of the protection of the patent

---

[192] *United States v. Line Material Co.,* 333 U.S. 287, 308 (1948).

[193] *Ethyl Gasoline Corp, v. United States,* 209 U.S. 346, 456 (1939) ("The patent law confers on the patentee a limited monopoly, the right to exclude all others from manufacturing, using or selling the invention. . . . The extent of that right is limited by the definition of his invention, as its boundaries are marked by the specification and claims of the patent. . . . He may grant licenses to make, use or vend, restricted in point of space or time, or with any other restriction upon the exercise of the granted privilege, save only that by attaching a condition to his license he may not enlarge his monopoly and thus acquire something which the statute and the patent together did not give."); *United States v. Studiengesellschaft Kohle,* 670 F.2d 1122, 1128 (D.C. Cir. 1981); *cf., USM Corp. v. SPS Technologies, Inc.* 694 F.2d 505, 513 (7th Cir. 1982).

2.12 THE LAW AND THE BASIC OPTIONS

are evaluated and balanced against the benefit of increased competition in markets covered by the patent and the benefit of permitting the patent owner to earn revenue from licensing.[194] Any analysis under this test must identify and distinguish effects in markets that would arise simply by the existence or enforcement of the licensed patents from effects that would not necessarily arise in that way.

If the competition "limited" by a license involves products within the scope of the licensed patents, it is difficult to identify any anticompetitive effect from the "limitation." For purposes of determining the legality of the patent owner's exploitation of an invention, the apparent short-run loss resulting from limited use of the invention during its term necessarily arises from granting the patent and has no effect on the legality of the patent owner's mode of exploitation.

The most significant limits on licensing options were developed to identify and punish patent owners who were deemed to be pursuing this effect—"extending the scope" of the patent's effects. Beginning in the early part of this century, the Supreme Court created rules to prevent "extensions of the patent monopoly." Throughout this century, the courts have frequently concluded that licensors were licensing the rights, especially patents, to acquire market power which did not inherently exist by virtue of those rights.[195] The courts, particularly the Supreme Court, condemned various provisions that theoretically might be used to achieve this purpose.[196]

---

[194] The courts historically condemn licenses as patent misuse or as against public policy without balancing of procompetitive and anticompetitive effects. The courts simply asked whether the agreement constituted an attempt to limit competition beyond the scope of the patent. If it did, the patent had been misused and was unenforceable until the offending conduct had stopped and its effects fully dissipated. If it did, the offending provisions were contrary to public policy, and were declared unenforceable. Because the provisions were not enforced, the licensee was permitted to ignore them.

[195] For example, *Zenith Radio Corp. v. Hazeltine Research, Inc.*, 395 U.S. 100, 136 (1969); *Brulotte v. Thys Co.*, 379 U.S. 29, 32–33 (1964); *United States v. Line Material Co.*, 333 U.S. 287, 308 (1948); *Morton Salt Co. v. G.S. Suppiger Co.*, 314 U.S. 488 (1942); *B.B. Chem. Corp. v. Ellis*, 314 U.S. 495, 496–497 (1942); *Ethyl Gasoline Corp. v. United States*, 309 U.S. 436, 456 (1940); *cf., Jefferson Parish Hosp. Dist. No. 2 v. Hyde*, 466 U.S. 2, 16–17 (1984) *(dicta); Blonder-Tongue Laboratories, Inc. v. Univ. of Illinois Foundation*, 402 U.S. 313, 343 (1971) *(dicta)*.

[196] The Court first declared such provisions unenforceable. Licensees coerced into accepting undesired terms could simply capitulate, then ignore them. Even though

(d) Evaluating the Potential Effects of Licensing in Markets for Products beyond the Reach of the Rights

When is an "extension" strategy potentially profitable? To acquire market power the rights do not provide, an owner must forgo current revenue to induce a licensee to do something that the owner could not compel it to do by enforcing the patent, such as agreeing not to buy a noninfringing product from another company. If that company may sell that product without infringing the patent and the buyer may use it without infringing, the patent alone does not provide control over its sale. The buyer will not give up its ability to buy from the company without receiving something in return.

The licensee will not agree to avoid purchases from the other company without receiving something in return. Indeed, if the buyer recognizes that its agreement may lead to the elimination of that company and to the owner acquiring market power in a product that a licensee uses, the licensee realizes that its agreement will make it even worse off in the future. The only thing the owner has to offer is a lower price for the license than it could otherwise have charged.

This extension strategy makes sense only if the owner will earn a sufficient return on this "investment" in trying to acquire market power. The market power must not only be successfully acquired. The market power must also be successfully exploited to earn a profitable rate of return on the investment made to acquire it. If entry and exit from that market is relatively easy for existing companies or if that market is subject to potential entry by companies with new and better products, the market power may not be sufficiently profitable or may not last long enough to permit such returns to be captured.

While the extension strategy is not likely to be potentially profitable in many situations, the Supreme Court found that patent owners frequently employ this strategy.[197]

---

unenforceable terms cannot possibly hurt the economy, the Court later created a rule under which patent property rights are temporarily forfeited if a patent owner tries the impossible. The Court never has revealed the trick by which a patent owner coerces a licensee into complying with an unenforceable obligation.

[197] The Supreme Court was probably wrong about the owner's goals in many of those decisions. Ward S. Bowman, Jr., *Patent and Antitrust Law* (1973); Testimony of John W. Schlicher, *Hearings On S.1841 and S.1535*, pp. 177–198 (S. Hrg. 98–1008, 98th Cong., 2nd Sess. April 3, 1984); William F. Baxter, *Remarks to the National Association of Manufacturers on May 10, 1983*, CCH Trade Reg. Rep. § 50,447

2.12 THE LAW AND THE BASIC OPTIONS

(e) The Time Horizon for Judging Anticompetitive Effects

Where the law determines the legality of licenses by analyzing their actual or likely effects on competition, there are two time periods that the law sometimes considers. The decisions evaluating the legality of restrictions do not always rigorously analyze the effects of the agreement in each of those periods and balance the benefits and costs of effects in one period against the other.

The first time period is the effect of the license on competition in markets for products made and sold and for licenses under rights existing at the time of the agreement being considered. The law looks to effects in markets for existing products and rights. The second time period is the effect of the agreement on competition to produce future inventions that might lead to new products or modifications of existing products, or to supply future products that would embody or use the inventions made using the results of that further research and development. The law sometimes looks to the impact in markets for future products and future rights.

(1983); Abbott B. Lipsky, Jr., *Remarks to the ABA Antitrust Section,* November 5, 1981, CCH Trade Reg. Rep. § 50,434 (1981).

3

The Decision to License and Payments for Licenses

3.1	Acquiring Rights	177
3.2	Refusing to Use or License	178
3.3	The Amount of Royalty Payments	181
3.4	The Relation of Royalty Payments to the Scope of the Patent	185
3.5	The Relation of Royalty Payments to the Patent Term	192
3.6	The Relation of Royalty Payments to the Value of Rights in Different Uses or to Different Users—Discriminatory Royalties	200
3.7	The Relation of Royalty Payments to the Value of Rights to Different Users—Royalties Proportional to Use of a Patented Machine	211
3.8	The Relation of Royalty Payments to the Value of Rights to Different Users—Royalties Payable by Licensed Sellers and Licensed Buyers of a Single Product	213
3.9	Sharing Royalties with Licensees	215
3.10	Licensing in Exchange for Rights—Grantbacks	216

3.1 ACQUIRING RIGHTS

An intellectual property owner has an absolute right to acquire rights, refuse to use the rights, and refuse to license others. It is incredible that owners of intellectual rights often question their right to do research, acquire rights, and refuse to use or license the rights. Owners of all other types of property have this right. If the owner is under an obligation to use rights or permit others to use them, the "exclusive" rights granted by intellectual property law are illusory, the value of rights declines, and markets for rights cannot function.

The courts say the antitrust and patent misuse rules are not violated by a company inventing a new and superior product, obtaining a patent, becoming a sole supplier of the product in a market, and excluding all other potential suppliers by enforcement of the patent. This is true even where the effect of the patent is to give the company monopoly power in a market for a product and there is no fraud in obtaining the patent.[1] The same rule probably applies where the company contracts with outside researchers to make the inventions.[2]

---

[1] *United States v. E. I. du Pont de Nemours & Co.,* 118 F.Supp. 41, 212–214 (D. Del. 1953), *aff'd on other grounds,* 351 U.S. 377 (1956) ("Powers which are granted under a valid patent are not powers on which plaintiff may rely to establish monopolization. Mere possession of a validly issued patent cannot be made the basis for a prosecution under the monopoly provisions of the Sherman Act."); *Cole v. Hughes Tool Company,* 215 F.2d 924, 937 (10th Cir. 1954); *United States v. L. D. Caulk Co.,* 124 F.Supp. 693, 705 (D. Del. 1954); *but cf., S.C.M. Corp. v. Xerox Corp.,* 463 F.Supp. 983 (D. Conn. 1979) and 474 F.Supp. 589 (D. Conn. 1979), (where the court instructed the jury that monopoly power acquired or maintained by acquiring a patent was unlawful where the primary purpose of obtaining the patent was to block competition, rather than to protect the patent owners' own products), *aff'd* 645 F.2d 1195 (2d Cir. 1981).

[2] Compare, *United States v. R.C.A.,* 1958 C.C.H. Trade Cases ¶ 69,164 (S.D.N.Y.) (consent decree permits R.C.A. to acquire patents on inventions by R.C.A. em-

THE DECISION TO LICENSE AND PAYMENTS FOR LICENSES

The courts reach that result by saying that the purposes of antitrust and patent law are not in conflict. Hence, they have refused to use antitrust law to preclude any inventor from obtaining and enforcing rights, even when an economic monopoly in the supply of products is the result.

Similarly, a company does not violate the antitrust laws by obtaining or accumulating many patents based upon its own inventions. In 1950 in *Automatic Radio v. Hazeltine*,[3] a licensee raised the defense of patent misuse in an action to recover royalties. The basis for the defense was that the license agreement required the licensee to pay royalties based on sales, even though none of the patents were used. The Court stated, in that context, that "The mere accumulation of patents, no matter how many, is not in and of itself illegal." That statement has led the courts to reject antitrust claims alleging accumulation of patents but not alleging any anticompetitive use of those patents.[4] That statement has also been followed in infringement actions to reject the contention that mere accumulation of patents gives rise to a misuse defense.[5]

3.2 REFUSING TO USE OR LICENSE

Patent law and antitrust law also do not require that the patent owner use the patented invention or license others to do so.[6] A patent owner's uni-

---

ployees or contract consultants); *United States v. I.B.M.*, 1956 C.C.H. Trade Cases ¶ 68,245 (S.D.N.Y.). One court has found that the acquisition of patents based upon sponsored research may constitute misuse, when coupled with anticompetitive conduct, such as acquisition of other rights from others, monopolistic licensing practices, and improper use of litigation. *Xerox Corp. v. International Business Mach. Corp.*, 399 F.Supp. 451, 454–455 (S.D.N.Y. 1975).

[3] *Automatic Radio v. Hazeltine*, 339 U.S. 827, 834 (1950), *aff'ing* 176 F.2d 799 (1st Cir. 1949) and 77 F.Supp. 493 (D. Mass. 1948).

[4] *Cole v. Hughes Tool Company*, 215 F.2d 924, 934 (10th Ger. 1954); *Dollac Corporation v. Margon Corporation*, 164 F.Supp. 481, 62 (D. N.J. 1958), *aff'd on other grounds*, 275 F.2d 202 (3 R.D. Cer. 1960).

[5] For example, *Zenith Radio Corp. v. Radio Corp. of America*, 106 F.Supp. 561, 576 (D. Del. 1952) ("Ownership of patents—regardless of number—does not constitute misuse.").

[6] *Continental Paper Bag Co. v. Eastern Paper Bag Co.*, 210 U.S. 405, 426–430 (1908). *Accord., United States v. United Shoe Mach. Co.*, 247 U.S. 32, 57–58 (1 18) ("Indeed, we said in the *Paper Bag Patent Case* that he may keep his invention out of use."); *Hartford-Empire Co. v. United States*, 323 U.S. 386, 417–418, 431–433

3.2 REFUSING TO USE OR LICENSE

lateral refusal to license does not violate the antitrust laws.[7] Even where the patent owner has monopoly power, a unilateral refusal to license a patent to others cannot be the basis for an award of damages for violation of section 2 of the Sherman Act.[8] A patent owner may not, however, agree with others not to use or license the patent.[9]

In 1908 in *Continental Paper Bag*, a patent owner brought an action for infringement. The patent owner had never used the invention or licensed others to use it. The Court affirmed the grant of an injunction against infringement. The Court found that it was reasonable for the patent owner to use existing old machines rather than incurring the expense of building the new patented machines. As to not licensing others, the Court said:[10]

> As to the suggestion that competitors were excluded from the use of the new patent, we answer that such exclusion may be said to have been of the very essence of the right conferred by the patent, as it is the privilege of any owner of property to use or not use it, without question of motive.

The Court declined to decide whether a case might arise where, "regarding the situation of the parties in view of the public interest," a court might withhold relief.

In 1945, in *Special Equipment Co. v. Coe*,[11] the Supreme Court said that the Commissioner of Patents could not refuse to issue a patent on a

---

(1945), *modifying* 46 F.Supp. 541, 613 (N.D. Ohio 1942) ("There is no question but that, under the privilege conferred upon an inventor through the patent, a patentee alone has the right to make, use, or vend the patented article [citation omitted]. He may refuse to make, use or vend, and thus withhold the value of his invention from the public.").

[7] *United States v. United Shoe Machinery Co.*, 247 U.S. 32, 57–58 (1918) ("Therefore, he [the inventor] necessarily has the power of granting it to some and withholding it from others, a right of selection of persons and terms."); *Standard Oil v. United States*, 283 U.S. 163, 179 (1931); *Extractol Process v. Hiram Walker & Sons*, 153 F.2d 264, 268 (7th Cir. 1946).

[8] *SCM Corp. v. Xerox Corp.*, 645 F.2d 1195 (2d Cir. 1981). Cf., *Data General Corp. v. Grumman Systems Support Corp.*, 32 U.S.P.Q.2d 1385, 1414–1416 (1st Cir. 1994).

[9] *Blount Mfg. Co. v. Yale & Towne Mfg. Co.*, 166 F. 555, 560, 562 (D. Mass. 1909).

[10] *Continental Paper Bag Co. v. Eastern Paper Bag Co.*, 210 U.S. 405, 429 (1908).

[11] *Special Equipment Co. v. Coe*, 324 U.S. 370, 371–377 (1945).

product even though the owner of the patent said that it did not intend to sell that product. Special Equipment Company owned a patent on an apparatus for processing pears by cutting off the stems, splitting the pears, and coring them. The machine included, among other parts, a knife that cut the pear into half sections. That is the machine that the patent owner intended to sell. The patent owner conceded that it was seeking another patent on the same machine without the knife, because it might be possible for someone to make and sell such a machine, and the sales of that machine would reduce the sales of the patented machine.

The Commissioner of Patents refused to issue the patent. The Supreme Court said the Commissioner could not refuse to issue the patent. The Court said it was plainly "legitimate to use a patent on the subcombination as a means of preventing appropriation of others of petitioner's more important complete invention, which he is using, where there is absent, as there is here, any purpose to enlarge the monopoly of either invention." The Court said that if a petitioner makes two inventions and one of them includes the other in its entirety, it is "evident that the value of former [namely the entire machine] would be greatly impaired if the subcombination invention could be freely used by others."

In *Hartford-Empire,* the defendants had been found guilty of violating sections 1 and 2 of the Sherman Act and section 3 of the Clayton Act. In reviewing the terms of the lower court's order, the Court said that patent owners "have always enjoyed" the options to "set the price for its use by others, elect to use it himself and refuse to license it, or to retain it and neither use or license it."[12] The decree enjoined the defendants from applying for a patent with the intention of not making commercial use of the invention within four years.[13] The Court found that, "unless we are to overturn settled principles, the paragraph . . . must be eliminated."[14] It said:[15]

> A patent owner is not in the position of a quasi-trustee for the public or under any obligation to see that the public acquires the free right to use the invention. He has no obligation either to use it or

---
[12] *Hartford-Empire Co. v. United States,* 323 U.S. 386, 417 (1945).
[13] Id. at 432.
[14] Id. at 432–433.
[15] Id. at 432–433.

to grant its use to others. If he discloses the invention in his application so that it will come into the public domain at the end of the 17-year period of exclusive right he has fulfilled the only obligation imposed by the statute. This has been settled doctrine since at least 1896.

3.3 THE AMOUNT OF ROYALTY PAYMENTS

An intellectual property owner may charge any amount for granting permission to use the rights. The law relies on private decisions of owners and licensees to determine the value of the rights and the amount of payments. Licensees resist paying royalties on behalf of themselves (and therefore their customers). If licensees agree to the amount of the owner's demands, consumers are better off. Licensees will do so only if the information protected by the rights is more valuable than the payment. If the law requires that the amount not be excessive or unreasonable, the exclusive rights are exclusive in name only and the private value of the rights declines.

The courts have declined the few invitations to forbid "excessive" or "unreasonably high" royalties. The courts have said that a patent owner has the right to license in exchange for a price.[16] A patent owner may charge as high a royalty as it can obtain.[17] Ignoring one or two aberrational decisions, antitrust or misuse law does not concern itself with the amount licensees pay owners. Unlike some public utilities whose rates are regulated by an agency to permit only a reasonable rate of return, the patent laws provide no limits on the amount a patent owner may charge for a license.[18]

The business reasons for licensing and the effect of royalties on licensing profits, product output, and price were described in Chapters 1 and 2. The owner will attempt to charge royalties so that its licensees produce the quantity that would be produced by a monopolist of the product having the licensees' costs. This will generate maximum returns to

---

[16] *Standard Oil Co. v. United States,* 283 U.S. 163, 172, 179 (1931); *Hartford-Empire Co. v. United States,* 323 U.S. 386, 413–416 (1945).
[17] *Brulotte v. Thys Co.,* 379 U.S. 29, 33 (1964); *W.L. Gore & Associates v. Carlisle Co.,* 529 F.2d 614, 623 (3d Cir. 1976) F.2d 614, 623 (3d Cir. 1976).
[18] Section 2.3.(c).

the owner. In the patent context, the extent of use of the invention will be limited by the royalty, just as the extent of sales of the product are limited by the price. However, the goal of the patent system is achieved by permitting profit-maximizing licensing. The private value of an invention increases beyond that which would prevail if licensing were prohibited or royalties regulated to some lower level.

Sham licenses may be used to achieve anticompetitive output restrictions (section 1.10(m)). This possibility provides no basis for any general rule against "excessive" or "unreasonable" royalty provisions. Consider the example of Figure 2.1. For convenience, that figure is presented here as Figure 3.1.

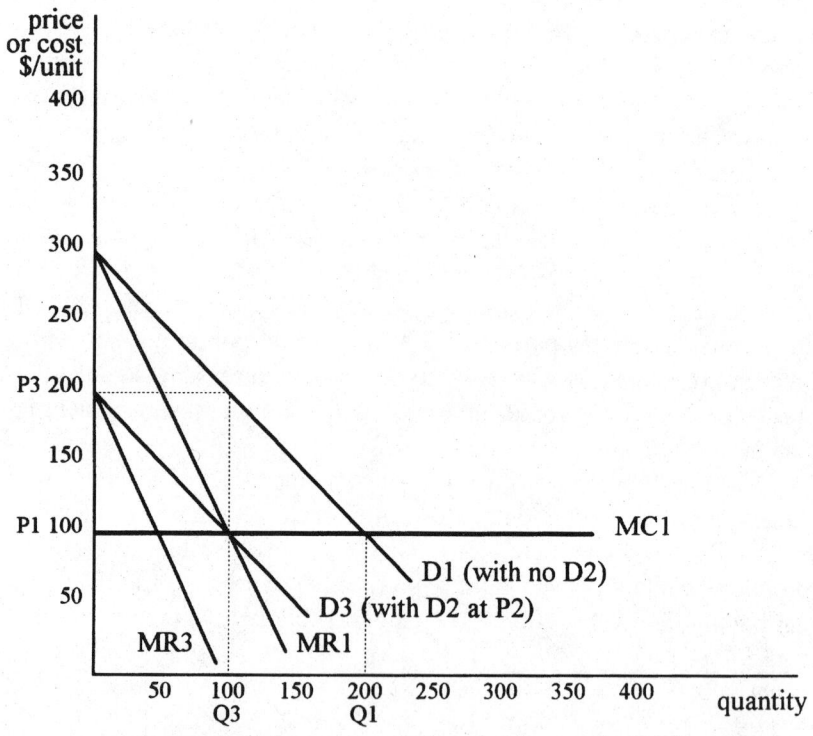

Figure 3.1(a). The Effects of Royalties on Old Product Profits and Sales

3.3 THE AMOUNT OF ROYALTY PAYMENTS

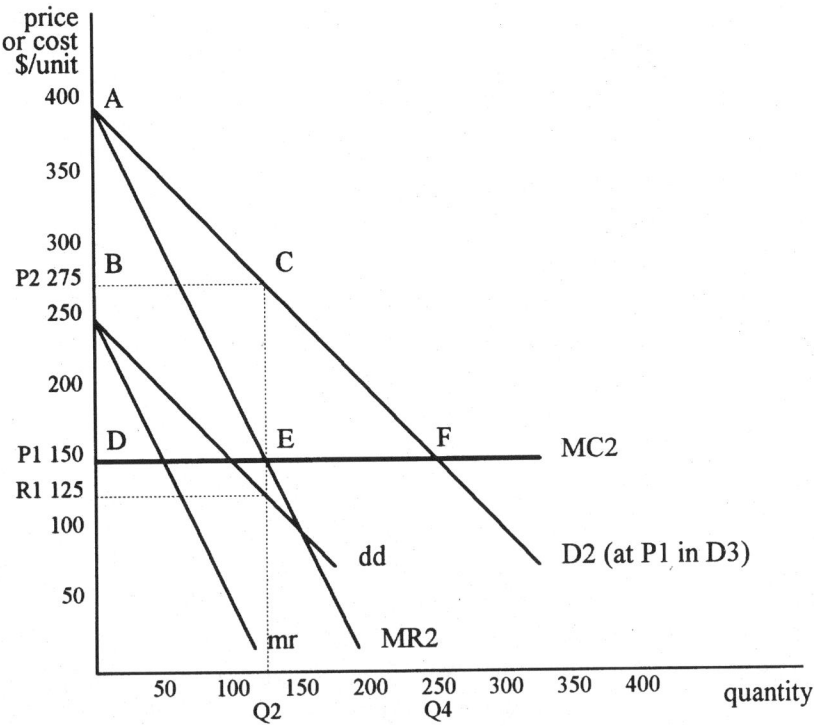

Figure 3.1(b). The Effect of Royalties on New Product Profits and Sales

Assume the invention of the new product. The patent owner is incapable of producing the product. If the patent owner were forced to produce the product, none would be made. Others are able to produce at cost, MC2. The patent owner may earn revenue and the invention used by licensing. The value of the invention is the difference between the cost of using it and the demand for product embodying it.

If licensees will produce the product, the demand for the invention is determined by subtracting production costs, MC2, from product demand, D2, to obtain derived demand, dd2, with its marginal revenue curve, mr2. Assume the costs of negotiating and enforcing the licenses are zero. The patent owner will license at a rate at which marginal licensing revenue is also zero. The royalty will be $R per unit. Licensees will treat that per-unit royalty as a cost and will produce Q2 units at price P2.

Assume that others are producing the old product, represented as D3 in Figure 3.1(a). For some users, that old product is a substitute for the new one. The owner of the new product patent may consider trying to eliminate competition between the old and new product suppliers. If those old product producers (and all other potential producers) would go away or limit production, this could shift upward the demand for the new product, D2, permit a higher royalty, and increase new product sales. To accomplish this, they must agree on and enforce reduced output levels for the old product. The old product suppliers may also want assurance that the owner will not reduce royalties to real licensees.

Should the law regulate royalty provisions to prevent such agreements? Suppose the patent owner and the old product producers (existing and potential) agree to attempt to limit output of the old product to 50 units and raise the price to P1 + $50 (a 50% increase). They try to figure out how to use a patent license to do that. The patent owner will grant them a sham license to produce the old product and they will pay a sham royalty of $50 per unit. This will raise their costs in just the right amount. However, no sane old product producer will agree to that license.

A one-way patent license with a one-way royalty payment does not provide a mechanism by which suppliers of substitutes can achieve anticompetitive restrictions under the guise of a license. Since the only restriction on the "licensee" is the royalty, the restriction on output applies only to the extent of the royalty. It is never in the interest of a "licensee" to limit its output simply to generate increased profits and turn all of those profits over to the patent owner. There must be a payback mechanism. To achieve output restrictions, the license must have some other "limitation" on output. In fact, the license imposes no real limitation because any "licensee" tempted to cheat may do so without fear of infringing the rights. Where a license scheme is devised for this purpose, royalties are more likely to be "low" than "high."

As discussed earlier, an agreement among owners of patents covering substitute products or methods fixing the royalty for licenses under those patents may violate section 1 of the Sherman Act.[19]

---

[19] Section 2.11(b) and 2.12(b).

3.4 THE RELATION OF ROYALTY PAYMENTS TO THE SCOPE OF THE PATENT

Antitrust and misuse law does limit the royalty base for patent licenses. A patent owner may base the formula for royalty payments on many different activities, including a licensee's sales measured in revenue or number of units. The licensee activities on which royalties are calculated is often called the *royalty base*. The nature of the royalty base does not raise antitrust or misuse issues, except in one circumstance. If royalties are based on products that could be made and sold without infringing the patent, and the patent owner conditioned the grant of the license on the payment of such royalties, the patent owner has misused the patent.[20]

In 1950, the Supreme Court said there was nothing wrong with a license agreement calling for royalty payments based upon a licensee's total sales, whether or not any of the patents were used.[21]

(a) The *Zenith* Rule on Royalty Payments

In 1969, the Supreme Court in *Zenith* v. *Hazeltine* said that a virtually identical agreement constituted patent misuse, where the patent owner was "conditioning the grant of a patent license upon payment of royalties on products which do not use the teaching of the patent. . . ."[22] Justice Harlan dissented. The Court said a patent owner "conditions" the license on such payments "where the patentee refuses to license on any other basis and leaves the licensee with the choice between a license so providing and no license at all."[23] The Court also said that, if there was misuse of this kind, it did not necessarily follow that there was a violation of the Sherman Act.

The Court said that "patent misuse inheres in a patentee's insistence upon a percentage-of-sales royalty, regardless of use, and his rejection of licensee proposals to pay only for actual use." The Court also said no

---

[20] *Zenith Radio CoLa. v. Hazeltine Research, Inc.*, 395 U.S. 100, 135–140 (1969).
[21] *Automatic Radio Mfg. v. Hazeltine Research, Inc.*, 339 U.S. 827, 830–833 (1950).
[22] *Zenith Radio Co. v. Hazeltine Research, Inc.*, 395 U.S. 100, 135–140 (1969). See United States v. Microsoft Corp., 1995-1 Trade Cas. (CCH) ¶ 71,027 (consent decree).
[23] Id. at 135.

inference of conditioning follows from a license provision measuring royalties by licensee's total sales.[24] Where the royalty base is agreed to for the mutual convenience and efficiency of the parties, there is no conditioning and no misuse. There is no misuse if the "licensee as well as the patentee would find it more convenient and efficient from several standpoints to base royalties on total sales than to face the burden of figuring royalties based on actual use."[25]

(b) The Competitive Effects

The Court declared such provisions harmful because they were, like tying arrangements, devices by which a patent owner could extend the "monopoly" of the patent to derive profits not arising from the patented invention:

> And just as the patent's leverage may not be used to extract from the licensee a commitment to purchase, use, or sell other products according to the desires of the patentee, neither can that leverage be used to garner as royalties a percentage share of the licensee's receipts from sales of other products; in either case, the patentee seeks to extend the monopoly of his patent to derive a benefit not attributable to use of the patent's teachings.

It is unlikely that a patent owner and the suppliers of unpatented products could use sham licenses and sham royalty payments to limit competition. The Court seems to be concerned that a patent owner may accomplish without the cooperation of competitors what he and they would be unable to accomplish working together. Suppose General Motors proposed to other automobile manufacturers that they each pay General Motors 10 percent of their sales to limit competition. They refuse. Would General Motors propose to pay each of them 11 percent of their sales to buy their cooperation with the plan? Subsidizing one's competitors seems a very poor device for limiting competition.

---

[24] Id. at 138.
[25] Id. at 138; *Automatic Radio Mfg. v. Hazeltine Research, Inc.,* 339 U.S. 827, 830–833 (1950).

3.4 THE RELATION OF ROYALTY PAYMENTS

Consider Figure 3.2(a) and (b). Figure 3.2(b) shows the demand, D2, and supply, MC2, curves for the patented product, assuming that competitive unpatented products were sold without a "royalty" charge. Figure 3.2(a) shows the demand, D3, and supply, MC1, curves for a competitively supplied unpatented substitute product, assuming that patent royalties are based only on the patented product.

Under those conditions, the profit-maximizing royalty for the patented product is R2, the quantity of the patented product is Q2, and the quantity of the unpatented product is Q1. The value of the patent licenses is the difference between the demand, D2, and supply, MC2,

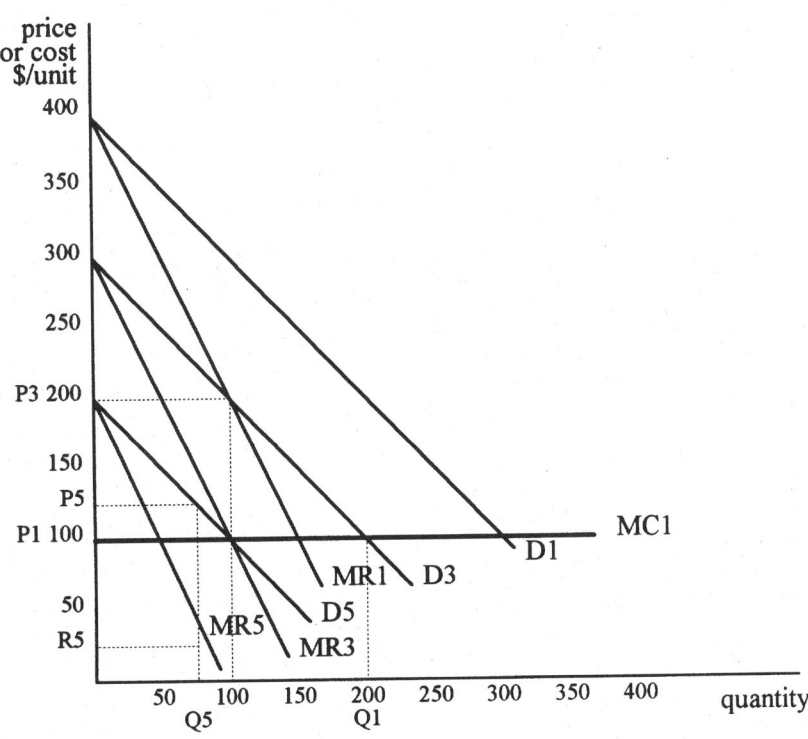

Figure 3.2(a). The Effects of the Royalty Base on Sales of Unpatented Substitutes

THE DECISION TO LICENSE AND PAYMENTS FOR LICENSES

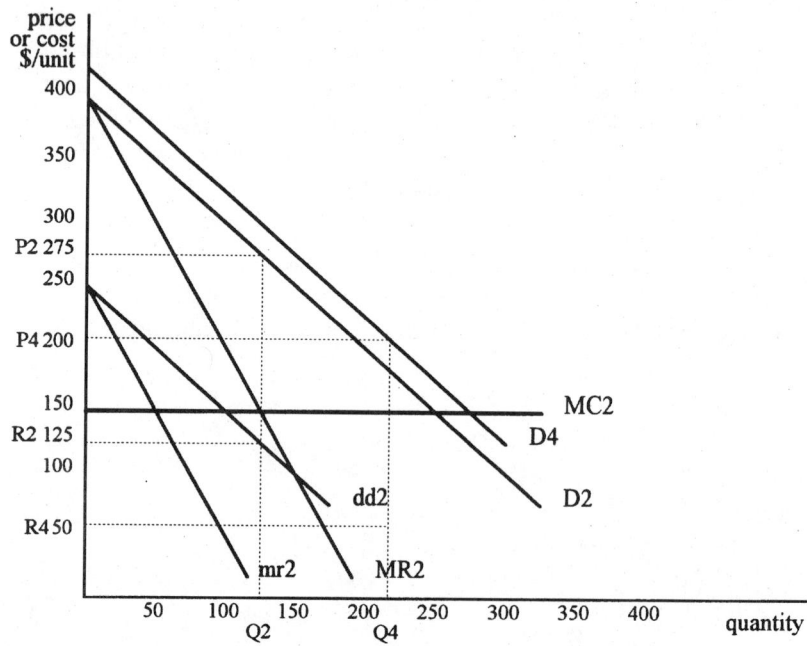

Figure 3.2(b). The Effects of the Royalty Base on Sales of a Patent Product

curves for the patented product. Assume that the companies that are the most efficient suppliers of the patented product also constitute all of the actual and potential suppliers of the old product.

If the potential suppliers of the patented product do not constitute most of the old product suppliers, the license is unlikely to reduce competition by limiting the supply of the old product. Unlicensed old product suppliers will preserve competition. Any one product producer will not go along unless all others are going along and cheaters can be detected and stopped. The actual and potential old product suppliers must also be the most efficient new product suppliers. Otherwise, a patent owner will decrease the value of the patent by raising the cost of producing the patented new product.

Assume that the patent owner offers to license all those companies and insists on a royalty base, including both patented and un-

3.4 THE RELATION OF ROYALTY PAYMENTS

patented products. The licensees will not agree to pay royalties on both patented and unpatented products at rate R2. That would require payments greater than what the patent is worth. Assuming that if royalty rate R4 is charged for the patented product and R5 for the unpatented products, it produces the same revenue as royalty rate R2 charged for only patented products. At royalty R5, the price for unpatented products will increase if all actual and potential producers agree to pay the royalty.

This will have the effect of shifting the demand for the unpatented products to the left, to D5, and shifting the demand for patented products to the right, to D4. The sum of the preroyalty shifting demand, D2 plus D3, must equal the sum of the postroyalty shifting demand. Given those new demand curves, the output of the patented product under this arrangement will increase from Q2 to Q4, and output of the unpatented product will decrease from Q1 to Q5.

However, it cannot be said that this effect is harmful. Any decrease in output of the unpatented product is offset by an increase in output of the patented product. The competitive process is not necessarily affected.

In the general situation, the likelihood of a patent owner significantly decreasing competition in the market including both patented and unpatented products depends on the market share of the licensees and the ease of entry into sales of the unpatented product. If there are many unlicensed suppliers of the unpatented product, output of the unpatented product will likely be unaffected because those other suppliers will continue to supply to Q1 and output of the patent product will increase to somewhere between Q2 and Q4. By this device, a patent owner does not necessarily affect competition in that general market.

If the effect of the license is to reduce competition in the market, and prices increase above P5 and P4, the patent owner loses and only his licensees seem to gain. The patent owner is stuck with earning royalties at R5 and R4. As output decreases due to lack of competition, the patent owner loses revenue.

For reasons that will be discussed later, there are situations in which patent owner revenue may increase by limiting competition among users of the invention, but this royalty provision is not a response to those situations. The only situation in which the patent owner comes out ahead is if the deal was a sham to start with, and even then, it will be ineffective for reasons discussed earlier. The Court's conditioning test seems to assure that the agreement is a harmless one.

(c) Procompetitive Reasons for Basing Royalties on Patented and Unpatented Products

The Court's explanation of this provision does not necessarily reveal any harm. However, the possibility of harm may be sufficient reason to condemn it, unless it provides a beneficial function. It does. This device may have the effect of reducing transaction costs and risk.

Significant administration costs for both patent owner and licensees may be involved in determining what transactions are within the scope of the patent. The licensees may not wish the patent owner to know sufficient technical details of their products to permit verification of compliance with the agreement. The scope of a patent is always somewhat unclear. The value of a patent is also incapable of exact determination. No one knows with any certainty the shapes of demand and cost curves over the life of a patent. However, the total market demand and supply conditions may be more readily predictable.

These factors increase the cost and risk to the parties of making agreements calling for royalties on only patented products. One method of reducing those costs and risks is to make the royalty base independent of the scope of the patent. In that way, the parties may predict with greater certainty the extent of the royalty obligations and reduce the costs of complying and enforcing the agreement. It is in the patent owner's and the licensees' interest to reduce those costs and risks.

The Court recognizes that this royalty base may serve that legitimate function. However, under the *conditioning* rule, this justification is only operative where the negotiation history shows that the licensee recognizes those benefits. By turning legality on negotiation history, the law fails to identify agreements based on their actual likely effects. Justice Harlan recognized that in his dissenting opinion.

A licensee may initially object to the broader rate base for a variety of reasons having nothing to do with the effect on competition between patented and unpatented products. It may not want enforcement costs reduced. It may prefer risk more than the patent owner. The li-

3.4 THE RELATION OF ROYALTY PAYMENTS

censee's objection and subsequent agreement says nothing about whether the agreement is more likely to reduce competition or reduce transaction costs. Indeed, in all cases, if the licensee objects, that is persuasive evidence that licensor transaction cost reduction or risk avoidance is at work. The law has it backward. In short, the effects of an agreement are not accurately identified by looking to whether a prospective licensee objected, then agreed.

(d)   An Alternative Interpretation of the *Zenith* Rule

There is a narrower reading of *Zenith*. *Zenith* is commonly understood to say that a patent is unenforceable if its owner grants a license only on condition that the licensee pay royalties on products that were made and sold without any use of the invention. The Court seemed to insist that the amount of those payments may not be based on activities that do not use the teachings of the patent.

However, the Court also said that a patent owner is entitled to insist on some payment whether or not the licensee uses the invention. It said the patent owner must be entitled to charge some fee representing the cost of dealing with the licensee. It also said the owner should be able to insist on money for simply granting the permission to use the patent. The Court said that if the royalty base was agreed to for the convenience and efficiency of the parties, then there was no reason to criticize the agreement.

None of these qualifications are permitted by the conditioning test. In other words, if the patent owner insisted on a payment based on activities that do not involve use of the patent and the licensee protested, the patents become unenforceable even though the patent owner's insistence may have been based upon an effort

> To recover the costs of granting a license,
>
> To capture the value of providing the licensee with an opportunity to use the inventions, or
>
> To reduce the transaction costs of calculating, collecting, and enforcing payment of royalties,

all of which the Supreme Court seemed to say were perfectly proper reasons for the patent owner to insist on payments.

This leads to a much different reading of *Zenith*. It is that the patent owner may condition the grant of a license on the payment of royalties on activities that do not use the invention, if based upon an effort to measure the value to the licensee of the opportunity to use the invention, to recapture the costs of granting the license, or to reduce the cost of negotiating, policing, and collecting royalties. The only prohibited ground under that test would be that royalties may not be based upon activities that do not use the invention in order to reduce competition between those products and the patented product.

That reading of *Zenith* seems a radical one. However, the actual holding in the *Zenith* case is simply that the lower Court's injunction was proper when it forbade conditioning the payment of royalties on products that do not use the teaching of the patent. The courts may always grant an injunction that would prohibit conduct that might be lawful in order to eliminate the effects of past violations or to provide effective, though overbroad, deterrence of them in the future. Therefore, a ruling on the scope of an injunction does not necessarily distinguish legal from illegal activities.

3.5 THE RELATION OF ROYALTY PAYMENTS TO THE PATENT TERM

(a) The *Brulotte* Rule on Royalty Payments

Prior to 1964, there was no limit on the term for royalty payments under a patent license. In *Brulotte v. Thys,* the Supreme Court, again with Justice Harlan dissenting, reviewed an agreement by which a patentee sold a patented hop-picking machine and granted a license to use the machine.[26] Hops are an agricultural product important to the brewing industry and its customers. Under the agreement, farmers in Washington received patented hop-picking machines. They also received a patent license. The license part of the transaction called for royalties based on

---

[26] *Brulotte v. Thys Co.,* 379 U.S. 29, 30, 33 (1964).

3.5 THE RELATION OF ROYALTY PAYMENTS

use by the farmer before and after expiration of the last patent "incorporated into the machine."

The Court declared that the patentee could not enforce the license to the extent that it called for royalties due after all the patents expired. The lower courts have followed this interpretation of *Brulotte*.[27] (See also sections 7.5 and 7.6) The Court said its decision did not preclude installment payments for machines leased or sold by the patent owner that continued beyond patent term.[28] *Brulotte* implied that a royalty obligation was unenforceable to the extent payments were based upon operations prior to the issuance of a patent. The Court in 1979 declared that *Brulotte* did not render all preissue payments unenforceable (see Chapter 7).[29]

(b) The Competitive Effects

The Court in *Brulotte* refused to enforce that part of the agreement by asserting that it had the same harmful effects as a tying arrangement. It was a device by which the patent owner could extend his patent "monopoly" to the period after it expired.

> A patent empowers the owner to exact royalties as high as he can negotiate with the leverage of that monopoly. But to use that leverage to project those royalty payments beyond the life of the patent is analogous to an effort to enlarge the monopoly of the patent by tying the sale or use of the patented article to the purchase or use of unpatented ones. See Ethyl Gasoline Corp. v United States, 309 US 436, 84 L ed 852, 60 S Ct 618; Mercoid Corp. v Mid-Continent Inv. Co. 320 US 661, 664–665, 88 L ed 376, 380, 381, 64 S Ct 268, and cases cited. The exaction of royalties for use of a machine after the patent has expired is an assertion of monopoly power in the

---

[27] *Modrey v. American Gauge & Machine Co.,* 478 F.2d 470, 474–475 (2d Cir. 1973); *Ar-Tik Systems, Inc. v. Dairy Queen, Inc.,* 302 F.2d 496, 510 (3d Cir. 1962).
[28] 379 U.S. at 31–32.
[29] *Aronson v. Quick Point Pencil Co.,* 440 U.S. 257, 261–264 (1979); *San Marino Electronic Corp. v. George J. Mayer Co.,* 155 U.S.P.Q. 617 (C.D. Cal. 1967) (no misuse where royalties paid during pendency of patent application and the term of the patent), *aff'd,* 422 F.2d 1285 (9th Cir. 1970).

THE DECISION TO LICENSE AND PAYMENTS FOR LICENSES

post-expiration period when, as we have seen, the patent has entered the public domain. We share the views of the Court of Appeals in Ar-Tik Systems, Inc. v Dairy Queen, Inc. 302 F2d 496, 510, that after expiration of the last of the patents incorporated in the machines, "the grant of a patent monopoly was spent" and that an attempt to project it into another term by continuation of the licensing agreement is unenforceable.

The effects of the *Brulotte* agreement are illustrated in Figure 3.3. Assume there is a patent on a product. The demand for the product over the first seventeen years is indicated by D1-17. Demand from years eighteen through twenty-five is D17-25. Assume that the patent owner licenses the patent nonexclusively to a number of licensees, with royal-

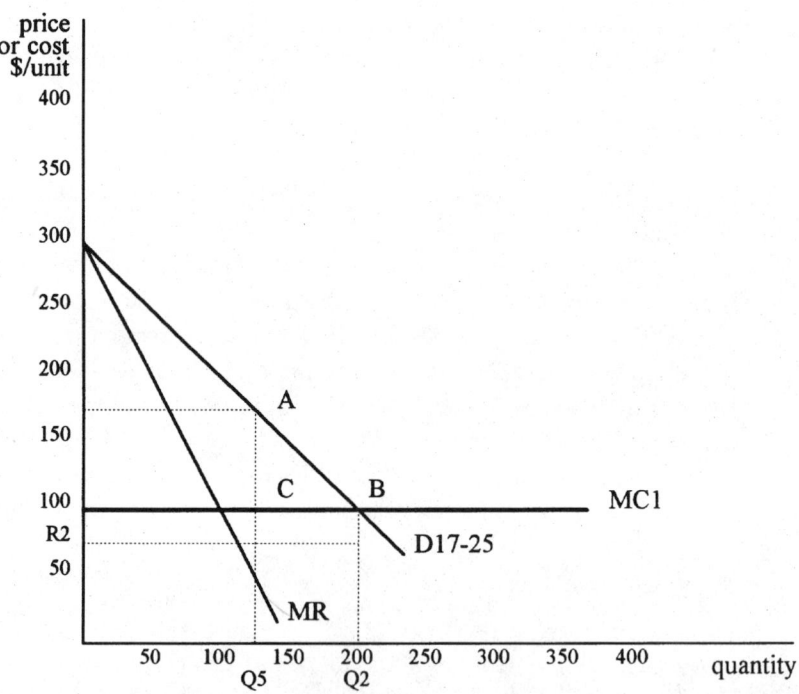

Figure 3.3(a). The Effect of Royalties on Sales After the Term

3.5 THE RELATION OF ROYALTY PAYMENTS

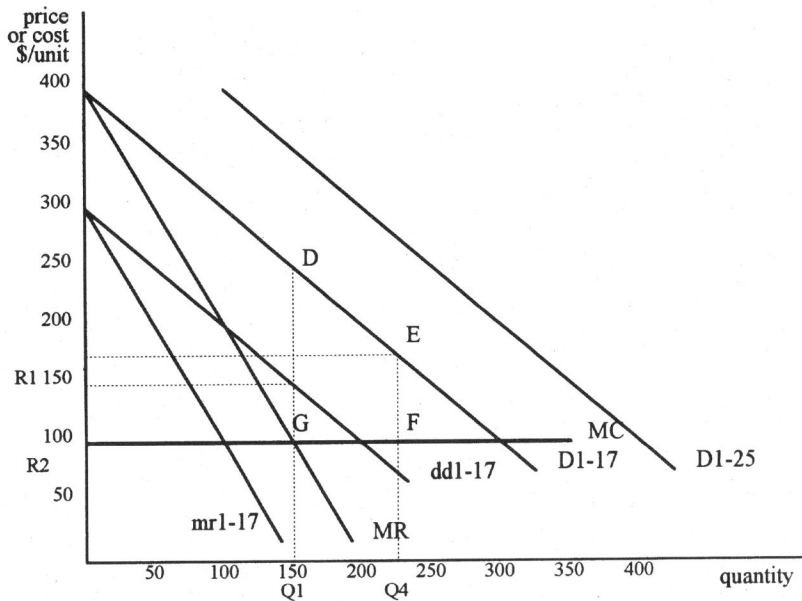

Figure 3.3(b)   The Effect of Royalties on Sales During the Term

ties at the rate R1 limited to the term of the patent. Under that license, Q1 units will be produced over the seventeen years at price P1. Q2 units will be produced over the next eight years.

If the patent owner asks that royalties be paid over the twenty-five year period, the royalty rate during the term must be lower. This is so because the value of the patent to the licensee is limited by the difference between the cost and demand during the term. After the term, all others will be able to use the invention freely in competition with those licensees. Unless that license provides them some additional benefit, the rate must be lowered to induce the licensees to agree to pay over the longer period.

Assume that royalty rate R2 paid over twenty-five years would yield the same revenue as rate R1 over seventeen years. Assume that the royalty shifting does not affect demand before or after the term. D1-17 and D17-25 do not change. Assume also that the royalty will have no ef-

THE DECISION TO LICENSE AND PAYMENTS FOR LICENSES

fect on competition in the period after expiration. Under that royalty rate R2, output over the first seventeen years will expand from Q1 to Q4 and output over the next eight years may decrease from Q2 to Q5.

If the royalty in the postexpiration period decreases production, the resource allocation loss from this agreement is the shaded area, ABC. The resource allocation gain from the agreement is the shaded area DEFG, the value minus the cost of increased production during the term. The net effect is indeterminate, assuming that the agreement provides no cost savings to the parties.

As in the case of royalties on unpatented competing products, the royalty provision is highly unlikely to limit competition in years 17 to 25. The agreement does not prevent unlicensed companies from entering in the postexpiration period. Companies may enter after expiration and supply the quantity between Q2 and Q5. If such entry occurs, there will be no loss in postexpiration resource allocation. This device does not provide a profitable mechanism to limit competition in the postexpiration period and separately exploit that limitation.

The use of the longer royalty term does not permit the patent owner to collect royalties based on the difference between the twenty-five-year demand curve, D1-25, and cost. The patent owner gains the potential to restrict quantity during the postexpiration period only to the extent it permits quantity to expand in the earlier period. The market power existing during the patent term can be exploited only once. Even if output is restricted in the postexpiration period, there is an offsetting benefit in that output has been greater during the patent term.

(c) Procompetitive Reasons for Basing Royalties on a Term Extending Beyond the Rights

If the extension of the payment period reduces the cost of producing or using the patent or operating under the license, the provision increases the value of the patent and increases innovation. The lengthened royalty term has certain benefits.

First, spreading royalties over a longer period helps the licensee defer costs. It is a device by which the patent owner assists in financing the cost of producing or using the new device. If the patent owner borrows at lower rates than its licensees, it may effectively reduce their bor-

3.5 THE RELATION OF ROYALTY PAYMENTS

rowing costs by permitting them to spread royalty payment over a longer period. It is highly likely that the seller of the agricultural machines in *Brulotte* had lower borrowing costs than its customers. The effect of that capital cost reduction is to permit greater use in the combined pre- and postperiod and increase the value of the patent to the extent of the cost reduction during the term.

Second, where a license includes several patents that expire at different times, such as a U.S. patent and all its foreign counterparts, providing for royalties at a constant rate until the last patent expires also reduces compliance and enforcement costs.

Finally, a patent may effectively "expire" by being held invalid in a judgment that would preclude all future enforcement against persons not subject to a contrary judgment. The probability and time of such a judgment is highly unpredictable. That uncertainty creates risk that the parties may wish to reduce or allocate to the best risk bearer. Reducing or properly allocating that risk effectively reduces the cost of bearing it. Spreading royalties over a period defined independently of that event may be a device to reduce risk costs. Those benefits of royalty spreading should not be ignored, as they are under current law.

(d) Other Implications of *Brulotte*

The *Brulotte* decision has four other interesting and largely ignored respects.

First, unlike the *Zenith* rule on payment of royalties on unpatented products and the tying rule, the limitation on collection of royalties after the patent expires is not limited to situations in which the patent owner conditioned the licensee on acceptance of that longer payment term. The Court in *Brulotte* did not inquire into the negotiating history of the term. There are many possible explanations. However, the most likely reason is the Court's remedy. While the Court said the provision was "illegal," it ruled only that the postexpiration royalties could not be collected. The bad provision was not enforceable to the extent it was bad.

The parties apparently did not argue in the Supreme Court about the obligation to pay royalties during the term of the patents. We do not know what the Court would have said about the enforceability of that obligation, or the enforceability of the patents. Most lower Courts have recognized that this decision did not declare that the patents were unenforceable.

This aspect of *Brulotte* raises an important distinction. It is whether the patent law provides any authority for a Court to declare unenforceable an economically "harmful" provision in a license, or provides any authority to declare the patent unenforceable.

Second, the patent owner was making and supplying hop-picking machines and licensing their use based upon the amount of hops picked. That royalty base had the effect of requiring farmers who used the machine more efficiently or more extensively to pay higher royalties on a per-machine basis than those who used it less efficiently or less extensively. By this agreement, the patent owner charged each customer-licensee what the market would bear on a licensee-by-licensee basis. The Court implied that this was entirely appropriate.[30] The Court in *Brulotte* gave tacit approval to economic discrimination, a strategy for exploiting a patent the Court criticized when accomplished by tying arrangements.

The effects of economic discrimination were illustrated in Chapter 1 (section 1.10(b)). The effect of the license is to charge each customer at a rate somewhat proportional to the value of the machine (and the patent) to it. The result of such royalties is highly likely to expand use of the invention during the patent term. The patent owner in *Brulotte* need not exclude the farmer whose value for the new machine is greater than its production cost but less than a single market clearing price. It is also more profitable, permitting patents to more effectively serve their purpose.

Third, the patent owner supplied both the patented machine and the license. The Court said that, if the payments after the patents expired were merely installment payments for the purchase of a machine, there would be no limit on the term over which they could be paid. However, the Court said that, because the payments seemed to be royalty payments for a license, those payments must cease when patents expire, even though the machine continued to be useful.

Hence, as Justice Harlan pointed out, the patent owner's only mistake was writing the agreement in a manner which permitted Justice Dou-

---

[30] *See, Extractol Process v. Hiram Walker & Sons,* 153 F.2d 204, 265, 267–268 (7th Cir. 1946); *Cold Metal Process Co. v. McLouth Steel Corporation,* 141 F.Supp. 487, 490 (E.D. Mich. 1941), *aff'd,* 170 F.2d 396, 370 (6th Cir. 1948).

3.5 THE RELATION OF ROYALTY PAYMENTS

glas to find that the payments were for the patent license rather than payments for an installment sale or lease of a machine. The division of payments between the license and the machine is entirely arbitrary. Any lease or sale of a machine, without a license under the patent, does not give the owner the right to use it. The value of such a machine is zero. Likewise, a license without a machine is useless. Together they have value. The user cares only about the total value and total price.

The assignment of separate prices to the two is without economic significance. After *Brulotte,* the assignment has considerable legal significance. The result of *Brulotte* is to treat manufacturing patent owners more favorably than nonmanufacturing patent owners. Only patent owners supplying products can lawfully assign long-term payments to the product. A patent owner without a product may not. *Brulotte* creates undesirable incentives for patent owners to integrate into product selling. This unnecessarily limits the value of many inventions.

Fourth, the *Brulotte* decision implicitly found that it was entirely lawful for a patent owner to sell the patented machine, separately license the right to use the machine and collect royalties based on its use. The lower courts found this arrangement proper prior to and after *Brulotte*.[31] This result seems to violate the Court's pronouncement that the sale of a patented machine "exhausts the patent monopoly." If the "patent monopoly" is "exhausted" as to the machine sold, is not the patent owner collecting royalties on "unpatented products" and seeking to "extend the monopoly?"

Why did the Court in *Brulotte* not ask whether the patent owner had insisted that purchasers of machines no longer subject to patent rights pay royalties for a license they do not need? The answer must be that the patent rights are not always "exhausted" by the sale. *Brulotte* recognizes that "exhaustion" occurs only when the parties agree, expressly or implicitly, that it does. That recognition in *Brulotte* as applied to postsale royalty payments should also apply to all other postsale restrictions. Unfortunately, it has not always been applied. For example, some lower

---

[31] *In Re Yarn Processing Patent Validity Litigation,* 541 F.2d 1127 (5th Cir. 1976); *Extractol Process v. Hiram Walker & Sons,* 153 F.2d 204, 265, 267–268 (7th Cir. 1946); *Cold Metal Process Co. v. McLouth Steel Corporation,* 141 F.Supp. 487, 490 (E.D. Mich. 1941), *aff'd,* 170 F.2d 396, 370 (6th Cir. 1948).

courts ignored this feature of *Brulotte* in finding that postsale license restrictions violate the antitrust laws based on the "exhaustion of the patent monopoly."[32]

3.6 THE RELATION OF ROYALTY PAYMENTS TO THE VALUE OF RIGHTS IN DIFFERENT USES OR TO DIFFERENT USERS—DISCRIMINATORY ROYALTIES

The Supreme Court has said a patent owner has the right to select its licensees and treat different licensees differently.[33] In the 1960s, the lower courts created limits to that right.

(a) The Shrimp Peeler Rule on Royalty Payments

A Gulf Coast shrimp canning company owned shrimp-peeling patents. The lower courts said the company violated the antitrust laws and misused the patents by licensing West Coast shrimp canners at a higher per-pound royalty rate than it charged Gulf Coast canners, with the effect of preventing competition between West Coast licensees and Gulf Coast licensees and the patentee, a Gulf Coast canner.[34] One district court

---

[32] *United States v. Galaxo Group Limited,* 302 F.Supp. 1, 4-11 (D.D.C. 1969) (agreement to supply patented bulk-form drugs to a licensee-purchaser who agreed that it "will not, without first obtaining [the sellers] consent, resell or re-deliver in bulk form" violated the Sherman Act), *final judgment,* 328 F.Supp. 709 (1971), *rev'd on other grounds,* 410 U.S. 52 (1973); *United States v. Ciba Geigy Co.,* F.Supp. (D. N.J. 1976) (supply agreement restricting purchasers of bulk-form drug from (a) reselling in finish dosage form not in combination with other drugs, and (b) reselling in other than combination form approved by the seller violated the Sherman Act). At least one court has declined to find misuse in these circumstances. *Chemagro Corporation v. Universal Chemical Co.,* 244 F.Supp. 486, 489 (E.D. Tex. 1965).
[33] *United States v. United Shoe Machinery Co.,* 247 U.S. 32, 58 (1918); *Standard Oil Co. v. United States,* 283 U.S. 163, 179 (1931); *United States v. E.I. du Pont de Nemours & Co.,* 113 F.Supp. 41, 224 (D. Del. 1953).
[34] *LaPeyre v. F.T.C.,* 366 F.2d 117 (5th Cir. 1966), *aff'ing sub nom Grand Caillou Packing Co. Inc.,* CCH Trade Reg. Rep., FTC Complaints, Orders, Stipulations; 16, 927 (F.T.C. 1964); *Peelers Co. v. Wendt,* 260 F.Supp. 193 (W.D. Wash. 1966); *Laitram Corp. v. King Crab,* 244 F.Supp. 193 (W.D. Wash. 1966); *Laitram Corp. v. King Crab,* 244 F.Supp. 9, *mod.,* 245 F.Supp. 1019 (D. Alaska 1965).

3.6 THE RELATION OF ROYALTY PAYMENTS

pushed the discrimination idea to its limits and found that the refusal to license is the ultimate discrimination. That court found that a refusal to license for personal rather than business reasons constituted discrimination and justified withholding an injunction against infringement.[35] A later amendment to the Patent Act affirmed the right to refuse to license.[36]

Since the Shrimp Peeler cases, infringers have frequently alleged that charging different royalty rates to different licensees constitutes misuse or violation of the antitrust laws or both. With the exception of the Shrimp Peeler cases, the courts have found no misuse or antitrust violation in particular cases.[37] They sometimes try to articulate a standard. In one case, the court said that to sustain a claim of royalty discrimination a licensee must show at least that (1) it took a license, (2) it was charged a royalty rate higher than that charged to its competitors, (3) in all "relevant" particulars it and the competitors were similarly situated, (4) the royalty rate was an important part of its production cost, and (5) the royalty thereby caused substantial impairment of competition.[38]

The wildcard is what factors are "relevant." The courts should not be involved in asking this question. The different rate proves that there was something different about the situations. Whatever the nature of that difference, there is no reason why a patent owner should not be able to take it into account. The standard stifles a licensing mechanism exceedingly valuable both for patent owners and for the country. If the stan-

---

[35] *Allied Research Products, Inc. v. Heatbath Corp.*, 300 F.Supp. 656, 657 (N.D. Ill. 1969) (The court found that a patent owner's refusal to grant a license solely for personal rather than business reasons constituted "discrimination," justifying the court's withholding injunctive relief. That decision is unique.).
[36] 35 U.S.C. § 271(d).
[37] *La Salle Street Press v. McCormick & Henderson, Inc.*, 445 F.2d 84, 95 (7th Cir. 1971); *Carter-Wallace, Inc. v. United States*, 449 F.2d 1374, 1381–1382 (Ct. Cl. 1971); *Bela Seating Co., Inc. v. Polaron Products, Inc.*, 297 F.Supp. 489 (N.D. Ill. 1960), *aff'd*, 438 F.2d 733 1738 (7th Cir. 1971); *Honeywell, Inc. v. Sperry Rand Corp.*, 180 F.Supp. 673 (D. Minn. 1973); *Pemco Products v. General Mills*, 155 F.Supp. 433, 437 (N.D. Ohio 1957), *aff'd*, 261 F.2d 302 (6th Cir. 1958); *Congoleum Industries, Inc. v. Armstrong Cork Company*, 366 F.Supp. 220, 232 (E.D. Pa. 1973), *aff'd*, 510 F.2d 334 (3d Cir. 1975); *Mobil Oil Corporation v. W.R. Grace & Company*, 367 F.Supp. 207, 251 (D. Conn. 1973); *Hanks v. Ross*, 200 F.Supp. 605, 623 (D. Md. 1961).
[38] *Honeywell, Inc. v. Sperry Rand Corp.*, 180 F.Supp. 673, 763 (D. Minn. 1973).

dard were applied to all other respects in which licensees are treated differently, the result would be full public utility regulation of patents. The courts, not patent owners, would decide the rights, the products, the territory, the term, the termination rights and all other provisions of economic significance.

(b) The *USM* Rule on Royalty Payments

In 1982, Judge Richard Posner in *USM v. SPS* made clear that there is no sensible basis for a general rule against economic discrimination by patent owners[39] (section 2.7(b)). However, Judge Posner did not refuse to apply the current rule. Rather, he found that the charge of misuse by royalty discrimination was not established because competition among licensees was unlikely to be limited.

(c) The Competitive Effects

The royalty base and royalty term rules seek to preclude restrictions on competition between unpatented and patented products or between unpatented products and products unpatented due to the term expiring. Royalty discrimination rules strike at "restrictions" on competition between suppliers of a patented product. The reason owners employ economic dicrimination is described in section 1.10(b).

What will be the impact of royalty differences for shrimp-peeler inventions? There is some demand for peeled shrimp in the United States prior to the invention. Assume the processing costs of both West Coast and Gulf Coast canners prior to the invention are equal. Assume that there is perfect competition among shrimp sellers. The industry will supply some quantity of peeled shrimp. The patent owner has some share of that market.

Assume the improved shrimp-peeling machine inventions would reduce the costs by 50 percent for the patent owner and for the West Coast and Gulf Coast canners. The demand for that invention is obtained by subtracting the postinvention cost from preinvention cost to obtain derived demand.

---

[39] *USM Corporation v. SPS Technologies,* 694 F.2d 505 (7th Cir. 1982).

3.6 THE RELATION OF ROYALTY PAYMENTS

It would seem to be in the patent owner's interest to license all canners at the same royalty rate or simply confine the use of the machine to itself, "monopolize" the shrimp canning business, and produce at some quantity and price. The availability of the preinvention canning technology limits the ability of the patent owner to limit output and price. Unless there is some other problem, both of those options would lead to the same output and price.

If the costs of different licensees are the same, the patent owner seems to have nothing to gain by charging the West Coast canners a higher royalty per unit of product sold than the Gulf Coast canners. How does one explain why a patent owner might charge competing licensees selling an identical product different royalties? Suppose that the costs of the West Coast and Gulf Coast canners prior to the invention were not the same. Suppose the West Coast canners' per-unit cost was higher than the Gulf Coast canners' cost. If Gulf Coast canners have capacity to supply the whole market, the West Coast canners would be out of business. Therefore, there must be some consumers the Gulf Coast canners cannot supply at a cost below the West Coast canners.

Prior to the invention, there are prevailing prices to the Gulf Coast canners' customers and to the West Coast canner's customers. Assume that the invention saves all canners 25 percent of their cost per unit. Hence, the per-unit cost savings to high-cost West Coast canners is greater than per-unit savings to low-cost Gulf Coast canners. Assume, the savings per unit from the machine to the West Coast canner is twice that for a Gulf Coast canner.

The patent owner takes this into account and charges the West Coast canners a per-unit lease or royalty rate that is twice the per-unit rate to the Gulf Coast canners. The patent owner charges each what the machine (and the invention) is worth to it. The West Coast canners remain at a significant, though smaller, cost disadvantage. The patent owner increases the revenue over what would be earned from a single rate. This will encourage innovation. It is not possible to predict whether output of shrimp under single or multiple royalties would be greater.

If it is illegal to charge different rates, the patent owner might license only the Gulf Coast canners, since they are significantly more efficient. This would leave the West Canners *worse off* than they would be if they were charged the "discriminatory" rate.

It is difficult to imagine a situation in which different royalty rates for different licensees would be anticompetitive. Different royalty rates for use or sale of a patented product only "restricts" use of the invention. That is not a "harm" which should lead to illegality. Restrictions on use of the invention are a necessary part of granting patents. Discriminatory royalties provide no opportunity for a invention producer to acquire some market power that the patent does not give it. Discriminatory royalties provide no obvious mechanism to aid a "cartel" (that is, horizontal) agreement to limit competition.

(d) Procompetitive Reasons for Discriminatory Royalties

By separately charging what each licensee is willing to pay, a patent owner increases revenue from use of the invention. This effect is procompetitive. Even if the law (wrongly) considered restrictions on use of the invention as an anticompetitive harm, charging different royalties to different licensees is likely in most cases to increase use of the invention, not decrease it. If the patent owner may discriminate costlessly and perfectly, the underuse "loss" vanishes. Each user having some utility for the invention will be permitted to use it. Each use that is valuable will be satisfied. To the extent that the patent owner is deterred by present law from doing so, due to the risk that a court will some day disagree with the owner's assessment of the differences between licensees, the country forgoes this important benefit.

(e) Baxter's Parable Illustrating the Market Effects of Discriminatory Royalties

In 1971, William F. Baxter explained the effects of the Shrimp Peeler rule (and other laws against economic discrimination) in the following article titled simply "A Parable."[40]

---

[40] William F. Baxter, "A Parable," *Stanford Law Review* **23,** 973. Copyright © (1971) by the Board of Trustees of the Leland Stanford Junior University. Reprinted with permission of the *Stanford Law Review* and Fred B. Rothman & Co.

3.6 THE RELATION OF ROYALTY PAYMENTS

A Parable*

William F. Baxter†

While visiting recently in the Emerald City, the federal capital of the land of Oz, I had occasion to hear a judicial opinion read in a case thought by the citizenry to be of considerable moment. No doubt I did not fully understand its implications, but nevertheless I investigated the background of the controversy and now report on the events in the hope that those concerned with similar matters here may understand more fully than I.

Throughout Oz and particularly in Emerald City, corn-on-the-cob is a highly prized delicacy. Of the 50 provinces of Oz, corn will grow in only one, Iwa. In all other provinces the soil contains some ingredient, not fully understood, that Oz agronomists call the X-factor and that wholly inhibits corn.

To be more precise, until recent years the plant could be grown only in East Iwa, for the soil of West Iwa, though it did not contain the X-factor, did contain a substance called the Y-factor that also prevented the growth of corn; but unlike X, Y posed a problem that, as we shall see, proved soluble. The presence of Y in the soil of West Iwa was particularly regrettable, for water was far more abundant in West than in East Iwa, and West Iwa was potentially the best corn country of all of Oz, since corn requires much water.

Several hundred farmers grew corn in East Iwa and sold it throughout Oz at prices that would seem high to us but that, in Oz, merely reflected the pervasive preference for corn over other foodstuffs and its relative scarcity.

The economists in Oz often quibbled over the question whether East Iwa corn farmers should be regarded as earning monopoly profits. Many East Iwa farmers had acquired their land by homestead—or at prices very much lower than those now prevailing—prior to the time corn

---

*For several years Professor Baxter has made copies of "A Parable" available to the students in his class on Government Regulation of Business. At the *Law Review*'s request, he has consented to have the document reproduced in these pages. Long a beneficiary of the service provided by the *Index to Legal Periodicals,* the *Stanford Law Review* confidently entrusts "A Parable" to the indexers' sound discretion.
†A.B. 1951, J.D. 1956, Stanford University. Professor of Law, Stanford University.

THE DECISION TO LICENSE AND PAYMENTS FOR LICENSES

was introduced in Oz and hence before the special value of the land was perceived. The incomes of those farmers, net of all other expenses, yielded an enormous return on the capital they originally had invested in land acquisition. Other corn farmers, however, had acquired their land at very high prices after its corn-growing potential was recognized, and their incomes, net of other expenses, yielded only a normal return on the capital they had invested in land acquisition. Some economists chose to say the first group of farmers, but not the second, earned monopoly profits; other economists thought it more useful to say that neither farm group earned monopoly profits—that the land investment of the first class should not be regarded as the price of acquisition but rather the price foregone by the decision of each to continue to hold the land and farm it instead of selling it at a high price to some other farmer. Certainly it is true that only the first group could be viewed as enjoying a specially favorable position: As a practical matter East Iwa cornlands were frequently bought and sold, so anyone in Oz was free to buy land and start farming corn, but, given prevailing land prices in East Iwa, that course offered no comparative attraction.

Corn farmers required fertilizer, and scores of companies manufactured fertilizer in Oz, including twenty or so in East Iwa. They competed vigorously and earned only a normal return on investment. One of these manufacturers, Dee Company, devoted large sums to research on the Y-factor in West Iwa soil. Eventually Dee discovered that the Y problem could be solved completely by repeated applications of fertilizer to which had been added a cheap chemical compound, Zilch, so Dee obtained a product patent from the federal government on the compound. As a consequence of this discovery, corn production in West Iwa became possible—indeed, many predicted that West Iwa would rapidly become a more profitable corn farming area than East Iwa because of its abundant water supply.

As real estate markets fluctuated frenetically in both parts of Iwa, Dee explored the process of manufacturing fertilizer containing Zilch. Several considerations were clear: Zilch was valueless outside West Iwa. If Dee was to recapture its research investment—and it hoped to recapture that and a little bit more—it would have to do so from sales of Zilch in West Iwa during the 17-year term of the patent. Fertilizer with Zilch would have to be priced much higher than ordinary fertilizer, but

3.6 THE RELATION OF ROYALTY PAYMENTS

Dee concluded West Iwa corn growers could afford the price given the high value of corn, low land costs, and cheap water.

Further, Dee found that the cost of adding Zilch to ordinary fertilizer was trivial. It decided to continue selling fertilizer in East Iwa and elsewhere in addition to selling Zilch fertilizer in West Iwa, and it discovered that the cheapest way to conduct this joint operation was to add Zilch to all its fertilizer early in the manufacturing process and then to add the words "Contains Zilch" to labels of those bags intended for the West Iwa market. The presence of Zilch in fertilizer sold elsewhere was ignored. It did no good, but it did no harm either. Dee therefore sold its new fertilizer in competition with all other manufactures in East Iwa and elsewhere, and it sold chemically identical but differently labeled Zilch fertilizer to the newly established corn farms in West Iwa at a price per bag several times as high as the price charged elsewhere.

Within a few years total corn production in Oz increased greatly, and corn prices fell. In East Iwa the price of farm land fell, and a certain hostility emerged there toward Dee Company and toward West Iwa corn competitors. In West Iwa, lands now suitable for corn farming came to be devoted to such farming, but they rose in value only modestly. Through the very high price of the essential Zilch fertilizer, most of the windfall gain that would otherwise have accrued to holders of West Iwa farm lands because of their newly achieved suitability for corn growing was extracted by the Dee Company.

The people of Oz, quite clearly, had been much benefited by this sequence of events. Corn was far more plentiful than before, its price was lower, and its price was destined to become lower still when the patent expired and Zilch fertilizer became available at prices that no longer reflected the supranormal profits flowing to Dee as its statutory reward for the Zilch discovery. But strangely, those most directly affected by the events were unhappy. The East Iwa farmers complained that Dee had destroyed the value of their lands. West Iwa farmers complained that Dee was suppressing and misappropriating the value of their lands. Consumers protested that corn prices would be lower still if the price of Zilch fertilizer were not so outrageous. And Dee lamented what seemed to it to be ingratitude all around.

A group of West Iwa corn farmers eventually brought a series of suits against Dee Company. In the first of these cases they accused Dee

THE DECISION TO LICENSE AND PAYMENTS FOR LICENSES

of engaging in price discrimination and thereby destroying their ability to compete with East Iwa farmers. Dee protested that destruction of West Iwa farmers' ability to compete was a consequence Dee would view with horror since they represented the only market in which the research costs of Zilch could be recovered. "More generally," Dee argued with some logic but in vain, "it is inevitably contrary to the self-interest of a seller to impose so large a price differential that a class of customers paying a highly profitable price is forced out of business." The court, however, held that when a single seller sells the same product to two groups who compete with one another and demands a higher price of one than of the other, it manifestly impairs competition between the groups, and commanded Dee to desist.[1]

After this judgment, Dee, perceiving the error of its ways, changed its mode of operation. It established two production lines, making ordinary fertilizer not containing Zilch on one and Zilch fertilizer on the other. Its costs of operation were somewhat increased, and it could charge no more than the going competitive price for ordinary fertilizer, so Zilch fertilizer thereafter sold at a slightly higher price than before. Dee was no longer selling the same product at different prices and was apparently in compliance with the judicial mandate, but predictably most parties affected became more unhappy than before. Dee sold less Zilch fertilizer at these higher prices, and its prospect of amortizing the research cost of Zilch became doubtful. Corn prices increased, to the displeasure of consumers, and West Iwa lands fell in value, causing outrage among farmers there.

Paradoxically, the only persons pleased by the outcome were the East Iwa farmers, who had been named codefendants in the first suit because they were the "wrongful beneficiaries" of the objectionable price discrimination. The increase in corn prices, attended by no change in their operating costs, redounded to their advantage, and the value of their lands rose.

As perhaps was inevitable, West Iwa farmers brought suit again, and again they were victorious. The Court, on this occasion, ruled that

---

[1] *Cf.* Grand Caillou Packing Co., FTC Docket No. 7887, 1964 TRADE REG. REP. ¶ 16,927 (June 4, 1964), *enforced in part sub nom.* La Peyre v. FTC, 366 F.2d 117 (5th Cir. 1966).

3.6 THE RELATION OF ROYALTY PAYMENTS

the prohibition against price discrimination was not as limited as its prior decision might have suggested. The court said:

> It is plain that West Iwa farmers are more impaired in their ability to compete than before and that the beneficent purpose of the price discrimination law has not been achieved. Looking to that purpose for interpretive guidance, we now see that the prohibition must extend to discriminatory sales of the same, or of *closely related,* products. That the two types of fertilizers sold by Dee are closely related is made manifest by the fact that the difference between them was artificially imposed by Dee to evade our prior judgment and has no functional purpose.[2]

For Dee Company only one step was possible: It halted the manufacture of ordinary fertilizer. The disappearance of one from the scores of competitors in that market had no observable effect. Dee's costs of manufacturing Zilch fertilizer again increased, however, since the firm was now of uneconomically small size, and once again Dee was induced to raise the price of Zilch with the same consequences as before: less Zilch fertilizer was sold, Dee's ability to recover its research expenditures was impaired, West Iwa farmers lost more of the corn market to East Iwa farmers, corn prices and East Iwa land prices rose, and the land prices of the victorious West Iwa farmers fell.

One final round of litigation was mercifully brief. West Iwa farmers; perceiving that their earlier victories had had unexpected consequences, sought a new court order requiring Dee to reduce the price of Zilch fertilizer; and, in the event that the court was unwilling to grant them that relief, they asked that the several earlier court orders be revoked. On this occasion Dee was victorious. Chief Judge Patman, in the last of his now famous trilogy of opinions, held with respect to the first

---

[2] Emphasis in original. *Cf.* McWhirter v. Monroe Calculating Machine Co., 76 F. Supp. 456, 460 (W.D.Mo. 1948) (different models of calculating machines held to be products of like grade and quality because they all possessed keyboards with keys, representing numerals and figures, that could be pressed down to perform addition, subtraction, multiplication, and division). *But cf.* Atalanta Trading Corp. v. FTC, 258 F.2d 365, 371 & n.5 (2d Cir. 1958) (Canadian bacon, ham, and pork shoulders are not closely related products, notwithstanding that all derive from the pig).

request that Dee's monopoly over Zilch was entirely legal and consistent with the purpose of the patent laws to encourage research on problems such as the Y-factor in soil; and he denied the second request on the ground that the earlier opinions had been necessary and appropriate to protect the citizens of Oz from the baleful consequences of price discrimination.

As I now review these events, I am puzzled by the emphasis placed, in all the court opinions, on the propriety of the monopoly that underlay the entire sequence. In the last case, of course, the assault was directly upon the monopoly and its propriety was dispositive. But in the first two cases the assault was on symptoms of the monopoly, and it occurs to me that the lesson to be learned from those cases applies equally well to any instance of monopolistic power, provided only that the legal system is unable or unwilling to eliminate it. But my ruminations may well be unsound, for Oz is a strange country and I am often puzzled by its customs.

3.7 THE RELATION OF ROYALTY PAYMENTS TO THE VALUE OF RIGHTS TO DIFFERENT USERS— ROYALTIES PROPORTIONAL TO USE OF A PATENTED MACHINE

Brulotte v. Thys Co. was described earlier (sections 3.5(a) and (d)). A patentee sold a patented hop-picking machine and granted a license to use the machine.[41] Payments were based upon the amount of hops picked. This required farmers who used the machine more extensively to pay more on a per-machine basis than those who used it less extensively. The decision implies this was entirely appropriate. The lower courts have approved similar arrangements.[42]

In 1917 in *Motion Picture Patents,* the Supreme Court suggested this strategy was "evil."[43] The patent covered a part of motion picture projectors. The Motion Picture Patents Company owned the patent. Motion Picture Patents granted a license to the Precision Machine Company to make and sell projectors. The Precision Machine Company agreed to sell machines only "under the restriction and condition that such . . . machine shall be used solely for exhibiting or projecting motion pictures containing the inventions of reissued letters patent No. 12,192, leased by a licensee of the licensor while it owned said patents and upon other terms to be fixed by the licensor and complied with by the user while said machine is in use and while the licensor owned said patents (which other terms shall only be the payment of a royalty or rental to the licensor while in use)." The Precision Machine Company also agreed to attach a plate to every machine showing the date of the machine part patent and containing the words:[44]

> The sale and purchase of this machine gives only the right to use it solely with moving pictures containing the invention of reissued

---

[41] *Brulotte v. Thys Co.,* 379 U.S. 29, 30, 33 (1964).
[42] *Extractol Process v. Hiram Walker & Sons,* 153 F.2d 204, 265, 267–268 (7th Cir. 1946); *Cold Metal Process Co. v. McLouth Steel Corporation,* 141 F.Supp. 487, 490 (E.D. Mich. 1941), *aff'd,* 170 F.2d 396, 370 (6th Cir. 1948).
[43] *Motion Picture Patents Co. v. Universal Film Mfg. Co.,* 243 U.S. 501, 508, 516–518 (1917).
[44] Id. at 506–507.

patent No. 12,192, leased by a licensee of the Motion Picture Patents Company, the owner of the above patents and reissued patent, while it owned said patent, and upon other terms to be fixed by the Motion Picture Patents Company and complied with by the user while it is in use and while the Motion Picture Patents Company owns said patents. The removal or defacement of this plate terminates the right to use this machine.

The license also said that Precision would not sell a machine for less than a price set by the Motion Picture Patents Company. Precision agreed to pay a royalty of $5 on some machines and a percentage of selling price on others.

Justice Clarke condemned the right of the patent owner to specify the payment of a royalty or rental for use of the machine during the time the machine was used and the patent existed. Justice Clarke noted that this right had been exercised by the patent owner to impose a charge on the purchaser "graduated by the size of the theater in which the machine was to be used."

Justice Clarke noted that the Motion Picture Patents Company received $5 on each machine sold. Because 40,000 machines had been sold, the patent owner had "already received over $200,000 for the use of its patented invention." What the patent owner was attempting to do by "this device" was to collect "during the life of the patent . . . many times this amount through the use of the same invention, after its machines had been sold and paid for." A patent owner who reserved the right to set a royalty for use of the machine had the power to do great "evil":[45]

> A restriction which would give the plaintiff such a potential power for evil over an industry which must be recognized as an important element in the amusement life of the nation, under the conclusions we have stated in this opinion, is plainly void, because wholly without the scope and purpose of our patent laws, and because, if sustained, it would be gravely injurious to the public interest, which we have seen is more a favorite of the law than is the promotion of private fortune.

---

[45] Id. at 519.

3.8 ROYALTIES PAYABLE BY LICENSED SELLERS

The Supreme Court declared it "evil" for a patent owner to obtain royalties proportional to the value of its invention to different users for the purpose of earning maximum profits.

As I noted above, the Court in *Brulotte* gave tacit approval to economic discrimination, a strategy for exploiting a patent the Court criticized when accomplished by tying arrangements.

3.8 THE RELATION OF ROYALTY PAYMENTS TO THE VALUE OF RIGHTS TO DIFFERENT USERS— ROYALTIES PAYABLE BY LICENSED SELLERS AND LICENSED BUYERS OF A SINGLE PRODUCT

Patent owners frequently license companies that do business with each other. The licenses sometimes fail to specify the royalty obligations of the parties when one licensee sells a product to another licensee that re-sells the product. There is an issue whether it is enforceable for a patent owner to license both the sale and resale of a patented product and collect royalties on both sales.

The exhaustion doctrine says that a patent owner that sells the patented product without condition has no claim for infringement against a purchaser (section 6.9). The same rule applies where a licensee makes an authorized and unconditional sale.[46] The most commonly cited statement is the Supreme Court's pronouncement in *Adams v. Burke*:[47]

> The right to manufacture, the right to sell and the right to use are each substantive rights, and may be granted or conferred separately by the patentee.
>
> But, in the essential nature of things, when the patentee, or the person having his rights, sells a machine or instrument whose sole value is in its use, he receives the consideration for its use and he parts with the right to restrict that use. The article, in the language of the court, passes without the limit of the monopoly.

---

[46] *Keller v. Standard Folding Bed Co.*, 157 U.S. 659, 666–667 (1895); *Hobble v. Jennison*, 149 U.S. 355, 362–364 (1893); *Adams v. Burke*, 84 U.S. 453 (1873). See also, section 6.7 and 6.9.

[47] *Adams v. Burke*, 84 U.S. 453, 456–457 (1873).

Bloomer v. McQuewan, 14 How., 459; *Mitchell v. Hawley, ante,* 3221. That is to say, the patentee or his assignee *having in the act of sale received all the royalty or consideration which he claims for the use of his invention in that particular machine or instrument,* it is open to the use of the purchaser without further restriction on account of the monopoly of the patentee's. [emphasis added]

In these decisions, the Court sometimes said that a patent owner is entitled to only one royalty of each product.[48] The Supreme Court has sometimes equated the payment of an agreed royalty with the purchase of a patented product.[49]

I am aware of no decision in which a patent owner has collected royalties from licensees on both the first sale and a subsequent sale of a product sold in the same form by each. However, I am aware of no decision expressly holding that it would be unenforceable for a patent owner to make such agreements. If the policy underlying these decisions is that a patent owner may collect only once for the exercise of all of the rights granted in a particular patent (whether received as a royalty or a purchase price), the policy is violated by a series of agreements that would require royalty payments by one licensee on exercise of the rights and by its supplier or customer having the same rights.[50]

This assumes that each licensee is using the same patents and same rights to make a single product. Separate royalty-bearing licenses to practice separate claims of a patent or different steps of a process have

---

[48] *Mitchell v. Hawley,* 83 U.S. 322, 323–324 (1872).
[49] *Keeler v. Standard Folding Bed Co.,* 157 U.S. 659, 666 (1895).
[50] *In Re Thorpe,* 777 F.2d 693, 695 (Fed. Cir. 1985) ("The sales by Lisle were authorized by the . . . license agreement. Resale [by the licensee's customer] did not create a sublicense. Edwards [the patent owner] is not entitled to a royalty payment each time a tool is resold."); *cf., Aro Mfg. Co. v. Convertible Top Co.,* 377 U.S. 476, 510 (1964) (The Court found that it would be inconsistent with public policy to allow a patent owner to collect damages from a component supplier, Aro, after the patent owner received the equivalent of a royalty from the seller, Ford, of the product using the component.).

3.9 SHARING ROYALTIES WITH LICENSEES

been approved by the lower courts.[51] Separate royalty-bearing licenses to practice different rights are also lawful. For example, the lower courts have permitted a patent owner to license one class of licensees to make and sell the patented product only to another class of licensees having royalty-bearing licenses to use the product.[52]

3.9 SHARING ROYALTIES WITH LICENSEES

The patent owner may authorize another to grant sublicenses and may share sublicense royalties with that person.[53] However, in *In Re Yarn Processing Patent Validity Litigation*,[54] the owner of a "combination of patents" manufactured and sold machinery for performing the patented processes. The owner also licensed competing manufacturers. The patent owner had acquired at least some of the patents from others. However, the licensed manufacturers were not the source of any of the licensed patents. Those licensees were authorized to make machines and to sell them only to machine users, who were separately licensed by the patent owner to use the machines and who paid royalties at a rate determined by the patent owner. The patent owner agreed to pay each manufacturing licensee the same percentage (33%) of user royalties that the owner collected from users of that manufacturer's machines. The user royalty payments were between two to six times the initial selling price of ma-

---

[51] *SCM Corp. v. Radio Corp. of America,* 318 F. Supp. 433 (S.D.N.Y. 1970) (separate royalty-bearing licenses to practice separate claims of a patent are lawful); *Eastern Venetian Blind Co. v. Acme Steel* Co., 188 F.2d 247, 252–253 (4th Cir. 1951) (separate royalty-bearing licenses to practice different steps of a patented process are lawful).

[52] *Duplan Corp. v. Derring Milliken, Inc.,* 444 F.Supp. 648, 661–664, 669–671 (D.S.C. 1977), *aff'd in pertinent part,* 594 F.2d 979 (4th Cir. 1979); *In re Yarn Processing Patent Validity Litigation,* 541 F.2d 1127, 1135 (5th Cir. 1976); *Extractol Process, Ltd. v. Hiram Walker & Sons, Inc.,* 153 F.2d 264, 268 (7th Cir. 1946).

[53] *Standard Oil Company v. United States,* 283 U.S. 163, 168–171 (1931).

[54] *In Re Yarn Processing Patent Validity Litigation,* 541 F.2d 1127 (5th Cir. 1976).

chinery. The court held that, in the circumstances, the agreement to share user royalties constituted fixing of machine selling price and a *per se* violation of the Sherman Act.

3.10 LICENSING IN EXCHANGE FOR RIGHTS—GRANTBACKS

The misuse rules condemn potentially beneficial agreements to prevent any possibility of a patent owner "extending the scope" of the patent. The actual effects of any particular agreement are not evaluated. There is one notable exception—the one having perhaps the most direct potential for scope extension. This should not, of course, suggest that the grantback rules be tightened up on owners.

The competition that an inventor or patent owner would most like to eliminate is competition from suppliers of substitute inventions or rights. There are few reported decisions of agreements under which a patent owner attempts to limit such competition by requiring its licensees not to invent substitute inventions or not to acquire licenses under substitute technology. The reason is probably that attempts to limit that type of competition would cost more than they are worth. To be profitable, the restriction must encompass a significant part of the existing or potential suppliers of those inventions or rights. It is likely to be too costly to identify them. They are also likely to be too numerous to attempt to control.

However, there are many reported cases of agreements by a patent owner that its licensee will assign or license to the patent owner inventions or patents developed later by the licensee. Such provisions are commonly called *grantbacks*. In theory, a grantback may serve to decrease the value to the licensee of producing substitute inventions and to deter competition in making them. However, the assignment or license back of substitute rights is not flatly prohibited by any antitrust or misuse rule!

(a) The *Transparent-Wrap* Rule

In 1947, in *Transparent-Wrap,* the Supreme Court reviewed the enforceability of an agreement in which the owner of a business sold it to

3.10 LICENSING IN EXCHANGE FOR RIGHTS—GRANTBACKS

another company.[55] The seller granted that buyer a trademark license and an exclusive license under a patent on the machines to make and sell the machine under patents then owned or later acquired by the seller. The buyer-licensee agreed to pay royalties. The buyer-licensee also promised to assign to the licensor "improvement patents applicable to the machine and suitable for use in connection with it." The buyer-licensee received a license under any assigned improvement patents in accord with the terms of the exclusive license. However, the buyer-licensee would not be required to pay any additional royalty based upon those assigned improvement patents. The licensor brought an action to require the buyer-licensee to assign certain patents on improvements.

The Supreme Court found that the agreement was enforceable and was not unlawful on its face under the antitrust laws. The Court, reversing the Second Circuit Court of Appeals, held that "the inclusion in the license of the condition requiring the licensee to assign improvement patents is not per se illegal and unenforceable."[56]

The Court said that, in certain circumstances, grantback provisions may be used to violate the antitrust laws:[57]

> We are quite aware of the possibilities of abuse in the practice of licensing a patent on condition that the licensee assign all improvement patents to the licensor. Conceivably the device could be employed with the purpose or effect of violating the anti-trust laws. He who acquires two patents requires a double monopoly. As patents are added to patents the whole industry may be regimented. The owner of a basic patent might thus perpetuate his control over an industry long after the basic patent expired. Competitors might be eliminated and an industrial monopoly perfected and maintained. Through the use of patent pools or multiple licensing agreements the fruits of invention of an entire industry might be systematically funneled into the hands of the original patentee.

---

[55] *Transparent Wrap Mach. Corp. v. Stokes & Smith Co.*, 329 U.S. 637 (1947).
[56] Id. at 648.
[57] Id. at 646.

The Court of Appeals on remand found no antitrust violation had been proved under a rule of reason standard. The Court of Appeals, in an opinion by Judge Learned Hand, found no "double monopoly".[58]

The Supreme Court's decision is important in several respects. First, the Court said the Court of Appeals was wrong to hold the provision unenforceable under the misuse standard of *Morton Salt*. The Court affirmed that where the "public policy" articulated in *Morton Salt* condemned a practice, the Court could refuse to enforce the offending provision and refuse to enjoin infringement that resulted from the failure to comply with it. The Court expressed concern about whether it had authority to declare the assignment unenforceable. The Court noted that Congress had provided that patents were assignable. There was no statutory limitation on the type of consideration that could be paid for the assignment. The Court said patent was "a species of property" and "for purposes of the assignment statute of the same dignity as the other property which may used to purchase patents." The Court felt that it would be interfering with the enforceability of patent assignments if it condemned an agreement in which the assignment is made in exchange for a patent license.

It seems incredible to believe that the misuse rule would not have been developed if Congress had passed a statute saying "a patent shall be licensable in law by an instrument in writing" and did not limit the type of consideration that could be given for it. This decision suggested that it might have been.

Second, the Court noted that the assignment might put the buyer-licensee at a "real competitive handicap." However, it noted that "the competitive handicap or disadvantage which he suffers is no greater and no less whether the consideration for the assignment be the right to use the basic patent or something else of value." The implication seems to be that if a licensee's agreement to restrain its activities would be lawful and enforceable if obtained for money, it ought also to be enforceable when the consideration is a patent license. If that is true, then most if not all of the misuse and enforceability rules vanish.

---

[58] 161 F.2d 565, 567 (2d Cir.), *cert. denied,* 331 U.S. 837, *rehearing denied,* 332 U.S. 787 (1947).

3.10 LICENSING IN EXCHANGE FOR RIGHTS—GRANTBACKS

Third, the Court said that the assignment provision did not violate the public policy against preventing a patent owner from using it "to acquire a monopoly not embraced in the patent." The Supreme Court said that "[o]ne who uses one patent to acquire another is not extending his patent monopoly to articles governed by the general law or as respects which neither monopolies nor restraints of trade are sanctioned. He is indeed using one legalized monopoly to acquire another legalized monopoly." More importantly, the Court again expressed new-found concern about the lack of any congressional command making the provision illegal:[59]

> It is true that for some purposes the owner of a patent is under disabilities with which owners of other property are not burdened. Thus where the use of unpatented materials is tied to the use of a patent, a court will not lend its aid to enforce the agreement though control of the unpatented article falls short of a prohibited restraint of trade or monopoly [citation omitted]. There is a suggestion that the same course should be followed in this case since the tendency of the practice we have here would be in the direction of concentration of economic power that might run counter to the policy of the anti-trust laws. The difficulty is that Congress has not made illegal the acquisition of improvement patents by the owner of basic patent. The assignment of patents is indeed sanctioned. And as we have said, there is no difference in the policy of the assignment statute whatever consideration may be used to purchase the improvement patents. And apart from violations of the anti-trust laws to which we will shortly advert, the end result is the same whether the owner of a basic patent uses a license to obtain improvement patents or uses the wealth which he accumulates by exploiting his basic patent for that purpose. In sum, a patent license may not be used coercively to exact a condition contrary to public policy. But what falls within the terms of the assignment statute is plainly not *per se* against the public interest.

---

[59] 329 U.S. at 645.

One would suppose the same is true of an agreement to pay money or an agreement to buy certain products even though there is no federal statute providing for such agreements.

Fourth, the Court said that it was too conjectural from the face of this agreement whether the enforcement of the condition would decrease the licensee's incentives to make inventions, because it is bound to turn over to the licensor the "products of its inventive genius." The Court said that the argument had no persuasive force. It said the buyer-licensee could use the improvements it developed without payment of an additional royalty. It said the license under the basic patent permitted the improvements to be put to immediate use and exploited by the licensee. It said that whether exploitation of "the improvement patents would be increased but for the agreement depends on vicissitudes of business too conjectural on this record to appraise."

The significance of those remarks is that the Court was unwilling to condemn a provision simply because it might have in some circumstances the effect of decreasing incentives to make inventions. The grant of the license under the basic patent, in the Court's view, increased the licensee's incentives. Even if the assignment back decreased those incentives, the Court was unwilling to attempt to decide the net effect. If that analysis is applied to all license provisions, there will be far fewer situations in which the Courts will be able to say that the effect of an agreement would always be to decrease competition outside the scope of a patent. The "vicissitudes of business" may lead to a different result.

Fifth, the Court said that the agreement "could be employed with the purpose or effect of violating the antitrust laws." However, "the inclusion in the license of the condition requiring the licensee to assign improvement patents is not *per se* illegal and unenforceable."

On remand, the lower court found no antitrust violation. The lower court found no unreasonable restraint in the period prior to the expiration of the basic patent because, during that period, the improvement patents added nothing to the defendant's control of the product. Even if the improvement patents related to machines not covered by the basic patent during its term, the court said there was no proof that the machines covered by the improvements would be "important competitors" with the machines made under the basic patents. Therefore, there was no reason for finding that the restraint on competition was "unreasonable." The lower court said

3.10 LICENSING IN EXCHANGE FOR RIGHTS—GRANTBACKS

that, to the extent that the improvement patents could be used after the basic patent expired, the licensor's control over the industry will be no greater than would have been the control those patents gave the licensee.

(b) The Applications of *Transparent-Wrap*

Later that same year, in *United States v. National Lead Co.*,[60] the Court reviewed the judgment and order of the district court which found that National Lead and du Pont violated section 1 of the Sherman Act by entering patent cross-license agreements, where the control of the patents and the manner they were used gave National Lead and du Pont "domination and control of the titanium pigment business." National Lead and du Pont sold over 90 percent of the titanium pigments and compounds in the United States.

The district court ordered National Lead and du Pont to grant to any applicant a nonexclusive license under existing patents or patents to be acquired in the next five years at a "uniform, reasonable royalty."[61] It provided that the grant may "at the option of the licensor, be conditioned upon the reciprocal grant of a license by the applicant, at a reasonable royalty, under existing patents and patents to be obtained in the next 5 years."

The Court held that this provision was within the discretion of the district court in framing relief. The Court noted the district court's explanation that the grantback was needed to prevent the licensor from being put at a competitive disadvantage to its licensee, who has "this extraordinary advantage of being able to take everything for itself and keep everything it has."[62]

In *United States v. E.I. du Pont de Nemours & Co.*,[63] an action for alleged violation of section 2, the government "attacked [the] validity of" a license agreement. As part of the settlement of an infringement action, du Pont granted an exclusive license to Sylvania under du Pont's basic patent on moisture-proof cellophane. Among other things, Sylva-

---

[60] *United States v. National Lead Co.*, 332 U.S. 319, 335–336, 359–360 (1947).
[61] Id. at 335–336.
[62] Id. at 359–360.
[63] *United States v. E.I. du Pont de Nemours & Co.*, 118 F.Supp. 41, 223–225 (D. Del. 1953), *aff'd on other grounds,* 351 U.S. 377 (1956).

nia was obligated to offer licenses to du Pont under patents it might later develop "which fell within the field of the basic moisture-proof patent." The Court found that, under the test laid down in the Second Circuit's opinion on remand in *Transparent-Wrap,* there was no showing that this provision had "restrictive effects." Three dissenting Justices, including Justice Douglas, who wrote the majority opinion in *Transparent-Wrap,* would have found that this agreement violated the Sherman Act.[64]

In cases where grantback provisions standing alone are alleged to violate the antitrust laws, the courts analyze with the provisions under the rule of reason. In applying the rule of reason to grantback provisions, the courts have determined its reasonableness by balancing the effect of the provision on competition and efficiency in use of the licensed invention, competition in the development of improvement inventions, and competition and efficiency in use of improvement inventions.

The courts identify various facts as bearing on that determination:

1. Whether the grantback is of an assignment or an exclusive license rather than a nonexclusive license (which satisfies the licensor's interest in remaining competitive with its licensee),
2. If exclusive, whether the licensee retains the right to use the improvement patent,
3. Whether the grantback includes the right of the licensor to grant sublicenses and, if so, whether it requires such sublicensing
4. Whether the grantback is limited to the scope of the licensed patents or whether the licensee's patents might cover competing products or processes which would not infringe the licensed patent,
5. Whether the grantback is limited to patents which a licensee acquires during the term of the license and whether the license grantback runs for a term beyond the term of the license,
6. Whether the grantback rights may be used by the licensor royalty-free or require a royalty payment,
7. Whether the grantbacks cover "an entire industry,"

---

[64] 351 U.S. at 419–420 n.10.

3.10 LICENSING IN EXCHANGE FOR RIGHTS—GRANTBACKS

8. Whether the parties have any market or monopoly power,
9. Whether the parties to the license are competitors, and, in hindsight,
10. Whether the agreement has deterred the licensee from making inventions and, if the licensee has made any inventions, their competitive significance and the extent to which they have been used.

The lower courts have uniformly held, in the absence of other restrictions, that a grantback of a nonexclusive license does not violate the antitrust laws or constitute misuse.[65] In the absence of other restraints, the courts have sometimes found grantbacks of exclusive licenses or assignments to be legal,[66] and have sometimes found them illegal.[67]

---

[65] *Binks Manufacturing Co. v. Ransburg Electro-Coating Corp.*, 281 F. 2d 252, 259 (7th Cir. 1960), cert. dismissed, 366 U.S. 211 (1961); *Barr Rubber Products Co. v. Sun Rubber Co.*, 277 F.Supp. 484 (S.D.N.Y. 1967), *aff'd in part, rev'd in part*, 425 F.2d 1114 (2d Cir. 1970), cert. denied, 400 U.S. 878 (1970) (Licensor "sought and obtained from its licensees promise of licenses from them under any patented improvement in the process"); *Well Surveys Inc. v. McCullough Tool Co.*, 199 F.Supp. 374, 395 (N.D. Okla. 1961), *aff'd*, 343 F.2d 381 (10th Cir. 1975), *cert. denied*, 383 U.S. 933 (1966); *International Nickel Co. v. Ford Motor Co.*, 166 F.Supp. 551, 565 (S.D.N.Y. 1958).

[66] *Santa Fe–Pomeroy Inc. v. P & Z Co., Inc.*, 569 F.2d 1084, 1101–1102 (9th Cir. 1978) (assignment of improvements legal where there were many competitive methods to the license methods, there was no evidence that the grantback had deferred improvements, and licensee was free to use any of the assigned improvement without additional royalty); *Zajizek v. Koolvent Metal Awning Corp.*, 283 F.2d 127, 131–132 (9th Cir. 1960), *cert. denied*, 365 U.S. 859 (1961) (assignment of improvements); *Swofford v. B.W., Inc.*, 251 F.Supp. 811, 820–821 (S.D. Tex. 1966), *aff'd*, 395 F.2d 362 (5th Cir. 1968), *cert. denied*, 393 U.S. 935 (1968); *Sperry Products, Inc. v. Aluminum Co. of America*, 171 F.Supp. 901, 936–938 (N.D. Ohio 1959), *aff'd in part*, 285 F.2d 911 (6th Cir. 1960), *cert. denied*, 368 U.S. 890 (1961) (assignment of improvement was legal on the basis of "an examination of all relevant market factors and their economic consequences").

[67] *Duplan Corp. v. Deering Milliken Inc.*, 440 F.Supp. 648 (D.S.C. 1977), *aff'd in part*, 594 F.2d 979 (4th Cir. 1979), *cert. denied*, 444 U.S. 1015 (1980) (requirement that a licensee assign patent relating to an area broader than that covered by the license was illegal because that requirement "substantially enhanced and extended" monopoly of the licensed patent).

Where agreements combine grantbacks with additional restrictions, both exclusive and nonexclusive grantbacks have been held to be illegal. Thus, in *U.S. v. General Electric Co.*,[68] assignment grantbacks employed in conjunction with price-fixing agreements were held to violate the antitrust laws. In another *U.S. v. General Electric Co.*,[69] a requirement that licensees grant back nonexclusive licenses under their own developments was held illegal, where the defendant was found to have engaged in a broad scheme to monopolize an industry and to have used the grantbacks to eliminate competition after its basic patents had expired. In *U.S. v. Aluminum Co. of America*,[70] a company found to have monopolized an industry was held, as part of the remedy for that violation, not to be entitled to condition license grants to competitors on a nonexclusive, royalty-free grantback under the licensee's own improvements.

(c) The Competitive Effects

The most fundamental distinction that should apply to such agreements is whether the grantback is confined to rights in complementary or substitute inventions. That distinction is not easy to make prospectively.

The day a basic patent expires, a product embodying what was previously a complementary improvement becomes, from the point of view of the owner of the basic patent, the principal substitute. It should never be unlawful to grant back, whether by assignment, exclusive license, or a nonexclusive license, inventions that are useful only in combination with the licensed patent if those rights granted back continue only during the term of that patent.

All other agreements should be evaluated based on the extent to which they decrease competition in the production of substitute inventions. If the licensees constitute only a small percentage of the potential makers of substitute inventions, it is unlikely that grantbacks will reduce competition in any significant way. If they do, that harm should be balanced against the benefits of grantback provisions.

Grantbacks may increase the level of investment in improvement

---

[68] *U.S. v. General Electric Co.*, 80 F.Supp. 989, 1005–1006 (S.D.N.Y. 1948).
[69] *U.S. v. General Electric Co.*, 82 F.Supp. 753, 815 (D. N.J. 1949).
[70] *U.S. v. Aluminum Co. of America*, 91 F.Supp. 333, 410 (S.D.N.Y. 1950).

3.10 LICENSING IN EXCHANGE FOR RIGHTS—GRANTBACKS

inventions by reducing uncertainty about the economic value of the improvements. Grantbacks may be preproduction invention agreements in which the owner of a patent gives others an option to make improvements and supply rights to them to the patent owner. The license under the existing patent is the consideration for that option. Without that grantback, the efficiency of producing improvement inventions may decrease as potential efficient improvers are denied licenses.

4

The Nature of Products and Rights Supplied Together—Tying and Package Licensing

4.1	Supplying Tangible Products with a License—Tying Arrangements	229
4.2	The Law Applied to Tying Arrangements	229
4.3	The Theory of Tying—Acquiring a "Limited Monopoly" beyond the Scope of the Rights	239
4.4	The Competitive Effects of Tying Arrangements	239
4.5	The Leading Decisions and Statutes on Extending the Rights	247
4.6	Licensing More than One Patent or Copyright in a Single Agreement—Package Licensing	279

4.1 SUPPLYING TANGIBLE PRODUCTS WITH A LICENSE—TYING ARRANGEMENTS

Tying arrangements have been used by rights owners from the beginning. The law initially encouraged their use, then condemned them with every available legal device.

4.2 THE LAW APPLIED TO TYING ARRANGEMENTS

In general, a tying arrangement is the sale of one product (called the "tying product") only on condition that the buyer purchase a separate product from the seller (called the "tied product"). The rules on tying arrangements arose out of the Supreme Court's conclusion that tying agreements are used by rights owners to attempt to obtain a "limited monopoly" in a market beyond the reach (or *scope*) of the rights or to restrict competition in such a market. For example, in *Morton Salt,* the Court said:[1]

> It thus appears that respondent is making use of its patent monopoly to restrain competition in the marketing of unpatented articles, salt tablets, for use with the patented machines, and is aiding in the creation of a limited monopoly in the tablets not within that granted by the patent. A patent operates to create and grant to the patentee an exclusive right to make, use and vend the particular device described and claimed in the patent. But a patent affords no immunity for a monopoly not within the grant, Interstate Circuit v. United States, 306 US 208, 228, 230, 83 L ed 610, 621, 622, 59 S Ct 467; Ethyl Gasoline Corp. v. United States, 309 US 436, 456, 84 L ed

---

[1] *Morton Salt Co. v. G. S. Suppiger,* 314 U.S. 488, 491 (1942).

852, 861, 60 S Ct 618, and the use of it to suppress competition in the sale of an unpatented article may deprive the patentee of the aid of a court of equity to restrain an alleged infringement by one who is a competitor.

The Court's earliest and perhaps the most influential expression of this theory occurred in 1917 in *Motion Picture Patents*.[2] In *Motion Picture Patents,* a patent owner licensed a company to make and sell motion picture projectors having a patented films feeding part. The seller put a notice on the projector that the purchase gives the right to use it only with films leased from the patent owner. The Court held that the "restriction" in the notice on the machine was ineffective, because its effect would be to "extend the scope of its patent monopoly."

> [The] restriction is invalid because such a film is obviously not any part of the invention of the patent-in-suit; because it is an attempt, without statutory warrant, to continue the patent monopoly on this particular character of film after it [the film patent] has expired, and because to enforce it would be to create a monopoly in the manufacture and use of moving picture films, wholly outside of the patent-in-suit [, the machine patent,] and the patent law as we have interpreted it.

In the 1930s, *Motion Picture Patents* was extended to render unenforceable similar restrictions in licenses to use patented processes or parts of patented articles.[3] In these cases, the patent owners granted licenses to use a patented process or to make and use a patented combination article only with unpatented materials or components obtained from the owner (or a licensee authorized to sell materials or components). The Court declared the restrictions unenforceable. Hence, the sale of ma-

---

[2] *Motion Picture Patents Co. v. Universal Film Mfg. Co.,* 243 U.S. 501, 508, 516–518 (1917).
[3] *Leitch Mfg. Co. v. Barber Co.,* 302 U.S. 458 (1938) (process patent); *Carbice Corp. v. American Patents Devel Corp.,* 283 U.S. 27, 30–35 (1931) (patented combination).

4.2 THE LAW APPLIED TO TYING ARRANGEMENTS

terials or components for the licensee's use was not contributory infringement.

At about the same time, similar developments were taking place in antitrust law. In the 1930s and 1940s, the Supreme Court held that the sale or lease of a patented product (the tying product) only on condition that the buyer purchased a different product (the tied product) may violate section 1 of the Sherman Act or section 3 of the Clayton Act.[4] A license can be the tying product. In the 1940s, the Court also declared that the antitrust rule applied where a patent owner supplied a "license" to a system on condition the licensee obtain an "unpatented" component from it or another licensee.[5]

In addition to the existence of the tying arrangement, the Court declared that a section 1 violation occurred only where the patent owner possessed sufficient economic power over the tying product to impose the tie-in and a not insubstantial amount of commerce in the tied product is affected. The Court said a Clayton Act section 3 violation was established if either one of those two additional elements were established.[6]

The Court also declared that, where the tying product was patented or was a patent license, there was a presumption of sufficient economic power over that product to establish an antitrust violation.[7] In antitrust

---

[4] *International Salt Co. v. United States* 332 U.S. 391 (1947) (Sherman Act, section 1 and Clayton Act, § 3); *International Business Machines Co. v. United States,* 298 U.S. 131 (1936) (Clayton Act, §3).

[5] *Mercoid Corp. v. Mid-Continent Co.,* 302 U.S. 661, 664–665, 667 (1944); *Mercoid Corp. v. Minneapolis-Honeywell Reg. Co.,* 320 U.S. 680, 682–684 (1944). This rule was foreshadowed, if not adopted, earlier by the lower courts. *B.B. Chemical Co. v. Ellis,* 117 F.2d 829, 834–836 (1st Cir. 1941), *aff'd,* 314 U.S. 495 (1942); *Philad Co. v. Lechler Laboratories,* 107 F.2d 747, 748 (2nd Cir. 1939).

[6] Tying arrangements prescribed by § 3 of the Clayton Act apply only to "goods, wares, merchandise, machinery, supplies and/or other commodities." 15 U.S.C. § 14. The few existing cases hold that § 3 does not apply where the tying product is a license under patents. *Advance Business Systems and Supply Co. v. S.C.M. Corp.,* 415 F.2d 55, 64 (4th Cir. 1969); *United States v. Investors Diversified Services, Inc.,* 102 F.Supp. 645 (D. Minn. 1951); *United States v. Western Union Telegraph Co.,* 53 F.Supp. 377, 381 (S.D.N.Y. 1943).

[7] *International Salt v. United States,* 332 U.S. 392, 395, (1947) (patented machine); *United States v. Loew's, Co., Inc.,* 371 U.S. 38, 45 (1962) ("The requisite economic power is presumed when the tying product is patented. . . .); *Rex Chain-Belt, Inc.*

THE NATURE OF PRODUCTS AND RIGHTS SUPPLIED TOGETHER

cases, the courts have found that special business circumstances may justify a tying arrangement.[8]

A patent misuse defense based upon a tying arrangement requires proof that the patent owner sold a patented product or granted a license on condition that the purchaser or licensee buy an unpatented product or material from the owner. Until 1988, a misuse defense did not require proof that the seller or licensee had any economic power in the tying product or that a not insubstantial amount of commerce was affected.[9] In 1988, section 271(d) of the Patent Act was amended to change the law on tying arrangements. Congress added subsections 4 and 5 to section 271(d):[10]

> (d) No patent owner otherwise entitled to relief for infringement or contributory infringement of a patent shall be denied relief or deemed guilty of misuse or illegal extension of the patent right by reason of his having done one or more of the following: . . . (4) refused to license or use any rights to the patent; or (5) conditioned the license of any rights to the patent or the sale of the patented product on the acquisition of a license to rights in another patent or purchase of a separate product, unless, in view of the circumstances, the patent owner has market power in the relevant market for the patent or patented product on which the license or sale is conditioned.

---

v. Harco Products, Inc., 512 F.2d 993, 1000 n.1, 1003 (9th Cir. 1975), *cert. denied,* 423 U.S. 831 (1975) (patent license); *Duplan Corp. v. Deering Milliken, Inc.,* 444 F.Supp. 648, 673 (D. S.C. 1977), *aff'd in pertinent part,* 594 F.2d 979 (4th Cir. 1979) (patent license); *cf., Standard Oil v. United States,* 337 U.S. 239, 307 (1949); *Times-Picayune Publishing Co. v. United States,* 345 U.S. 594, 608, 611–612 n. 30 (1953); *Northern Pacific R. Co. v. United States,* 356 U.S. 1, 10 n.8, 18 (1958).

[8]*Standard Oil Co. v. United States,* 337 U.S. 293, 305–306 (1949); *International Salt Co. v. United States,* 33 U.S. 392, 397–398 (1947); *International Business Machines Corp. v. United States,* 298 U.S. 131, 138–140 (1936); *Jerrold Electronics Corp. v. Westcoast Broadcasting Co.,* 34 F.2d 653 (9th Cir. 1965), *cert. denied,* 382 U.S. 817 (1965); *United States v. Jerrold Electronics Corporation,* 187 F.Supp. 545 (E.D. Pa. 1960), *aff'd per curiam* 365 U.S. 567 (1961); *Dehydrating Process Co. v. A.O. Smith Corp.,* 292 F.2d 653, 655–657 (1st Cir. 1961); *Electric Pipe Line v. Fluid Systems, Inc.,* 231 F.2d 370, 371–372 (2d Cir. 1956).

[9]*Morton Salt Co. v. G. S. Suppinger Co.,* 314 U.S. 488, 491–494 (1942).

[10]35 U.S.C. § 271(d).

4.2 THE LAW APPLIED TO TYING ARRANGEMENTS

That change seemed simply to limit the prohibition on tying arrangements (and package licensing) in one respect: The patent owner must have market power in the relevant market for the tying product. The business-justification antitrust rule has never been applied to a case involving a patent misuse defense.

The law is not entirely settled where the seller or licensor owners a patent on the tied product. Section 3 of the Clayton Act makes tying arrangements unlawful whether or not the tied product is patented.[11] Some courts have found that, in certain circumstances, there is no patent misuse where the tied product was patented.[12] Other courts have found that there was misuse even though the tied product was patented.[13]

---

[11] *International Business Machines Corp. v. United States,* 298 U.S. 131, 136–138 (1936); *cf., Ethyl Gasoline Corp. v. United States,* 309 U.S. 436, 458–459 (1940) ("The patent monopoly of one invention may no more be enlarged for the exploitation of a monopoly of another than for the exploitation of a unpatented article or for the exploitation or promotion of a business not embraced within the patent."); *Ohio-Sealy Mattress Mfg. v. Sealy,* 585 F.2d 821, 833–835 (7th Cir. 1978), *cert. denied,* 99 S.Ct. 1267 (1979) ("We quite agree with Ohio that a patented product, like any other, may be illegally tied."); *but cf., Transparent-Wrap Machine Corp. v. Stokes & Smith Co.,* 329 U.S. 637, 644–646 (1947); *Automatic Radio Mfg. Co. v. Hazeltine Research, Inc.,* 339 U.S. 827, 832–834 (1950).

[12] *Rex Chainbelt, Inc. v. Harco Products, Inc.,* 181 U.S.P.Q. 432, 435 (C.D. Cal. 1973), *aff'd,* 512 F.2d 993 (9th Cir. 1975), *cert. denied,* 423 U.S. 831 (1975); *Federal Sign & Signal Corp. v. Bangor Punta Op., Inc.,* 357 F.Supp. 1222, 1228, 1240 (S.D.N.Y. 1973) (no misuse where "... plaintiff was preceding in good faith to rely on the validity of its Liston patent, which covers the ... device."); *United States v. Consolidated Car-Heating Co., Inc.,* 87 U.S.P.Q. 20, 23–24 (S.D.N.Y. 1950) (no Sherman Act violation where a patent owner agreed to "loan" its licensee a patented electric furnace and required, as a condition of the license to use it to manufacture dentures with patented alloy, that the licensee purchased patented alloy for use in the furnace only from the patent owner or its authorized dealers; "Defendant, by reason of its ownership of the patent on the Ticonium alloy, is the only person entitled to manufacture the alloy. Therefore there can be nothing illegal in the defendant's requiring the laboratories to obtain the alloy only from it or from its authorized dealers."); *cf., Libbey-Owens-Ford Glass Co. v. Sylvania Industrial Corp.,* 64 F.Supp. 516, 517–518 (S.D.N.Y. 1945), *appeal dismissed,* 154 F.2d 814, 815–816 (2d Cir. 1946) (no misuse where a single patent had claims covering the composition sold and the process of using them).

[13] *Popiel Brothers, Inc. v. Schick Electric, Inc.,* 356 F.Supp. 240, 250–251 (N.D. 111. 1972), *aff'd on other grounds,* 494 F.2d 162 (7th Cir. 1974) (misuse where plaintiff "has declined to assert its apparatus patent against defendants, choosing instead

THE NATURE OF PRODUCTS AND RIGHTS SUPPLIED TOGETHER

A common element of an antitrust claim and a misuse defense is that the seller or licensor conditions the sale of the tying product or the grant of the license on the purchase of another product. Some courts have found no conditioning if the patent owner had never been asked for a separate license under the patent and, accordingly, had never refused to grant it.[14] However, the court has found conditioning even where the patent owner sold an unpatented material capable of use in a patented process and the law operated to supply an implied license to use the process.[15]

Where the patent owner offers a separate license to use the patent rights with materials, parts, or components from any source, the courts have said the terms of the separate license must be definite and must be the same as or more favorable to the licensee than the terms of any license the patent owner grants to purchasers of materials, parts, or components from it.[16] In other words, the royalties under both options

---

to use the method patent to suppress competition by the defendant in the sale of hair curling appliances."); *Baldwin-Lima-Hamilton Corp. v. Tatnall Meas. Sys. Co.,* 169 F.Supp. 131 (E.D. P.A. 1958), *aff'd,* 268 F.2d 365 (3rd Cir. 1959) ("The monopoly which the patent law grants with respect to an article covered by one patent may not be utilized to aide the patentee to exploit another article even though it is covered by another patent."); *cf., Jacquard Knitting Machines Co. v. Ordnance Gauge Co.,* 106 F.Supp. 59, 65–66 (E.D. Pa. 1952), *aff'd,* 213 F.2d 503 (3rd Cir. 1954)(misuse where patent owner did not charge infringement of the patent on the tied product); *Philad Co. v. Lescher Laboratories,* 107 F.2d 747, 748–749 (2d Cir. 1939) (misuse where tied product patent was not in suit); *Mercoid Corp. v. Minneapolis-Honeywell Reg. Co.,* 320 U.S. 680, 684 n.1 (patent on the tied product was owned by a third party so that, as to the parties in action, it ". . . is an unpatented device.").
[14]*Ansul Company v. Uniroyal Co., Inc.,* 306F 541, 562 (S.D.N.L) (1969), *aff'd in part* 448 F.2d 472 (2d Cir. Supp. 1971), *cert. denied,* 404 U.S. 1018 (1972); *Federal Sign Signal Corp. v. Bangor Punga Op. Inc.,* 357 F.Supp. 1222, 1240 (S.D.N.Y. 1973). *Compare, B.B. Chemical Co. v. Ellis,* 117 F.2d 832, 837–838 (1st Cir. 1941), *aff'd,* 314 U.S. 495 (1942); *Rex Chambelt Inc. v. Harco Products, Inc.,* 512 F.2d 993, 1001 n.2 (9th Cir. 1975), *cert. denied,* 423 U.S. 831 (1975) ". . . the fact that no one has yet asked for a direct license (and consequently no one was refused one) is evidence that there is no economic tying effect or misuse present . . . however, it is not conclusive of the point.").
[15]*B.B. Chemical Corp. v. Ellis,* 314 U.S. 495, 496–497 (1942); *Leitch Mfg. Co. v. Barber Co.,* 30 U.S. 458, 460–463 (1938).
[16]*Ansul Company v. Uniroyal Co. Inc.,* 306 F.Supp. 541, 563, 564 (S.D.N.Y 1969), *aff'd in pertinent part,* 44 F.2d 872, 882.N4 (2d Cir. 1971) (misuse were the offer to competitors to sell the unpatented material for the use in the method was "unreasonable and discriminatory"); *National Foam System v. Urquhart,* 202 F.2d 659, 662–664 (5th Cir.

4.2 THE LAW APPLIED TO TYING ARRANGEMENTS

must not be higher for the licensee who chooses not to purchase materials.

The decisions desrcibing owners' efforts to avoid this problem are legion. A couple of early examples are described here, and many others are confined to the notes.[17] For example, in *Barber Asphalt Corp. v. La*

1953); *Dehydrators, Ltd. v. Petrolite Corporation*, 117 F.2d 183, 184–187 (9th Cir. 1941); *Barber Corp, v. La Fera Greco Contr. Co.*, 116 F.2d 211, 214–216 (3rd Cir. 1940); *Urquhart v. United States*, 109 F.Supp. 409, 411–412 (Ct. Cl. 1953). *Compare, Congolium Industries Inc. v. Armstrong Cork Co.*, 366 F.Supp. 220, 228 (E.D.P. 1973), *aff'd*, 510 F.2d 334 (3rd Cir. 1975) *cert. denied*, 421 U.S. 988 (1975); *Hall Laboratories v. Springs Cotton Mills*, 112 F.Supp. 29, 32 (W.D. S.C. 1953), *aff'd*, 208 F.2d 500 (4th Cir. 1953); *Calhoun v. United States*, 339 F.2d 665, 668–670 (Ct. Cl. 1964); *Rohm and Haas Co. v. Corning Fiberglass Corp.*, F.Supp. 196 U.S.P.Q. 726, 734, 742–743 (N.D.A.l.a. 1977); *Watson Packer, Inc. v. Dresser Industries, Inc.*, F.Supp. 193 U.S.P.Q. 552, 559–560 (N.D. Tex. 1977); *Printing Plates Supplies Co. v. Crescent Engraving Co.*, 246 F.Supp. 654, 672–674 (W.D. Mich. 1965); *United States Gypsum Company v. National Gypsum Company*, 387 F.2d 799, 802 (7th Cir. 1967), *cert. denied*, 39 U.S. 988 (1968) (". . . there could be no misuse if the terms on which a license is available to those wishing to use [unpatented] tape manufactured by others are reasonably comparable to the terms for one who uses the patentee's tape.").

[17]*A. L. Smith Iron Co. v. Dickson*, 52 F.Supp. 566, 567–568 (D. Conn. 1943), *rev'd on other grounds*, 141 F.2d 3, 7 (2d Cir. 1944) (patent unenforceable even though licensee's selling unpatented bands of the patented combination hatch cover (a) separately stated the purchase price for the part and a specified amount per hatch cover for royalty when parts were purchased from them, and, (b) offered to grant a separate license to make, use, and sell the combination with parts from any source at the same amount per hatch cover, where there was evidence that "identical royalty agreements were not contemplated" and there was "no guarantee" to purchasers from others who might obtain licenses that "they may not be at a competitive disadvantage because of varying terms on the royalty agreements . . . even though the royalty might be stated at a fixed amount. . . ."); *Urguhart v. United States*, 109 F.Supp. 409, 411–412 (Ct. Cl. 1953) (patent owner misused patents on a method of producing fire-extinguishing foam where (a) it licensed manufacturers of unpatented foam stabilizers to make and sell that material at a royalty of 15 percent of the net selling price of the material and with a notice to purchasers that an unstated part of the purchase price was for a license to practice the process, and (b) offered a direct license to users for a royalty of 10 cents per pound, which the Court in 1953 found to be a higher rate per gallon than the royalty paid by the manufacturing licensee); *National Foam System v. Urguhart*, 202 F.2d 659, 662–664 (5th Cir. 1953) (same); *Ansul Company v. Uniroyal, Inc.*, 306 F.Supp. 541, 563–564 (S.D.N.Y. 1969), *aff'd in pertinent part*, 448 F.2d 872, 882 n.4 (2d Cir. 1971) (misuse where patent owners' offer to license competitors to sell the unpatented material for use in the patent method was "unreasonable and discriminatory"; license offered to competitors at $8.25 per gallon is higher than consideration paid by its cus-

THE NATURE OF PRODUCTS AND RIGHTS SUPPLIED TOGETHER

Fera Greco Contr. Co.[18] the court found misuse. The patent owner, through a licensee, sold unpatented emulsion at a price per gallon with a statement that the price included all royalties due. The royalty was

---

tomers for an implied license, which consideration was calculated as the difference between the patent owner's sale price and the cost of unpatented materials); *Solvex Corp. v. Freeman,* 459 F.Supp. 440, 442–446 (W.D. Va. 1977) (jury verdict on written interrogatories finding misuse where separate license was "on more onerous terms" when the thread is purchased from a competitor and there was refusal to license thread-manufacturing competitors); *cf., Rex Chainbelt, Inc. v. Harco Products Inc.,* 512 F.2d 993, 1002, n.3a. (9th cir. 1975), *cert. denied,* 423 U.S. 831 (1975) ("A great economic disparity in alternatives will just as effectively create or enforce a tie as the absence of choice."). Compare, *Sonobond Corporation v. Uthe Technology, Inc.,* 314 F.Supp. 878, 879–881 (N.D. Cal. 1970) (material issues of fact preclude summary judgment of misuse even though the amount of royalty a licensee pays "could vary" depending upon whether it purchased unpatented components from the patent owner, its manufacturing licensee, or a nonlicensed source; royalty for separate license of 6 percent of net sales of product including unpatented component creates less uncertainty than *Barber* and *Dehydrators*); *Watson Packer, Inc. v. Dresser Industries, Inc.,* 193 U.S.P.Q. 552, 559–560 (N.D. Tex. 1977) (no misuse where (a) owner of method patent offered to license users at royalty of $60 on each job performed using the method with a service company other than the patent owner and "no royalty" would be payable when the patent owner performed the services, (b) the patent owner offered to license defendant prior to suit, and (c) the defendant made a profit of $300 to $350 per job); *Rohm and Haas Co. v. Owens-Corning Fiberglas Corp.,* 196 U.S.P.Q. 726, 734, 742–743 (N.D. Ala. 1977) (no misuse where owner of method patents sold components designed, promoted, and sold for use in an infringing manner expressly stating that the price included a 4-cent-per-pound royalty, explained that a separate license could be acquired "simply by paying the same royalty rate," and offered to sell components at a price excluding the royalty where actual use was noninfringing); *Congoleum Industries, Inc. v. Armstrong Cork Company,* 366 F.Supp. 220, 228 (E.D. Pa. 1973), *aff'd,* 510 F.2d 334 (3rd Cir. 1975), *cert. denied,* 421 U.S. 988 (1975) (no misuse where "agency agreement" required use of a label license at a fixed royalty rate, granting of a user license upon request and granting of a license to other vendors at the patent owner's request); *Hall Laboratories v. Springs Cotton Mills,* 112 F.Supp. 29, 32 (W.D. S.C. 1953), *aff'd,* 208 F.2d 500 (4th Cir. 1953) (no misuse where royalty of 2 cents per pound of unpatented material whether purchased for patent owner or others and the patent owner sells the material excluding the royalty for unpatented uses); *Calhoun v. United States,* 339 F.2d 665, 668–670 (Ct. Cl. 1964) (no misuse where owner of patented packing construction licensed manufacturers to make and sell unpatented rings for use in the patented construction upon payment of royalty of one-quarter cent per construction unit, purchasers being licensed to use the rings under the patent and a direct license from patent owner to users of rings from any source was available and specified the same license rate); *Calhoun v. State Chemical Mfg. Co.,* 153 F.Supp. 293, (N.D. Ohio 1957) (same).
[18]*Barber Asphalt Corp. v. La Fera Greco Contr. Co.,* 116 F.2d 211, 214–216 (3rd Cir. 1940).

4.2 THE LAW APPLIED TO TYING ARRANGEMENTS

stated as 1 cent per square yard of concrete covered in practicing the patented process. The licensee also offered to grant a separate license at 1 cent per square yard of concrete covered. However, the licensee paid the patent owner a royalty of 2 cents per gallon. The court said the difference in rate bases established conditioning. In *Dehydrators, Limited v. Petrolite Corporation*,[19] a patent owner sold unpatented turkey red oil with no specified royalty charge for use in the patented process. The court said it misused the patent from 1933 to 1938 even though it offered a separate license to users for a royalty of 1 cent per 42 gallons of pipeline oil recovered by the process. The court said it misused the patent from 1938 to 1940, even though it offered a separate license for a royalty equal to the difference between the price of turkey red oil on the open market and the price of the patent owner's turkey red oil, such that the treating cost to the user was the same regardless of the source.

The law had difficulty deciding whether a patent owner does anything wrong by conditioning the grant of a patent license on the purchase of a product that the patent law of indirect infringement gives the patent owner the exclusive right to sell. In 1944, in the *Mercoid* cases, the Court held that the misuse and antitrust rules applied where patent owner (through licensees) supplied a "license" with an "unpatented" material, part, or component which was not a staple article of commerce and had no substantial noninfringing use.[20]

In 1952, Congress enacted a statutory definition of infringement in partial response to *Mercoid*. The 1952 Act defined *infringement* in three sections.[21]

(a) Except as otherwise provided in this title, whoever without authority makes, uses or sells any patented invention, within the United States during the term of the patent therefor, infringes the patent.

---

[19]*Dehydrators, Limited v. Petrolite Corporation,* 117 F.2d 183, 184–187 (9th Cir. 1941).
[20]*Mercoid Corp. v. Mid-Continent Co.,* 302 U.S. 661, 664–665, 667 (1944); *Mercoid Corp. v. Minneapolis-Honeywell Reg. Co.,* 320 U.S. 680, 682–684 (1944). This rule was foreshadowed, if not adopted, earlier by the lower courts. *B.B. Chemical Co. v. Ellis,* 117 F.2d 829, 834–836 (1st Cir. 1941), *aff'd,* 314 U.S. 495 (1942); *Philad Co. v. Lechler Laboratories,* 107 F.2d 747, 748 (2d Cir. 1939).
[21]35 U.S.C. § 271(a)–(c).

(b) Whoever actively induces infringement of a patent shall be liable as an infringer.

(c) Whoever sells a component of a patented machine, manufacture, combination or composition, or a material or apparatus for use in practicing a patented process, constituting a material part of the invention, knowing the same to be especially made or especially adapted for use in an infringement of such patent, and not a staple article or commodity of commerce suitable for substantial noninfringing use, shall be liable as a contributory infringer.

Congress also added section 271(d), which provided:[22]

(d) No patent owner otherwise entitled to relief for infringement or contributory infringement of a patent shall be denied relief or deemed guilty of misuse or illegal extension of the patent right by reason of his having done one or more of the following: (1) derive revenue from acts which if performed by another without his consent would constitute contributory infringement of the patent; (2) licensed or authorized another to perform acts which if performed without his consent would constitute contributory infringement of the patent; or (3) sought to enforce his patent right against infringement or contributory infringement.

In 1980, the Court held in *Dawson Chemical Co., Inc. v. Rohm and Haas Co.*,[23] that section 271(d) precluded a finding of misuse, where the rule of contributory infringement as defined in section 271(c) would prohibit the sale of the "tied" product, if sold by someone other than the patent owner. *Dawson* was a case where the owner supplied a product and the "license" under a process patent was implied. Section 271(d) does not deal with the issues arising where the patent owner utilizes tie-ins to exploit patents other than process or "combination" patents. Finally, the

---

[22]35 U.S.C. § 271(d) (1952).
[23]*Dawson Chemical Co., Inc. v. Rohm and Haas Co.*, 448 U.S. 176 (1980), *affirming*, 599 F.2d 685 (5th Cir. 1979).

section does not apply where the product supplied has uses other than with the patented invention.

4.3 THE THEORY OF TYING—ACQUIRING A "LIMITED MONOPOLY" BEYOND THE SCOPE OF THE RIGHTS

Most antitrust and misuse rules that condemn restrictions in "vertical" licenses are based in theory on the tying decisions. As discussed in Chapter 3, the Supreme Court said that its limits on royalty payments were extensions of this idea. The Supreme Court concluded that tying agreements are used by rights owners to attempt to obtain a "limited monopoly" in a market beyond the scope of the rights or to restrict competition in such a market. Expressions of this idea are quoted in the previous section from *Morton Salt* and *Motion Picture Patents*.

Tying agreements require a licensee to buy an unpatented product. However, this does not mean that competition in the sale of that unpatented product is restricted in any meaningful sense or that the patent owner is attempting to acquire a monopoly, even a "limited monopoly." Was the Morton Salt Company trying to obtain a monopoly and raise the price of all salt by requiring its canning machine customers to buy its salt? If an individual sells her house on condition that the buyer also take her car, General Motors and Ford will not notice. Restraining competition in the automobile market is probably the furthest thing from her mind. If she owns a can opener patent and licenses a company to make and sell can openers if it agrees to buy her car, she may be found to have misused her patent to attempt to monopolize the automobile industry.

4.4 THE COMPETITIVE EFFECTS OF TYING ARRANGEMENTS

There are many reasons for owners of intellectual property rights to employ tying arrangements. The problem with the law on tying arrangements is that it sometimes prohibits beneficial agreements having noth-

THE NATURE OF PRODUCTS AND RIGHTS SUPPLIED TOGETHER

ing to do with acquiring "limited monopolies" or restraining competition in unpatented products.

Consider a partially hypothetical example involving three complementary products—motion picture projectors, motion picture theater operation, and motion picture film making.[24] There is some existing demand and supply of projectors, theaters, and films. Assume there are many suppliers of those products. They are supplied under competitive structural conditions. Someone now improves the projector and patents the improvement. What should it do?

(a) Supply All Complements—Full Vertical Integration

The first option is full vertical integration into all three businesses. The patent owner could make the new projectors, acquire or build theaters, equip them with the projectors, acquire or build a motion picture studio, make movies, and show them in its theaters. If the patented projectors dramatically improve picture or sound quality, and the owner is as efficient as others in running theater and film studios, exploitation in that manner would result in the owner obtaining some share of the new markets for theaters and films. Its share would depend on the value of its projectors. The owner may displace some current theaters and studios. This strategy would not raise antitrust or misuse issues.

(b) Supply the Protected Product—Partial Vertical Integration

The next option is vertical integration into only one of those businesses. Full integration may not be a viable alternative for the owner. It has no expertise in operating theaters or producing films. It does know something about making projectors.

The patent owner might consider making and selling patented projectors for the highest price it may get. Given the existing supply of theaters and films, there will be some demand for the improved projector.

---

[24]For those wishing a more recent version of this situation, read *projector* as operating system software, *theater* as computer, and *film* as application software.

4.4 THE COMPETITIVE EFFECTS OF TYING ARRANGEMENTS

At the market-clearing price for these projectors, the demand for old projectors shifts downward and demand for theaters and films may go up.

(c) Supply the Protected Product with an Express Royalty-Bearing License—Partial Integration with Economic Discrimination

The patent owner may consider the possibilities for profitable discrimination. The owner will recognize that different theaters catering to different kinds of people will use projectors with different intensities to show different kinds of films. Hence, a single price for projectors may not maximize profits. More revenue might be earned if separate prices could be charged to theaters based upon the different values of the improved projector to them.

The patent owner would consider selling the projectors and negotiating patent licenses with each theater. The price for projectors would be lower. The license royalty would be based on the value of use to each licensee, such as a percentage of theater revenue. However, negotiating, policing, and collecting royalties under those licenses will be expensive. There are thousands of theaters. Those costs may gobble up the increased revenue. However, this alternative would not raise antitrust or misuse problems.

Notice that this pricing device also reduces the risk borne by the theaters of adopting the new projectors. The initial cost of switching to the new projector is reduced. If the new technology turns out not to work or to work less well than expected, the theaters have a smaller investment to lose.

(d) Supply the Protected Product at Price Proportional to Intensity of Use—Partial Integration with Economic Discrimination

Is there a way to discriminate without negotiating all these licenses? The value of the projector to different theaters is somewhat proportional to the amount of time it is used. The patent owner would consider attaching a meter to its projectors, and sell or lease them at a price, or rent them based on the metered use. This device would not measure or "meter" the value of the invention as well as would a meter attached to the theater's cash registers or ticket machines. However, it would measure value better than a lump sum projector payment. The owner would continue to incur the cost of negotiating, policing, and collecting payments under sales and lease agreements. These costs may render this possibility unprofitable. However, this alternative would not raise antitrust or misuse problems.

(e) Supply the Protected Product and a Complementary Product to Meter Intensity of Use—Partial Integration with Economic Discrimination

The owner may next consider tie-ins. The patent owner might seek to accomplish the same basic goals at lower transaction costs by selling or leasing the projectors with a simple license to use them only with films purchased from the patent owner. The patent owner would again price the projector lower than the sale option. It would buy or lease films at market prices and supply them to theaters at above-market prices. Theaters using more films or using them more frequently would, in effect, pay a higher projector "royalty."

The patent owner's ability to charge a higher price for films does not necessarily reflect any market power in the general market for films. It may reflect only the fact that a patent owner has not charged as high a price as it could have for projectors and collects "royalties" based on film supplies. The patent owner does not necessarily eliminate any film supplier. The film-producing industry may be as competitively structured as ever. To the extent that the owner is able to collect a price higher than the "market" price for films, it is able to do so only because theaters (that is, projector users) place that higher value on the improved projector.

Depending on supply conditions in the film market, the patent owner may or may not obtain market power in the film market. Moreover, to the extent that it does, this effect should not necessarily mean that consumers are harmed. The benefits from increased returns for use of the invention and potentially increased use of the invention during the term of the patent may more than offset the costs from any resulting reduction in the supply of films.

4.4 THE COMPETITIVE EFFECTS OF TYING ARRANGEMENTS

There are other reasons why a projector patent owner might wish to require its use with films obtained from it having nothing to do with acquiring a film monopoly.

(f) Supply the Protected Product and a Complementary Product that Would Be Supplied by a Single Seller—Reducing the Harm from Monopoly Supply of a Complement

First, it may be trying to reduce the losses from an existing film monopoly held by others. A film monopoly will hurt the owner's profits. There are only so many consumer dollars to be divided among the patent owner, projector suppliers, theater operators, and film makers. If film makers capture a larger share, there is a smaller share left for the others.

Suppose that films are supplied by a noncompetitive market. If the patent owner could reduce the price and increase the supply of films, the demand for projectors would be greater and the value of the invention greater. In that situation, the patent owner might agree to supply projector customers with films at below the market prices and charge a higher price for the projector. This projector price will be above the most profitable price it could obtain if films are supplied by a film monopolist.

(g) Supply the Protected Product and a Complementary Product at Prices that Encourage Use in Low-Cost Proportions

Second, the patent owner might use a tie-in to encourage the licensee to use both projectors and film in the most efficient proportions. The patent owner might use a tie-in because the demands for projectors and films are related in such a way that it may earn greater revenue by reducing the price of projectors below the "monopoly" price and supplying films at greater than the "competitive" price. This might happen even if all theaters are identical and economic discrimination is not the goal. This assumes that theaters can use projectors and films in different ratios. This is a type of *variable input substitution* problem.

For many products, different ratios of components, materials, or other inputs may be used to make a final product. An inefficient ratio of variable inputs will be used if their relative prices do not accurately reflect their true relative costs. If the price for one input greatly exceeds its cost and the prices of others are close to cost, too little of the relatively expensive input will be used and too much of the others. The same problem may arise where complementary products are purchased and used by the ultimate consumer.

(h) Supply the Protected Product and a Complementary Product to Assure Compatibility and Quality

Third, the restriction may assure in the lowest-cost way that the films supplied are technically compatible with the projector. The Supreme Court has declared that a licensor, like a product supplier, may lawfully dictate minimum quality specifications to its licensees and customers. For example, a patent owner may require that lessees of its patented machines use them only with supplies of specified standards necessary to assure proper functioning of the machine.[25]

(i) Supply a Complementary Product to Reduce the Transaction Costs of Express Licensing

Fourth, owners may sell a product used in a patented method or system to reduce the transaction costs of expressly licensing users individually. The owner of a patent may be unable to capture any of the value of the invention if its only options are to use the invention or to grant express licenses in exchange for royalties. Owners of process and system patents are frequently unable to directly exploit the invention.

The process or system may be used or made by thousands or millions of people or firms. The patent owner cannot possibly capture much of its value by vertical integration. Eli Whitney could not possibly have exploited a cotton gin patent by acquiring every cotton plantation or every cotton mill in the United States. Likewise, it would be extraordinarily expensive to grant thousands of written licenses. The costs of negotiating, policing, and enforcing licenses to each user may exceed the value of the process or system to them.

---

[25]*International Salt Co. v. United States,* 332 U.S. 392, 397–398 (1947); *International Business Machines Corp. v. United States,* 298 U.S. 131, 138–140 (1936).

4.4 THE COMPETITIVE EFFECTS OF TYING ARRANGEMENTS

When tying arrangements are used to reduce transaction costs of licensing, the owner seeks to convey a license with the product. It may do so by a notice on the label or package. If the law operates to imply a license if the owner says nothing to the buyer, the owner may reduce its "licensing" costs even further by saying nothing. It does not matter to the owner whether the product is useful only with the patented process or system or has other uses, so long as all the people who use the patented process or system also acquire and pay for a "license" by purchasing the product from the owner.

Often, this means that the owner must have a low-cost remedy against infringement. However, enforcement action against all process users and system makers is likely to be relatively expensive for the same reason transaction costs were large. Unless enforcement costs are also low, this form of "licensing" may be of little use to the owner. The doctrines of contributory infringement seek to reduce the cost of infringement suits by permitting actions against other component or material suppliers. The patent rule makes other suppliers of some unpatented product liable for infringement to reduce the number of suits that must be brought to stop the infringement. In 1944, the Supreme Court in *Mercoid v. Mid-Continent* essentially held that the contributory infringement remedy was not available against suppliers of materials and components if the process or system patent owner was also supplying those products.[26] As discussed earlier, Congress changed that result for certain products.

One would assume that the policy of reducing the costs of infringement actions would also apply to reducing the costs of licensing. Reducing the costs of permitting use is as valuable as reducing the costs of stopping use. Hence, one might suppose that any tying arrangement for the purpose of reducing transaction costs would be permissible. The nature of the product would not be dispositive.

A patent owner should probably be permitted to reduce transaction costs by supplying any type of product to meter use of any type of invention. Indeed, the supply of a product having many unpatented uses is less likely to restrict competition in the general market for that product than the supply of a product having no other uses. If the product has no other uses, and entry into the business is difficult for reasons other than the patent, the tying arrangement may provide a source of lasting

---

[26]*Mercoid Corp. v. Mid-Continent Inv. Co.*, 320 U.S. 661, 664–665 (1944).

market power after the patent expires. The Patent Act may confine this area of permission to supplying a product having a single use.[27]

(j) Supply the Protected Product and a Complementary Product to Acquire Market Power in Supply of the Complement

However, the patent owner may be trying to acquire a monopoly in film production. Under that possibility, the patent owner has no market power as a film maker. It considers sacrificing potential profits from the projector business to increase its market share in films. The patent owner will be able to capture a share of the market for films only if it sacrifices profits it could have made from selling projectors. The patent owner will be able to profit from acquiring a share of the market for films only if it acquires some market power. It must acquire such a large share that restricting its output decreases total industry output sufficiently to raise price without inducing new entry or increased production by the remaining film makers. For this to be sensible, the discounted present value of those future profits must be greater than the present-day profits forgone to obtain this position.

Even then, any decrease in output in the film market is accompanied by an increase in output of projectors. Theater owners will purchase films from the patent owner only to the extent that the additional cost of doing so is offset by the benefits from obtaining at a lower cost. Theaters using unpatented projectors are free to continue to do so. The suppliers of films to such theaters are not affected by the restriction. The only part of the film industry affected by the restriction is the part which benefits from use of the patented projector.

There is no reason to believe that theater-goers will be adversely affected unless the patent owner's market power in film making is likely to survive the expiration of the patent. During the term, theater-goers may not be worse off. Theater owners may show films at the same rate and price as they had before the patent issued. Increased use of the projectors may offset decreased output of films. Theater-goers are adversely affected only if the film monopoly lasts beyond the term of the patent.

In short, for this strategy to be profitable, the owner must have market power in the market for projectors, theaters that use projectors must

---
[27]There is uncertainty about the interpretation of section 271(d)(5).

4.5 THE LEADING DECISIONS AND STATUTES ON EXTENDING THE RIGHTS

constitute the predominant source of demand for the films, and entry into both markets must be difficult.[28]

4.5 THE LEADING DECISIONS AND STATUTES ON EXTENDING THE RIGHTS

(a) *Heaton-Peninsular Button-Fastener*

In 1896, the Court of Appeals for the Sixth Circuit in *Heaton-Peninsular Button-Fastener Co. v. Eureka Specialty Co.*[29] recognized the utility of tying arrangements for metering the value of the rights to different licensees. The patent owner owned several patents on machines for fastening buttons to shoes. The machines automatically attach the buttons to the shoes by stapling them in the proper place. The staples had to be the right size and shape for use in the machine. However, in every other respect, the staples were ordinary metal staples. The patent owner manufactured and sold the machines. The owner's machines had a metal label saying:

> CONDITION OF SALE
>
> THIS MACHINE IS SOLD AND PURCHASED TO USE ONLY WITH FASTENERS MADE BY THE PENINSULAR NOVELTY DO., TO WHOM THE TITLE TO SAID MACHINE IMMEDIATELY REVERTS UPON VIOLATION OF THIS CONTRACT OF SALE.

The defendant sold staples to the patent owner's customers. The Sixth Circuit declared that the defendant indirectly infringed the machine patent.

The Sixth Circuit acknowledged that there was no patent on the staples. The staples were not within the "direct monopoly of the patent" any more than were the buttons or the shoes. The defendant said that declaring the sale of staples to be indirect infringement would "create a monopoly in an unpatented article." The Sixth Circuit said it would not.

The Sixth Circuit first asked whether those who purchased machines from the patent owner directly infringed the patent by using them

---

[28]William F. Baxter, "The Viability of Vertical Restraints Doctrine," *California Law Review* **75,** 933 (1987).
[29]*Heaton-Peninsular Button-Fastener Co. v. Eureka Specialty Co.,* 77 F. 288, 296–800 (6th Cir. 1896).

contrary to the notice, namely with staples they purchased from someone else. The Sixth Circuit concluded that the patent owner sold the machine subject to a restricted license to use it only with staples made by the patent owner. The purchaser's use was not authorized by that license and would constitute infringement.

The Sixth Circuit then asked whether that restriction was contrary to public policy and unenforceable, because the patent owner was using "his monopoly as to create another monopoly in an unpatented article." The Sixth Circuit said that the property rights of a patent owner, like all other property rights, were subject to the "general law of the land." The Sixth Circuit then asked whether there was a public policy that limited the rights of a patent owner to define the terms of licenses because those terms may create a "monopoly in the unpatented article."

The Sixth Circuit said that the first public policy to consider was that favoring "wide liberty in the making of contracts." The Sixth Circuit then analyzed the economic effects of the restriction the patent owner had employed. Suppose, said the Court, that the patented machine dramatically reduced the cost of making shoes. The patent owner could go into the business of manufacturing shoes. If it wished, it could sell its shoes for a price slightly lower than the cost to anyone else of making shoes using alternative techniques and acquire a monopoly in selling shoes. The "monopoly" would be a monopoly only in shoes fastened with buttons. No one would say that monopoly was illegitimate or "obnoxious to public policy," because the "great consuming public" was benefited by the invention and its exploitation in that way. Other shoe manufacturers may not like what had happened. However, the interest of consumers controlled.

If that method of exploitation was not obnoxious to public policy, the court asked, why was it obnoxious to policy for the patent owner by a system of licenses to permit others to use the machine on condition that they bought some minor part of the shoe, such as the button fastener, from the patent owner? The court noted that the thing that affected makers of wire staples for shoe manufacture was the invention of a machine that, by reason of its "simplicity, superior capabilities, its cheapness, and accuracy," had driven all other methods of fastening buttons to shoes out of use. Use of those machines gave rise to a large market for wire sta-

4.5 DECISIONS AND STATUTES ON EXTENDING THE RIGHTS

ples "adapted in size and shape to use with the new mechanism." The market for other sizes and shapes of staples for button fastening disappeared. To the extent that the patent owner wished to be the sole supplier of staples adapted for that use, it controlled the market for staples only to the extent the patented machine was better and cheaper than other ways of attaching staples and would last only unless superseded by yet better and cheaper devices.

The invention destroyed the demand for staples not adapted for use with the machine and created the demand for staples fitted for that use. Because the patent forbids anyone from using the machines, the patent destroys the market for staples fitted for that use. If a monopoly in unpatented staples results, that monopoly is simply incidental to the monopoly in the use of the invention, is legitimate, and is not obnoxious to public policy.

The court noted that requiring machine users to buy staples from the patent owner "may or may not result in the engrossment of the market for staples." The device would give the patent owner no control over the markets for staples for uses other than in the patented machine. If staples adapted in size and form for use in the patented machine are also capable of use in other machines, then the patent owner may have no monopoly in the market for staples.

The court also asked why the patent owner would want to be the only supplier of staples adapted for that use. The court said that the fasteners were used as "counters" by which a royalty proportional to actual use of a machine was determined. In other words, the button-fastening machine is more valuable to a purchaser who uses it to make a larger number of shoes. It is desirable for the patent owner to be able to charge different royalties to users depending upon the value of the machine to them. If the law prohibits patent owners from using staples for counters, they will have to resort to more expensive ways of charging machine users in some way proportional to the value of machines to them. They will attach expensive tamper-proof counters to the machines and inspect them every few months and send bills. They may simply trust their users to count the number of staples they use or the number of shoes they make and engage in expensive audits from time to time to make sure that users are not cheating. Public policy would certainly not favor the waste that would result from these other ways of metering use of the machine.

THE NATURE OF PRODUCTS AND RIGHTS SUPPLIED TOGETHER

(b) *Henry v. A.B. Dick*

In 1912, in *Henry v. A.B. Dick*,[30] the Supreme Court adapted the views of the Sixth Circuit expressed in *Heaton Button-Fastener*. The Court's opinion was written by Justice Lurton, formerly a judge on the Sixth Circuit Court of Appeals and the author of the opinion in *Heaton Button-Fastener*. The A.B. Dick Company owned two patents covering a duplicating machine known as the "Rotary Mimeograph." The machine used stencils and ink to duplicate documents. A.B. Dick made and sold mimeograph machines. Each machine bore this notice:

> LICENSE RESTRICTION
> THIS MACHINE IS SOLD BY THE A.B. DICK CO. WITH THE LICENSE RESTRICTION THAT IT MAY BE USED ONLY WITH THE STENCIL PAPER, INK AND OTHER SUPPLIES MADE BY A.B. DICK COMPANY, CHICAGO, U.S.A.

This defendant, Sidney Henry, sold the owner of a machine a can of ink suitable for use in the machine. Henry knew about the notice on the A.B. Dick machine and sold the ink knowing that it would be used in the machine. A.B. Dick sued Henry for contributing to infringement by the owner of the machine.

In an opinion by Justice Lurton, four Justices affirmed the decision that Henry was a contributory infringer. Three Justices dissented. Justice Lurton devoted most of the opinion to the question of whether the owner would directly infringe the patent by using the machine with ink obtained from Henry. Justice Lurton's opinion asked whether A.B. Dick could sell the patented machine and retain part of the exclusive right to use the machine, namely, the right to use it with ink or other supplies obtained from anyone other than A.B. Dick. Justice Lurton concluded that a patent owner could sell a patented machine and, by conditions or restrictions imposed at the time, retain some of the exclusive rights in the use of the machine.

Justice Lurton also asked whether this limitation was lawful. As he had in *Heaton Button-Fastener*, Justice Lurton found no basis in the

---

[30]*Henry v. A.B. Dick Co.*, 224 U.S. 1, 25–36 (1912).

4.5 DECISIONS AND STATUTES ON EXTENDING THE RIGHTS

Patent Act or the Sherman Act to declare the restriction unlawful. Justice Lurton rejected the argument that a restriction of this kind "gives to a patentee the power to extend his monopoly so as to cause it to embrace any subject, not within the patent, which he chooses."

Justice Lurton said that stencils, ink, and other articles used in the machine would continue to be unpatented. Ink and similar articles could be sold for any purpose save one—"they may not be sold to a user of one of the patentee's machines with the intent that they shall be used in violation of the license." The effect of the restriction is to preserve the patent owner's rights against contributory infringement. The doctrine of contributory infringement had the same consequence whether or not the patent owner was selling supplies. The sale of supplies to someone to infringe the patent was prohibited. Justice Lurton recognized the conflict. Hence, he asked whether "the doctrine of contributory infringement operates to extend the monopoly of the patent over subjects not within it. . . ." He concluded that the doctrine did not.

Justice Lurton did not see how the doctrine could affect any market other than the market for the sale of supplies to users of the patented machine. That was a market that the patentee created by inventing a new machine. If the patent owner kept the machine to itself and used its own ink, no one else would have sold ink for use in the patented machines. By selling the machine subject to the restriction, the patentee "took nothing from others and in no wise restricted their legitimate market." Justice Lurton noted that the lower courts had rejected the same argument when they applied the rule of contributory infringement to preclude the sale of one element of a patented combination.

For Justice Lurton, A.B. Dick had simply devised a better way to reap benefits of its discovery. It sold the machine at its cost and took its "profit" by selling supplies, rather than charging a higher price for the machines and not selling supplies. The restriction was lawful.

(c) *Motion Picture Patents*

In 1914, Congress changed the antitrust statutes by adding section 3 of the Clayton Act. Section 3 prohibited the sale of a product, whether patented or unpatented, on the condition that the purchaser not deal in the goods of another, if the effect was substantially to lessen competition.[31]

In 1917, the Supreme Court reversed its position in *Henry*.[32] In *Motion Picture Patents,* the patent covered a part of motion picture projectors that fed the film through the machine. Projectors using the patented part had improved picture quality and exposed films to less wear. This permitted a single reel of film to be used more times. The Motion Picture Patents Company owned the patent. Motion Picture Patents also owned a patent that related in some way to motion picture films.

In 1912, Motion Picture Patents granted a license to the Precision Machine Company authorizing that company to make and sell projecting machines. The Precision Machine Company agreed to sell machines only "under the restriction and condition that such . . . machine shall be used solely for exhibiting or projecting motion pictures containing the inventions of reissued letters patent No. 12,192, leased by a licensee of the licensor while it owned said patents and upon other terms to be fixed by the licensor and complied with by the user while said machine is in use and while the licensor owned said patents (which other terms shall only be the payment of a royalty or rental to the licensor while in use)." The Precision Machine Company also agreed to attach a plate to every machine showing the date of the machine part patent and containing the words:[33]

> THE SALE AND PURCHASE OF THIS MACHINE GIVES ONLY THE RIGHT TO USE IT SOLELY WITH MOVING PICTURES CONTAINING THE INVENTION OF REISSUED PATENT NO. 12,192, LEASED BY A LICENSEE OF THE MOTION PICTURE PATENTS COMPANY, THE OWNER OF THE ABOVE PATENTS AND REISSUED PATENT, WHILE IT OWNS SAID PATENT, AND UPON OTHER TERMS TO BE FIXED BY THE MOTION PICTURE PATENTS COMPANY AND COMPLIED WITH BY THE USER WHILE IT IS IN USE AND WHILE THE MOTION PICTURE PATENTS COMPANY OWNS SAID PATENTS. THE REMOVAL OR DEFACEMENT OF THIS PLATE TERMINATES THE RIGHT TO USE THIS MACHINE.

---

[31]15 U.S.C. § 15.
[32]*Motion Picture Patents Co. v. Universal Film Mfg. Co.,* 243 U.S. 501, 508, 516–518 (1917).
[33]Id. at 506–507.

4.5 DECISIONS AND STATUTES ON EXTENDING THE RIGHTS

The license also said that Precision would not sell a machine for less than a price set by the Motion Picture Patents Company. Precision agreed to pay a royalty of $5 on some machines and a percentage of selling price on others.

It is unclear from the opinion whether the Motion Picture Patents produced and leased motion picture films. The implication from the language in its license to Precision was that it did not. Motion Picture Patent presumably granted licenses to others under its film patent to make and lease films, and licensed Precision to make and supply projectors.

Precision sold a projector to the 72nd Street Amusement Company, which operated a playhouse in New York City. The projector had the required plate. In August 1914, the reissue patent 12,192 related to films expired. Later that year, the Prague Amusement Company leased the 72nd Street Playhouse and began showing films.

After the film patent expired, the Universal Film Manufacturing Company made two films and sold them to the Universal Film Exchange, which in turn supplied them to the Prague Amusement Company for use on the projectors. The patent owner sent a letter to the 72nd Street Amusement Company and to the Universal Film Exchange notifying them that they were infringing the patent on the projectors. The patent owner then commenced an action against Prague, the theater operator, the Universal Film Exchange, the film seller, and Universal Film Manufacturing Company, the maker of the films.

The Supreme Court affirmed the decision of the Second Circuit Court of Appeals that there was no infringement by any of the defendants. The District Court had apparently held that the limitation on use of the machines by a notice attached to the machine was "invalid" and that 72nd Street Amusement Company, the purchaser of the machine, and its lessee, the Prague Amusement Company, had an "implied license" to use the machine as it had been used. Justice Clarke's opinion for five members of the Court affirmed those decisions. Justice McReynolds concurred in the result only. Justice Holmes, with Justices McKenna and Van Devanter, dissented.

Justice Clarke said there were two questions. The first was whether the owner of a patent on a machine could license someone to sell it and "by a mere notice attached to it limit its use by the purchaser . . . to films which are no part of the patented machine, and which are not patented?"

THE NATURE OF PRODUCTS AND RIGHTS SUPPLIED TOGETHER

The other question was whether a patent owner could license someone to sell the machine and "by a mere notice attached to such machine, limit the use of it by the purchaser . . . to terms not stated in the notice, but which are to be fixed, after sale, by such assignee [patent owner], in its discretion?" In other words, the Supreme Court said it was limiting its decision to whether the restrictions in the notice were to be given effect or ignored.

Justice Clarke declared the restrictions in the notice "invalid," as had the lower courts. Because the restrictions were "invalid," the use of the machines with films from another supplier did not constitute direct infringement. Accordingly, there was no infringement for the Universal Film Exchange to assist by supplying film.

Justice Clarke's decision left intact the contributory infringement remedies available to the owner's patents on machines, who did not wish to exploit the patents by selling machines or by licensing others to sell machines. However, Justice Clarke's opinion was very important to the owners of all other machine patents. Justice Clarke's opinion deprived those patent owners of one of the most efficient ways of capturing the value from the use by others of their inventions. The first but not the only victim was the Motion Picture Patents Company.

For reasons discussed earlier, the Motion Picture Patents Company may have had no interest in obtaining a monopoly in the supply of motion picture films, either for itself or, even more implausibly, its licensee. Rather, the Motion Picture Patents Company was simply trying to meter the value of its machines to the 40,000 theaters that were using them by the time of the action. Motion Picture Patents was trying to capture the value of the invention to those different theaters in the most efficient way—by revenues derived from leasing films.

The success of Motion Picture Patents' ability to meter that use depended upon its ability to supply, through another licensee, all of the films used in those machines. If the number of film production companies was much smaller than the number of theaters, the rights against contributory infringement may have been vital to the patent owner's method of exploiting the machine invention. If one other film company could lawfully supply films and the Motion Picture Patents Company's only remedy was 40,000 actions for direct infringement, the enforcement costs made this form of exploitation unworkable.

4.5 DECISIONS AND STATUTES ON EXTENDING THE RIGHTS

Justice Clarke determined the "invalidity" of the notice by saying it depended upon the scope of the right to "use" the invention granted in the statute. To interpret the meaning of the right to "use" a patented machine, Justice Clarke turned to "three rules long established by this Court, applicable to the patent law." The first was that the "scope of every patent is limited to the invention described in the claims contained in it, read in light of the specification." The second was that "the patentee received nothing from the law which he did not have before, and that the only effect of his patent is to restrain others from manufacturing, using, or selling that which he has invented."

From those "rules," Justice Clarke proceeded to condemn the restriction, because its effect would be to "extend the scope of its patent monopoly." The "restriction is invalid because such a film is obviously not any part of the invention of the patent-in-suit; because it is an attempt, without statutory warrant, to continue the patent monopoly on this particular character of film after it [the film patent] has expired, and because to enforce it would be to create a monopoly in the manufacture and use of moving picture films, wholly outside of the patent-in-suit [, the machine patent,] and the patent law as we have interpreted it."

Justice Clarke declared that the restriction in the notice was outside the scope of patent rights because it was not a restriction on use of the machine. It was a restriction only on use of materials. This linguistic tour de force sufficed for Justice Clarke to declare that the patent law had nothing whatsoever to do with the validity of the restriction. Justice Clarke said of the notice:[34]

> The grant [of the patent] is of the exclusive right to use the mechanism to produce the result with any appropriate material, and the materials with which the machine is operated are no part of the patented machine or of the combination which produces the patented result. . . . Both in form and in substance the notice attempts a restriction upon the use of the supplies only, and it cannot, with any regard to propriety and use of language, be termed a restriction upon the use of the machine itself.

---
[34] Id. at 512–513.

> Whatever the right of the owner may be to control by restriction the materials to be used in operating the machine, it must be derived from the general law from the ownership of the property in the machine, and it cannot be derived from or protected by the patent law. . . .

Justice Clarke's assertion to the contrary, the only restriction was on use of the machine with certain materials, or use of certain materials with the machine. It was not a restriction on use of films only, since as Justice Clarke noted earlier in his opinion, without use of the patented projectors, it was impossible to show films "successfully." Justice Clarke said the validity of the restriction must be determined under the "general law." Justice Clarke never did identify the "general law" that condemned the restriction. Justice Clarke did note that Congress had enacted a provision of the antitrust laws that seemed directly related to the practice. However, Justice Clarke said it was unnecessary to apply the congressional solution.

Justice Clarke's opinion also referred to a third "long established rule." It was that "the primary purpose of our patent laws is not the creation of private fortunes for the owners of patents, but is 'to promote the progress of science and useful arts. . . .' " Justice Clarke[35] said that the patent "monopoly granted to inventors was never designed for their exclusive profit or advantage; the benefit to the public or community at large was another and doubtless the primary object in granting and securing that monopoly." As Justice Clarke put it, the Court had never "modified this statement of the relative importance of the public and private interests involved in every grant of a patent."

In other words, Justice Clarke perceived that the interest of the public was somehow inconsistent with patent owners earning "private fortunes" or obtaining "profit or advantage." Under a property rights theory, it is the goal of patent law to permit patent owners to capture as much of the profits from use of the invention as possible. Since the supply of films operates to lower transaction costs incurred by patent owners, and enhance their "private fortunes," the rule was potentially suspect to Justice Clarke if some other "public" interests can be invoked to limit it.

---

[35] 62 U.S. 322 (1859).

4.5   DECISIONS AND STATUTES ON EXTENDING THE RIGHTS

Justice Clarke disposed of the idea that the public would benefit from the practice of selling a patented machine at cost and collecting royalties based on the number of units of some material used with the machine. Justice Clarke said this was the "clearest possible condemnation of the practice adopted." Because the patent owner obtained its "entire profit" from the sale of supplies, that proved that the owner "intends to and does derive its profit, not from the invention on which the law gives it a monopoly, but from the unpatented supplies with which it is used, and which are wholly without the scope of the patent monopoly. . . ."

Unlike Justice Lurton, Justice Clarke did not believe that the profit that the patent owner derived from selling films was derived entirely from the value of the invention. Justice Holmes, with Justices McKenna and Van Devanter, recognized that it was, and dissented on that basis.

The Supreme Court said that it was deciding whether a patent owner could reserve rights by a notice attached to the machine. The Court said that it was not deciding whether the use of the patented machine could "validly" be restricted to specific supplies by a "special contract between the owner of a patent and the purchaser or licensee." The Court implied that it might be possible to sell machines and sign written licenses with users containing the same language that the Motion Picture Patents Company put on the notice attached to the machine. However, the transaction costs of doing so would frequently be large. The *Motion Picture Patents* decision was not rendered moot by a sea of written license agreements between machine sellers and purchasers. It was too late for the Motion Picture Patents Company and any other patent owner unfortunate enough to have relied on the *Heaton Button-Fastener* case and put the notice containing the restriction on the machine. The 40,000 theaters that owned projectors bearing the notice were not about to sign a license. They could use any films they wanted and could use them without paying a royalty. They had no incentive to sign a license agreement that the Supreme Court implied that the Motion Picture Patents Company might have lawfully required them to sign earlier.

Motion Picture Patents left the doctrine of contributory infringement intact. However, the decision effectively eliminated the rule's value to the owners of machine patents that were most efficiently exploited by the patent owner or a licensee supplying the machine. If the patent owner or its licensee supplied the machine and attempted by a notice on the machine to reserve rights against contributory infringement, the Supreme Court had said the attempted reservation was ineffective.

(d) *Carbice*

In the 1930s, *Motion Picture Patents* was extended to render unenforceable similar restrictions in licenses to use patented processes or parts of patented articles.[36] In these cases, the patent owners granted licenses to use a patented process or to make and use a patented combination article only with unpatented materials or components obtained from the owner or a licensee authorized to sell materials or components. The Court declared the restrictions unenforceable. Hence, the sale of materials or components for the licensee's use was not contributory infringement.

The *Motion Picture Patents* decision left open one other inefficient possibility for the owners of patented machines to meter use of their inventions by supplying materials. The Motion Picture Patents company lost its ability to do so by supplying the machines. Suppose the patent owner did not supply the machines. Suppose the patent owner simply went into the business of supplying materials for use in the machine and turned its back on its customers' making the machine for themselves or having someone else supplying it to them for use with those materials. Could the patent owner supply materials or the components and invoke its contributory infringement remedies, when others contributorily infringed?

In 1931, the Supreme Court in *Carbice Corp. v. American Patents Dev. Corp.*[37] said no. The American Patents Development Corporation owned a patent on a package for transporting ice cream. The patent claimed a package having an insulated compartment containing solid carbon dioxide, dry ice, situated so that the compartment containing the dry ice was surrounded completely by the ice cream. The patented "package" therefore was made and used only when a container of insulating material had dry ice and perhaps even ice cream in it.

---

[36]*Leitch Mfg. Co. v. Barber Co.*, 302 U.S. 458 (1938) (process patent); *Carbice Corp. v. American Patents Devel. Corp.*, 283 U.S. 27, 30–35 (1931) (patented combination).
[37]283 U.S. 27 (1931).

4.5 DECISIONS AND STATUTES ON EXTENDING THE RIGHTS

American Patents Development licensed the Dry Ice Corporation under its package patent. The Dry Ice Corporation made and sold dry ice. The Dry Ice Corporation gave its dry ice customers notice in each invoice that the shipment was on the condition the dry ice be used only in containers obtained from or approved by the Dry Ice Corporation, and that containers obtained from or approved by the Dry Ice Corporation be used only with dry ice of the Dry Ice Corporation. The Court noted the Dry Ice Corporation had never supplied containers and had never insisted that containers be purchased from it. Hence, customers were free to purchase containers (without dry ice) from anyone they wished.

Another company, Carbice, began selling dry ice to an ice cream maker intending to have that company use it in the patented packages. Carbice advertised its dry ice for that purpose and guaranteed that its dry ice was as good as that of the Dry Ice Corporation. The patent owner brought an action for infringement against Carbice, the competing dry ice seller.

The Second Circuit Court of Appeals said there was contributory infringement.[38] Judge Swan's opinion, joined in by Judge Learned Hand and Judge Augustus Hand, said that *Motion Picture Patents* did not prevent a finding of contributory infringement. *Motion Picture Patents* said the restriction in the notice was invalid only because the unpatented film formed no part of the patented machine. The dry ice was a component of the package as defined by the claims.

Judge Swan said that the ice cream manufacturer, Marchiony, purchased nothing from the Dry Ice Corporation except dry ice. The Motion Picture Exchange sold films to a theater that bought a projector from a licensee. The ice cream maker bought nothing from the patent owner or its licensee that was used in connection with the defendant's dry ice. Hence, there was no transaction with the patent owner or licensee to give rise to a "license" for the ice cream manufacturer to make the completed package.

Judge Swan considered the possibility that the ice cream company might have the right to reuse containers that it purchased from others for initial use with dry ice from the Dry Ice Corporation, and reuse with dry ice from Carbice. Even if the ice cream company was reusing contain-

---

[38]38 F.2d 62, 65 (2d Cir. 1930).

ers that it had used previously with dry ice from the Dry Ice Corporation, Judge Swan said that would be to reconstruct the patented package and not within the rights of a purchaser.

The Supreme Court reversed. The Court declared that American Patents Development was attempting to use the patent to obtain a monopoly in the market for dry ice.[39] The Supreme Court said that the patent owner was attempting to extend its package monopoly to obtain for its licensee a monopoly in selling dry ice. Accordingly, the Supreme Court said the action for infringement against a competing dry ice supplier should be dismissed.

Justice Brandeis's opinion for the Supreme Court did not address either of the points that had been depositive to the Court of Appeals for the Second Circuit. Justice Brandeis, like Justice Clarke thirteen years earlier, did not discuss the rule of contributory infringement. Justice Brandeis simply said that the only business of the Dry Ice Corporation was making and selling dry ice. The defendant Carbice sold dry ice. Justice Brandeis said Carbice was charged with contributory infringement because it sold dry ice to "customers" of the Dry Ice Corporation with "knowledge" that the dry ice would be used by the customer in patented packages.

Brandeis said the owner of the patent could prohibit entirely the sale and use of transportation packages, and grant licenses on terms "consistent with the limited scope of the patent monopoly." Justice Brandeis asserted that the patent owner "may not extract as the condition of a license that unpatented materials used in connection with the invention shall be purchased only from the licensed; and if it does so, relief against one who supplies such unpatented materials will be denied."

Justice Brandeis said that the relief sought was indistinguishable from that denied in *Motion Picture Patents*. Justice Brandeis said that *Motion Picture Patents* meant that a patent owner could not derive its profit from sale of unpatented supplies used with the invention. He said that the monopoly could be "so expanded" that the owner of a patent "might conceivably monopolize the commerce in a large part of unpatented materials used in its manufacture." The owner of a patent on a machine might secure a "partial monopoly" on unpatented supplies. The owner of patent on a process might secure a "partial monopoly" on an

---

[39]*Carbice Corp. v. American Patents Development Corp.*, 283 U.S. 27 (1931).

4.5 DECISIONS AND STATUTES ON EXTENDING THE RIGHTS

unpatented material employed in it. The owner of this patent might "conceivably secure a limited monopoly" of dry ice and ice cream.

From this, Justice Brandeis concluded the Dry Ice Corporation "has no right to be free from competition in the sale of solid carbon dioxide." The patent owner could not obtain relief because its licensee, the Dry Ice Corporation, was attempting "without sanction of law, to employ the patent to secure limited monopoly of unpatented material used in applying the invention."

The problem with Justice Brandeis's analysis was that the Dry Ice granted no licenses, much less licenses conditioned on the purchase of dry ice from Dry Ice. Dry Ice simply sold dry ice. If the purchaser of the dry ice obtained a license, it was only because the law implied a license. The license did not continue after the dry ice had vanished into the atmosphere.

Justice Brandeis seemed to insist that, if the patent owner wished to retain its rights against contributory infringement, it would have to avoid exploiting the patent by engaging in the sale of an unpatented component of a patented machine or an unpatented material supply used in a patented process. In order to obtain the enforcement cost savings that arise from contributory infringement remedies, the patent owner would have to sacrifice the transaction cost savings involved in engaging in activities that would be contributory infringement, namely, selling a component or supplies and collecting "royalties" as part of the selling price and in proportion to use of the invention by different users.

In order to obtain efficiency in enforcement, the patent owner would have to forgo efficiency in exploitation. The only other option was to retain the efficiencies in exploitation and forgo the efficiencies of contributory infringement. Justice Brandeis seemed to want the patent owner to sue ice cream manufacturers one at a time.

The patent owner's response to that decision was to announce to the industry that the Supreme Court had not declared the patent invalid, but had precluded it from bringing actions against dry ice companies. Hence, the patent owner said it would henceforth commence actions for infringement against those who made and used complete transportation packages using dry ice purchased from anyone other than the Dry Ice Company.

Carbice asked the Court to grant a further hearing. The Supreme Court accepted that request and summarily declared the patent invalid. In so doing, the Court avoided the necessity of having to explain exactly what it expected the patent owner to do to comply with its earlier decision. Did it have to buy its way out of the license granted the Dry Ice Company and stay out of the dry ice business? Did it have to grant licenses to users to buy dry ice from anyone and, if so, at what rates? Did it have to license competing dry ice suppliers? By declaring the patent invalid, the Supreme Court avoided the necessity of answering these questions. The Court eliminated the issue by eliminating the patent.

(e) *Leitch*

In 1938, the Supreme Court confirmed in *Leitch v. Barber* that the *Carbice* rule applied in the same way to process patents.[40] The Barber Company owned a patent on a process of making a concrete road by applying a film of bituminous emulsion to fresh concrete to retard evaporation during curing. The Barber Company supplied bituminous emulsion to road builders.

Another company, Leitch Manufacturing Company, began selling bituminous emulsion to road builders knowing that it would be used in the patented process. Barber sued Leitch for contributory infringement. The Court of Appeals for the Third Circuit concluded that there was contributory infringement and nothing in *Carbice* to prohibit that relief.

The Supreme Court, in an opinion by Justice Brandeis, reversed that decision. As he had in *Carbice,* Justice Brandeis said nothing about the doctrine of contributory infringement. Justice Brandeis said that the patent owner had done something wrong. What did Barber do wrong? Barber sold bituminous emulsion, an "unpatented staple article of commerce produced in the United States by many concerns and in common use by the customers for many purposes." Barber sought to use the patent "to secure a limited monopoly in the business of producing and selling the bituminous material for practicing and carrying out the patented method."

How? Justice Brandeis said Barber did not engage in road building, did not grant written licenses to road builders, and did not even "seek to make road builders pay a royalty for employing the patented method." Rather, Barber adopted a "method of doing business which is the practical equivalent of granting a written license with the condition that the patented method may be practiced only with emulsion purchased from

---

[40]*Leitch Mfg. Co. v. Barber Co.,* 302 U.S. 458, 460 (1938).

4.5 DECISIONS AND STATUTES ON EXTENDING THE RIGHTS

it." Justice Brandeis said that if a road builder buys emulsion from Barber, "the law implies authority to practice the invention." Justice Brandeis did not explain why the law implied that authority. Justice Brandeis then said that Barber sued a competing supplier of the material who sold to road builders for that use.

Barber used the patent to "suppress competition in the production and sale of staple unpatented material for this use in road building." If Barber sold the material and the doctrine of contributory infringement precluded everyone else from selling the material for that use, it would seem that the patent law, not the Barber Company, "suppressed competition" in selling the material. Justice Brandeis did not want to blame the law or abolish the rule of contributory infringement. Rather, he seemed determine to blame Barber.

He did that by simply asserting that the "patent did not confer upon the Barber Company the right to be free from competition in supplying unpatented material to be used in practicing the invention. . . ." Justice Brandeis said that proposition was "settled by the rule declared in the *Carbice Corp.* case." Those words come very close to saying that *Carbice* means there is no action for contributory infringement. If patents confer no rights against contributory infringement, Justice Brandeis's statement is true. If the rule against contributory infringement does grant such rights, his statement is false. If *Carbice* is that broad, there was no escape.

Justice Brandeis said Barber tried to limit the *Carbice* case to situations in which the patent owner entered into a "contract or agreement aimed at expansion of the patent monopoly." Barber argued that there had to be a "contract or notice" that attempted to "expand the patent monopoly" by limitations, restrictions, or conditions in an agreement. The Barber Company said it had done none of these things. It simply sold bituminous emulsion, without condition, restriction, or limitation and, whatever rights the purchasers have, they are the rights "implied by law."

Justice Brandeis would have none of it. Justice Brandeis said *Carbice* denied relief on the "broad ground that the owner of the patent monopoly, ignoring the limitation 'inherent in the patent grant,' sought by its method of doing business to extend the monopoly to unpatented material used in practicing the invention."

The Leitch company lost its rights against contributory infringement because it sold the product under circumstances in which customers obtained an implied license to carry out the patented process. Justice Brandeis asserted that the Barber Company was not trying to obtain a "royalty" for use with its invention. Rather the Barber Company was attempting to acquire some "limited monopoly."

Barber was likely to have had nothing of the kind in mind. There were many other uses for bituminous emulsion. The Barber Company probably had no hope of becoming a bituminous emulsion monopolist for all uses. The "limited monopoly" that concerned Justice Brandeis was a limited monopoly of bituminous emulsion for use with the invention. However, a "monopoly" in the supply of bituminous emulsion for that use is of no greater value to Barber than the value of the invention. The only purpose of supplying bituminous emulsion was likely to have been that to reduce the cost of transactions with road builders and provide a return for use of the invention proportional to the amount of use by different road builders. Those building longer, wider roads paid more than those building shorter, narrower ones.

(f) *Morton Salt* and *B.B. Chemical*

In the years after *Carbice* and *Leitch,* patent owners attempted to continue to obtain the efficiencies in exploitation that resulted from supplying components or materials, while satisfying the *Carbice* rule, by offering to their customers a separate license to use the process or make the patented machine with components or materials obtained from any source. While they were sometimes successful in this endeavor, they often were not. The lower courts declared that to satisfy the Supreme Court rules, the terms of the separate license had to be definite and had to be the same as or more favorable than the terms of the "license" that the patent owner granted to purchasers of materials or components from it.[41]

These developments forced patent owners to make a decision to exploit the invention inefficiently and enforce it efficiently or exploit it efficiently and enforce it inefficiently. In 1942, that changed.

---

[41]*Compare Urquhart v. United States,* 109 F.Supp. 409, 411–412 (Ct. Cl. 1953); *Al Smith Iron Co. v. Dickson,* 52 F.Supp. 566, 567–568 (D. Conn. 1943), *rev'd on other grounds,* 141 F.2d 3 (2d Cir. 1944); *Dehydrators Ltd. v. Petrolite Corporation,* 117 F.2d 183, 184–187 (9th Cir. 1941); *Barber Asphalt Corp. v. La Fera Greco Contr. Co.,* 116 F.2d 211, 214–216 (3rd Cir. 1940).

4.5 DECISIONS AND STATUTES ON EXTENDING THE RIGHTS

In 1942, the Court went a step further. In *Morton Salt Co. v. G.S. Suppiger Co.*[42] and *B. B. Chemical Co. v. Ellis*,[43] the Supreme Court declared that a patent owner dealing in materials rendered the patent entirely unenforceable against contributory infringement and direct infringement. In *Morton Salt,* a patent owner leased a patented salt-dispensing machine to canners under a license to use it on the condition that only the patent owner's salt tablets be used with the machine. The patent owner brought an action for infringement against a maker of infringing machines. The Court held that the patent was unenforceable even against a machine seller. The Court found the patent unenforceable even though there was no evidence of any injury to competition sufficient to establish a violation of the antitrust laws, section 3 of the Clayton Act. In *B. B. Chemical,* a companion case, the Supreme Court declared that this type of exploitation also eliminated all rights against those who induced infringement. The Court also declared that it was "without significance" that this was the only practical way of licensing others to use the invention.

After *Morton Salt* and *B. B. Chemical,* a patent owner's choice was to exploit the invention efficiently and not enforce it at all, or exploit it inefficiently and enforce the patent. Since no enforcement renders the patent valueless, the patent owners opted not to exploit the inventions efficiently. Inefficient exploitation necessary to retain their rights was better than no exploitation.

(g) The *Mercoid* Cases

The language in *Leitch* that bituminous emulsion was a staple article of commerce having many other uses suggested that perhaps the *Carbice* and *Leitch* rules did not apply to materials useful only in practicing the invention. There seemed to be little support for that idea based on *Motion Picture Patents* and *Carbice.* In *Motion Picture Patents,* the Supreme Court said that the only practical way to show a film was to use a projector with a patented film-feeding mechanism. In *Carbice,* the Supreme Court said that there had been no significant commercial production of

---

[42] 314 U.S. 488, 491 (1942).
[43] 314 U.S. 495, 496–497 (1942).

dry ice before the production by the Dry Ice Corporation and that 90 percent of the Dry Ice Corporation's sales were for use in the patented package. The fact that films and dry ice were useful almost only in the patented machine or to make a patented package did not seem to matter.

In the late 1930s and early 1940s, patent owners argued that *Carbice* and *Leitch* did not apply if the patent owner was selling a part, component, or material that had no substantial noninfringing use. If the component or material had no substantial noninfringing use, its sale by anyone else was, under the prevailing rule, presumptively constituted contributory infringement. If selling such a product constituted infringement and would be enjoined, there seemed to be little reason to consider that product to be "unpatented" or to consider that the patent owner who wished to sell the product was "extending its patent monopoly." It was the rule of contributory infringement, not the patent owner's conduct, that brought the sale of that product within the patent "monopoly." The lower courts generally rejected that distinction.[44]

In 1944, in *Mercoid Corp. v. Mid-Continent Co.*,[45] the Supreme Court confirmed that there was no exception for a product that had no use other than in an infringing machine or process. The Supreme Court in the *Mercoid* cases declared the patent owner forfeited its rights against contributory infringement by licensing a company to sell a part of a patented combination, even though the part had no other use.

The Mid-Continent Company owned the Cross patent for a home heating system. The patent claimed a "combination" having three main components—a motor-driven stoker to feed fuel into a furnace, a room thermostat to control feeding of fuel by the stoker, and a stoker switch that responded to low temperature in the furnace and caused the stoker to feed fuel to prevent the fire from going out.

The Mid-Continent Company granted Minneapolis-Honeywell an exclusive license to make, use, sell, and sublicense others to make, use, and sell, systems. Minneapolis-Honeywell paid royalties to Mid-Continent based on sales of stoker switchers that were used in systems embodying the Cross patent. Minneapolis-Honeywell produced and sold

---

[44]*B.B. Chemical Co. v. Ellis,* 117 F.2d 829, 834–836 (1st Cir. 1941), *aff'd,* 314 U.S. 495 (1942); *Philad Co. v. Lechler Laboratories,* 107 F.2d 747, 748 (2d Cir. 1948).
[45]320 U.S. 661, 664–665, 667 (1944).

4.5 DECISIONS AND STATUTES ON EXTENDING THE RIGHTS

stoker switches and advertised that the right to use the Cross system patent was only granted to the user when stoker switches of Minneapolis-Honeywell were purchased and used in the system.

Mid-Continent and Minneapolis-Honeywell were not in the business of installing heating systems in homes throughout the United States. The Supreme Court did not ask why the patent owner or its exclusive licensee were not in that business. It is not far-fetched to assume that the installation of the patented system could be conducted far more efficiently by numerous local companies designing systems specifically for the many kinds of furnaces, feed motors, and thermostats found in homes throughout the United States. What those mechanics would lack was the stoker switch to prevent the fire from going out during periods of relatively warm whether.

Minneapolis-Honeywell made and sold that switch. Minneapolis-Honeywell also apparently granted sublicenses to other companies to sell switches. The Court did not say whether the switches sold by Minneapolis-Honeywell had any uses other than in a Cross system. The Mercoid Company also made and sold stoker switches. The Mercoid stoker switches had no use other than in the Cross system. The Supreme Court assumed that Mercoid sold those switches for the purpose and with the intent that they be used to make an infringing system. For that reason, the Court of Appeals had declared Mercoid guilty for contributory infringement and had enjoined those sales.

The Supreme Court, with Justices Frankfurter, Roberts, and Jackson dissenting, declared that Mid-Continent could not obtain relief. It employed the patent to secure a "limited monopoly" in an "unpatented material or device [that] is itself an integral part of the structure embodying the patent." Justice Douglas' opinion for the court had said that *Carbice, Leitch, Morton Salt,* and *B.B. Chemical* meant that the "owner of the patent may not employ it to secure a limited monopoly of an unpatented material used in applying the invention." Justice Douglas said that, where the owner did so, both "direct and contributory infringement suit were disallowed. . . ."

Justice Douglas perceived the case as merely raising the question whether the same rule applied, if the device sold was an integral part of the patented system, rather than a material consumed in the operation of a patented machine or process. Justice Douglas said there was no difference "in principle." Justice Douglas's explanation was mainly a rehash of things the Court had said in *Motion Picture Patents* and *Carbice*.

Justice Douglas also said that a patent was "privilege which is conditioned by public purpose." To protect "the public interest," the "limits of the patent are narrowly and strictly confined to the precise terms of the grant." The "necessities or conveniences of the patentee do not justify any use of the monopoly of the patent to create another monopoly."

Justice Douglas did not explain what "monopoly" the Mid-Continent was trying to obtain. Its stoker switches had no use other than in the Cross patent. The market for stoker switches was derived entirely from the market for patented systems. The separate monopoly that Justice Douglas wanted to stamp out simply did not exist.

Mid-Continent had nothing to gain by a monopoly in stoker switches. Rather, Mid-Continent was almost certainly trying to exploit the market for the patented system in the most efficient way, namely, by supplying switches to the thousands of home heating contractors and installers to use with the best motors and thermostats available in particular situations.

Justice Douglas would have had no objection to Mid-Continent hiring thousands of people to run around the country granting written licenses to thousands of homeowners, or hiring thousands of people to go into the home heating installation business. However, it would have been enormously wasteful for Mid-Continent to do so.

When Justice Douglas said the "necessities or convenience" of patentees did not justify Mid-Continent's method of exploitation, Justice Douglas meant that the ability and desire of a patent owner to capture the maximum possible value from use of its invention was not important.

Justice Douglas's comments about limiting patents to the "precise terms of the grant" were obviously inconsistent with the existence of the doctrine of contributory infringement that, in all instances, enjoined activities not within the "precise terms" of the grant. If they had been, there would be direct infringement. As had Justice Brandeis before him, Justice Douglas said not a word about the law of contributory infringement or the reasons the courts had developed the rule.

4.5 DECISIONS AND STATUTES ON EXTENDING THE RIGHTS

Justice Douglas's only comment was that the "result of this decision, together with those which have proceded it, is to limit substantially the doctrine of contributory infringement." He said that "[w]hat residuum may be left we need not stop to consider." The only residuum was for situations in which the patent owner engaged in using or selling complete systems or processes or licensed others to do so. Any effort to achieve transaction cost savings by supplying parts or components resulted in forfeiting contributory infringement remedies and, depending upon the way it was done, all other remedies.

Justice Douglas said not one word about the impact of the decision on incentives to make inventions. Justices Roberts and Frankfurter in separate opinions tried to say that Justice Douglas's opinion did not mean that the doctrine of contributory infringement ceased to exist. However, both Justices said the decision was correct because it was simply an application of the *Carbice* rule.

They said *Carbice* was premised on the view that the sale of components by others was not contributory infringement, because the use of the components by their customers was not direct infringement. Those Justices probably drew that conclusion because the Court in *Carbice* had referred to sales by Carbice of dry ice to the patent owner's "customers." However, it was clear from Justice Brandeis's opinion that the decision did not turn on that fact. Indeed, the facts seemed clear enough that, while the ice cream company in *Carbice* bought dry ice from the patent owner's licensee and from Carbice, that company did not use the dry ice from Carbice with anything that it had purchased from the patent owner. There was simply nothing from which the Court could imply a license in the Carbice Company's customers based on some transaction with the patent owner. Justice Frankfurter's effort to save the rule seemed to fall short.

Justice Jackson alone analyzed the effect of the contributory infringement doctrine and the effect of the patent owner's supplying unpatented materials or components. Unlike Justices Brandeis and Douglas, Justice Jackson said a patent was simply property. Justice Jackson noted that, if the law did not exclude others from selling what he called "strategic unpatented elements" of the patented combination, "the patented system is so vulnerable to competition has to be almost worthless."

Justice Jackson recognized that without a contributory infringement remedy, enforcement costs may be so great as to render many patents worthless. On the other hand, Justice Jackson was also concerned that permitting the contributory infringement doctrine resulted in the exclusion of others from selling old devices. He recognized that the rule precluded selling old devices only by those who "knowingly and intentionally" sold the device for use in a patented combination. However, Justice Jackson said that the "less legal rights depended on someone's state of mind the better."

Justice Jackson seemed to believe that the rule of contributory infringement might be applied erroneously with sufficient frequency that unpatented component sales would be enjoined, even though they were sales for some other use. Justice Jackson said the real issue was whether to leave combination patents with "little value" or whether to give them value and take the risk of adverse "economic effects" on the sale of elements that are not a part of a "legal monopoly." On balance, Justice Jackson concluded that the potential costs of the second effect were greater than the potential benefits of the first, and said, in that situation, the patent owner should have remedies only against direct infringement.

In a companion case, *Mercoid Corp. v. Honeywell*,[46] the Supreme Court reached the same conclusion in an action by Minneapolis-Honeywell against Mercoid for infringement of Honeywell's Freeman patent. The patent covered a system for controlling hot-air furnaces. The system included three thermostats for its operation.

Rather than grant a single exclusive license, as had Mid-Continent, Honeywell granted five licenses to "its manufacturing competitors" to make and sell a furnace control that included a thermostatic switch, useful in a Freeman system. Honeywell offered to license Mercoid under the same terms granted to its other five licensees. Mercoid refused the license. The furnace control was sold with the notice that it included a license to make one installation of a Freeman heating system.

The Court found that the furnace control was something less than a complete claimed invention. The Court also said that the furnace control provided the sequence of operations that was the "precise essence

---

[46]320 U.S. 680 (1944).

4.5 DECISIONS AND STATUTES ON EXTENDING THE RIGHTS

of Freeman's advance in the art." Mercoid also supplied furnace controls that had no use other than accomplishing the operations of the Freeman patent. Mercoid defended its action on the basis that Honeywell had done something wrong and counterclaimed saying that Honeywell had violated the antitrust laws.

The Court of Appeals had rejected both the defense and the antitrust claim. The Supreme Court in another opinion by Justice Douglas reversed, saying that the effort "to control competition on this unpatented device plainly violates the anti-trust laws. . . ." Honeywell could not obtain "any decree which directly or indirectly helps to subvert the public policy which underlies the grant of its patent."

Justice Douglas did not explain how the Court reached the conclusion that Honeywell was trying to monopolize the supply of furnace controls for use in the Freeman system, when it had licensed the five other companies to sell them and had tried to license Mercoid on the same terms.

After *Mercoid v. Honeywell,* a patent owner that wished to exploit the invention at lowest transaction cost not only forfeited all of its rights to prevent infringement, it also subjected itself to a claim for treble damages under the antitrust laws. The Supreme Court did not explain how Mercoid could conceivably have been damaged by Honeywell's activities.

The law of contributory infringement became relatively unimportant after this series of decisions. The rights against contributory infringement were likely to reduce enforcement costs in the same type of situations where a patent owner engaging in the same activity could reduce transaction costs. If it was most efficient for the patent owner to capture the value of the invention by supplying components or parts, it was also likely for others to capture that value in that way. Contributory infringers were highly likely to arise.

If the patent owner wished to exploit the invention by selling the components or parts or by licensing others to do so, it destroyed the enforceability of the patent and subjected itself to damages. The only door left open to owners of combination patents was to integrate into supplying the completed patented product or directly granting licenses to users to make and use it. If that was too expensive, the patent simply vanished in economic significance. The only other hope the Supreme Court left for patent owners was to obtain a patent that covered the precise product that it sold, and nothing more.

(h) *Special Equipment*

In 1945, one year after the *Mercoid* cases, in *Special Equipment Co. v. Coe*,[47] the Supreme Court in an opinion by Justice Stone said that the Commissioner of Patents could not refuse to issue a patent on a component or part of a larger system, even though the owner of the patent said that the only reason it was seeking that patent was to have an action for direct infringement against someone who might sell the component or part.

Special Equipment Company owned a patent on an apparatus for processing pears by cutting off the stems, splitting the pears, and coring them. The machine included, among other parts, a knife that cut the pear into half sections. That is the machine that the patent owner had intended to sell. The patent owner conceded that it was seeking another patent on the same machine without the knife, because it might be possible for someone to make and sell such a machine, and the sales of that machine would reduce the sales of the patented machine.

The Commissioner of Patents refused to issue the patent. The Supreme Court said the Commissioner could not refuse to issue the patent. In the context, Justice Stone said that "[c]ontrol of the part could not be used as a means of enlarging an already acquired control [through patent] of the whole." Justice Stone said that "obviously licensing the subcombination [, the part], which is less useful than the whole, would not, in any circumstances disclosed by the record, be a practical means of enlarging the use of the whole."

Justice Stone said the failure to "acquire control of the whole would be a legitimate reason for wishing to acquire and retain control of a part, if it involves a patentable invention." Justice Stone said it was plainly "legitimate to use a patent on the subcombination as a means of preventing appropriation of others of petitioner's more important complete invention, which he is using, where there is absent, as there is here, any purpose to enlarge the monopoly of either invention."

---

[47]324 U.S. 370, 371–377 (1945).

4.5 DECISIONS AND STATUTES ON EXTENDING THE RIGHTS

Justice Stone said that if a petitioner makes two inventions and one of them includes the other in its entirety, it is "evident that the value of former [namely the entire machine] would be greatly impaired if the sub-combination invention could be freely used by other."

In other words, one year after *Mercoid,* six members of the Supreme Court declared that the value of a patent on a machine would be greatly impaired if parts could be supplied by others. They said it did not enlarge the "monopoly" of the whole machine for the inventor to acquire control of a part. If those Justices really believed that, their concurrence in the *Mercoid* decisions seems clearly to have been mistaken. Justices Douglas, Black, and Murphy, in dissent, said exactly that.

Justice Douglas also said that it was "a mistake . . . to conceive of a patent as but another form of private property." Justice Douglas said it was a mistake to subordinate the "public purpose of the grant to the self-interest of the patentee." Justice Douglas did not suggest what should be substituted for the self-interest of patentees or suggest any theory to justify a patent system, if the property theory were discarded.

Curiously, Justice Douglas said that if the patent owner was trying to acquire a patent on a part or component of a larger machine and was not proposing to sell that part or component, the patent should not be issued. That would leave the inventor's only remedy against sellers of components or parts to be an action for contributory infringement, which remedy Justice Douglas had been so instrumental in eliminating as useful. However, this time six justices refused to go along.

(i) The 1952 Amendment to the Patent Act

In 1952, Congress enacted a statutory definition of infringement in partial response to *Mercoid.* Congress amended the Patent Act to include for the first time a section expressly defining infringement.[48] That section expressly provided that whoever sells a component of a patented machine or combination, or a material for use in practicing a patented process, constituting a material part of the invention, knowing the same to be especially made or adopted for use in infringement of the patent

---

[48] 35 U.S.C. § 271 (1976).

and not a staple article or commodity of commerce for substantial noninfringing use, is libel for contributory infringement.[49] Congress also added section 271(d), quoted earlier (section 4.2).

Section 271 said the doctrine of contributory infringement existed. Congress also seemed to signal that it wished to make it possible for patent owners to achieve the transaction cost savings of supplying parts, components, or materials and preclude their sale by others. However, it did not become clear until 1980 that patent owners could do so without granting or offering to grant written licenses to makers or users of complete systems or processes, and without offering the same licenses to other suppliers of materials, components, or parts.

(j) *Dawson*

In 1980, the Court held in *Dawson Chemical Co., Inc. v. Rohm and Haas Co.*[50] that section 271(d) precluded a finding of misuse where the rule of contributory infringement as defined in section 271(c) would prohibit the sale of the "tied" product, if sold by someone other than the patent owner. The case involved a process patent. The process required use of a certain chemical. The patent owner sold a chemical useful in carrying out the process. The sale of that chemical by another would constitute contributory infringement of the patent. The owner also supplied its customers with instructions for performing the patented process. The owner stated its intention not to grant licensees to other chemical manufacturers or to process users who obtained their chemical from another source. The Court found that section 271(d) precluded a finding of misuse.

The Supreme Court, with Justices White, Brennen, Marshall, and Stevens dissenting, held that the owner of a process patent did not engage in patent misuse by selling a material useful only in carrying out the process and refusing to grant written licenses to process users or to other material sellers. The Court's opinion, by Justice Blackmun, said

---

[49]35 U.S.C. § 271(c).
[50]*Dawson Chemical Co., Inc. v. Rohm and Haas Co.*, 448 U.S. 176 (1980), *affirming,* 599 F.2d 685 (5th Cir. 1979).

4.5 DECISIONS AND STATUTES ON EXTENDING THE RIGHTS

that section 271(d) precluded a finding of misuse where the patent owner sold a material that if sold by another would have constituted contributory infringement (in that it had no other uses), provided instructions for performing the process, and stated that it would not grant licenses to other manufacturers of the material or to process users obtaining their materials from other sources.

Justice Blackmun, unlike Justices Brandeis and Douglas before him, discussed the doctrine of contributory infringement. Justice Blackmun opened by noting that the doctrine of contributory infringement enabled a patentee to obtain relief against those whose "acts facilitate infringement by others" and had been part of the law since *Wallace v. Holmes* in 1871. Justice Blackmun also noted that the "idea" that a patentee should be denied relief if it attempted illegally "to extend the scope of its patent monopoly" was of more recent origin and probably went back to *Motion Picture Patents.*

Unlike Justices Brandeis and Douglas before him, Justice Blackmun noted that the two concepts were closely related and needed to be considered together. Justice Blackmun returned to the origins of the doctrine in *Wallace v. Holmes* and noted that the purpose of the rule was to reduce enforcement costs by eliminating the need for a patent owner to engage in the "almost insuperable task of finding and suing all" those directly infringing a patent. Justice Blackmun noted that, if enforcement costs against direct infringers were very high, others could capture the profits from use of the invention by supplying a product that facilitated infringement by others and, as a practical matter, be insulated from remedies by the sheer cost of enforcement against them. Justice Blackman said the doctrine was necessary to "protect patent rights from subversion," noting Judge Taft's explanation in *Thomas-Houston Electric Co. v. Ohio Brass.*

Unlike Justices Brandeis and Douglas, Justice Blackmun noted that an injunction against contributory infringement inevitably suppressed "competition in an unpatented article of commerce." However, Justice Blackmun also noted that "proponents of contributory infringement" defended that result, because it reduced enforcement costs and because "the market for the unpatented article flows from the patentee's invention."

Justice Blackmun said that the case before the Court seemed to bear significant factual similarity only to the *Leeds & Catlin* and *Mercoid* cases. Those decisions involved the sale of articles that were "essential to the patented inventions, and that were unsuited for any commercial non-infringing use." Justice Blackmun said that the "majority of cases" in which the misuse doctrine developed involved efforts by patent owners to "extend patent protection to control staple articles of commerce."

Justice Blackmun found in sections 271(c) and 271(d) a "compromise" between the rules of contributory infringement and patent misuse. Justice Blackmun said that section 271(c) adopted a "restrictive definition of contributory infringement" that distinguished between staple and nonstaple articles of commerce. Justice Blackmun said the sale of dry ice in the *Carbice* case would not have been contributory infringement. Justice Blackmun did not note that, at the time of the *Carbice* decision, 90 percent of the dry ice sold by the patent owner and all of the dry ice sold by the defendant was used in the patented package.

Justice Blackmun said that it would never be necessary to invoke patent misuse to prevent a patent owner from enjoining the sale of a product with noninfringing uses. Congress had eliminated infringement liability in those cases. In order to say that, Justice Blackmun had to ignore section 271(b), which plainly adopted the formulation of the Second Circuit Court of Appeals in *Individual Drinking Cup*. The sale of a staple article could constitute infringement where the seller did something in addition to the sale to induce the customer to make the complete patented product or use the patented process, such as by advertising that the product could be used in that way.

Having concluded that a patent owner could never obtain an injunction against the sale of "so-called staple articles of commerce," Justice Blackmun was led to the view that Congress intended to permit a patent owner to supply nonstaple articles, namely articles with no noninfringing use and to refuse to license others to sell those products without engaging in patent misuse. Justice Blackmun said a patentee may sell a "non-staple article himself while enjoining others from marketing that same good without his authorization." In that way, Justice Black-

4.5 DECISIONS AND STATUTES ON EXTENDING THE RIGHTS

mun said that the patent owner is able to "control the market for that product."

Justice Blackmun also noted that the section authorized the patent owner to license others to engage in conduct that would be contributory infringement. This ability to license would be worthless if the patent owner had no power to enjoin them in the absence of a license. Justice Blackmun said that the patent owner's sale of the unpatented material and its refusal to license others to sell it, while bringing action for contributory infringement, did allow the patent owner to "suppress competition in the market for an unpatented commodity." That was precisely what the statute expressly protected.

The accused infringer argued that the patent owner was not merely engaging in the conduct described in section 271(d). That section said that it was not misuse to do one or more of three things: sell a product, the sale of which would constitute contributory infringement; license someone else to sell such a product; and enforce the patent against infringement or contributory infringement. The patent owner sold such product, sought to enforce the patent against contributory infringement, and refused to license others to sell the product.

Justice Blackmun said the section permitted such licensing but did not require it and that to require the granting of such licenses would run contrary to the long settled view that "the essence of a patent grant is the right to exclude others from profiting by the patented invention." Justice Blackmun correctly noted that, if section 271(d) required such licensing, the patentee would be forced to forfeit the protection against contributory infringement because it would be forced to authorize infringement. Noting that compulsory licensing was a rarity in the patent system, Justice Blackmun said that there was no misuse even though the patent owner refused to grant such licenses.

Justice White, with Justices Brennen, Marshall, and Stevens, dissented, saying that the section protected patent owners from charges of misuse only if they granted licenses to all those who did not purchase the material from them.

The theoretical economic damages originally conceived in the tying area underlie much of the law dealing with other types of agreements. The deficiencies of the tie-in rules infect other areas. Hence, a fundamental change in the tie-in rules would require the courts to reanalyze other types of restriction. That reevaluation would lead to major changes.

(k) The 1988 Amendment to the Patent Act

In 1988, section 271(d) of the Patent Act was amended to change the law on tying arrangements, package licensing, and, perhaps, grantbacks.[51] That section now provides:[52]

> (d) No patent owner otherwise entitled to relief for infringement or contributory infringement of a patent shall be denied relief or deemed guilty of misuse or illegal extension of the patent right by reason of his having done one or more of the following: (1) derived revenue from acts which if performed by another without his consent would constitute contributory infringement of the patent; (2) licensed or authorized another to perform acts which if performed without his consent would constitute contributory infringement of the patent; (3) sought to enforce his patent rights against infringement or contributory infringement; (4) refused to license or use any rights to the patent; or (5) conditioned the license of any rights to the patent or the sale of the patented product on the acquisition of a license to rights in another patent or purchase of a separate product, unless, in view of the circumstances, the patent owner has market power in the relevant market for the patent or patented product on which the license or sale is conditioned.

This change seemed simply to limit the prohibition on tying arrangements and package licensing in one respect: The patent owner must have market power in some market before separate markets are likely to be adversely affected. However, statements by Congressmen accompanying the change suggested a much broader interpretation (section 2.7(c)).

---

[51] 35 U.S.C. § 271(d).
[52] 35 U.S.C. § 271(d).

4.6 LICENSING MORE THAN ONE PATENT OR COPYRIGHT IN A SINGLE AGREEMENT— PACKAGE LICENSING

Licenses commonly include more than a single patent or copyright. There is no general antitrust or misuse prohibition against such a license.

(a) The Law

In the 1940s, the Court considered a case involving the licensing of a block or package of copyrighted movies to theaters. The Court held that a copyright owner violated section 1 of the Sherman Act by compelling a licensee to accept an entire block or package of films.[53] Mandatory package leasing of copyrighted motion picture films was found to constitute a violation of the Sherman Act in 1948. In *United States v. Paramount Pictures, Inc.*, the Court declared:[54]

> Block-booking is the practice of licensing, or offering for license, one feature or group of features on condition that the exhibitor will also license another feature or group of features released by the distributors during a given period. . . . Block booking prevents competitors from bidding for single features on their individual merits. The District Court held it illegal for that reason and for the reason that it "adds to the monopoly of a single copyrighted picture that of another copyrighted picture which must be taken and exhibited in order to secure the first." That enlargement of the monopoly of the copyright was condemned below in reliance on the principle which forbids the owner of a patent to condition its use on the purchase or use of patented or unpatented materials. . . . The court enjoined defendant from performing or entering into any license in which the right to exhibit one feature is conditioned on the licensee's taking one or more other features.

* * *

---

[53]*United States v. Loew's, Inc.*, 371 U.S. 38, (1962); *United States v. Paramount Pictures*, 334 U.S. 131, (1948).
[54]*United States v. Paramount Pictures, Inc.*, 334 U.S. 131, 156–158 (1948)

We do not suggest that films may not be sold in blocks or groups, when there is no requirement, express or implied, for the purchase of more than one film. All we hold to be illegal is a refusal to license one or more copyrights unless another copyright is accepted.

That rule was reaffirmed in *United States v. Loew's, Inc.*[55] The Court in *Loew's* identified two alleged "adverse effects on free competition resulting from [the] illegal block booking." The first was that "television stations forced by appellants to take unwanted films are denied access to films marketed by other distributors, who, in turn, were foreclosed from selling to the stations." Second, "[a] substantial portion of the licensing fees represented the cost of the inferior films which the stations were required to accept."

In *Loew's* the Court also said that there "may be rare circumstances in which the doctrine we have enunciated under § 1 of the Sherman Act prohibiting tying arrangements involving patented or copyrighted tying products is inapplicable." The Court said "it [is] difficult to conceive of such a case, and the present case clearly is not one." That language may mean that conditioning a license under one copyright on the acceptance of a license under another is not *per se* unlawful and therefore subject to rule of reason analysis.

The Court again considered package licensing in 1979 in *Broadcasting Music Inc. v. Columbia Broadcasting System*.[56] Thousands of owners of music copyrights granted nonexclusive licenses to two licensing organizations and authorized them to grant nonexclusive licenses to thousands of people or companies wishing to perform or play such music. Each licensing organization offered only a "blanket" license under all copyrights licensed to it for a price determined by the organization. Because the copyright owners retained the right to grant individual licenses to users, there was no conditioning and no illegal package licensing. The Court also held the "blanket" license did not constitute a *per se* violation of section 1 as a price-fixing agreement. The Court declared that the agreement served a legitimate purpose of reducing transaction costs of granting licenses.

---

[55]*United States v. Loew's, Inc.*, 371 U.S. 38 (1962).
[56]*Broadcasting Music Inc. v. Columbia Broadcasting System*, 441 U.S. 1, 24 (1979).

4.6 LICENSING MORE THAN ONE PATENT OR COPYRIGHT

The Supreme Court has said twice that compulsory package licensing of patents is misuse. In *Automatic Radio Mfg. Co. v. Hazeltine Research*,[57] the Supreme Court said that its decisions "have condemned schemes . . . conditioning the granting of a license under one patent upon the acceptance of another and different license," citing *Paramount Pictures*. Similarly, in *Zenith Radio Corp. v. Hazeltine Research*,[58] the Court of Appeals found compulsory package licensing to constitute both misuse and an antitrust violation. That issue was not raised in the Supreme Court. The lower courts have applied the package-licensing principle in finding patent misuse where a patent owner conditioned the grant of a license under one patent on the acceptance of a license under another patent.[59]

Some courts have refused to find illegal package licensing where the invention of one patent in the package may not be used without infringing the other patent.[60] A few lower courts have suggested that mandatory package licensing of patents is also permissible where it is difficult or impractical to set a separate royalty for each patent.[61]

As explained earlier (section 2.7(b)), some Courts of Appeals have said that the misuse standard is the same as the antitrust rule of reason standard, unless the practice is one which the Supreme Court has specifically declared to be misuse *per se*. The Supreme Court has never held that compulsory package licensing of patents constitutes either a violation of the antitrust laws or patent misuse. Therefore if this test is rigor-

---

[57]*Automatic Radio Mfg. Co. v. Hazeltine Research,* 339 U.S. 827 (1950).
[58]*Zenith Radio Corp. v. Hazeltine Research,* 395 U.S. 100 (1969).
[59]*Automatic Radio Mfg. Co. v. Hazeltine Research, Inc.,* 339 U.S. 827, 831 (1950); *Beckman Instruments, Inc. v. Technical Development Corp.,* 433 F.2d 55, (7th Cir. 1970); *Compton v. Metal Products, Inc.,* 353 F.2d 38, (4th Cir. 1971); *Shea v. Blaw-Knox Co.,* 388 F.2d 761, (7th Cir. 1968); *Hazeltine Research v. Zenith Radio Corp.,* 388 F.2d 25, (7th Cir. 1967), *aff'd in part, rev'd on other grounds,* 395 U.S. 100 (1969); *Hensley Equipment Co. v. Esco Corp.,* 383 F.2d 252, (5th Cir. 1967); *American Securit Co. v. Shatterproof Glass Corp.,* 268 F.2d 769, (3rd Cir. 1959); *Hazeltine Research, Inc. v. Zenith Radio Corp.,* C.C.H. Trade Cases. ¶ 71, 355 (N.D. Ill. 1965); *cf., Ethyl Gasoline Corp. v. United States,* 309 U.S. 436, 459 (1944).
[60]*International Mfg. Co. v. Landon, Inc.,* 336 F.2d 723 (9th Cir. 1964) (no violation of the Sherman Act to require package licensing of patents covering activities which cannot be carried out without infringing all patents in the group, that is, blocking patents).
[61]*Compare, Hull v. Brunswick Corp.,* 704 F.2d 1195, 1200–1201 (10th Cir. 1983).

ously applied, compulsory package licensing would not constitute patent misuse unless the overall effect of the license tends to restrain competition unlawfully in an appropriately defined relevant market. None of the reported package-licensing patent cases applies that standard.

If it is applied, one might expect the courts to find that compulsory package licensing of patents rarely produces anticompetitive effects. It is difficult to conceive of any anticompetitive harm from the practice. An offer to license one or ten patents at the same rate does not inevitably force the licensee to accept the package or to pay greater royalties. The license does not compel the licensee to use the inventions of all (or even any) of the licensed patents. Royalty payments will depend on the rate base. The licensee may pay less under the smaller package because some products may fall outside the scope of the patents of the limited package, and outside of the payment base. Hence, it is not possible to say that this offer compels the prospective licensee to take licenses it does not want. Moreover, granting a license under patents does not foreclose any other supplier of patent licenses from dealing with the licensee. The licensee need not use any of the patents that it does not want to use. And even if a license does use some of the licensed patents, it may also license other patents from other patent owners. A theater's lease of copyrighted films may require that all the films be exhibited.

There are also procompetitive benefits from reduced transaction costs and increased licensing revenue. However, the Federal Circuit's rule of reason test will be employed in connection with mandatory package licensing of patents because the Supreme Court has condemned mandatory package licensing of copyrights as *per se* unlawful and has said that the same rule applies to patents.

A critical element which distinguishes a license under more than one patent from an illegal package license is proof of conditioning. The Supreme Court has not defined how conditioning may be proved. The Supreme Court has not decided whether an offer to license one or ten copyrights or patents constitutes a compulsory package if payments are at the same rate whether ten or one are licensed. The reasons given by the Supreme Court for finding the practice harmful also do not help answer the question.

In *Loew's,* the Court suggested that package licensing permitted the patent owner to obtain more money from the licensee, which was forced

4.6 LICENSING MORE THAN ONE PATENT OR COPYRIGHT

to license copyrights it did not want. An offer to license one or ten patents at the same rate does not inevitably force the licensee to accept the package or pay the same or greater royalties. It may pay less under the smaller package because activities may fall outside the scope of all of the patents of the limited package. Hence, it is not possible to say that the offer compels the prospective licensee to take licenses it does not want.

There have been several lower court decisions finding patents unenforceable for compulsory package licensing.[62] In other situations, the courts have found no refusal to license fewer than all the patents in the package.[63]

Where the actual royalty payments for the complete package will necessarily be significantly less than the payments for the more limited license, the Court of Appeals in *Hazeltine v. Zenith* found that this "economic coercion" proved improper conditioning. In *Hazeltine v. Zenith,* the patent owner offered two separate deals to the prospective licensee, which refused both. The District Court found both to involve economic coercion to force acceptance of the package. The Court of Appeals agreed on the second and disagreed on the first. The first offer was for

---

[62]*Hazeltine Research, Inc. v. Zenith Radio Corp.,* 388 F.2d 25, 33–35 (7th Cir. 1967), *aff'd in part, rev'd in part,* 395 U.S. 100, *on remand,* 418 F.2d 21 (7th Cir. 1969), *rev'd on other grounds,* 401 U.S. 321 (1976); *American Securit Co. v. Shatterproof Glass Corp.,* 268 F.2d 769, 775–777 (3d Cir. 1959), *cert. denied,* 361 U.S. 902 (1959).

[63]*Hull v. Brunswick Corp.,* 704 F.2d 1195 (10th Cir. 1983) (no misuse where patents were initially licensed at a royalty rate of 7 percent for each product using any one patent; one licensee subsequently requested a modification to provide individual rates for each patent and the patent owner refused; "None of these facts demonstrates that Hull's ultimate refusal to renegotiate the royalty structure forced Brunswick to pay for patents it did not want. . . ."); *Hensley Equip. Co. v. Esco Corp.,* 383 F.2d 252, 265 n.24 (5th Cir.), *modified,* 386 F.2d 442 (5th Cir. 1967); *McCullough Tool Co. v. Well Surveys, Inc.,* 343 F.2d 381, 408–410 (10th Cir. 1965), *cert. denied,* 383 U.S. 933 (1966); *Apex Elec. Mfg. Co. v. Altorfer Bros. Co.,* 238 F.2d 867, 871–872 (7th Cir. 1956) (owner of three patents granted licenses under one, two, or three patents at the licensee's option for a "minimum royalty of fifty cents"); *GAF Corp. v. Eastman Kodak Co.,* 519 F.Supp. 1203 (S.D.N.Y. 1981) ("Further, GAF's contention that it was coerced into accepting Kodak's patent packages . . . is without support, especially in view of the fact that GAF did not protest the terms of the license agreements, . . . or produce overwhelming evidence that demands . . . for something less than the license package would have been rejected. . . .").

a license under any one patent at 50 percent of the annual fixed royalty charge for the package of over 500 patents, for any two patents at 80 percent of the annual charge, and for any three or more at 100 percent of the charge. The District Court found that offer was an attempt "by economic coercion to force the taking of the package."

The Court of Appeals found that conclusion erroneous because the formula "allowed licensees to save money by taking licenses of less than three patents." The Court of Appeals noted that eight TV manufacturers had taken licenses under only one patent and there were only three of the patents in general use at the time of the offer. The defendant had rejected the offer at a time when its discussion with the patent owner had narrowed to a single patent. The second offer, which both courts found to establish misuse, was an offer of a license (1) to use nine color TV patents at an annual royalty of $435,000, (2) to use all color TV patents for an annual royalty of $500,000, or (3) for the package of all monochrome and color TV patents at an annual rate of $150,000. Since the payment for the package was much lower than the payment for the smaller groups, the courts found conditioning. The Court of Appeals found the support for that decision in *Loew's,* where the Supreme Court approves an injunction against "economic coercion."

Other decisions imply that the economic unreasonableness of the royalty terms offered by the patent owner may be a basis for finding misuse. In 1980, the Fourth Circuit said in *Western Elec. Co. v. Stewart-Warner Corp.:*[64]

> We think the above contention as to misuse by Stewart-Warner is not well taken. This is not a case in which Western refused to grant Stewart-Warner any license other than a license of a package of patents, as in *American Securit Co. v. Shatterproof Glass Corp.,* 268 F.2d 769 (3rd Cir. 1959). Here, Western would not take a grant-back license so as to lower the cash royalties to be paid by Stewart-Warner. The fact that Stewart-Warner would have preferred to pay less cash, with the balance payable by a grant-back of a license to operate under its patents, is insufficient to make out a case of coercive package licensing. In order to prevail on this

---

[64]*Western Elec. Co. v. Stewart-Warner Corp.,* 631 F.2d 333, 338–339 (4th Cir. 1980).

4.6 LICENSING MORE THAN ONE PATENT OR COPYRIGHT

claim, Stewart-Warner must have shown that Western did not give it a choice to take a license under the Derick-Frosch patent alone or in combination with other patents on reasonable terms. *Well Surveys, Inc. v. Perfo-Log, Inc.,* 396 F.2d 15 (10th Cir. 1968). Stewart-Warner has not made such a showing. It is undisputed that Western gave it the choice to take the Derick-Frosch patent alone at one rate of royalty or a combination of the Derick-Frosch patent with other patents at different royalty rates. As *Well Surveys* teaches, "freedom of choice is the controlling question," at p.18. This makes important the finding of the district court that "viable economic alternatives were made available to Stewart-Warner by Western through the application of its royalty reduction formula." Stewart-Warner has not shown this finding to be clearly erroneous.

In *Mobil Oil Corporation v. W.R. Grace & Company*,[65] a district court refused to find that an offer of a license under 40 patents at 8 percent or a license under 5 patents at 7.4 percent constituted misuse. The court noted that "[a] simple comparison of the number of patents encompassed against the price variable of the royalty is not a fair and true test of the dollar value of the licensees [*sic:* licenses], especially where the composition of the patented products are so intertwined as to be almost inseparable."

Where a prospective licensee requests a license under part of the package and the patent owner offers such a license only at the same royalty rate, the law is unclear whether misuse is established. The courts have split in deciding whether conditioning exists if the patentee requires that the licensee pay the same royalty regardless of the number of patents licensed.[66]

---

[65]*Mobil Oil Corporation v. W.R. Grace & Company,* 367 F.Supp. 207, 245–250 (D. Conn. 1973).

[66]*Hazeltine Research, Inc. v. Zenith Radio Corporation,* 388 F.2d 25, 33–35 (7th Cir. 1967), mod., 395 U.S. 100 (1969); *Rocform Corp. v. Acitelli-Standard Concrete Wall, Inc.,* 367 F.2d 678, 681 (6th Cir. 1966) (package licensing held to constitute misuse where, upon expiration of the "most important" patent, there was no royalty rate reduction or any clause permitting termination by the licensee, even in the absence of evidence that the licensee had requested a license under fewer patents and was refused); *Binks Mfg. Co. v. Ramsberg Electro-Coating Corp.,* 281 F.2d 252 (7th Cir. 1960) *cert. granted,* 364 U.S. 926 (1960), *cert. dismissed,* 366 U.S. 211 (1961); *Well Surveys, Inc. v. Perfolog, Inc.,* 396 F.2d 15, 18 (10th Cir. 1968); *Amer-*

The District Court in *American Securit* said the same result follows where rates are the same. In *American Securit,* the owner of 35 patents was ordered by a consent decree to grant licenses at reasonable rates to "any, some or all" of the patents. The patent owner initially offered a license under all 35 patents at a royalty of $.02 per square foot of glass regardless of the number of patents used. The prospective licensees asked for a more limited license. The patent owner indicated that it would issue the limited licenses with the same royalty terms. The court found "package licensing, compulsory, as distinguished from voluntary," where (1) the patent owner testified that it did not grant licenses on an individual basis, (2) only package licenses were actually granted, and (3) the patent owner "refuse[d] . . . to set royalties on specified groups of patents." Based on these facts, the Court of Appeals concluded that the patent owner's policy was to license only on a package.[67] However, the District Court's opinion suggests that the royalty rate proposal alone would have established misuse.[68] To the same effect is *Sheller-Globe Corp. v. Milsco Manufacturing Co.*[69] Other decisions suggest that insistence on the same rate is not inherently coercive. At least one District Court refused to find misuse where the patent owner offered a license under a single patent or a package at the same royalty rate.[70]

A few courts have suggested that the package licensing prohibition precludes conditioning the grant of a license under patents on the acceptance of a license under trade secrets or know-how.[71]

---

ican Security Co. v. Shatterproof Glass Corp., 268 F.2d 769, 775–777 (3rd Cir. 1959).
[67]*American Security Co. v. Shatterproof Glass Corp.,* 268 F.2d 769 (3rd Cir. 1959).
[68]154 F.Supp. 890, 895.
[69]*Sheller-Globe Corp. v. Milsco Manufacturing Co.,* 206 U.S.P.Q. 42, 67–68 (E.D. Wisc. 1979), *aff'd on other grounds,* 636 F.2d 177 (7th Cir. 1980).
[70]*Studiengesellschaft Kohle v. Northern Petrochemical,* 225 USPQ 194, 197, 199–220 (N.D. Ill. 1984) ("Plaintiff's offer to grant defendant a license under all its patents at no extra charge beyond the rate for a license under the '115 patent is not misuse."), *rev'd on other grounds,* 784 F.2d 351 (Fed. Cir. 1986).
[71]*Technograph Printed Circuits Ltd. v. Bendix Aviation Corp.,* 218 F.Supp. 1 (D. Md. 1963), *aff'd per curiam on other grounds,* 327 F.2d 497 (4th Cir. 1964); *U.S. v. Westinghouse Electric Corp.,* 200 U.S.P.Q. 514, 523 n.40 (N.D.Cal. 1978); *cf., Duplan Corp. v. Deering Milliken,Inc.,* 444 F.Supp. 648, 673, 695–698 (D. S.C. 1977), *aff'd in pertinent part,* 594 F.2d 979 (4th Cir. 1979) (patent misuse but no antitrust violation where licenses under patents are tied to licenses under other patents and technical information).

4.6 LICENSING MORE THAN ONE PATENT OR COPYRIGHT

(b) The Theory of the Law on Package Licensing

Like most other rules, the package licensing rule grew out of the rule against tying arrangements. The tying law does not seem to compel these packaging licensing rules. The alleged evil of tying arrangements seems inapplicable. The patent owner does not acquire a "limited monopoly" over products not within the scope of the patent. The patent owner already has any available market power in the supply of licenses under the other patents. A "package only" policy can create no further market power in their supply. Rather, the rules against package licensing seem to rest more on the fact that the Supreme Court once said in the context of resale price fixing that "[t]he patent monopoly of one invention may no more be enlarged for the exploitation of a monopoly of another . . . than for the exploitation of an unpatented article. . . ."[72]

Moreover, granting a license under patents does not foreclose any other supplier of patent licenses from dealing with the licensee. The licensee need not use any of the patents that it does not want to use. And even if it does, it may also license other patents from other patent owners. The situation may be different for leasing motion picture films to theaters and television stations. Such leases require the theater or station to show the films.

(c) Royalties and Package Licensing

While the law is not entirely clear, there is no general prohibition against a uniform royalty rate over the entire term of a license under multiple patents expiring at different times. There are two Court of Appeals decisions that say that it is misuse to license a package of patents and not reduce the royalty rates as individual patents expire. In *Rocform Corp. v. Acitelli-Standard Concrete Wall, Inc.,* the Sixth Circuit said:[73]

> The dissent also contends that a flat price for use of a number of patents is permissible practice up to the termination date of "the last necessary patent."

---

[72]*Ethyl Gasoline Corp. v. United States,* 309 U.S. 436, 459 (1944).
[73]*Rocform Corp. v. Acitelli-Standard Concrete Wall, Inc.,* 367 F.2d 678 (6th Cir. 1966) (with one Judge dissenting).

We believe this is too broad a contention. We do not deal here (as did the Supreme Court in Brulotte v. Thys Co., supra) with the sale of a piece of machinery which incorporated a number of patents. Rather we deal with a licensing arrangement where one important patent (about to expire) is grouped with others of longer duration for "leverage." Cf. American Securit Co. v. Shatterproof Glass Corp., supra.

We believe such a contract, when it contains no diminution of license fee at the expiration of the most important patent and contains no termination clause at the will of the licensee, constitutes, in effect, an effort to continue to collect royalties on an expired patent. Brulotte v. Thys Co., supra; American Securit Co. v. Shatterproof Glass Corp., supra.

American Securit Co. [74] says the same thing. At least one court has followed *American Securit* on that issue.[75]

In 1964, the Supreme Court held that a license agreement would not be enforced to the extent that it called for royalties after all the licensed patents used expired.[76] Based on the reported decision, royalties did not decrease as patents expired. The Supreme Court did not find the patent unenforceable on that basis. Most courts have held that this fact alone does not constitute patent misuse.[77]

---

[74]*American Securit Co. v. Shatterproof Glass Corp.*, 268 F.2d 769 (3rd Cir. 1959).
[75]*Duplan Corp. v. Deering Milliken Corp.*, 444 F.Supp 648, 697–699 (D. S.C. 1977), aff'd per curiam, 594 F.2d 979 (4th Cir. 1979).
[76]*Brulotte v. Thys Co.*, 379 U.S. 29 (1964).
[77]*Hull v. Brunswick Corp.*, 704 F.2d 1195 (10th Cir. 1983); *Beckman Instruments, Inc. v. Technical Develop. Corp.*, 433 F.2d 55, 60–61 (7th Cir. 1970); *In Re Yarn Processing Patent Validity Litigation*, 561 F.2d 1127, 1141–1142 (5th Cir. 1976); *Well Surveys, Inc. v. Perfolog, Inc.*, 396 F.2d 15, 17–18 (10th Cir. 1968); *Shea v. Blaw-Knox Co.*, 388 F.2d 761, 765 (7th Cir. 1968) (No misuse where license included two patents, royalties were paid at $250 per unit for any product using either patent, there was no request for a license under one patent alone, and plaintiff was willing to license individually); *McCullough Tool Co. v. Well Surveys, Inc.*, 343 F.2d 381 (10th Cir. 1965); *GAF Corp. v. Eastman Kodak Corp.*, 519 F.Supp 1203, 1236 (S.D.N.Y. 1981); *Carter Prods. v. Colgate-Palmolive Co.*, 164 F.Supp. 503, 525–526 (D. Md. 1958), aff'd, 269 F.2d 299 (4th Cir. 1959); cf., *Lessona Corp. v. Varta Batteries, Inc.*, 522 F.Supp. 1304, 1340–1343 (S.D.N.Y. 1981) (". . . the extension of the five percent royalty rate to the later-remaining patent is no more ev-

4.6 LICENSING MORE THAN ONE PATENT OR COPYRIGHT

(d) The Competitive Effects

The economics of package licensing suggest that there is no necessary economic harm. There are several reasons why a patent owner or copyright owner would seek to license as a package other than to restrict competition in the supply of patent licenses.

First, where patents relate to the same use, it is impossible to negotiate a separate royalty on a patent-by-patent basis. The royalty for any one patent depends on the royalty for another.

Second, different licensees may place different values on the separate patents. By placing a single value on the package and offering the package to all potential licensees, the patent owner achieves to some degree a charge to different licensees at rates reflecting those different values without the costs of negotiating a separate license with each licensee under different groups of patents and at different royalty rates. No licensee will pay more than what all the patents in the package are worth to it. A license tied to the purchase of a product has at least the potential of limiting competition in a general market for the unpatented "tied" product. A package license cannot conceivably restrict competition between the supply of the "tied" (or "unwanted") patent and substitute patents. A licensee will not use inventions which are not profitable to use. A licensee is not foreclosed from acquiring a license under the substitute patents of others. The license under the "tied" patent cannot affect competition in the supply of competing licenses.

Third, an individual licensee may have decreasing demand for additional licenses. After a licensee has a license under one patent, the value of an additional related patent is likely to be less. In that situation, an all-or-none offer may generate more revenue than a single price for each license.

Finally, and perhaps most importantly, package licensing may reduce the costs of negotiation and enforcing licenses. Package licensing may or may not increase the use of the inventions or the copyrighted works. However, it is highly unlikely that package licensing "extends the scope" of any patent or copyright.

---

idence of patent misuse, absent 'conditioning' or coercion, than the payment of such a royalty on the sale of a product applying one but not both of the patents while both patents remain in force.").

5

The Nature and Scope of Licensed Rights—Exclusivity, Field of Use, Price, Quantity, Territory, Customer and Cross-Licensing

5.1	Assigning the Rights to Others	293
5.2	Granting an Exclusive License	295
5.3	Exclusive Dealing—Restrictions against a Licensee Dealing in Substitute Products	297
5.4	Field of Use Restrictions	299
5.5	Price Restrictions	307
5.6	Quantity Restrictions	314
5.7	Territorial Limitations	319
5.8	Customer Limitations	322
5.9	Cross-Licensing and Limitations on the Grant of Licenses	322

5.1 ASSIGNING THE RIGHTS TO OTHERS

Chapter 1 described the reasons a technology producer may wish to put those rights in the exclusive possession of one user (section 1.10). One way to do that is sell the rights. Antitrust law limits the freedom of the owner to assign the rights. The misuse rules largely leave this option alone. The antitrust limits are the intellectual property version of the limits on mergers and asset acquisitions. Rivalry may be limited by a single firm acquiring enough other firms supplying substitutes to obtain market power. Similarly, the owner of one intellectual properties right may attempt to limit rivalry by acquiring intellectual properties rights to substitute products.

The acquisition of patents is subject to section 7 of the Clayton Act. A patent is an asset for this purpose.[1] An exclusive license under the patent is probably also an asset for that purpose.[2] An acquisition violates section 7 only if the effect may be substantially to lessen competition or tend to create a monopoly. Sections 1 and 2 of the Sherman Act also apply. In determining whether the acquisition of patents violates the antitrust laws, some of the factors the courts have considered are:[3]

---

[1] *SCM Corp. v. Xerox Corp.*, 463 F.Supp. 983 (D. Conn. 1978), *aff'd*, 645 F.2d 1195 (2d Cir. 1981); *In Re Yarn Process Patent Validity Litigation*, 398 F.Supp. 31, 35 (S.D. Fla. 1975), *aff'd in part, rev'd in part*, 541 F.2d 1127 (5th Cir. 1976); *Dole Valve Co. v. Perfecton Bar Equip., Inc.*, 311 F.Supp. 459, 463 (N.D. Ill. 1970).
[2] See *United States v. Lever Bros.*, 216 F.Supp. 887, 889 (S.D.N.Y. 1963); *United States v. Columbia Pictures Corp.*, 189 F.Supp. 153, 181–182 (S.D.N.Y. 1960).
[3] *United States v. United Shoe Machinery Co.*, 247 U.S. 32, 48–54 (1918); *United States v. United Shoe Machinery Co.*, 110 F.Supp. 295, 332–333 (D. Mass. 1953), *aff'd per curiam*, 347 U.S. 521 (1954); *United States v. Winslow*, 227 U.S. 202, 217–218 (1913); *SCM Corp. v. Xerox Corp.*, 645 F.2d 1195 (2d Cir. 1981); *In Re Yarn Processing Patent Validity Litigation*, 398 F.Supp. 31, 53 (S.D. Fla. 1975), *aff'd in part*, 541 F.2d 1127 (5th Cir. 1977); *United States v. Aluminum Company of America*, 91 F.Supp. 333, 391–392 (S.D.N.Y. 1950); United States v. S.C. Johnson & Son, 1995-1 Trade Cas. (CCH) ¶ 70,884 (N.D. Ill. 1994) (consent decree).

The impact of the agreement on competition between the parties before and after the assignment;

Whether the acquired patents are substitutes for or complements of patents owned by the acquiring party;

The commercial significance of the acquired patent;

Whether the acquisition was made to settle potential or actual patent litigation; and

Whether the acquired patents were used by the acquiring party.

The acquisition of patents based on independent research of others may also be one feature of an agreement to unreasonably restrain trade in violation of section 1. In *United States v. Singer*,[4] the Court held that Singer, an American manufacturer of household sewing machines, conspired with two other sewing machine suppliers, Gegauf and Vigorelli, to use Singer patents to exclude Japanese companies from the U.S. market.[5] Singer and the others entered several agreements to settle patent controversies. One agreement was a cross-license agreement between Singer and Gegauf. Each licensed the other under its U.S. patents and applications.[6] Subsequently, Gegauf assigned a U.S. application, and any patent which might be granted on it, to Singer. Singer instituted infringement actions and other proceedings against Japanese manufacturers.[7] The Court held that the Sherman Act did not permit Singer to agree with Gegauf and Vigorelli to enforce the patent "to the benefit of all three parties" rather than to protect its own machine.[8]

The acquisition of patents is also sometimes a feature of agreements among companies to pool their patents. Those patents may be assigned to an entity or company that acts as the licensing agent for the pooled patents (section 5.9).

---

[4] 374 U.S. 174 (1963).
[5] Id. at 175, 189.
[6] Id. at 179–180, 190, n.7.
[7] Id. at 187–188.
[8] Id. at 193–195.

5.2 GRANTING AN EXCLUSIVE LICENSE

By an exclusive license, the owner agrees that it will not use the rights or license others. The courts have held that the mere granting of an exclusive license does not violate the antitrust laws.[9] An exclusive license may be designed to avoid externalities between one licensee and another potential licensee. Subject to the limits discussed in the previous section, exclusive licenses have been declared lawful.

Chapter 1 described the potential effects of exclusive licensing (sections 1.10(c)–1.10(e)), and these effects were illustrated in Figures 1.9 and 1.10. Assume that the patent owner must license a product patent. However, investments in needed research, development, and promotion would produce external benefits for other producers of the product. If the invention is licensed nonexclusively, any one licensee that contemplates those investments will recognize the benefits for licensees that make no similar investment. This licensee will be reluctant to invest. By granting an exclusive license, the patent owner provides the licensee with incentives to make such investments which will be "protected" by the patent.

Those investments increase the value of the product and the invention, beyond that which nonexclusive licensing could achieve. The exclusive license increases average costs, but increases demand by a greater amount. Hence, exclusive licensing may lead to greater profits (and output) than nonexclusive licensing.

The exclusive licensee will treat royalties as a cost. Assume the licensee has market power. This licensee will determine marginal revenue, raise price, and restrict quantity. Both the patent owner and the economy lose by that additional restriction on output. The patent owner loses and the economy loses. It is in the patent owner's and society's interest to limit the exclusive licensee's independent exploitation of that market power. Licensors may seek to prevent such restrictions on output by minimum quantity requirements, by increased minimum royalty rates if annual production is low, or by maximum prices.

---

[9]*Virtue v. Creamery Package Mfg. Co.*, 277 U.S. 8, 36–37 (1913); *United States v. E.I. du Pont de Nemours & Co.*, 118 F.Supp. 41, 224 (D. Del. 1953); *cf., Bement v. National Harrow Co.*, 186 U.S. 70, 94 (1902).

An exclusive license might also reduce rivalry. Assume that a certain company possesses substantial market power in the market for a product and that entry by the patent owner with the new patented product would reduce that power. An exclusive license from the patent owner to the existing company eliminates that potential competition. However, the law properly does not treat all exclusive licenses as unlawful. If the license does not reduce rivalry between the existing product and the potential substitute, or is unlikely to enhance market power, the grant of an exclusive license is lawful.

The owner and its licensee will not always be able to predict whether total exclusivity for the entire term of the rights is mutually advantageous. They may wish to provide for some exculusivity and leave open the option granting another license. They may simply provide that this option will be available by mutual consent.

Where the patent owner agrees that it will grant additional licenses only with the consent of existing licensees, two courts in the 1950s said that agreement violated section 1 of the Sherman Act.[10] However, in each case, the licenses also restricted the licensees' selling price. Hence, the finding of an antitrust violation did not necessarily rest on the fact that the licenses gave licensees "veto power" over the grant of additional licenses. The Supreme Court affirmed both decisions in *per curiam* opinions. Notwithstanding those courts' criticisms of licensee "veto power," the courts say an agreement to grant added licenses only with the consent of existing licensees is judged by the rule of reason.[11]

A patent license may provide that a licensee be given the benefit of more favorable terms granted in other licenses.[12]

---

[10]*United States v. Krasnov,* 143 F.Supp. 184, 200–202 (E.D. Pa. 1956), *aff'd per curiam,* 355 U.S. 5 (1957); *United States v. Besser Mfg. Co.,* 96 F.Supp. 304, 311 (E.D. Mich. 1951), *aff'd,* 343 U.S. 444 (1952).

[11]*Mannington Mills, Inc. v. Congoleum Industries, Inc.,* 610 F.2d 1069–1073 (3rd Cir. 1979) (alleged conspiracy among patent owner and its foreign licensees to cancel foreign license of another licensee; see section 2.7(b)); *Moraine Prods. v. ICI America, Inc.,* 538 F.2d 134, 143–146 (7th Cir. 1976). Compare, *Bement v. National Harrow Co.,* 186 U.S. 70, 94 (1902); *Burger Laboratories, Ltd. v. R.K. Laros Co.,* 209 F.Supp. 639 (E.D. Pa. 1962), *aff'd per curiam,* 317 F.2d 455 (3rd Cir. 1963).

[12]*General Tire & Rubber Co. v. Firestone Tire & Rubber Co.,* 349 F.Supp. 333,

5.3 EXCLUSIVE DEALING—RESTRICTIONS AGAINST A LICENSEE DEALING IN SUBSTITUTE PRODUCTS

In 1914, Congress enacted section 3 of the Clayton Act.[13]

Section 3 prohibits the sale of a product on the purchaser's agreement not to deal in competitive products, where the effect of the agreement is likely to be a significant reduction in competition in some market. That section applies only to tangible property. It is not applicable to licensing.

In 1940, the Supreme Court said *in dicta* that a patent owned "may not . . . condition the license so as to control the conduct by the licensee not embraced in the patent monopoly. . . ."[14] In the 1940s, two Courts of Appeal found patent misuse based on a licensee's agreement to refrain from dealing in products that competed with the licensed products.[15] Those courts said misuse was established without proof that the agreement was likely to have any adverse effects on competition. Later cases generally followed suit and said that a patent owner misuses the patent by requiring the licensee not to deal in competing products.[16] One recent decision declined to go alone based on the misuse standards described earlier[17] (section 2.7).

In one of those decisions, the Court of Appeals also found misuse based on the owner's agreement not to deal in competing unpatented products.[18] Again, the court did not require proof of adverse effects on

---

344–345 (N.D. Ohio 1972); *Technograph Printed Circuits, Ltd. v. Bendix Aviation Corp.*, 218 F.Supp. 1, 51 (D. Md. 1963); *cf., U.S. v. U.S. Gypsum Co.*, 333 U.S. 364, 389 (1948).

[13] 15 U.S.C. § 15.

[14] *Ethyl Gasoline Corp. v. United States*, 309 U.S. 436, 458–459 (1940).

[15] *McCullough v. Kammerer Corp.*, 166 F.2d 759 (9th Cir. 1948) (misuse); *National Lockwasher Co. v. George K. Garrett Co.*, 137 F.2d 255 (3rd Cir. 1943) (misuse).

[16] *Berlenbach v. Anderson & Thompson Ski Co.*, 329 F.2d 782 (9th Cir. 1964) (misuse); *Krampe v. Ideal Industries, Inc.*, 347 F.Supp. 1384 (N.D. Ill. 1972); but *cf., Radio Corp. of America v. United Radio & Electric Corp.*, 50 F.Supp. 206 (D. N.J. 1926).

[17] *Keystone Retaining Wall Systems v. Westrock*, __F.Supp.__, 22 U.S.P.Q. 2d 1001, 1008 (D. Ore. 1991).

[18] *McCullough v. Kammerer Corp.*, 166 F.2d 759 (9th Cir. 1948).

competition, and did not leave it open for the patent owner to prove any justification for the agreement.

There is not a Supreme Court decision holding that this practice is always misuse. Hence, the misuse standards incorporating analysis of effects seem to apply (section 2.7).

The reason those courts gave for the rigid misuse rule was that the only possible effect of such restrictions was to extend the patent monopoly to unpatented products and to acquire a broader monopoly than the patent granted. Such agreements may not have that effect. A licensee's agreement not to deal in competitive unpatented products may avoid the free-rider problem arising when the licensee's investment has external benefits for products sold in competition with the patented product.

An exclusive license may be designed to avoid externalities between one licensee and other potential licensees. Exclusive licenses are lawful for that purpose. An agreement not to deal in competitive products may be designed to avoid externalities between the patented product and unpatented products (section 1.10(c)). The gains in profits from sales of the patented product from such agreements are beneficial. The costs from any loss of rivalry between the patented and unpatented products are harmful. The predominant effect will vary from case to case. If (1) the patented product constitutes a small part of the market, (2) the licensees agreeing to the restriction account for only a small percentage of the market, or (3) entry is easy, the restriction is unlikely to have any serious detrimental effect on rivalry.

The courts were wrong to assume that an agreement not to deal in competitive products is always a method by which the patent owner acquires a broader monopoly. The categorical prohibition of such agreements makes exploitation of the patent by making and selling products more profitable than exploiting the same patent by licensing. A product producer can achieve the benefits of increased investment by unilateral decisions about dealing in competitive products. A patent owner not in a position to produce cannot do the same thing. Licensing becomes a disfavored mode of exploitation. The result is wasteful vertical integration into production.

Standing alone, the licensee's agreement not to sell competing unpatented products is not likely to be an effective way for competitors to limit competition under the guise of a license. Each company agreeing

5.4 FIELD OF USE RESTRICTIONS

not to sell the unpatented product becomes a competitor in selling the patented product.

5.4 FIELD OF USE RESTRICTIONS

A patented invention may have many different uses with different values. Patent owners frequently grant exclusive or nonexclusive licenses limited to particular types, kinds, styles, or sizes of products. Such restrictions are frequently referred to as *field of use restrictions*. The Supreme Court has found that a patent owner does not violate the antitrust laws or engage in patent misuse by a field of use restriction in a vertical patent license.[19] Where a single firm acting alone grants licenses under existing patents owned or lawfully acquired by it, the courts have uniformly approved a limitation on the types or kinds of products the licensee may produce and sell. There have been dozens of decisions approving so-called field of use limitations in vertical agreements.[20]

---

[19]*General Talking Pictures Corp. v. Western Electric Co.,* 304 U.S. 175, *reh'g granted,* 304 U.S. 587, *aff'd on reh'g,* 305 U.S. 124 (1938); *Bement v. National Harrow Co.,* 186 U.S. 10, 72–73, 93–94 (1902); *Rubber Co. v. Goodyear,* 9 Wall 788, 799 (1869). In *Bement,* the patent owner granted a license to make and sell "float spring tooth harrows" and frames of the kind shown by a sample in the possession of the licensee and described in the license. The licensee agreed that it would not, during the license, make or sell any (patented) harrow other than licensed styles, and the licensor agreed that it would not license any other person to make or sell the style licensed to licensee. The Court held that this license did not violate the Sherman Act.

[20]*A. & E. Plastik Pak Co., Inc. v. Monsanto Co.,* 396 F.2d 710 (9th Cir. 1968); *Armstrong v. Motorola, Inc.,* 374 F.2d 764 (7th Cir. 1967), *cert. denied,* 389 U.S. 830 (1967); *Coats Loaders & Stackers, Inc. v. Henderson,* 233 F.2d 915 (6th Cir. 1956); *Hazeltine Research v. Admiral Corp.,* 183 F.2d 953 (7th Cir. 1950), *cert. denied,* 340 U.S. 896 (1950); *Automatic Radio Mfg. Co. v. Hazeltine Research,* 176 F.2d 799 (1st Cir. 1949), *aff'd on other grounds,* 339 U.S. 827 (1950); *Turner Glass Corp. v. Hartford Empire Co.,* 173 F.2d 49, 53 (7th Cir. 1948), *cert. denied,* 338 U.S. 830 (1949); *Duplan Corp. v. Deering Milliken, Inc.,* 444 F.Supp. 648, 671 (D. S.C. 1977), *aff'd in part, rev'd in part on other grounds,* 594 F.2d 974 (4th Cir. 1979); *United States v. Ciba-Geigy Corp.,* 508 F.Supp. 1118, 1149–1151 (D. N.J. 1976); *Ansul Co. v. Uniroyal, Inc.,* 306 F.Supp. 541 (S.D.N.Y. 1969), *aff'd in part, rev'd in part on other grounds,* 448 F.2d 872 (2d Cir. 1971), *cert. denied,* 404 U.S. 1018 (1972); *Bela Seating Co. v. Poloron Prods., Inc.,* 297 F.Supp. 489 (N.D. Ill. 1968), *aff'd,*

THE NATURE AND SCOPE OF LICENSED RIGHTS

(a) The *General Talking Pictures* Rule on Limited Fields of Use

In 1938, the Supreme Court found that a vertical patent license limited to products of a specified type or description is not misuse and, implicitly, not a violation of the antitrust laws. In *General Talking Pictures Corp. v. Western Electric Co.*,[21] the license involved patents on vacuum tube amplifiers. The patent owner, Western Electric, essentially retained rights to products using those amplifiers in the so-called commercial field. The "retained" commercial field included talking picture equipment for use in theaters. The owner granted nonexclusive licenses to products useful in the so-called private field. The private field included amateur radio reception. The owner granted nonexclusive licenses to others to make and sell equipment only for radio reception. One nonexclusive licensee in the radio field made amplifiers and sold them to General Talking Pictures knowing that General intended to include them in equipment for use in theaters. General had actual notice of that licensee's limited license and knew that the license did not authorize the sale of amplifiers for that use. The Court, in a five-to-one decision, held that both the licensee and purchaser were guilty of infringement and would be enjoined. The Court held the restrictions enforceable and not patent mis-

---

438 F.2d 733 (7th Cir. 1971), *cert. denied*, 403 U.S. 922 (1971); *Barr Rubber Prods. Co. v. Sun Rubber Co.*, 277 F.Supp. 484 (S.D.N.Y. 1967); *aff'd in part, rev'd in part on other grounds*, 425 F.2d 1114 (2d Cir. 1970), *cert. denied*, 400 U.S. 878 (1970); *Chemagro Corp. v. Universal Chemical Co.*, 244 F.Supp. 486 (E.D. Tex. 1965); *Reliance Molded Plastics, Inc. v. Jiffy Products*, 215 F.Supp. 402 (D. N.J. 1963), *aff'd per curiam*, 337 F.2d 857 (3rd Cir. 1964); *Harte & Co., Inc. v. L. E. Carpenter & Co.*, 138 U.S.P.Q. 578 (S.D.N.Y. 1963); *Kaz Mfg. Co. v. Chesebrough-Pond's, Inc.*, 211 F.Supp. 815 (S.D.N.Y. 1962), *aff'd*, 317 F.2d 679 (2d Cir. 1963); *Eversharp, Inc. v. Fisher Pen Co.*, 204 F.Supp. 649 (N.D. Ill. 1961); *Sperry Products, Inc. v. Aluminum Co. of America*, 171 F.Supp. 901 (N.D. Ohio 1959), *aff'd on this issue, rev'd in part on other grounds*, 285 F.2d 911 (6th Cir. 1960), *cert. denied*, 368 U.S. 890 (1961); *Deering, Milliken & Co. v. Temp-Resisto Corp.*, 160 F.Supp. 463 (S.D.N.Y. 1958), *rev'd in part on other grounds*, 274 F.2d 626 (2d Cir. 1960); *United States v. Birdsboro Steel Foundry & Mach. Co.*, 139 F.Supp. 244 (W.D. Pa. 1956); *Westinghouse Elec. Corp. v. Bulldog Elec. Prods. Co.*, 106 F.Supp. 819 (N.D. W.Va. 1952), *aff'd*, 206 F.2d 574 (4th Cir. 1953), *cert. denied*, 346 U.S. 909 (1953); *Atlas Imperial Diesel Engine Co. v. Lanova Corp.*, 79 F.Supp. 1002 (D. Del. 1948); *cf., United States v. Ethyl Gasoline Corp.*, 27 F.Supp. 959 (S.D.N.Y. 1939), *aff'd*, 309 U.S. 43 (1940).

[21]*General Talking Pictures Corp. v. Western Electric Co.*, 304 U.S. 175 (1937), *reh'g granted* 304 U.S. 87, *aff'd on reh'g* 305 U.S. 124 (1938).

5.4 FIELD OF USE RESTRICTIONS

use. The Court approved these licenses in very broad terms, noting particularly the absence of any effort to "extend the scope of the monopoly":[22]

> Pertinent words of the license are these: "To manufacture . . . and to sell only for radio amateur reception, radio experimental reception and radio broadcast reception. . . ." Patent owners may grant licenses extending to all uses or limited to use in a defined field. *Rubber Company v. Goodyear,* 9 Wall. 788, 799–800. *Gamewell Fire-Alarm Telegraph Co. v. Bradley Co.,* Fed. Cas. No. 4,015, 7 Fed. Cas. 946, 947. Robinson on Patents, §§ 808, 824. Unquestionably, the owner of a patent may grant licenses to manufacture, use or sell upon conditions not inconsistent with the scope of the monopoly. *Bement v. National Harrow Co.,* 186 U.S. 70, 93. *United States v. General Electric Co.,* 272 U.S. 476, 489. There is here no attempt on the part of the patent owner to extend the scope of the monopoly beyond that contemplated by the patent statute. *Cf. Cabrice Corp. v. American Patents Corp.,* 283 U.S. 27, 33. *Leitch Mfg. Co. v. Barber Co.,* U.S. 458.

On rehearing, the Court made clear that the granting of "licenses extending to all uses or limited in use to a defined field"[23] was a valid and legally enforceable restriction:[24]

> Any use beyond the valid terms of a license is, of course, an infringement of a patent. Robinson on Patents, § 916. If where a patented invention is applicable to different uses, the owner of the patent may legally restrict a licensee to a particular field and exclude him from others. Transformer Company was guilty of an infringement when it made the amplifiers for, and sold them to, Pictures Corporation. And as Pictures Corporation ordered, purchased and leased them knowing the facts, it also was an infringer.
> The question of law requiring decision is whether the restriction in the license is to be given effect. That a restrictive license is

---
[22] Id. at 181.
[23] Id. at 181.
[24] 305 U.S. at 126, 127.

legal seems clear. *Mitchell v. Hawley,* 16 Wall. 544. As said in *United States v. General Electric Co.,* 272 U.S. 476, 489, the patentee may grant a license "upon any condition the performance of which is reasonably within the reward which the patentee by the grant of the patent is entitled to secure." The restriction here imposed is of that character. The practice of granting licenses for a restricted use is an old one, *see Rubber Company v. Goodyear,* 9 Wall 788, 799, 800; *Gamewell Fire-Alarm Telegraph Co. v. Brooklyn,* 14 F. 255. So far as appears, its legality has never been questioned.

In 1903, the Court reached the same result in an antitrust case.[25]

Since the decision in *General Talking Pictures* in the late 1930s, only a few decisions have found patent misuse or an antitrust violation based on a limit to any particular style, type, or kind of product embodying a licensed patent. Those few decisions usually involve patents directed to parts or components or to processes of making a product and the limitation is on the nature of the "unpatented" end product that includes the part or was made by the process. Those issues commonly arise where the restriction purports to apply to products, parts, or components purchased from the patent owner or a licensee.

The basis for the decision approving field of use restrictions is that competition in markets for existing products is competition that the patent owner may control by virtue of its patents. The owner is under no obligation to permit the maximum amount of competition in that market. It may decline to use or license the patent and prevent the selling of products that use an invention covered by the patent.

Where field of use restrictions are used to prevent competition which would have existed in the absence of a license agreement, their use may violate the Sherman Act.[26] Where the patent owner grants licenses it was not obligated to grant, and limits them to particular types of products that use patented inventions, the courts find such limitations lawful, because the patent owner is permitting competition that he had the right

---

[25] *Bement v. National Harrow Co.,* 186 U.S. 70, 93–94 (1903).
[26] *United States v. Associated Patents,* 314, F.Supp. 74, (E.D. Mich. 1955), *aff'd per curiam,* 350 U.S. 196 (1956) (pooled patents licensed to define exclusive, non-competitive fields); *United States v. Hartford-Empire Co.,* 46 F.Supp. 451 (N.D. Ohio 1942), *mod.,* 323 U.S. 386 (1945).

5.4 FIELD OF USE RESTRICTIONS

to prevent entirely. The patent owner is not attempting to limit competition in some markets that would arise notwithstanding the existence and enforcement of the patents. The license does not limit competition between the patented product and products that could lawfully have been marketed in competition with them. The purpose of the patent law to reward inventions is served. No purpose of the antitrust law is offended. Therefore, the courts would treat the agreement as entirely lawful.

(b) The Competitive Effects

The effects of field of use restrictions in situations such as that in *General Talking Pictures* are illustrated in section 1.10(b). There the preinvention demands for amplifiers for use in movie theaters and those for home use in radio receivers are described by respective demand and supply curves. Assume the invention increases the demand for those uses as shown in the postinvention demand curves. The profit-maximizing royalty rates for the respective uses are different.

In order for the patent owner to maximize its profits from those different demands, it must be able to license them at different rates. If it chooses, as the patent owner did in *General Talking Pictures,* to license different companies in different fields, then it must be able to prevent the licensee in the lower-royalty field from selling to customers for use in the higher-royalty field. Field of use restrictions serve that purpose. They result in greater revenue for the patent owner. The effect on the use of the invention depends on the relationship between the effect of the royalty rates on price and on output. Where there are only two uses for the invention and each is licensed at separate rates, the output may be greater or less than what it would be with a single royalty rate and no restriction. However, such restrictions do not limit competition with any previous products. That competition continues and limits the demand for the invention.

Where there are more than two fields, the impact of field of use restrictions is almost inevitably to increase invention use compared with the single-field, single-price alternative. The effect of field of use restrictions is identical in that respect to one type of tying arrangement. The courts are willing to recognize the different values of the invention in different uses when they are spelled out in a license. Where it is too expensive to license each individual user, and the only mechanism for

THE NATURE AND SCOPE OF LICENSED RIGHTS

distinguishing different values between different uses and users is tying arrangements, the courts have become blind to these benefits.

(c) The *General Talking Pictures* Rule on Field of Use Limits on Purchasers from a Licensee

The courts have not recognized the economic value of field of use restrictions in all contexts. *General Talking Pictures* held that, where a patent owner grants a license to make and sell patented products for a limited use, a purchaser of a patented product from such a licensee with notice of the limitation is bound by it. If the purchaser uses the product for an unlicensed use, it is guilty of infringement.

(d) The Application of the Rule on Field of Use Limits on Purchasers from a Licensee

In spite of the Supreme Court's ruling, some lower courts declared in the 1950s and 1960s that a patent owner may not make and sell a patented product and limit the field of use of a purchaser.[27] These decisions were confined primarily to antitrust actions. In one case, a lower court declined to find misuse based on a field of use restriction applied to a purchaser.[28]

---

[27] *Hensley Equipment Co. v. Esco Corp.*, 383 F.2d 252, 262–264 (5th Cir. 1957) (license agreement restricting use and sale of patented parts purchased from the licensor to machinery manufactured by licensee or its dealers constituted *per se* violation of the Sherman Act in restricting resale of parts); *United States v. Glaxo Group Limited*, 302 F.Supp. 1, 4–11 (D. D.C. 1969) (agreement to supply patented bulk-form drug to a licensee-purchaser who agreed that it "will not, without first obtaining [the sellers] consent, resell or re-deliver in bulk form" violated the Sherman Act), *final judgment*, 328 F.Supp. 709 (1971), *rev'd on other grounds*, 410 U.S. 52 (1973); *United States v. Ciba Geigy Co.*, 508 F.Supp. 1118, 1126–1147 (D. N.J. 1976) (supply agreement restricting purchasers of bulk-form drug from (a) reselling in finish dosage form not in combination with other drugs, and (b) reselling in other than combination form approved by the seller violated the Sherman Act); *Baldwin-Lima-Hamilton Corp. v. Tatnal Meas. Sys. Co.*, 169 F.Supp. 1, (E.D. Pa. 1958), *aff'd per curiam*, 268 F.2d. 395 (3rd Cir. 1959); *cf., United States v. Univis Lens Co., Inc.*, 316 U.S. 241, 249–253 (1942); *Ethyl Gasoline Corp. v. United States*, 309 U.S. 436, 455–461 (1940).

[28] *Chemagro Corporation v. Universal Chemical Co.*, 244 F.Supp. 486, 489 (E.D. Tex. 1965).

5.4 FIELD OF USE RESTRICTIONS

The lower courts reached those decisions without explaining why those cases were not controlled by *General Talking Pictures,* which found that such a restriction was enforceable against a purchaser of the patented product from a licensee if the purchaser had notice of the restriction.

The "logic" by which the courts have condemned resale field of use restrictions was based on longstanding judicial *dicta* that the first sale of a patented product "exhausts the patent monopoly" (sections 6.5–9). The effect of "exhaustion" was that the postsale restrictions were viewed as restrictions on unpatented products.

The costs of an across-the-board prohibition against field of use restrictions on purchasers of a patented product are illustrated by the following example. If the licensee in the home field sells at lower, home-field prices to users for theater use, licensees in the theater field will be unable to make any sales. This destroys the value of the restriction to the patent owner. There is no reason why the sale of a product necessarily "exhausts the patent monopoly." The sale may be accompanied by an express license to the purchaser spelling out the rights granted and retained.

Those decisions stood until the late 1970s. In 1977, in *Continental T.V., Inc. v. G.T.E. Sylvania, Inc.,*[29] the Supreme Court held that all nonprice vertical resale restrictions were not *per se* violations of the Sherman Act and were to be judged under the rule of reason. That decision did not involve a patented product or a patent license. However, the decision seemed to require that resale field of use restrictions violate the antitrust laws only if found to unreasonably restrain competition under the circumstances.

In 1992, the Court of Appeals for the Federal Circuit in *Mallinckrodt v. Medipart* confirmed that, under *General Talking Pictures,* a purchaser of a patented product infringes the patent when it uses the product in violation of a lawful restriction or condition on use specified by the seller at the time of the sale.[30] The court found that the purchaser infringed even though the seller was the patent owner (section 6.9(c)).

---

[29]*Continental T.V., Inc. v. G.T.E. Sylvania, Inc.,* 433 U.S. 36 (1977).
[30]*Mallinckrodt, Inc. v. Medipart, Inc.,* 976 F.2d 700, 701 (Fed. Cir. 1992). That court also discussed the exhaustion doctrine in *Intel Corp. v. ULSI System Technology, Inc.,* 995 F.2d 1566, 1568–1569, 1571–1576 (Fed. Cir. 1993).

(e) The Application of the Rule on Field of Use Limits to Products Made by a Patented Process

The approval of field of use restrictions also generally extends to restrictions on the sale of unpatented products made by patented processes or patented machines.

However, in one instance, the owner of a patent on a process for making an old but valuable chemical catalyst granted to one U.S. licensee an exclusive license to make and "sell" the unpatented catalyst using the process.[31] It granted licenses to other companies limited to making and using such catalysts in their polymer manufacturing operations. One district court found that these agreements did not constitute patent misuse.[32] Later, another district court held that they violated the Sherman Act. The Court of Appeals reversed on the ground that the purported exclusive license to sell the unpatented catalyst was lawful where the process was the only economically viable one (section 2.6).

The Court of Appeals said the restriction had no impact on competition in the catalyst market beyond that which would take place if the patent owner granted an unlimited exclusive license to make and use the process. Since an exclusive license would be lawful, the licenses granted were lawful. The court did not suggest how its "analysis" could reach any different conclusion if the process was one of many available processes for making the product. However, the court seemed to think there might be a problem if the owner of less valuable rights tried the same thing. The court's opinion did not identify what the patent owner was trying to accomplish by its licensing strategy.

Again, the patent owner may have wished to limit its licensees to particular products or marketing areas to achieve economic discrimination or encourage investment that might generate external benefits for other licensees. The process patent could have different values based upon the end products produced, and the costs of alternative processes

---

[31] *United States v. Studiengesellschaft Kohle, M.B.H.*, 426 F.Supp. 143 (D. D.C. 1976), *rev'd*, 628 F.2d 142, 146–149 (D.C. Cir. 1980) (grant of nonexclusive licenses under patented process to manufacturers to make and use unpatented chemicals and grant to a "competing" manufacturer of a nonexclusive license to make and an "exclusive" license to sell the chemical in the United States violated the Sherman Act).
[32] *Ethyl Corporation v. Hercules Powder Company*, 232 F.Supp. 453 (D. Del. 1964).

for making those end products. Hence, different licenses limited to producing particular kinds of unpatented products may be profit maximizing and perhaps output expanding. Even if one licensee receives the "exclusive right to sell" an unpatented product, the agreement has no effect on that licensee's ability to use the old or other alternative technology to make and sell the same product. An exclusive license does not constitute an agreement by the licensee not to use unpatented technology.

The use of a process may also generate downstream externalities in development and marketing. Hence, it may be desirable to grant exclusive licenses in a product field to eliminate those externalities.

The legality of the restriction should not be based on whether output under the agreements is greater or less than output under exclusive licensee or patent owner production. That test ignores the benefit from increased profitability from use of the restriction. If one attempts to evaluate the lawfulness of particular restrictions by comparing output under the agreements to some other state of affairs, the only useful comparison is the output in the market under the agreements with the restriction compared with the output which would have prevailed had the invention not been made at all. Any comparison of two marketplace conditions, which *assumes* both the existence and some use of the invention, ignores that licensing is permitted (but not compelled) in order to give incentives to produce the invention in the first place. Any such comparison assumes either that the patent system does not work or that the reduction in the percentage of the value captured by the patent owner will not lead to any reduction in innovation.

5.5 PRICE RESTRICTIONS

The history of antitrust and misuse law follows a similar pattern in addressing restrictions on the prices at which licensees sell, the quantities they sell, the territories in which they may sell, and the customers to whom they may sell. Practices are declared legal and later declared illegal. The law again has often failed to distinguish economically harmful from beneficial agreements.

Minimum price, maximum quantity, exclusive territory, and exclusive customer restrictions may be useful to restrict rivalry among suppliers of substitutes under the guise of license agreements. Exclusive field of use restrictions may be used for the same purpose. Rivals may be selling or have the ability to sell substitute products without infringing patents. They may be tempted to try to eliminate or limit that competition by a series of sham license agreements. Those agreements may assign exclusive fields, exclusive territories, or exclusive customers. They may set minimum prices or maximum quantities. The courts attempt to identify such sham agreements and treat them appropriately (section 2.11).

However, the proper hostility to sham agreements has from time to time led courts to broadly condemn certain restrictions even though they are used in vertical agreements for purposes other than restricting competition.

(a) The Competitive Effects

An owner may wish to control minimum price or maximum quantity to induce licensee investments that enhance the value of the rights. These devices may provide more flexible controls than granting "exclusivity" to one (or a few) licensees. These controls may also seek to prevent a "low-royalty" licensee from defeating economic discimination. If these controls do not enhance licensee efficiency, they are contrary to the owner's interest.

If there are externalities in providing further development and marketing services and those services are not provided, the demand for the patented product may be low. With a higher-level investment in development and marketing, the demand for the product can be expanded. If more than one licensee is needed to manufacture at a minimum cost, granting an exclusive license to one licensee would result in inefficient production. The value of the patent could be increased if several licenses were granted and each licensee induced to increase its investment.

If the patent owner could induce that additional investment, it could charge a higher royalty rate and earn significantly greater revenue. In order to induce the licensees to make the additional investment, the patent owner may charge a royalty rate and set a minimum price at a level that would be profit maximizing for licensees that made the desired investments. The patent owner may also set a maximum quantity to achieve

5.5 PRICE RESTRICTIONS

the same thing. Given that minimum price or maximunm quantity, non-price competition among the licensees with respect to development and marketing services may induce the additional costs and the consequent expansion of demand. If the license is nonexclusive, a royalty alone cannot provide those incentives.

Minimum prices and maximum quantities may also be useful to an owner that wishes to produce and sell in a market with strong scale economies in demand or supply, see section 1.10(d). The owner may license so that its product is adopted by users at a faster rate than substitutes. Multiple sources may induce users make asset specific investments they would otherwise shun. Multiple sources may also be necessary simply to grow at the necessary rate relative to other products. However, unless the owner is also able to exceed the rate of growth of its licensees, the licensees may survive and the owner disappear as a producer. These restrictions may be devices for the owner to control the rate of growth by its licensees and help assure the owner's survival as producer.

Price and quantity restrictions may also be useful to supplement grants of exclusive positions to licensees. Exclusivity may create the successive monopoly problem. The owner's controls for this purpose are now exactly the opposite of those discussed above. The owner wishes to set maximum prices and minumum quantities. Those controls may help maximizing licensing profits by limiting a licensee's exercise of market power. In order to prevent such licensees from limiting output, raising price, and limiting the owner's royalty income, the owner may set a maximum price for licensee sales or set a minimum quantity.

(b) The *General Electric* Rule

In 1902 and again in 1926, the Supreme Court found no Sherman Act violation by a patent owner independently fixing prices for its manufacturing licensee's sale of patented goods.[33] In one of those cases, the patent owner, General Electric, made and sold patented electric lights and granted a license to Westinghouse to make and sell lights. The license provided that Westinghouse would sell at prices and terms of sale spec-

---

[33] *United States v. General Electric Co.*, 272 U.S. 476, 478–479, 488–494 (1926); *Bement v. National Harrow Co.*, 186 U.S. 70, 72, 93 (1902).

THE NATURE AND SCOPE OF LICENSED RIGHTS

ified by General Electric and would use the type of distribution system used by General Electric. General Electric distributed its patented lights only through agents who agreed to sell at prices fixed by General Electric. The Court stated the following test:[34]

> Conveying less than title to the patent, or part of it, the patentee may grant a license to make, use and vend articles under the specification of his patent for any royalty and upon any condition the performance of which is reasonably within the reward which the patentee by the grant of the patent is entitled to secure. . . . The patentee may make and grant a license to another to make and use the patented articles, but withhold its right to sell them. . . . If the patentee goes further, and licenses the selling of the articles, may he limit the selling by limiting the method of sale or price? We think he may do so, provided that the conditions of sale are normally and reasonably adapted to secure pecuniary reward for the patentee's monopoly.

The Court found it reasonable for a patent owner selling the patented product to fix the prices at which the licensee sells. The Court said the licensee's price "will necessarily affect" the price at which the patent owner sells its goods. Therefore, the patentee should be permitted to control it.[35] The Court did not notice that price controls may enhance the owner's profits from exploitation even though it is not selling.

A patent owner may benefit from enhanced efficiency of exploitation by minimum prices or maximum quantities whether or not the patent owner is a manufacturer and seller. If *General Electric* is read to say the only legitimate interest of a patent owner is protecting its own sales, the courts could find that minimum price restrictions are unlawful if the licensor is not a producer.

One lower court interpeted *General Electric* to permit price restrictions only where the licensed patent completely covers the product.[36] Some lower courts have found that the *General Electric* decision did not

---

[34] 272 U.S. at 489–490.
[35] *Compare, United States v. Huck Manufacturing Co.,* 382 U.S. 1197 (1965), *aff'g by an equally divided court,* 227 F.791 (D. Mich. 1964).
[36] *United States v. General Electric Co.,* 82 F.Supp. 753, 767–778, 776–777, 813–817, 873–876, 881–883, 901–905 (D. N.J. 1949).

5.5 PRICE RESTRICTIONS

permit a patentee to fix the price of unpatented products of patented machines or processes.[37] Conversely, the lower courts have held that it did not constitute patent misuse to fix the maximum quantity of unpatented end products under a license covering a patented process[38] (section 5.6). As shown above, there is no reason for believing that price and quantity restrictions serve any different functions when the patent covers a machine or process rather than an end product.

(c) Price Limits under Cross-Licensed Patents—*Line Material*

In 1948 in *United States v. Line Material,* the Supreme Court found a Sherman Act violation where separate owners of complementary patents relating to a single product cross-licensed each other and provided licenses under both patents to manufacturers fixing the price for sale.[39] The patents were complementary in the sense that only when both patents were used in a single product could the public and the patentees obtain full benefit of the efficiencies provided by both inventions.[40]

The Court, with three Justices dissenting, distinguished *General Electric* on the basis that the license involved patents owned by different patent owners.

If the patents in that action had covered two competing products, the decision might be sound. In that instance, the cross-licensing and minimum price provisions could provide a basis for limiting competition between competing patented products. However, one patent related to a product and the second patent related to an improvement. The cross-licensing could not eliminate competition. Because no competition is possible without the cross-licensing, there was no reason for treating this situation differently. The effect of that ruling may be to force the owner of the basic patent to market a product not using the improvement. If it

---

[37] *Cummer-Graham Co. v. Straight Side Basket Corp.,* 142 F.2d 646 (5th Cir. 1944); *Barber-Colman Co. v. National Tool Co.,* 136 F.2d 339 (6th Cir. 1943); *Sylvania Industrial Corp. v. Visking Corp.,* 132 F.2d 947 (4th Cir. 1943).
[38] *Q-Tips, Inc. v. Johnson & Johnson,* 109 F.Supp. 657 (D. N.J. 1951); *Ethyl v. Hercules Power Company,* 232 F.Supp. 453 (D. Del. 1964).
[39] *United States v. Line Material Co.,* 333 U.S. 287, 293–297, 305–315 (1948). This categorical rule has been followed. *In Re Yarn Processing Patent Validity Litigation,* 541 F.2d 1127, 1135 (5th Cir. 1976).
[40] Id. at 281.

does so, it may use the minimum price clauses. The invention covered by the improvement patent will not be used and an inferior product is marketed.

(d) Price Limits on Resale—*Bauer*

Through a number of decisions, the Court limited lawful price fixing to the first authorized sale. In 1913, in *Bauer & Cie v. O'Donnell*,[41] the patent owner or its licensees sold a patented product with a notice on the package that the product is "licensed by us for use and sale at a price not less than $1 dollar." The notice said that "the purchase is an acceptance of the condition."

The Court declared that a purchaser of that product who resold for less than one dollar was not guilty of infringement. The Court found the notice ineffective to limit the right of the purchaser to sell. The Court said that the patent owner received no royalty based on the subsequent sale.[42] The Court also said the patent right to sell was exercised by the first sale.[43]

The Court recognized that resale price restrictions might be required to induce distributors and retailers to "create and maintain a market." However, it dismissed that important observation by saying that consideration "could have had little weight" in framing the patent and copyright acts.[44]

The restrictions may have been necessary to create incentives for licensees to make investments that would increase the value of the rights. This would also further the government's purpose for granting rights. However, because those considerations "could" have had little weight in framing the statutes, the Court dismissed the primary justification for the restriction. The Court did not bother to say whether a different result would have been forthcoming if Congress had given those considerations much weight.

Basically, the only reason the Supreme Court refused to enforce resale price restrictions was that it had condemned them with respect to

---

[41] *Bauer & Cie v. O'Donnell,* 229 U.S. 1, 8–9 11, 18 (1913).
[42] Id. at 6.
[43] Id. at 16–17.
[44] Id. at 13.

5.5 PRICE RESTRICTIONS

unpatented products in the *Dr. Miles*[45] decision in 1911 and with respect to a copyrighted book in the *Bobbs-Merrill*[46] decision in 1908. In *Dr. Miles,* the Court found that provisions in an agreement fixing the price for resale of an unpatented product were contrary to public policy and therefore void.

(e) Resale Price Limits—*Univis Lens* and *Ethyl Gasoline*

In the 1940s, the Supreme Court further limited the right of a patent owner to fix prices. In *United States v. Univis Lens Co.*[47] and *Ethyl Gasoline Corp. v. United States,*[48] the patent owner granted a license to sell a patented product fixing the price at which the licensee sells. The owner made and sold the patented product to that licensee for resale in *Ethyl.* The owner, through another licensee, made and sold an unpatented product useful only in making a patented product in *Univis.* In each case, the patent owner received no royalties based on its licensee's sales at the fixed prices. The Court said both agreements violated section 1.

These cases made it clear that fixing the resale price of patented articles sold by the patent owner is illegal, even though the patent owner expressly licenses the resellers to sell at certain prices. The same result was applied if the patent owner made and sold an unpatented product useful to that licensee only in making the patented product. These decisions put price fixing out of the reach of patent owners who make all or part of the patented product.

The basis for these decisions was that the first sale of the product "exhausted the patent monopoly." Therefore, the patents could not justify fixing the purchaser's selling price. Merely because the patent owner sells a patented product does not necessarily mean it has no interest in the level of investment by purchasers. The Court also noted that the purchasers paid no royalties on their sales. Even if the returns to the patent owner are in the form of the price of a product, that does not affect the patent owner's legitimate interest in achieving an increase in investment by its customers.

---

[45] *Dr. Miles Medical Co. v. Park's Sons Co.,* 220 U.S. 373 (1911).
[46] *Bobbs-Merrill Co. v. Straus,* 210 U.S. 339 (1908).
[47] *United States v. Univis Lens Co.,* 316 U.S. 241, 243–245, 249–251 (1942).
[48] *Ethyl Gasoline Corp. v. United States,* 309 U.S. 436, 446–448, 452, 457 (1940).

(f) Price Limits in Licenses used for Cartel Administration

The patent owner's right to restrict the licensee's price or quantity applies only to vertical agreements, that is, agreements between suppliers of complementary products or services. If the restriction results from an agreement among licensees primarily to limit rivalry among them that would occur without the license, price or quantity restrictions are illegal. The courts have been quick to note that such agreements are not reasonably related to the patent owner increasing the efficiency of use of the patent, but rather have the purpose of maximizing returns to licensees by merely limiting competition.

A patent owner's right to restrain trade in a patented article does not include the right to do so in concert with licensees or other patentees and the legality of restraints resulting from the combination are judged by the standards of the Sherman Act.[49]

For example, in 1942, the Court held in *United States v. Masonite Corp.*,[50] that certain agreements violated the Sherman Act because they were not reasonably related to the patent owner's earning maximum returns from the patented article, but rather had the purpose of maximizing returns to the patent owner and its competitors by fixing the price at which they sell the patented article. The patent owner, pursuant to an agreement among itself and its competitors, entered substantially identical "agency" agreements to establish those competitors as agents for distribution of the patent owner's product at fixed minimum prices.

5.6 QUANTITY RESTRICTIONS

Patent owners have also limited the quantity that licensees may sell over a certain time period. Does the antitrust law or the law of patent misuse prohibit a patent license that limits the licensee to selling a maximum quantity of the patented product?

---

[49] *United States v. New Wrinkle, Inc.*, 342, U.S. 371, 374, 378–380 (1952); *United States v. United States Gypsum Co.*, 333 U.S. 364, 399–401 (1948); *Standard Sanitary Mfg. Co. v. United States*, 226 U.S. 20, 39–49 (1912); *Newburgh Moire Co. v. Superior Moire Co.*, 237 F.2d 283 (3rd Cir. 1956); *United States v. Vehicular Parking, Ltd.*, 54 F.Supp. 828, 837 (D. Del. 1944).
[50] *United States v. Masonite Corp.*, 314 U.S. 265, 276–280 (1942).

5.6 QUANTITY RESTRICTIONS

(a) The Law

The decisions say that a maximum quantity restriction on licensee sales, standing alone, is not an antitrust violation and does not give rise to a defense of patent misuse. Prior to the Sherman Act in 1890, the courts recognized the enforceability of a limitation on the quantity of licensee sales.[51] In 1899, the Supreme Court established that an agreement between competitors to divide markets is a *per se* violation of the Sherman Act.[52]

There are few decisions addressing whether maximum quantity restriction on licensee sales violates the antitrust laws or constitutes patent misuse. In two cases, the lower courts found no antitrust violation and no misuse.[53]

In 1953 in *United States v. du Pont,* the government alleged that du Pont violated Section 2 of the Sherman Act. The government asserted that du Pont had monopolized particular cellophane markets by its patent licensing and other practices. Du Pont owned a number of patents that covered moistureproof cellophane. It granted a license under the moisture-proof patents to Sylvania. Sylvania agreed to pay a royalty of 2 percent of its net selling price of patented cellophane. The royalty increased on Sylvania's sales that exceeded a certain percentage of the combined sales of Sylvania and du Pont. The royalty would increase to 30 percent of the net selling price or $0.20 per pound, whichever was greater, on Sylvania sales in excess of 20 percent of the combined sales of such cellophane in 1933 by du Pont and Sylvania. For nine years after 1933, Sylvania's threshold share for increased payments was increased by 1 percent per year. Additional royalties were computed on an annual basis.

Under the agreement, Sylvania cross-licensed du Pont under certain Sylvania patents. Du Pont agreed to pay royalties of 2 percent of its net selling price and 20 percent or 30 percent of the net selling price of

---

[51]*Aspinwall Manuf'g Co. v. Gill,* 32 F. 697, 698 (D. N.J. 1887) ("Of course, the defendants cannot pretend that their license to build 100 machines gave them any right to build any more than that. . . .").
[52]*Addyston Pipe & Steel Co. v. United States,* 175 U.S. 211, 237, 241 (1899).
[53]*United States v. E.I. du Pont de Nemours & Co.,* 118 F.Supp. 41, 149–158, 211–214, 226 (D. Del. 1953), *aff'd on other grounds,* 351 U.S. 377 (1955); *Q-Tips, Inc. v. Johnson & Johnson,* 109 F.Supp. 657, 659–660 (D. N.J. 1951) and 108 F.Supp. 845, 871 (D. N.J. 1952), *aff'd in pertinent part,* 207 F.2d 509 (3rd Cir. 1953).

products sold by du Pont in excess of 80 percent of the combined sales of du Pont and Sylvania in 1933. For each of the nine years after 1933, 1 percent was deducted from the 80 percent to mark the limit for that year above which du Pont was obligated to pay the additional royalty.

The district court found that the provision for increased royalties had no impact on Sylvania's production, because in each year Sylvania sales were below the threshold for increased royalties. It also found that royalties paid did not impair Sylvania's ability to compete. In addition, the court found that "royalties never prevented Sylvania from expanding its production, and Sylvania never considered the royalties an impediment to its ability to produce and expand."

The government urged that the Sylvania license was a predatory act, which supported the finding that du Pont had unlawfully acquired and maintained a monopoly. The court rejected that contention. It seemed to do so on both legal and factual grounds. The opinion suggests that limiting Sylvania's quantity by the escalating royalty provision was entirely lawful:[54]

> As patentee du Pont had [the] right to fix royalties at graduated scales on [the] amount of Sylvania's production. *United States v. General Electric Co.,* 272 U.S. 476, 47 S.Ct. 192, 71 L.Ed. 362; *General Talking Pictures Corp. v. Western Electric Co.,* 305 U.S. 124, 59 S.Ct. 116, 83 L.Ed. 81. No limitation of production by Sylvania under its own patents existed or is charged.
>
> In its contention of suppression of competition and assertion of monopoly power, plaintiff fails to come to grips with the fact that throughout the period that graduated royalties were in effect, Sylvania's entire moistureproof production fell within valid claims of the broad product patent.... On these facts, there is no authority to support the contention that it would have been in any way illegal under the Sherman Act for du Pont to limit Sylvania's production. The cases are to the effect [that the] owner of a valid product patent may by license restrict production of the licensee to a specified quantity, at a specified place.

---

[54] 118 F.Supp. at 226.

5.6 QUANTITY RESTRICTIONS

However, the court also noted that the evidence was clear that the royalty provisions did not limit Sylvania's production.

In 1951 in *Q-Tips, Inc. v. Johnson & Johnson*[55] the Q-tip company owned a patent covering a machine used for making medical swabs. The swabs themselves were not patented. The Q-tip company granted one license to make and use with the patented machine which limited "the number of unpatented double-tipped cotton tips that may be produced." In an action for infringement of the patent, the defendant alleged that the patent owner had misused its patent by this limitation and asserted a counterclaim under the antitrust laws. The defendant sought summary judgment dismissing the infringement complaint on the basis of this defense. The court denied the motion. The court rejected the defendant's argument that the patent owner was attempting to obtain an unlawful monopoly in the unpatented swabs. It found both the tie-in cases and price-fixing cases inapplicable.[56]

Both *du Pont* and *Q-Tips* were decided shortly after the district court's 1949 decision in *United States v. General Electric Co.*[57] In this action, the government charged a wide range of alleged violations of the Sherman and Clayton Acts. These included charges relating to General Electric's patent licenses with lamp manufacturers. Some of these licenses were the so-called "B" licenses. Each of the B licensees received the right to make electric lamps and sell them in the United States. Each B licensee was limited to sales in any one year of a fixed quota or percentage based on General Electric's total net dollar sales for that year. The B licensees paid royalties at a rate of 3.5 percent of General Electric's prices for the corresponding type of lamps and an additional 20 percent of the licensee's net sales in any year in excess of 5 percent over its quota for that year. If a licensee sold an amount 10 percent in excess of its quota, this constituted a breach. The B license included no restriction on the price at which the licensee sold.

General Electric's type "A" license with Westinghouse included restrictions on Westinghouse's sales prices. General Electric argued that

---

[55]*Q-Tips, Inc. v. Johnson & Johnson,* 109 F.Supp. 657 (D. N.J. 1951).
[56]Id. at 660.
[57]*United States v. General Electric Co.,* 82 F.Supp. 753, 767–778, 776–777, 813–817, 873–876, 881–883, 901–905 (D. N.J. 1949).

"it is entirely proper to grant licenses under machine or process patents with quantity restrictions as distinguished from price restrictions on the product, since quantity restrictions are a direct restriction on the extent of use of the licensed machine or process." General Electric also defended the legality of the price restriction of the Westinghouse license.

The lower court found the price restriction illegal, because General Electric did not own a patent completely covering the lamps. The court also held that the B licensees were guilty of conspiring with General Electric in violation of the Sherman Act, relying in the main on *United States v. Line Material Co.*,[58] a case involving price restrictions.[59] The court concluded that there was a "lack of valid patent support to sustain price, quantity and export limitations in the incandescent electric lamp domestic licenses in existence after 1933." It concluded that General Electric and its B licensees had violated section 2 of the Sherman Act. The court's general conclusion that there was an antitrust violation noted the quantity restrictions in the B licenses.

Again, quantity restrictions are common features of "licenses" alleged to have the primary purpose and effect of limiting rivalry among "licensees" that would supply substitutes in the absence of the license.[60]

(b) The Competitive Effects

The effects were dicussed earlier. The law does not always perceive the effects I described. The decisions indicate that restrictions on the maximum quantity of a patented product that may be sold do not constitute patent misuse or a violation of the antitrust laws. This is true only where there are no other restrictions in the agreement having an anticompetitive effect and the agreement is unilaterally imposed by the patent owner in its own economic interest and without agreement among or for the benefit of its licensees. In spite of the decided cases, there is some reason to believe that the legality of quantity restrictions is open to question.

---

[58]*United States v. Line Material Co.*, 333 U.S. 287 (1948).
[59]82 F.Supp. at 882–883.
[60]*American-Equipment Co. v. Tuthill*, 69 F.2d 406 (7th Cir. 1934); *Rubber Tire Wheel Co. v. Milwaukee Rubber W. Co.*, 154 F. 358 (7th Cir. 1907).

The uncertainty about the legality of price restrictions in patent licenses creates uncertainty about the legality of quantity restrictions. Quantity restrictions are at least as restrictive, and potentially more restrictive, of competition as price restrictions.

Suppose that several companies selling products in a market wish to limit competition under the guise of a license. They agree that one of them will license the others under a commercially unimportant patent for a nominal royalty. The licenses will provide that no licensee will sell more than 20 percent of the total market in any year. There is no easy way for a licensee to avoid the restriction. If the licenses fixed a minimum price, a licensee could profitably cheat by upgrading the quality of its product and capturing a larger share of industry profits. Under a quantity restriction, the licensees do not have that alternative way of competing for additional sales. The economic reality is that a restriction on maximum quantity is the practical equivalent to the restriction on minimum price. Hence, there is some reason to believe that price and quantity restrictions would be treated similarly. Because of the question about the legality of price restrictions, there is also a question about the legality of quantity restrictions.

5.7 TERRITORIAL LIMITATIONS

While the law has placed significant restrictions on the use of price and quantity restrictions in licenses, the law has generally treated as lawful restrictions on the territories within the United States where manufacturing licensees may sell, unless the restriction is employed as part of an agreement between rivals to eliminate competition.[61] The courts have held that a patent owner may limit the licensee's right to make, use, or sell a patented product to a particular territory within the United States.[62]

---

[61]However, one case suggests that, as in case of price restrictions, a patentee may not grant a license limiting the place of sale or use of an unpatented product of a patented machine or process. *In Re Amtorg Trading Corp.,* 75 F.2d 826 (C.C. P.A. 1935).

[62]*Bement v. National Harrow Co.,* 186 U.S. 70, 92–93 (1902); *Adams v. Burke,* 17 Wall. 453 (1873); *Brownell v. Ketham,* 211 F.2d 121, 128 (9th Cir. 1954) ("It is a

The only apparent basis for that difference in treatment is a provision in the Patent Act on assignment of patents, which states in part:[63]

> Applications for patents, patents, or any interest therein, shall be assignable in law by an instrument in writing. The applicant, patentee, or his assigns or legal representatives may in like manner grant and convey an exclusive right under his application for patent, or patents, to the whole or any specified part of the United States.

The courts also approved various restrictions that seek to limit the import or export of patented products. The courts have said it does not violate the antitrust laws for an owner of U.S. and foreign patents to grant a license under the foreign patent and receive the licensee's express agreement not to sell in the United States.[64] Likewise, where a patentee of both U.S. and foreign patents sells the patented product in a foreign country with notice that the product is not to be imported or sold within the United States, a purchaser from the patentee with notice who resells in the United States is guilty of infringement.[65]

Restrictions on exports have received similar treatment. One court held that it is lawful to grant a license under a U.S. patent that limits the license to sales to customers in the United States and includes the licensee's agreement not to sell for export from the United States.[66] However, another decision suggests that it is unsettled whether the licensee's agreement not to sell in the United States for export is lawful.[67]

As in the case of price restrictions, the courts have limited the patentee's ability to limit the area where a patented product may be

---

fundamental rule of patent law that the owner of a patent may license another and prescribe territorial limitations."); *cf., Ethyl Gasoline Corp. v. United States,* 309 U.S. 436, 456 (1940).

[63] 35 U.S.C. § 261 (1982).

[64] *Dunlop Company Limited v. Kelsey-Hayes Company,* 484 F.2d 401, 417 (6th Cir. 1972).

[65] *Dickerson v. Timing,* 84 Fed. 192, 195 (8th Cir. 1897); *Dickerson v. Matheson,* 57 Fed. 524 (2d Cir. 1893).

[66] *Brownell v. Ketcham Wire & Mfg. Co.,* 211 F.2d 121, 129 (9th Cir. 1954) (holding that such a license does not violate the antitrust laws).

[67] *Compare, Extractol Process Ltd. v. Hiram Walker & Sons,* 153 F.2d 264, 267–268 (7th Cir. 1946) (suggesting that a sale in the U.S. for use outside the U.S. is not infringement).

5.7 TERRITORIAL LIMITATIONS

resold. It is unclear under current law whether the patent owner has the right to restrict the place of use or resale by a U.S. purchaser of a patented product (see sections 6.5 to 6.9).

The Supreme Court has sometimes acknowledged the right of a patent owner to expressly limit the rights of a purchaser.[68] However, the Court held in *Adams v. Burke* and *Hobbie v. Jennison*[69] that, if a patent owner assigned the rights to make, use, and sell in a limited territory, those purchasing from that assignee in the assigned territory could use the articles anywhere without infringing the patent. In *Keeler v. Standard Folding Bed Co.*,[70] the Court found that such a purchaser could also resell the products outside the territory. In each of these situations, the patent owner did not limit the assignee's right to sell to sales for use or resale in the assigned territory. In addition, the assignee did not condition the sale on the purchaser's agreement to use or resell the product only in the territory. The Court in *Hobbie* said that the patent owner could bind a territorial assignee to conditions that would prevent it from interfering with another assignee. The Court in *Keeler* declined to say "[w]hether a patentee may protect himself and his assignees by special contracts brought home to the purchasers. . . ."

Where an express agreement is made with the purchaser limiting its use to a certain area, the lower courts have sometimes enjoined use by a purchaser outside the area. In *Skeeball Co. v. Cohen*,[71] the patentee sold an amusement device, conveying title to the purchaser and licensing use only within a certain area. The defendant bought a device from purchaser and used it in another area. The court held that the restriction was valid and the patentee was entitled to an injunction.

In 1977, the Court in *Continental T.V., Inc. v. G.T.E. Sylvania, Inc.*[72] held that nonprice vertical resale restrictions were not *per se* violations of the Sherman Act and were to be judged under the rule of reason. That decision overruled the *per se* rule in *United States v. Arnold Schwinn &*

---

[68] *Mitchell v. Hawley*, 83 U.S. 544 (1872).
[69] *Adams v. Burke*, 84 U.S. 453 (1873); *Hobbie v. Jennison*, 149 U.S. 355 (1893) (territorial assignee who sold to a buyer in the territory knowing the buyer intended to use the product outside the territory, is not liable for infringement).
[70] *Keeler v. Standard Folding Bed Co.*, 157 U.S. 659 (1895).
[71] *Skeeball Co. v. Cohen*, 286 Fed. 275 (E.D.N.Y. 1922).
[72] *Continental T.V., Inc. v. G.T.E. Sylvania, Inc.*, 433 U.S. 36 (1977).

Co.[73] While *G.T.E. Sylvania* did not involve a patented product, that decision seems to require that resale territorial restrictions violate the antitrust laws only if they are found, under all the circumstances, to be unreasonable.

5.8 CUSTOMER LIMITATIONS

There have been few decisions involving licenses that limited sales to particular customers or types of customers. The few decisions suggest that a patent owner may grant a license to sell restricted to a prescribed customer or class of customers.[74] The courts have sometimes permitted the owner to achieve this result by licensing different rights to different types of companies. A licensee may be authorized to sell only to licensees under other patents.[75] The licensee may also be permitted to sell only to licensees under other claims of the same patent.[76]

5.9 CROSS-LICENSING AND LIMITATIONS ON THE GRANT OF LICENSES

The law has rejected the view that the owner of a lawfully acquired patent has a general obligation to license third parties on some reasonable basis. There is no such obligation, even if the owner has a monopoly in a market and a license is necessary for others to compete in that market.[77] The

---

[73] *United States v. Arnold Schwinn & Co.,* 388 U.S. 365 (1967).

[74] *In Re Yarn Processing Patent Validity Litigation,* 541 F.2d 1127, 1135 (5th Cir. 1976) (a license under process patents to make machinery to perform the process and to sell only to persons licensed by the patent owner to use the process, does not violate the Sherman Act); *Westinghouse Electric & Mfg. Co. v. Cutting & Washington Radio Corp.,* 294 Fed. 671 (2d Cir. 1922).

[75] *Deering Milliken & Co. v. Temp-Resisto Corporation,* 160 F.Supp. 463, 478–482 (S.D.N.Y. 1958); *but cf., Ethyl Gasoline Corp. v. United States,* 309 U.S. 436 (1940); *United States v. Univis Lens Co.,* 316 U.S. 241 (1942).

[76] *SCM Corporation v. Radio Corporation of America,* 318 F.Supp. 433 (S.D.N.Y. 1970).

[77] *For example, SCM Corp. v. Xerox Corp.,* 645 F.2d 1195, 1206 (2d Cir. 1981); *cf., Berkey Photo, Inc. v. Eastman Kodak Co.,* 603 F.2d 263, 281 (2d Cir. 1979) (a monopolist has no obligation to predisclose details of its new products to competitors). The "essential facilities" doctrine of antitrust law has not (yet) been applied to in-

5.9 CROSS-LICENSING

reason is that an obligation to license undercuts the value of the patent and reduces the incentives the patent system seeks to create.

Similarly, the law has not required separate owners of independently developed patents to license third parties on some reasonable basis, even if together they account for a "monopoly" share of a market and they have licensed each other. In *Standard Oil Co. v. United States,* 283 U.S. 163, 172 (1930)[78] the Court declared:

> The government next contends that the royalties violate the Sherman Law because the fees charged are onerous. The argument is that the competitive advantage which the three primary defendants [who cross-licensed each other under competing cracking processes] enjoy of manufacturing cracked gasoline free of royalty, while licensees must pay to them a heavy tribute in fees, enables these primary defendants to exclude from interstate commerce cracked gasoline which would, under lower competitive royalty rates, be produced by possible rivals. This argument ignores the privileges incident to ownership of patents. Unless the industry is dominated, or interstate commerce directly restrained, the Sherman Act does not require cross-licensing patentees to license at reasonable rates others engaged in interstate commerce. The allegation that the royalties charged are onerous is standing alone, without legal significance; and, as will be shown, neither the alleged domination, nor restraint of commerce, has been proved. [citations and footnote omitted]

Standard Oil leaves open the possibility that cross-licensing patent owners may not have the usual privileges of patent ownership (whether to charge what the market will bear or to license only to limited fields). However, because the Court found no "domination or restraint of commerce," it did not explain what those different privileges of cross-licensing owners might be.

Separate companies commonly license each other under their patents. Cross-licenses may contain limitations on the ability of those companies to grant licenses under their separate patents to third parties.

---

tellectual property licensing. *See, Data General Corp v. Grumman Systems Corp.,* 32 U.S.P.Q 2d 1385 (1st Cir. 1994).
[78] *Standard Oil Co. v. United States,* 283 U.S. 163, 172 (1930).

The legality of cross-license agreements and licenses under the cross-licensed patents are evaluated under the rule of reason. The rule of reason permits evaluation of both so-called procompetitive and anticompetitive effects and attempts to determine the net effect.

Again, there are three "markets" in which agreements between owners of different patents may have potential anticompetitive effects. The first is the competition between patent owners in selling products that each could make under its patents at the time of the agreement without infringing the patents of the other. There is the competition between a patent owner and a licensee in selling existing products not covered by the licensed patents. There is the competition that might exist between patent owners to license patent rights existing at the time of their agreement. In each case, the effects are in markets for existing products and rights. The second is competition to improve existing products by future research and development. The third is the competition in the markets for future products that might be made possible by future research and development by patent owners and their licensees.

The courts have a vague sense that cooperation among patent owners may limit competition in ways that would not have occurred had those patent owners competed in their use of their inventions and their licensing policies and practices. For example, the Court in *Hartford Empire Co. v. United States* said that the effects of a license that allocated exclusive, noncompeting fields to the owners are harmful, where the owners of those patents cover potentially competing products.[79] By coordinating the exploitation of those potentially competing products, the competition that might have existed between them is eliminated. Where the patents are blocking or complementary, the courts in general have been inclined to find that the limitations in licenses do not have the effect of eliminating competition.

Cross-licensing in itself is not unlawful.[80] Nonexclusive cross-licenses of competing patents are also not necessarily unlawful. In *Standard Oil Co. v. United States*,[81] the Court found that nonexclusive cross-licensing of competing petroleum-cracking process patents did not

---

[79] *Hartford Empire Co. v. United States*, 323 U.S. 386, 400–401 (1944).
[80] *For example, Apex Electrical Manufacturing Co. v. Altorfer Brothers Co.*, 238 F.2d 867, 873 (7th Cir. 1956).
[81] *Standard Oil Co. v. United States*, 283 U.S. 163, 170–172 (1930).

5.9 CROSS-LICENSING

unreasonably restrain trade in unpatented gasoline where the use of the processes did not give owners and licensees a "dominant" position in the market for all gasoline, and where the parties had the right to sublicense under all patents but only at rates fixed by the agreement.

Cross-license agreements have been generally condemned in three situations.

The first involves findings that the licenses were a sham and were merely a vehicle for parties who would otherwise compete to reduce that rivalry.[82]

The second is where the cross-licenses had the effect of placing all significant patents under the control of the cross-licensing parties, who allocated rights to each other and to third parties to operate exclusively in noncompetitive fields. In *Hartford Empire Co. v. United States*,[83] patents relating to glass-making machinery were accumulated by Hartford by internal development, by purchase, and by pooling. Competing and conflicting patents were pooled or cross-licensed. Fields of use were assigned among the participating companies to use the patents to make certain types of glass. Production quotas were assigned within some of the fields. The Court concluded:[84]

> In summary, the situation brought about in the glass industry, and existing in 1938, was this: Hartford, with technical and financial aid of others in the conspiracy, had acquired, by issue to it or assignment from the owners, more than 600 patents. These, with over 100 Corning controlled patents, over 60 Owens patents, over 70 Hazel patents, and some 12 Lynch patents, had been, by cross-licensing agreements, merged into a pool which effectively controlled the industry. This control was exercised to allot production in Corning's field to Corning, and that in restricted classes within the general container field to Owens, Hazel, Thatcher, Ball and such other smaller manufacturers as the group agreed should be licensed. The result was that 94% of the glass containers manufactured in this country on feeders and formers were made on machinery licensed under the pooled patents [footnote omitted]

---

[82] *United States v. New Wrinkle, Incorporated,* 342 U.S. 371 (1952).
[83] *Hartford Empire Co. v. United States,* 323 U.S. 386, 400–401 (1944).
[84] Id. at 400.

In *United States v. Associated Patents Inc.*,[85] certain machine tool manufacturers formed a holding company and assigned their patents to the company. The holding company granted each member of the pool an exclusive license for a particular field. That license provided that no other licenses would be issued except with the consent of the manufacturer having an exclusive license for the field requested. The Court found that arrangement violated section 1 of the Sherman Act without finding that the pooling manufacturers dominated the industry.

Third, where owners of competing patents agree to limit their competition in the manner in which they exploit those patents, and the patents "dominate" the markets in which they sell, the courts have condemned those agreements because they limited the opportunities for additional parties to obtain rights and operate in one or more markets reserved to the cooperating parties. In other words, where "pools" of potentially competing patents are formed that dominate the markets to which the licenses relate, and those parties jointly control the exploitation of those rights, the courts have condemned those agreements under section 1 of the Sherman Act.

In *United States v. Krasnov*,[86] two companies that accounted for 62 percent of the sales in a market cross-licensed each other under certain important patents and agreed not to grant any further licenses without the consent of both parties. In addition, the parties fixed prices and co-operated with respect to bringing infringement actions. The court found the agreements to violate sections 1 and 2 of the Sherman Act.

In *Hazeltine Research v. Zenith Radio Corp.*,[87] the owners of radio and television transmission and reception patents in Canada, Great Britain, and Australia pooled their patents (by cross-licensing other pool members who manufactured radios and televisions in the country of the particular pool and granting "the pool" the exclusive right to license the patents of the members), and agreed to refuse to license companies to sell televisions and radios in the country of the pool unless those prod-

---

[85] *United States v. Associated Patents Inc.*, 134 F.Supp. 74 (E.D. Mich. 1955), *aff'd per curiam sub nom. Mack Investment Co. v. United States,* 350 U.S. 960 (1956).
[86] *United States v. Krasnov*, 143 F.Supp. 184, 198 (E.D. Pa. 1956), *aff'd per curiam* 355 U.S. 5 (1957).
[87] *Hazeltine Research v. Zenith Radio Corp.*, 239 F.Supp. 51 (N.D. Ill. 1965), *aff'd in part, rev'd in part,* 395 U.S. 100 (1969).

5.9 CROSS-LICENSING

ucts were manufactured in the country of the pool. This agreement precluded foreign manufacturers from obtaining licenses.

In that action, Zenith manufactured televisions in the United States. It requested and was denied a license by the Canadian pool. It did not request a license from the other pool, but the Court found that if it had it would have been refused. The Court did not find that it would have been unlawful for any individual patent owner to license its patents to authorize the sale of products made in the country of the pool. The restriction alone was not unlawful. The agreement to improve it was.

The District Court found that all three pools violated the Sherman Act. It found that the patents in the pool in Great Britain were dominant, but made no similar finding in Canada or Australia. The Supreme Court affirmed the finding of a violation of section 1 of the Sherman Act with respect to the Canadian pool, even though there was no finding of dominance. The Supreme Court found that "[t]he chief purpose of the [Canadian] pool was to protect the manufacturing members and licensees from competition by American and other foreign companies seeking to export their products into Canada."[88] The Court noted that the members of the Canadian pool were "competing" business concerns and patentees.[89]

Finally, in *Mason City Tent and Awning Co. v. Clapper*,[90] the owner of a patent on a heat deflector for tractors and owner of a patent as a component of a deflector granted a license to three companies to sell deflector units. The owners agreed to not grant any additional licenses without the consent of *all* parties to the agreement; that is, the other owner and all three licensees. This was found to be a *per se* violation:[91]

> ... That is so because the patent laws were designed to only protect the patentee, and his assigns, in the whole or partial enjoyment of the fruit of his invention, and any restraint upon competition created by a license agreement that does not inure to the patentee, or his assigns, is not protected by the patent laws. Hence it is held that an agreement by a patentee which gives a non-exclusive licensee

---
[88] Id. at 115.
[89] Id. at 118.
[90] *Mason City Tent and Awning Co. v. Clapper*, 144 F.Supp. 754, 756 (W.D. Mo. 1956).
[91] Id. at 767.

a veto power in the selection of other licensees, is invalid according to Sherman Act standards.

We think said agreement is also violative of Section 2 of the Act, in that it manifests an attempt to monopolize, by the combining of non-competing patents in a single agreement, by competitors, and gives to the parties to the agreement veto power over patent rights that are not referable to their individual business, the patents or licenses granted, and this is true, even though the licensees may have continued to compete with each other in the manufacture and sale of tractor covers after the execution thereof. They were jointly given an exclusive market and control thereover by the terms of said agreement and not singularly as a consequence of patent privileges acquired. *United States v. Line Material Co.,* 33 U.S. 287, 68 S.Ct. 550, 92 L.Ed. 702.

In the decisions condemning cross-license agreements that limit a patent owner's freedom to license his patent without the consent of another party to the arrangement, the courts have often found or implied that it was significant that the patents covered competing products or processes. In situations where the patents are blocking or complementary, the courts have been less inclined to condemn the agreements, whether or not dominance was found. When the courts refer to patents as blocking, they seem to be referring to situations in which patents owned by different companies could be used in the manufacture or sale of a single product. Without authority to use all the patents, the courts seem impressed by the notion that the most desirable potential product may not be made at the lowest cost.

For example, in *International Manufacturing Co. v. Landon Inc.,*[92] the court said:[93]

> The pooling of patents, licensing all patents in the pools collectively, and sharing royalties is not necessarily an antitrust violation. In a case involving blocking patents such an arrangement is the only reasonable method for making the invention available to the public.

---

[92] *International Manufacturing Co. v. Landon Inc.,* 336 F.2d 723 (9th Cir. 1946) *cert. denied,* 379 U.S. 988 (1965).
[93] Id. at 729.

5.9 CROSS-LICENSING

In *United States v. Birdsboro Steel Foundry & Machine Co.*,[94] the court found that an exclusive cross-license agreement under blocking patents was lawful. The parties each made and sold cooling beds used in the steel industry. One company owned facilities suited to make small and intermediate-sized beds. The other company owned facilities capable of making large-sized beds. Each owned patents. Neither could, without a license from the other, make cooling beds containing the features desired by users, because those beds would contain inventions covered by patents of each party. There were also certain types of beds that neither could make, because the patents of one blocked use of certain inventions of the other.

The court found that the patents were blocking and that without the license they could not be used together. Mesta granted Birdsboro exclusive rights to sell beds for semifinished products. Birdsboro granted Mesta exclusive rights to sell beds for merchant mills. The court found the agreement lawful under the rule of reason, in spite of the allocation of exclusive fields:[95]

> The agreement in the instant case involves exclusive cross licenses....
>
> Viewing the agreement, however, as one of exclusive *cross* licensing, it is clear that such an agreement is not illegal per se and may even be desirable. In Standard Oil Co. v. United States, supra, the Court held, 283 U.S. at page 171, 51 S.Ct. at 424:
>
>> Where there are legitimately conflicting claims or threatened interferences, a settlement by agreement, rather than litigation, is not precluded by the Act.
>
> * * *
>
> An interchange of patent rights and a division of royalties according to the value attributed by the parties to their respective patent claims is frequently necessary if technical advancement is not to be blocked by threatened litigation.

---

[94] *United States v. Birdsboro Steel Foundry & Machine Co.,* 139 F.Supp. 244 (W.D. Pa. 1956).
[95] Id. at 259–261.

In a footnote the Court stated:

This is often the case where patents covering improvements of a basic process, owned by one manufacturer, are granted to another. A patent may be rendered quite useless, or "blocked," by another unexpired patent which covers a vitally related feature of the manufacturing process. Unless some agreement can be reached, the parties are hampered and exposed to litigation. And, frequently, the cost of litigation to a patentee is greater than the value of a patent for a minor improvement.

* * *

Nor does any illegality inhere in the fact that the licenses granted are limited in their fields of use. See General Talking Pictures Corp. v. Western Elec. Co.

* * *

The agreement here involved is not an agreement between actual or potential competitors in the manufacture of beds of the types covered by the agreement. The court is well aware that cross licensing agreements have been used in some cases to fix prices, to extend patent monopolies to unpatented subject matter, to regiment an industry, or otherwise to restrain lawful competition. But no such illegality appears in this case.

* * *

In the instant case defendants have not, through their agreement, either acquired a power or evidenced an intent to exclude competition from the cooling bed industry. Cf. United States v. Associated Patents, Inc., D.C., E.D.Mich., 1955, 134 F.Supp. 74, affirmed per curiam sub nom. Mac Investment Co. v. United States, 76 S.Ct. 432. Rather, they have served to increase competition in the cooling bed industry by facilitating the production of beds which could not otherwise have been produced, in an industry of which their Fisk-Peterson beds represent a minor part of the total production. Application of the "rule of reason," cf., United States v. United States Gypsum Co., 1948, 333 U.S. 364, 400–401, 68 S.Ct. 525,

5.9 CROSS-LICENSING

92 L.Ed. 746, to the evidence in this case does not lead to the conclusion that competition has been unlawfully restrained.

Even if the patents could be used separately, but covered complementary products rather than competing products, the courts are less inclined to condemn an exclusive cross-license agreement.[96]

In *Cutter Laboratories Inc. v. Lyophile-Cryochem Corp.*,[97] Sharp & Dohme made and sold drugs. It owned patents on freeze-dried drugs, processes, and machines. The Stokes company made and sold machines used in making drugs. It owned machinery patents. The two companies transferred "the exclusive power to issue licenses" under their patents in the field of freeze-dried drugs to a new corporation, Lyophile-Cryochem. The corporation granted the Stokes company an exclusive license to sell machinery and granted Sharp & Dohme a nonexclusive license to sell drugs. That corporation licensed third parties to use machinery and, presumably, sell drugs at royalties the Court found reasonable and nondiscriminatory. The court found the pool lawful, in view of the complementary nature of the drug and machinery businesses and the practice of licensing third parties. The court found:[98]

> The manner in which the agreements bring about this restraint of trade or monopoly, or both, says appellant, is by excluding Stokes from exploiting its present and future patents for freeze-dried medical products and excluding Sharp & Dohme from exploiting its present and future patents for machinery and apparatus, except to make and use such machinery for its own purposes. . . .
>
> It must be remembered that the patent laws give the patentee a monopoly. He may make, use or sell the patented product, license others, on an exclusive or non-exclusive basis, to do so, authorize the issuance of sublicenses, or assign the patent itself for a consideration. The sole limitation is, that he must not use his legitimate patent monopoly as a means of suppressing competition or ac-

---

[96] *For example, Baker-Cammack Hosiery Mills, Inc. v. Davis Co.*, 181 F.2d 550, 570 (4th Cir. 1950), *cert. denied* 340 U.S. 824 (1950).
[97] *Cutter Laboratories Inc. v. Lyophile-Cryochem Corp.*, 179 F.2d 80, 91–94 (9th Cir. 1949).
[98] Id. at 92–94.

quiring a monopoly outside of the area of monopoly which the patent grants. The legality of the agreements in this case depends, therefore, upon a comparison of the competitive situation which they create with the patent monopolies which each party would have in the absence of the agreements. Insofar as the parties agree to give Lyophile-Cryochem the exclusive power to issue licenses to outsiders, there is no extension of the patent monopoly because the licensing agent, unless it indulges in restrictive practices, not present here, is in no better bargaining position than its principals. As to the rights retained by or granted to the parties themselves under the agreements, the patents can be divided into two groups. First, there are the patents which each party owns within its own field, which each obviously would be just as free, but no more so, to exploit by making, using and selling in the absence of the agreements. . . . Thus, the objections to the agreements must be narrowed down to the cross-licensing rights granted under the second group of patents, consisting of those each party owns in the other's field. Stokes, interested in the manufacture of freeze-drying apparatus, conducts research for improvements in that apparatus. In the course of that research, it incidentally discovers improvements in freeze-drying processes and freeze-dried medical products. It is entitled to a patent monopoly on those improvements, but it cannot directly exploit those patents without going outside its normal field, which is machinery. Sharp & Dohme, on the other hand, is in a position to exploit the improvements. Moreover it is faced with the same problem, for it is in no position to exploit directly the improvements in machinery which it discovers in the course of its research. It is consistent with the spirit, as well as the letter, of the patent laws that each of these two companies should arrange to use the other in order to reap the rewards to which it is entitled as patentee and yet which it is in no position to reap by itself. Any patent owner who grants an exclusive license, reserving no right except to collect royalties, cuts himself off from practicing the art claimed in the patent until the patent has expired.

* * *

But conceding the patent pool did place the hands of the parties in a power to exclude competition from the industry by fixing prices

5.9 CROSS-LICENSING

or charging unreasonable royalties or other methods, that power by itself could not constitute unlawful monopolization, unless accompanied by a purpose or intent to exclude competition. United States v. Griffith, 334 U.S. 100, 68 S.Ct. 941, 92 L.Ed. 1236; American Tobacco Co. v. United States, 328 U.S. 781, 809, 814, 66 S.Ct. 1125, 90 L.Ed. 1575. The District Court found no such intent. There is no evidence of any exclusionary activities or otherwise which might evidence such intent; and, indeed, the reasonableness of exploiting legitimate patent monopolies negatives such intent.

Where the parties to a cross-license agreement agree that the combined patents will be licensed on a nonexclusive basis in all fields, the courts have been reluctant to condemn the agreement, even though the parties agree on the royalty rate that would be charged. In *Standard Oil,* four oil companies cross-licensed competing patents covering processes of making cracked gasoline. The agreements permitted each party to grant licenses to others under all the patents and provided for a division of royalties among the four in a certain way. Each company retained the right to license its own patents alone to outsiders. One of the three cross-licenses fixed the royalty to be charged outsiders; the second and third fixed the minimum royalty to be charged. The Court upheld the agreements to fix the royalties and minimums, however, on the basis that the combined patents did not dominate the gasoline industry and, therefore, their owners had no power to fix gasoline prices. The Court said that the cracked gasoline constituted only about 22 percent of total gasoline. From that it reasoned that eliminating competition among holders of competing process patents could not limit total gasoline output. In later decisions in which the parties and patents were found not to be dominant, and licenses were offered to reasonable to third parties, the courts have upheld the agreement.[99]

If a patent owner grants a nonexclusive license under its patents to sell certain products, and has agreed that no further licenses would be granted in that field without the licensee's consent, that agreement may violate the antitrust laws. If the licensor granted an exclusive license under its patents to that field, that agreement would not necessarily be

---

[99] *Baker-Cammack Hosiery Mills, Inc. v. Davis Co.,* 181 F.2d 550, 570 (4th Cir. 1950); *Sbicca-Dell Mac, Inc. v. Milius Shoe Co.,* 145 F.2d 389, 399 (8th Cir. 1944).

unlawful, even though the licensee's consent could be needed for the grant of further licenses.

The courts have found that a patent owner who grants nonexclusive licenses and agrees not to grant additional licenses without the consent of existing licensees violates the Sherman Act. Where the terms of an agreement give existing companies as licensees joint control over granting additional licenses and those companies' combined production would, if under unified control, give them market power, the courts have declared the agreement illegal. Such an agreement prevents competition in granting additional licenses for the sole benefit of the licensees.[100] In *United States v. Besser Mfg. Co.*,[101] the court found as follows:

> We believe that the contract under question goes further than is necessary to protect the patent monopoly of Gelbman and Andrus. It may well be that an exclusive license to one party would be valid, but here the patentees have joined hands with the two largest competitors in the industry and by terms of their agreement have virtually made it impossible for others to obtain rights under those patents. The contract even gives Stearns and Besser the power to restrict competitions—present and future—by requiring their joint consent before licensing others. It is this combination requiring collective action that primarily invalidates the agreement. We believe it clear that the parties intended this contract to be a means whereby control of the industry could be acquired and competition eliminated. For what other reason would Besser or Stearns want the consent of the other before approving a licensee suggested by the patentees? And where it is apparent as it is here, that the contract is to eliminate competition, it must be held illegal.

The courts also say a patent owner may violate the antitrust laws by an agreement with certain licensees to terminate the rights of another

---

[100] *United States v. Krasnov*, 143 F.Supp. 184 (E.D. Penn. 1956) *aff'd per curiam*, 355 U.S. 5 (1957) (granting additional licenses required the consent of an assignor, the assignee licensor, and the two existing licensees; the licensees were the two dominant firms in the industry; and the licensor engaged in other anticompetitive conduct).
[101] *United States v. Besser Mfg. Co.*, 96 F.Supp. 304, 310–311 (E.D. Mich. 1951), *aff'd* 343 U.S. 444 (1951).

licensee.[102] In *Moraine Products v. ICI America, Inc.*,[103] the owner of a patent licensed two existing competitors and agreed that no further licenses would be granted without the agreement of the licensor and one of those licensees. The Court held that such an agreement was not a *per se* violation of the antitrust laws. Rather, its legality was determined under the rule of reason. It was remanded to the District Court for consideration of whether the restriction was for the purpose of limiting the grant of further licenses to competitors for the benefit of the licensee, rather than for maximizing revenue to the patent owner.

Because each of these decisions involved the possibility that a nonexclusive licensee would prohibit further licensing solely to further its own competitive advantage and without respect to the value of that limitation to the patent owner, the courts have treated these agreements harshly. However, where a limitation on the right of an owner to grant licenses is related to profit-maximizing exploitation of the invention by that owner, such as by granting an exclusive license, these decisions have not been applied. The law is clear that not all exclusive licenses are illegal, even though an exclusive license prevents the owner from granting additional licenses without the licensee's consent. Hence, the decisions relating to a licensee's veto power do not invalidate all exclusive grants.

---

[102] *For example, Mannington Mills v. Congoleum Industries, Inc.*, 610 F.2d 1059, 1072–1073 (3rd Cir. 1979) (reserving judgment whether a *per se* or rule of reason analysis applied).
[103] *Moraine Products v. ICI America, Inc.*, 538 F.2d 134 (7th Cir. 1976).

6

Licenses Deemed to Arise from Sale of a Product—Implied Licenses and Exhaustion of Rights

6.1	Licenses Arising from the Sale of a Product	339
6.2	A License May Be Express or Implied	340
6.3	The Circumstances that Imply a License	341
6.4	The Legal Theory of Exhaustion	348
6.5	The Origins of the Exhaustion Doctrine—*Bloomer*	351
6.6	Exhaustion Applies Only to Authorized, Unconditional Sales—*Mitchell*	354
6.7	Some Early Applications of Exhaustion—*Adams, Hobbie, Keeler*	357
6.8	The Development of Antitrust and Misuse Limits to Exhaustion—*Henry, Bauer, Motion Picture Patents*	363
6.9	The Modern Exhaustion Doctrine	366

6.1 LICENSES ARISING FROM THE SALE OF A PRODUCT

Patent law developed two rules to limit the owner's rights against activities involving products obtained from the patent owner or someone it had licensed to supply them—the *implied license doctrine* and the *exhaustion doctrine*. The Patent Act says nothing about these issues. Under the Patent Act, the only excuse for infringement is that the patent owner "authorized" the acts that would otherwise constitute infringement.[1] Under the Act, the issue is, "Did the owner authorize the activity?" The courts have vacillated between determining the nature of the agreement between the patent owner and the purchaser and imposing rules prescribing the purchaser's and owner's rights regardless of their understanding.

Assume the product sold by a patent owner or its licensee is not a complete patented product. The product sold is a component or part useful in making a patented product or carrying out a patented process. In that situation, the law historically determines the parties' rights based on rules governing implied licenses. The other rule, sometimes called the "exhaustion" rule, was typically applied where the patent owner or its licensee sold a complete patented product.

The law has not clearly defined when the rights of the parties are determined under the exhaustion rules or under implied license rules. In at least one early decision, the Supreme Court said that the exhaustion doctrine was merely one application of the implied license rule.[2]

---

[1] 35 U.S.C. § 271(a).
[2] *Henry v. A.B. Dick,* 224 U.S. 1, 23–24 (1912), *overruled on other grounds,* 243 U.S. 502 (1917) ("An absolute and unconditional sale operates to pass the patented thing outside the boundaries of the patent, because such a sale implies that the patentee consents that the purchaser may use the machine so long as its identity is

LICENSES DEEMED TO ARISE FROM SALE OF A PRODUCT

These doctrines may defeat the intent of unwary patent owners. The law prohibiting tying arrangements sometimes traps rights owners that did not give a thought to licensing. The owner may simply sell a product. The tying problem may arise because the law supplied the "license" to which the product was inadvertently, yet unlawfully "tied."

This license doctrine may defeat the intent of an unwary owner in another way. Rights owners often sell products other than those directly protected by the rights. For example, a patent owner may sell components or parts of a patented product or materials useful in carrying out a patented process. Those purchasers may use the components to make the protected product or system. Those purchasers may use the product to carry out the patented process. The owner may not have wished to license the rights to the purchaser or wished to separately grant licenses. The law may defeat these plans by creating a license the owner did not intend to grant. Purchasers having an implied license will rarely agree to pay for an express one or to cease using the rights.

6.2 A LICENSE MAY BE EXPRESS OR IMPLIED

The courts have declared that a license may be granted expressly or by conduct from which a license is inferred. In *DeForest Radio Tel. & Tel. Co. v. United States,* the Supreme Court said:[3]

> No formal granting of a license is necessary in order to give it effect. Any language used by the owner of the patent or any conduct

---

preserved. This implication arises, first, because a sale without reservation, of a machine whose value consists in its use, for a consideration, carries with it the presumption that the right to use the particular machine is to pass with it. The rule and its reason is thus stated in Robinson on Patents, Vol. 2, § 824: 'The sale must furthermore be unconditional. Not only may the patentee impose conditions limiting the use of the patented article, . . . upon his grantees and express licensees, but any person having the right to sell may, at the time of sale, restrict the use of his vendor within specific boundaries of time or place or method, and these will then become the measure of the implied license arising from the sale.' ").
[3]*DeForest Radio Tel. & Tel. Co. v. United States,* 273 U.S. 236, 241 (1927).

6.3 THE CIRCUMSTANCES THAT IMPLY A LICENSE

on his part exhibited to another, from which that other may properly infer that the owner consents to his use of the patent in making or using it, or selling it, upon which the other acts, constitutes a license and a defense to action for a tort. Whether this constitutes a gratuitous license or one for a reasonable compensation must of course depend upon the circumstances; but the relation between the parties thereafter in respect of any suit brought must be held to be contractual and not an unlawful invasion of the rights of the owner.

In *DeForest,* the Court found that AT&T, a licensee with the right to grant additional licenses, granted a license to the U.S. government to have patented products made for and used by it. During the war, AT&T notified the government that it would not interfere with the manufacture of the product, provided that it was understood that AT&T waived none of its patent rights or claims. AT&T also supplied the technical information needed to make the product. The Court found that, by this conduct, a license under the patent was granted, albeit one for which compensation would be subsequently agreed to.

The lower federal courts have sometimes said the legal basis for implying a license is equitable estoppel.[4] This approach suggests a *DeForest-*type test. A license is implied where the owner's conduct, under the circumstances, indicated that the owner consents to use of the rights.

6.3 THE CIRCUMSTANCES THAT IMPLY A LICENSE

Absent an express license and other inconsistent facts, the courts have often found an implied license from the sale by a patent owner (or an authorized sale by its licensee) of an unpatented material or component useful only in making a patented product or using a patented method.[5] In

---

[4] *For example, Bandag, Inc. v. Al Bolser's Tire Stores,* 750 F.2d 903, 924 (Fed. Cir. 1984); *Stickle v. Heublein, Inc.,* 716 F.2d 1550, 1559 (Fed. Cir. 1983).
[5] *United States v. Univis Lens Co.,* 316 U.S. 241, 249 (1942) ("[U]pon familiar principles the authorized sale of an article which is capable of use only in practicing the patent is a relinquishment of the patent monopoly with respect to the article sold."); *B.B. Chem. v. Ellis,* 314 U.S. 495, 497 (1942) (sale of chemicals useful only in

LICENSES DEEMED TO ARISE FROM SALE OF A PRODUCT

Dawson Chemical Co. v. Rohm & Haas Co.,[6] Rohm & Haas owned a patent on a method of using the chemical propanil having no other substantial use. The Supreme Court found that the "farmers who buy propanil from Rohm & Haas may use it, without fear of being sued for direct infringement, by virtue of an 'implied license' they obtain when Rohm & Haas relinquishes its monopoly by selling the propanil." In *Westinghouse Elec. & Mfg. Co. v. Independent W. Tel. Co.,*[7] one of the defenses was a claim of implied license because the amplifier used to infringe a radio patent had been purchased from Radio Corporation, a licensee. The product purchased could be connected by the operator to infringe or not infringe as he or she desired. The Court of Appeals rejected the defense of implied license:[8]

> If the article has other uses than in the patented combination, there is no basis to imply a license. *Gen. Elect. Co. v. Continental Lamp Works (C.C.A.),* 280 Fed. 846; *Edison, etc., Co. v. Peninsular, etc., Co.,* 101 Fed. 831, 43 C.C.A. 479. It is only when the article sold must be used in the patented combination, if it be used at all, that a license is implied.

Conversely, no license is generally implied where the product has noninfringing uses.[9] For example, in *Lawther v. Hamilton,*[10] the Court found no implied license where the patent owner, through an agent, sold a machine useful in practicing one patent. The purchaser used parts from that machine to make one for use in a process covered by another patent in suit. The court said:

---

patented process implies a license to do so); *Leitch Mfg. Co. v. Barber Co.,* 302 U.S. 458, 461 (1938) ("For any road builder can buy emulsion from it [the patent owner] for that purpose [of employing the patented method], and whenever such a sale is made, the law implies authority to practice the invention."); *Edison Electric Light Co. v. Peninsular Light Power & H. Co.,* 95 F. 699, 678–679 (W.D. Mich. 1899).
[6]*Dawson Chemical Co. v. Rohm & Haas Co.,* 448 U.S. 176, 186 (1980).
[7]*Westinghouse Elec. & Mfg. Co. v. Independent W. Tel. Co.,* 300 F. 748 (S.D.N.Y. 1924).
[8]Id. at 750.
[9]*Bandag, Inc. v. Al Bolser's Tire Store,* 750 F.2d 903, 924 (Fed. Cir. 1984).
[10]*Lawther v. Hamilton,* 124 U.S. 1, 11 (1887).

6.3 THE CIRCUMSTANCES THAT IMPLY A LICENSE

> They contend that by this transaction, Lawther [the patent owner] gave his consent to their use of his process. We do not think there is sufficient evidence of any such consent. The use of the rollers did not necessarily involve the use of the process, and there is not proof that anything was said about the process.

The apparent basis for this distinction is that the parties must have intended to give the purchaser the rights needed to make some profitable use of the product. Where an implied license is necessary to achieve that goal, a license will not be implied.

The courts have had difficulty deciding whether a purchaser of a single-use component or material always acquires a license or whether it obtains a license only where that fact and others indicate that the patent owner intended to give the purchaser a license. The decisions generally say the issue is to be decided under all the circumstances. Under that view, the purchaser of a single-use product from an authorized seller does not necessarily obtain a license. Other circumstances matter, and may matter more.

For example, the Court of Appeals for the Federal Circuit in 1986 in *Met-Coil Systems*[11] made clear that other facts are important. The court cited and quoted the statement in *United States v. Univis Lens Co.*[12] that:

> ... [U]pon familiar principles the authorized sale of an article which is capable of use only in practicing the patent is a relinquishment of the patent monopoly with respect to the article sold.

The Court of Appeals said that this "familiar principle" applies to a sale of "nonpatented equipment" only where (1) the equipment has "no noninfringing use" and (2) "the circumstances of the sale must 'plainly indicate that the grant of a license should be inferred.'"

Hunt v. Armour & Co.[13] was a suit for infringement of a patent on a chicken-plucking machine. One of the defenses was that the defendant had not infringed because it had purchased fingers for its machine from

---

[11] *Met-Coil Systems Corp. v. Korners Unlimited, Inc.*, 803 F.2d 684 (Fed. Cir. 1986).
[12] *United States v. Univis Lens Co.*, 316 U.S. 241, 249 (1942).
[13] *Hunt v. Armour & Co.*, 185 F.2d 722 (7th Cir. 1950).

a licensee authorized to make and sell the machine and fingers as replacement parts in machines. The Court of Appeals rejected this defense, stating:[14]

> Apparently it is defendant's view that by purchasing the fingers, which are covered by one group of claims in the patent, it automatically also obtained a license under the separate group of machine claims. However, each claim of a patent constitutes a separate grant of monopoly. . . . A mere sale does not import a license except where the circumstances plainly indicate that the grant of a license should be inferred. *Radio Corp. of America et al. v. Andrea et al.,* 2 Cir. 90 F.2d 612, 615. The defense of misuse of the patent is without merit and is overruled.

While the point is not discussed, it seems that the fingers purchased from a licensee had no use, except as a part of the patented machine. They could be used as replacement parts in licensed machines.

What circumstances matter? The most obvious is whether the seller gave notice to the buyer at the time of sale that no license was granted. The courts have often referred to this fact. This was illustrated by the Sixth Circuit Court of Appeals' decision in *Edison Electric Light Co. v. Peninsular Light, Power & H. Co.*[15] Thomas Edison patented a system for electrical distribution. The system involved an arrangement of wires and transformers. The system permitted the high voltage from the power distribution network to be reduced and used safely in a home wiring system. Edison had a separate patent on a particular house wiring system that was suitable for use in electric lighting.

The Edison Electric Light Company sold to a hotel the wiring and fixtures for connecting the hotel to a *power* distribution line and to use electric lighting. Edison Electric Light did not put any limitation on the use of the wiring or fixtures by the hotel and did not require that the hotel buy electricity from Edison Electric Light. At the time Edison Electric Light installed the wires and fixtures, the hotel had no alternative source

---

[14]Id. at 729. The same defense was rejected on the same ground in *Priebe & Sons Co. v. Hunt,* 188 F.2d 880, 884 (8th Cir. 1951).
[15]*Edison Electric Light Co. v. Peninsular Light, Power & H. Co.,* 101 F. 831, 832–837 (6th Cir. 1900).

6.3 THE CIRCUMSTANCES THAT IMPLY A LICENSE

of electrical power. Sometime later, an alternative source appeared, Lowell Light and Power. The Peninsular Company purchased power from Lowell Light and Power, changed the wiring outside the hotel to connect its lines to the hotel lighting system, and began supplying power. The Edison Electric Light Company sued the Peninsular Company.

The Peninsular Company supplied the power directly to the hotel for use in the ways described in Edison's patent. Rather, the court said Peninsular was not liable, because the hotel had an implied license to use the wiring and other facilities that Edison Electric Light had supplied to it. The court said that an implied license existed, because the apparatus installed by the Edison Electric Light Company was "particularly adapted for the use of Edison's inventions, and, as we interpret the facts and circumstances of the record, it is not capable of use under any other plan or system."

The court said that, if the Edison Electric Light Company wished to restrict the right of the purchaser to use it for purposes for which it was "particularly adapted," there must appear "some expressed or implied agreement by which the mode or time or place of use" has been limited. If the patent owner intended that the system could be utilized only so long as Edison Electric Light was supplying the current, the burden was on Edison Electric Light to inform the buyer at that time. Because the Edison Electric Light had not done so, the circumstances indicated that Edison intended that the owners of the hotel enjoy the advantages of the Edison system regardless of the source of electricity.

Other decisions confirm the importance of notice to the buyer. In *Radio Corporation of America v. Andrea*,[16] the Court of Appeals found no implied license. The patent owner sold vacuum tubes that were designed primarily for use in the patented receivers. However, there was a noninfringing use. The court considered that the owner provided a notice limiting the rights:

> A mere sale imports no license except where the circumstances plainly indicate that the grant of a license was inferred. It is not sufficient that these tubes were primarily designed for the use to which objection is made. The tubes could be used to replace others which

---

[16] *Radio Corporation of America v. Andrea,* 90 F.2d 612 (2d Cir. 1937).

345

had been sold by licensees; the Pilot Radio Corporation and the Stromberg Carlson Tel. Mfg. Company had noninfringing uses. Besides, the notices that the "tubes are to be used in systems already licensed for use" are explicit and clear. We recognized the effect of such notices in General Electric Co. v. Continental Lamp Works, Inc. The use of the tubes was an infringement at all times.

In *General Electric Co. v. Continental Lamp Works,*[17] the defendant relied on a defense of implied license because a patent owner sold the bases it used to make the infringing gas-filled light bulbs. The Court of Appeals found that the sale did not provide a license under the owner's bulb patent. The court noted noninfringing uses with unpatented bulbs and a notice to that effect brought home to the purchaser at the time of his purchase:[18]

> The standard medium base is used by all parties for the various types of lamps, patented and unpatented. It is used for the carbon lamp, which was covered by patents which have now expired.
>
> * * *
>
> The burden was upon the appellees to establish that the parties agreed, by a meeting of the minds, that the licenses contended for should be granted, or that when the bases were purchased, the parties understood, and the appellees had adequate reason to assume, that they had received an implied license under the circumstances, which estopped the appellant from denying that such was the intention of the parties at the time of the transaction. . . .
> . . . We think there was nothing in the sale of these bases which justified the claim of estoppel against the appellant enforcing its rights against infringers.
>
> * * *

So, where the owner of a patent sells a patented article subject to a restriction, the purchasers, with notice of this limitation, could ac-

---

[17] *General Electric Co. v. Continental Lamp Works,* 280 F. 845 (2d Cir. 1922).
[18] Id. at 849, 850, and 851.

6.3 THE CIRCUMSTANCES THAT IMPLY A LICENSE

quire no better right than strangers to infringe upon that part or claim of the monopoly still secured to the patentee. Dickerson v. Tinling, 84 Fed. 192, 28 C.C.A. 139. The sale of an element of a patented combination does not necessarily imply license to use the whole combination. There is always a question of what is a fair inference from the transaction. . . .

Suppose the seller gave notice to the buyer at the time of sale that the buyer was authorized to use the component or material in a limited way. The courts have had more difficulty deciding whether a patent owner may sell a component or material for one use, and reserve its rights against other uses by the purchaser. This situation is discussed in more detail in connection with the exhaustion rule. The Court of Appeals for the Federal Circuit has indicated that the owner may sell for limited uses and enforce the rights against other uses[19] (sections 2.7(b) and 5.4(d)).

Suppose the seller is a licensee. In this context, a circumstance is whether the owner gave the seller authority to make the sale. If a patent owner did not authorize its licensee to sell the product, the law is fairly clear that the purchaser acquires no license. Unauthorized sales create no license for the purchaser. This is discussed in later sections on exhaustion.

Another circumstance is whether the patent owner authorized a licensee to sell for the use made by the buyer. The courts have had more difficulty deciding whether a patent owner may authorize a licensee to make a sale of a component for one use, and reserve its patent rights against other uses of that component by the purchaser. There is support for the view that a purchaser acquires an unlimited license only where the seller is authorized to sell for use in an unlimited way. Where the seller is licensed to sell for limited uses, a purchaser with notice of it is probably bound by the limitation, provided the limitation is lawful and enforceable. Even where the licensee's authority is to sell for only limited uses, the courts have been unsure whether a purchaser is bound by the limitation if it does not know about the limitation.

The preceding chapter described how the law has limited the ability of the owner to apply license restrictions to purchasers of products.

---

[19]*Mallinckrodt v. Medipart*, 976 F.2d 700 (Fed. Cir. 1992).

LICENSES DEEMED TO ARISE FROM SALE OF A PRODUCT

The law has employed a variety of rules to limit enforcement of license restrictions against those who purchased the protected product from the owner or a licensee. Those rules are discussed in more detail in the following section. They are important because they often render impractical otherwise sound and lawful licensing strategies.

6.4 THE LEGAL THEORY OF EXHAUSTION

A commonly cited statement of exhaustion is the Court's pronouncement in *Adams v. Burke*:[20]

> The right to manufacture, the right to sell and the right to use are each substantive rights, and may be granted or conferred separately by the patentee.
>
> But, in the essential nature of things, when the patentee, or the person having his rights, sells a machine or instrument whose sole value is in its use, he receives the consideration for its use and he parts with the right to restrict that use. The article, in the language of the court, passes without the limit of the monopoly. *Bloomer v. McQuewan,* 14 How., 459; *Mitchell v. Hawley ante,* 3221. That is to say, the patentee or his assignee *having in the act of sale received all the royalty or consideration which he claims for the use of his invention in that particular machine or instrument,* it is open to the use of the purchaser without further restriction on account of the monopoly of the patentee's.
>
> * * *
>
> It seems to us that, although the right of Lockhart & Seelye to manufacture, to sell and to use these coffin lids was limited to the circle of ten miles around Boston, that a purchaser of a single coffin acquired the right to use that coffin for the purpose for which all coffins are used. That so far as the use of it was concerned, *the*

---

[20] *Adams v. Burke,* 84 U.S. 453, 456–457 (1873).

6.4 THE LEGAL THEORY OF EXHAUSTION

patentee had received his consideration, and it was no longer within the monopoly of the patent. [emphasis added]

In these decisions, the Courts have from time to time said that a patent owner is entitled to only one royalty of each product. In *Mitchell v. Hawley,* the Court said:[21] Patentees acquire by their letters patent the exclusive right to make and use their patented inventions and to vend the same to others to be used for the period of time specified in the patent, but when they have made one or more of the things patented, and have vended the same to others to be used, they have parted to that extent with their exclusive right, *as they are never entitled to but one royalty for a patented machine,* and consequently a patentee, when he has himself constructed a machine and sold it without any conditions, or authorized another to construct, sell, and deliver it, or to construct and use and operate it, without any conditions and the *consideration has been paid to him for the thing patented,* the rule is well established that the patentee must be understood to have parted to that extent with all his exclusive right, and that he ceases to have any interest whatever in the patented machine so sold and delivered or authorized to be constructed and operated. [emphasis added]

The Supreme Court has also equated the payment of an agreed royalty with the purchase of a patented product. In *Keeler v. Standard Folding Bed Co.,* the Court said:[22]

This brief history of the case shows that in *Wilson v. Rousseau,* 45 U.S. 4 How. 688, and cases following it, it was held that as between the owner of a patent, on the one side, and a purchaser of an article made under the patent on the other, *the payment of a royalty once, or, what is the same thing, the purchase of the article from one authorized by the patentee to sell it,* emancipates such article from any further subjection to the patent throughout the entire life of the patent.

---

[21] *Mitchell v. Hawley,* 83 U.S. 322, 323–324 (1872).
[22] *Keeler v. Standard Folding Bed Co.,* 157 U.S. 659, 666 (1895).

LICENSES DEEMED TO ARISE FROM SALE OF A PRODUCT

* * *

The conclusion reached does not deprive a patentee of his just rights, because no article can be unfettered from the claim of his monopoly without paying its tribute. [emphasis added]

If the policy underlying these decisions is that a patent owner may collect only once for the exercise of all of the rights to make, use, and sell granted in a particular patent (whether received as a royalty or a purchase price), that policy is violated by a series of agreements that would require royalty payments by one licensee on exercise of the rights to make, have made, use, and sell and by its supplier also having rights to make, use, and sell.[23] In *Aro Mfg. Co. v. Convertible Top Co.,* the Court found that it would be inconsistent with public policy to allow a patent owner to collect damages from a component supplier, Aro, after the patent owner received the equivalent of a royalty from the seller, Ford, of the product using the component:[24]

> To allow recovery of a royalty on Aro's sales after receipt of the equivalent of a royalty on Ford's sales, or to allow any recovery from Aro after receipt of full satisfaction from Ford, would not only disregard the statutory provision for recovery of "damages" only, but would be at war with virtually every policy consideration in this area of the law. It would enable the patentee to derive a profit not merely on unpatented *rather than* patented goods-an achievement proscribed by the Motion Picture Patents and Mercoid Cases, supra—but on unpatented *and* patented goods. In thus doubling the number of rewards to which a patentee is entitled "under our patent law as written," see Mr. Justice Black concurring in Aro I, 365 US at 360, 5 L ed 2d at 607, it would seriously restrict the purchaser's long-established right to use and repair an article which he has legally purchased and for the use of which the patentee has been compensated. See Adams v Burke, 17 Wall 453, 21 L Ed 700.

---

[23] *Compare, Aro Mfg. Co. v. Convertible Top Co.,* 377 U.S. 476, 510 (1964).
[24] Id. at 510.

And *In Re Thorpe,* 777 F.2d 693, 695 (Fed. Cir. 1985):

> The sales by Lisle were authorized by the . . . license agreement. Resale [by the licensee's customer] did not create a sublicense. Edwards [the patent owner] is not entitled to a royalty payment each time a tool is resold.

This assumes that each licensee is using the same patents to make a single product.[25] For example, the courts have permitted a patent owner to license one class of licensees to make and sell (but not use) the patented product only to another class of licensees having royalty-bearing licenses to use the product.[26]

6.5 THE ORIGINS OF THE EXHAUSTION DOCTRINE—*BLOOMER*

The basic idea is that a sale relinquishes, surrenders, or exhausts the rights. This idea appeared in 1852 in the Supreme Court's opinion in *Bloomer v. McQuewan.*[27] *Bloomer v. McQuewan* involved the Woodworth patent on planing machines. The patent issued in about 1828 for a fourteen-year term. In 1830, the patent owner conveyed to Collins and Smith the right to construct, use, and sell planing machines in Pennsylvania. In 1831 or 1832, Collins and Smith transferred to Barnet the exclusive right to construct and use "during the residue of the aforesaid fourteen years" no more than 50 machines in Pittsburg County. Pursuant to this agreement, the defendants made and used two planing machines.

---

[25] *SCM Corp. v. Radio Corp. of America,* 318 F. Supp. 433 (S.D.N.Y. 1970) (separate royalty-bearing licenses to practice separate claims of a patent are lawful); *Eastern Venetian Blind Co. v. Acme Steel Co.,* 188 F.2d 247, 252–253 (4th Cir. 1951) (separate royalty-bearing licenses to practice different steps of a patented process are lawful).

[26] *Duplan Corp. v. Deering Milliken, Inc.,* 444 F.Supp. 648, 661–664, 669–671 (D. S.C. 1977), *aff'd in pertinent part,* 594 F.2d 979 (4th Cir. 1979); *In Re Yarn Processing Patent Validity Litigation,* 541 F.2d 1127, 1135 (5th Cir. 1976); *Extractol Process, Ltd., v. Hiram Walker & Sons, Inc.,* 153 F.2d 264, 268 (7th Cir. 1946).

[27] *Bloomer v. McQuewan,* 55 U.S. 539 (1852).

LICENSES DEEMED TO ARISE FROM SALE OF A PRODUCT

In 1842, the patent expired, and was extended for seven additional years as provided in the Act of 1836. In 1845, Congress enacted a special law further extending the patent from 1849 to 1856. In 1845, the patent owner purported to assign to Bloomer the exclusive right to construct and use the machines in Pittsburg County during the first and second extensions. In 1850, Bloomer brought an action to enjoin the defendants' use of these two machines in Pittsburg during the term of the second extension. The Supreme Court held that the special act extending the term did not prevent the defendant's continued use of the machines. In this context, the Court coined the language:

> And when the machine passes to the hands of the purchaser, it is no longer within the limits of the monopoly. It passes outside of it, and is no longer under the protection of the Act of Congress.

This language seems to have nothing to do with the issues. The defendants had not purchased the machines. The defendants built them. The decision rested on some other idea.

A majority of the Court said that the defendants were not infringers, because the special act of Congress was not intended to limit rights "purchased" prior to the extension and the agreement did not expressly limit the time the machines could be used. The majority reached that conclusion by creating a distinction between a grant of the rights to make and sell machines and the right to use them. The majority said, if a patent owner granted someone the exclusive rights to make and sell at a particular place, the "purchaser buys" the rights with reference to the term of the rights the patent owner then possesses. A purchaser of rights to make and use has no claim to the extended rights, because he did not "purchase or pay for it."

However, if the patent owner grants someone the exclusive right to use a machine, the buyer does not care about the term of the patent. According to the majority, the value of the right to use the machine does not depend on the term of the patent. Because the purchaser buys use rights without regard to the term, the purchaser receives the extended rights to protect that expectation. In this context, the majority opinion said:[28]

---
[28] Id. at 549–550.

6.5 THE ORIGINS OF THE EXHAUSTION DOCTRINE—BLOOMER

> But the purchaser of the implement or machine for the purpose of using it in the ordinary pursuits of life, stands on different ground. . . . And when the machine passes to the hands of the purchaser, it is no longer within the limits of the monopoly. It passes outside of it, and is no longer under the protection of the Act of Congress. . . .
>
> Moreover, the value of the implement or machine in the hands of the purchaser for use, does not in any degree depend on the time for which the exclusive privilege is granted to the patentee; nor upon the exclusion of others from its use. . . . It is of no importance to him whether it endures for a year or twenty-eight years. . . . And in the case before us the respondents derive no advantage from the extension of the patent, because the patentee may place around them as many planing machines as he pleases; so as to reduce the profits of those which they own to their just value in an open and fair competition.

The Court is correct that the owner of a machine does not need patent law to preclude others from using the machine. However, the value of a patented machine to its owner depends very much on the extent of use of machines by others.

The defendants purchased the exclusive right to use up to 50 planing machines in Pittsburg county. They paid $4,000 for that right. They made two machines. Hence, they paid $2,000 per machine for the exclusive right to use such machines in Pittsburg county. The defendants are likely to have cared very much about the extent of use of patented machines by others in Pittsburg county and the duration of the remaining term of the patent. There is no other explanation for their seeking and paying for an exclusive right to use them in that area. The majority ignored the fact that the defendants purchased exclusive use rights.

Even if the defendants had purchased only nonexclusive use rights, they are also likely to have cared about the term of the patent. The value of the machines to them after the patent expires is likely to have been less than the value of the machines during the term. It is one thing to use a machine in competition with other purchasers during the term from authorized sources, and another to use it in competition with purchasers after the term from all sources.

The majority's contrary assertion is wrong. Justices McLean and Nelson recognized these errors and dissented. Justice McLean explained

LICENSES DEEMED TO ARISE FROM SALE OF A PRODUCT

why the value of patented machines depends on the term of the patent and why a purchaser of a right to use a machine for ten years should have no claim to use it longer.[29]

6.6 EXHAUSTION APPLIES ONLY TO AUTHORIZED, UNCONDITIONAL SALES—*MITCHELL*

Twenty years later in *Mitchell v. Hawley,* the Supreme Court declared that a purchaser of a patented machine did not always have the right to use it during the extended term of a patent. In *Mitchell v. Hawley,*[30] the patent covered a machine for making felt hats. The patent owner, James Taylor, granted to a Mr. Bayley "the exclusive right to make and use 'and to license to others the right to use the said machines' in the States of Massachusetts and New Hampshire, during the remainder of the original term of said letters patent. . . ." The license provided that "the licensee shall not . . . sell or grant any license to use the said machines beyond the expiration of the original term." The licensee Bayley had the right to obtain a similar license if the patent was extended upon paying further compensation.

Bayley built four machines and sold them "with the right to run" them during the original term. At the time of the sale, the buyers executed a license authorizing them to "run and use [them] for felting hats, in said Town of Haverhill, under Taylor's patent, bearing date as specified in the original letters patent. . . ." The patent expired and was extended under section 18 of the Act of 1934. The defendants apparently purchased the machines from the original buyers.

The purchasers continued to use the machines during the extended term. The Supreme Court held that continued use exceeded the purchaser's right to use and was infringement. The Court's explanation for this result is difficult to follow. The Court initially said that, if a patent owner authorizes another to construct and use a machine "without any conditions," the owner of the machine may use it until it wears out, in spite of extensions. The Court said:[31]

---
[29]Id. at 556–558.
[30]*Mitchell v. Hawley,* 83 U.S. 322, 324 (1872).
[31]Id. at 323.

6.6 AUTHORIZED, UNCONDITIONAL SALES—MITCHELL

> [A] patentee, when he has himself constructed a machine and sold it without any conditions, or authorized another to construct, sell, and deliver it, or to construct and use and operate it, without any conditions, and the consideration has been paid to him for the thing patented, the rule is well established that the patentee must be understood to have parted to that extent with all his exclusive right, and that he ceases to have any interest whatever in the patented machine so sold and delivered or authorized to be constructed and operated. Where such circumstances appear, the owner of the machine, whether he built it or purchased it, if he has also acquired the right to use and operate it during the lifetime of the patent, may continue to use it until it is worn out, in spite of any and every extension subsequently obtained by the patentee or his assigns. [citation omitted]

This implies that the issue is whether the licensee Bayley was granted rights to make and sell machines without any condition on the duration of right. If there were no conditions, Bayley and his customers had the right to continue the use. However, the Court did not pursue these implications of its statements. Rather, the Court paused to praise the distinction created in *Bloomer* between "purchasers" of rights to make and sell (whose rights end when the original patent expires) and purchasers of machines (whose rights continue forever):[32]

> Purchasers of the exclusive privilege of making or vending the patented machine hold the whole or a portion of the franchise which the patent secures, depending upon the nature of the conveyance, and of course the interest which the purchaser acquires terminates at the time limited for its continuance by the law which created the franchise, unless it is expressly stipulated to the contrary. But the purchaser of the implement or machine for the purpose of using it in the ordinary pursuits of life stands on different grounds, as he does not acquire any right to construct another machine either for his own use or to be vended to another for any purpose. Complete title to the implement or machine purchased becomes vested in the vendee by the sale and purchase, but he

---

[32] Id. at 323.

LICENSES DEEMED TO ARISE FROM SALE OF A PRODUCT

acquires no portion of the franchise, as the machine, when it rightfully passes from the patentee to the purchaser, ceases to be within the limits of the monopoly.

This implies that the defendants, as mere machine purchasers, always have the right to continue to use it as that use is outside "the limits of the monopoly." However, the Court then qualified the distinction in *Bloomer*. The Court said machine purchasers escape the "monopoly" only where the sale is "absolute, and without any conditions":[33]

Patented implements or machines sold to be used in the ordinary pursuits of life become the private individual property of the purchasers, and are no longer specifically protected by the patent laws of the State where the implements or machines are owned and used. Sales of the kind may be made by the patentee with or without conditions, as in other cases, but where the sale is absolute, and without any conditions, the rule is well settled that the purchaser may continue to use the implement or machine purchased until it is worn out, or he may repair it or improve upon it as he pleases, in same manner as if dealing with property of any other kind.

The Court then described the facts. The Court noted the licensee Bayley's agreement not to sell or grant any license to use beyond the original term and the language in the license to the purchasers "showing conclusively that the purchasers were referred to the original letters patent as the source of his authority." One expects the Court to conclude that the purchasers' rights were or were not "conditioned" by the term of the original patent, and the opinion to end. However, the opinion goes in a different direction. The Court does not ask about the terms of the sale from Bayley to the purchaser. Rather, the Court asked about the scope of Bayley's rights. The Court concluded that, because Bayley had no right to sell machines and give purchasers rights to use beyond the term, the purchaser had no such rights.[34]

---

[33] Id. at 323.
[34] Id. at 324.

6.7 SOME EARLY APPLICATIONS OF EXHAUSTION

Mitchell v. Hawley was clear about one thing—where a patented machine passes into the hands of the purchaser, it sometimes stays within the limits of the "monopoly." The *Bloomer v. McQuewan* language did not mean what it said.

Mitchell v. Hawley also seemed important because the result turned on what the parties provided in their agreements. In *Mitchell v. Hawley* the machine purchaser had no right to use during the extended term because (1) his seller had no right to create such a lengthy license, (2) the license the purchaser accepted was conditioned to use during the original term, or, perhaps, (3) both reasons.

This focus on what the agreements indicated the parties intended is very similar to what Justice McLean wrote about in his dissent in *Bloomer*. The patent owner Taylor wanted to sell any extension-term rights separately. He did not want transactions during the original term to reduce the value of the extension rights. This was clear to Bayley and should have been clear (or at least the Court thought so) to the purchaser. The Court reached a result to protect those intentions.

6.7 SOME EARLY APPLICATIONS OF EXHAUSTION— *ADAMS, HOBBIE, KEELER*

However, this lesson of *Mitchell v. Hawley* was quickly obscured. Following the decisions in *Bloomer v. McQuewan* and *Mitchell v. Hawley* on the time of permitted use, a number of Supreme Court decisions held that an unrestricted sale by an "assignee" or licensee in his territory gave the purchaser the right to use and sell the article elsewhere. In each of these situations, the seller had the right by assignment or license under the allegedly infringed patent to sell in a limited geographic area. In each decision, the Court found that the sale occurred in the licensed or assigned territory. In each, the Court concluded that the purchaser received the right to use or resell the article anywhere.

The first and most well-known of these decisions was *Adams v. Burke*, decided in 1873, about nine months after *Mitchell v. Hawley*.[35] The patent related to coffin lids. The patent owner assigned to the Lock-

---

[35] *Adams v. Burke*, 24 U.S. 453 (1873).

LICENSES DEEMED TO ARISE FROM SALE OF A PRODUCT

hart & Seelye company all of their interest in the patent for and in the area within ten miles of Boston. An undertaker accused of infringement traveled to Boston and purchased a coffin lid from Lockhart & Seelye "without condition or restriction." He took the coffin lid outside the ten-mile limit and used it to bury one of his customers.

The Supreme Court declared that neither the Patent Act nor the agreement of the parties contemplated that the purchaser would be a patent infringer if he used the coffin more than ten miles from Boston. Unfortunately for the law, the Court's only explanation was that, having received the purchase price, the patent owner and his other territorial assignees had no interest in where the coffin lid was used:[36]

> But, in the essential nature of things, when the patentee, or the person having his rights, sells a machine or instrument whose sole value is in its use, he receives the consideration for its use and he parts with the right to restrict that use. The article, in the language of the Court, passes without the limit of the monopoly. That is to say, the patentee or his assignee having in the act of sale received all the royalty or consideration which he claims for the use of his invention in that particular machine or instrument, it is open to the use of the purchaser without further restriction on account of the monopoly of the patentees. [citations omitted]

Justices Bradley, Swayne, and Strong dissented. Justice Bradley asked whether the policy of the Patent Act precluded territorially limited assignments. He noted that the Patent Act specifically authorized them, and concluded that "legislative policy" allowed a patentee to "divide up his monopoly territorially." Justice Bradley then examined the assignment to determine the nature of the rights granted to Lockhart & Seelye. He concluded that Lockhart & Seelye received an assignment of the right to make in the ten-mile area, to sell in that area, and to use in that area. Each right was "conveyed in precisely the same language."

Justice Bradley might at this point have been tempted to say Lockhart & Seelye could not convey rights that it did not possess, cite *Mitchell v. Hawley,* and declare the undertaker an infringer. Instead, he asked

---
[36] Id. at 456.

6.7 SOME EARLY APPLICATIONS OF EXHAUSTION

about the intention of the patent owner and Lockhart & Seelye. He concluded that the use outside a limited territory could defeat the purpose of granting territorially limited assignments. Such uses reduce the value of the invention in other territories and reduce the incentives of the patent owner or the assignees in other territories to invest in exploiting the invention. Only then did he conclude that Lockhart and Seelye could not transfer rights it did not possess.[37]

In 1893, in *Hobbie v. Jennison*,[38] the Supreme Court found that a seller possessing territorially limited rights to make and sell was not an infringer, even though he sold to a buyer knowing the buyer intended to use the article outside the seller's territory. A unanimous Supreme Court said the issue was controlled by *Adams v. Burks*.

The owner of a patent on pipe had assigned its rights in Michigan to the defendant. The owner had assigned its rights in Connecticut to the plaintiff. The defendant made pipe in Michigan and sold it to a Connecticut company "on board [railway] cars in Michigan." The Connecticut company paid the freight for delivery to Connecticut and installed the pipes in a steam-heating system in Hartford. The defendant knew the Connecticut company intended to use them in Connecticut.

The Court said there was no infringement because the patent owner or his assignee received all the consideration for the use of the pipe. However, the Court added that if a patent owner wanted to "protect himself and his assignees of exclusive territory," he may "bind every licensee or assignee" to "conditions that will prevent any other licensee or assignee from being interfered with." The Court noted that there were no conditions or restrictions on the defendant.

In 1895, in *Keeler v. Standard Folding Bed Co.*,[39] the Supreme Court declared that a purchaser could also resell the product outside the territory. Six Justices said the issue was controlled by the earlier decisions. "[O]ne who buys patented articles of manufacture from one authorized to sell them becomes possessed of an absolute property in such articles, unrestricted in time or place." The patent owner is not deprived

---
[37] Id. at 456–457.
[38] *Hobbie v. Jennison*, 149 U.S. 355 (1893).
[39] *Keeler v. Standard Folding Bed Co.*, 157 U.S. 659 (1895).

of his "just rights, because no article can be unfettered from the claim of his monopoly without paying its tribute." They added that any other rule would cause inconvenience and annoyance to the public in ways "too obvious to require illustration."

Justice Brown, with the Chief Justice and Justice Field, disagreed. The owner of a patent on folding beds had assigned the rights in Massachusetts to the plaintiff, Standard Folding Bed Co., and the rights in Michigan to the Welsh Folding Bed Company. The defendant, Cornelius Keeler, bought a carload of beds from the Welsh company in Grand Rapids, Michigan, shipped them to Massachusetts, and sold them in the plaintiff's territory.

Justice Brown said it was "somewhat startling" to permit a Massachusetts bed dealer, who knows the Massachusetts selling rights belong to another, to buy in Michigan and sell in Massachusetts. Justice Brown noted that three lower Courts had found that a purchaser does not have the right to resell outside the territory of his supplier. Justice Brown said that there is good reason to permit a purchaser, who "has once paid tribute to the patentee," to use the article anywhere. However, Justice Brown said that to permit a purchaser to buy in one territory for the sole purpose of selling in another territory would be "utterly destructive" of the rights of the owner in the resale territory.

It is likely that permitting purchase and resale would be more harmful to the attempted territorial grants than permitting only purchase and use. Transaction and transportation costs are likely to be much lower, and the volume of cross-territory transactions much larger, when dealers or distributors buy in one place and resell in another than when individual end users buy in one place and use in another. However, the effect on the patent owner's attempt to exploit the invention differently in different areas is merely a matter of degree. Users and resellers buying outside their territory both defeat the attempted division. There may be a good reason to permit certain users to defeat the division. It is to reduce information and transaction costs. I will explain why in a moment.

The other important question is the effect of the rule on the value of a patent. Justice Brown sensed that patent owners have some legitimate reason for exploiting their rights in this way. However, he had dif-

6.7 SOME EARLY APPLICATIONS OF EXHAUSTION

ficulty saying what they were. Justice Brown said the majority's rule was harmful because it would permit a patent owner to undersell his licensees and destroy them.[40] No sane patent owner would do that.

The problem is not to protect territorial assignees from the patent owner. It is to protect them from each other. Whether the patent owner is trying to achieve economic discrimination or to induce investments that may have external benefits, the owner's interest is to make sure the territorial divisions actually work. Justice Brown was on the right track when he focused on the competitive advantages one seller may have over others. He failed to recognize that it is in the patent owner's and, ultimately, the consumer's interests to make the territorial divisions effective.

The Court's explanations for the results leave much to be desired. The problem with the Court's analysis is that a patent owner who assigns exclusive territories to different licensees has a great deal of interest in where the products made by those licensees are ultimately used or resold.

It may be irrational for the owner to be totally content simply because everyone who uses the patented product paid for it. There are two reasons an inventor may be able to capture a greater part of the social value of the invention by assigning different licensees to exclusive, nonoverlapping territories.

First, the patent owner may do so if the product has a higher value to users in one territory than in another. The owner may be using exclusive territorially restricted licenses to achieve economic discrimination. Second, the owner may also be assigning exclusive territories to induce licensees to invest in support services, advertising, or promotional activities conducted most efficiently on a regional basis. If consumers in one territory are permitted to purchase in one territory and use in another, this may undermine the marketing and service benefits the patent owner is seeking to achieve by exclusive territories. If distributors are permitted to buy in one territory and sell in another, their activities may also undermine the purpose of the territorial limitation.

---
[40]Id. at 853.

For example, if the patent owner is using exclusive territories to achieve economic discrimination, its efforts may be undermined if distributors are permitted to buy in the lower-value, lower-price territory and resell in the higher-value, (and what the patent owner had hoped to be) higher-price territory. Similarly, if consumers or distributors from the service- and promotion-intensive territory are permitted to purchase in a less service-oriented, promotion-rich territory, they decrease the incentives the patent owner was attempting to create for the licensee providing intensive service and promotion. The Court was simply wrong to believe that patent owners have no interest in the products sold other than receiving the purchase price.

The Court's reasoning was deficient. The Court's results may have been entirely sensible. The reason is that information and transaction costs are likely to be reduced by requiring a seller to inform a purchaser of limitations on its right to use or resell a patented product.

In each of these cases, the patent owner and his territorial assignees or licensees did not inform the purchaser at the time of the transaction that the purchaser's rights to use or resell were limited. If restrictions of that kind are likely to apply only to a very small percentage of total purchasing transactions, the costs of engaging in those transactions are likely to be much lower if the law places the burden on the seller to inform the buyer of limitations, rather than requiring buyers to inquire in each instance about their existence. It is likely to be more efficient to require information of that kind to be exchanged only in those cases where the product is patented and the seller wishes to impose or is obligated to impose limitations.

In these cases, neither the patent owner nor his licensees provided that information. It was entirely sensible for the Court to declare, as it did in *Adams v. Burke,* that it would not "imply" any such limitation either as a matter of patent law or as a matter of contract law. Except for *Keeler,* the Supreme Court opinions seemed consistent with the view that patent owners could prevent undesired transactions between territories.

The Court said the owner could do so by express limitations or restrictions against the territorial assignee's right to sell in the territory for use or resale outside the territory or by express limitations or conditions on the purchaser's right to use or resell elsewhere. In 1911, the Court seemed to confirm this.

6.8 THE DEVELOPMENT OF ANTITRUST AND MISUSE LIMITS TO EXHAUSTION—*HENRY, BAUER, MOTION PICTURE PATENTS*

In 1911, in *Henry v. A.B. Dick Co.*, the Supreme Court declared that a patent owner could sell a patented product subject to restrictions on the permitted uses of the product by the purchaser.[41] *Henry* was discussed earlier.[42] The patent owner had two patents covering a "stencil-duplicating machine known as the 'Rotary Mimeograph'." The patent owner made and sold mimeograph machines. Each machine bore this notice:

> LICENSE RESTRICTION
> THIS MACHINE IS SOLD BY THE A.B. DICK CO., WITH THE LICENSE RE-
> STRICTION THAT IT MAY BE USED ONLY WITH THE STENCIL, PAPER, INK,
> AND OTHER SUPPLIES MADE BY A.B. DICK COMPANY, CHICAGO, U.S.A.

The defendant, Sidney Henry, sold the owner of a machine, a can of ink suitable for use in the machine. Henry knew about the license agreement and expected that his ink would be used in the A.B. Dick machine. A.B. Dick sued Henry for contributing to infringement by the owner. A majority of the Court said that the owner did not acquire an unlimited right to use the machine when she bought the machine.

The Court said that the owner's rights depended on the nature of the license under the patent that was express or implied from the circumstances of the sale. Justice Lurton, for the majority, said everyone agreed that a patent owner may effectively restrict the time, place, and manner of use of a patented machine. He said the "books abound in cases upholding the right of a patentee owner of a machine to license another to use it, subject to any qualification in time, place, manner, or purpose of use which the licensee agrees to accept." The contention was that a patent owner could not do the same thing if it sold the machine.

Justice Lurton said it had long been settled by cases such as *Mitchell* and *Adams* that a patent owner's sale of a patented machine "subject to no conditions" gives the purchaser the right to "use it where, when, and

---

[41]*Henry v. A.B. Dick Co.*, 224 U.S. 1, 17–25 (1912).
[42]Section 4.5(b).

LICENSES DEEMED TO ARISE FROM SALE OF A PRODUCT

how he pleases," and to "dispose of the same unlimited right to another." Justice Lurton then explained that an unlimited license was implied from an unconditional sale, because such a sale "implies that the patent owner consents" to unlimited use by the purchaser. This is the presumed or "implied" intent of the patent owner and the purchaser.

However, the patent owner and purchaser may have a different intent that will control whether a restricted license accompanies the sale. They may intend that the purchaser acquire all the property rights to the "materials composing a patented product" and only "some of" the uses included in the patent rights. The physical machine and the license are "separate things" and may be transferred separately. Justice Lurton then asked whether the type of restriction imposed was "lawful." He concluded that it was lawful.

The 1911 decision in *Henry v. A.B. Dick* seemed to clarify when a sale exhausted the patent rights and when it did not. Patent owners apparently had the assurance that they could sell patented products and separately license the patent rights, reserving some of them. For sixty years, the Supreme Court had seemed to say this was a viable way of exploiting the rights. However, beginning in about 1917, the Supreme Court shifted course. From 1917 to 1969, the Supreme Court declared unlawful many restrictions and conditions that patent owners used in their efforts to exploit the rights.

During that period, the Supreme Court concluded that the policy of patent law was not served by permitting patent owners to limit expressly the resale price of patented products or to limit the source of complementary products that could be used with a patented product. Because the sale of the product "carried it outside the patent monopoly," efforts by patent owners to limit the price of the subsequent sale price or the source of complementary products to be used with it were declared to be contrary to patent law and unenforceable. If patent owners have no legitimate interest in what happens to patented products after the first sale, as the Court had sometimes asserted prior to *Henry,* the restrictions they place on those products must have some illegitimate goal and should be illegal. These decisions provided fuel for the notion that purchasers of patented products could never infringe the patent, regardless of the nature of their agreement with the patent owner or a licensee.

The first type of restriction involved attempts by the patent owner to regulate the minimum prices at which purchasers resold the patented

6.8 THE DEVELOPMENT OF ANTITRUST AND MISUSE LIMITS

article. In 1913, in *Bauer & Cie v. O'Donnell,* the patent owner granted one license for the sale of the patented product.[43] The licensee sold the product in a package bearing a notice that the product:

> [I]s licensed by us for sale and use at a price not less than one dollar. Any sale in violation of this condition, or use when so sold, will constitute an infringement. . . . A purchase is acceptance of this condition. . . .

The defendant purchased the product from jobbers, who had resold the product for less than one dollar. The Court said that the patent law provided no basis for resale price maintenance. The Court asserted that "it was the intention of Congress to secure an exclusive right to sell, and there is no grant of a privilege to keep up prices . . . by notice restricting the price at which the article may be resold."

The Court ignored the attempt by the patent owner to license separately the right to use, saying it was "a perversion of terms to call the transaction in any sense a license to use the invention." Because the patent owner received no royalties on "use" or resale by jobbers, and the use right was unlimited, the Court found it a mere "play on words" to call the transaction a "license to use."

The Court declared void the attempt to fix the resale price of a patented article. The Court had previously reached the same conclusion for unpatented articles in *Dr. Miles Medical Co. v. Park and Sons Co.*[44] and for copyrighted books in *Bobbs-Merrill Co. v. Straus.*[45] Because the attempted restriction was void, the Court held that the purchaser's sales in violation of it did not constitute infringement under exhaustion principles. In other words, since the exclusive right to sell had been exercised and the buyer was free of any lawful restrictions, the buyer did not infringe by reselling below the minimum price.

The second type of decision found that the patent owner may not compel those using its patented machine or product to buy only from it the components or supplies used in such machine or product. Such use of a patent "to extend the scope of its patent monopoly" to unpatented

---

[43] *Bauer & Cie v. O'Donnell,* 229 U.S. 1 (1913).
[44] *Dr. Miles Medical Co. v. Park and Sons Co.,* 220 U.S. 373 (1911).
[45] *Bobbs-Merrill Co. v. Straus,* 210 U.S. 339 (1908).

components or supplies was declared invalid and unenforceable in a series of decisions from 1917 to 1944.[46] For example, in 1917 *Motion Picture Patents Co.,* the question decided was "[m]ay a patentee or his assignee license another to manufacture and sell a patented machine, and by a mere notice attached to it limit its use by the purchase or by the purchaser's lessee, to films which are no part of the patented machine, and which are not patented?"[47] The Supreme Court concluded that "such a restriction is invalid. . . ." The Court said the patent owner had no claim against the user of the machine, or the supplier of materials, in that case motion pictures.

Presumably the basis for the conclusion of noninfringement was that the purchaser received a license to use the machine in a limited way, the limitation was unenforceable, and therefore the purchaser had the right to use the machine in any way. The Court in *Motion Picture Patents* did not discuss the conclusions reached in *Henry v. A.B. Dick* about the different effects of a restricted and an unrestricted sale on the scope of the purchaser's rights. The majority in *Motion Picture Patents* did broadly say that "the decision" in *Henry v. A.B. Dick* "must be regarded as overruled." This implied that *Henry* was overruled with respect to the legality of one particular kind of restriction (namely to use the machine only with supplies purchased from the patent owner) and perhaps overruled with respect to the scope of a purchaser's rights depending on whether the sale was unconditional or unrestricted.

6.9 THE MODERN EXHAUSTION DOCTRINE

(a) *Univis Lens*

In 1942, the Supreme Court in *United States v. Univis Lens Co.*[48] summarized the exhaustion rule in *dicta* in an antitrust action:

---

[46]*Motion Picture Patents Co. v. Universal Film Co.*, 243 U.S. 502, 508, 516–518 (1917); *Carbice Corp. v. America Patents Corp.*, 283 U.S. 27 (1931); *Morton Salt Co. v. Suppiger Co.*, 314 U.S. 488 (1942); *cf., Leitch Mfg. Co. v. Barber Co.*, 302 U.S. 458 (1938) (process patents); *B.B. Chemical Co. v. Ellis*, 314 U.S. 495 (1942) (process patents).
[47]243 U.S. at 508.
[48]*United States v. Univis Lens Co.*, 316 U.S. 241, 249–250 (1942).

6.9 THE MODERN EXHAUSTION DOCTRINE

An incident to the purchase of any article, whether patented or unpatented, is the right to use and sell it, and upon familiar principles the authorized sale of an article which is capable of use only in practicing the patent is a relinquishment of the patent monopoly with respect to the article sold.

His monopoly remains so long as he retains the ownership of the patented article. But sale of it exhausts the monopoly in that article and the patentee may not thereafter, by virtue of his patent, control the use or disposition of the article.

(b) *General Talking Pictures*

It now seems clear that not all sales exhausted all the patent rights. In 1938 in *General Talking Pictures,* a company purchased patented amplifiers from a seller who held a license to "manufacture . . . and to sell only for radio amateur reception, radio experimental reception and radio broadcast reception."[49] The antitrust and misuse aspects of this decision were discussed earlier (section 5.4).

The seller had no license to sell amplifiers for use in theaters as a part of "talking picture" equipment. The purchaser knew that the seller was not licensed to sell for such use. The purchaser leased the amplifiers for use by a theater operator in talking picture equipment. When sued for infringement, the purchaser contended that the amplifiers in question were licensed for any and all purposes, because of their manufacture and sale by a licensee.

The Supreme Court rejected this contention and held both seller and purchaser guilty of infringement. The Court found that the limited grant was lawful and that there was no basis for treating the sale "as if made under the patent or the authority of their owner." Because the seller could not convey to the purchaser "what both knew it was not authorized to sell," both the seller and purchaser were infringers.

Rehearing was granted on the defense of license. The Court held to its previous decision, Justice Brandeis writing:[50]

---

[49]*General Talking Pictures Co. v. Western Electric Co.,* 304 U.S. 175, 179–180, 182 (1938), *on reh'g,* 305 U.S. 124, 127 (1938).
[50]305 U.S. at 127.

LICENSES DEEMED TO ARISE FROM SALE OF A PRODUCT

The question of law requiring decision is whether the restriction in the license is to be given effect. That a restrictive license is legal seems clear. *Mitchell v. Hawley,* 16 Wall. 544. As was said in *United States v. General Electric Co.,* 272 U.S. 476, 489, the patentee may grant a license "upon any condition the performance of which is reasonably within the reward which the patentee by the grant of the patent is entitled to secure." The restriction here imposed is of that character. The practice of granting licenses for a restricted use is an old one, *see Rubber Company v. Goodyear,* 9 Wall. 788, 799, 800; *Gamewell Fire-Alarm Telegraph Co. v. Brooklyn,* 14 F. 255. So far as appears, its legality has never been questioned. . . .

As the restriction was legal and the amplifiers were made and sold outside the scope of the license, the effect is precisely the same as if no license whatsoever had been granted to Transformer Company. And as Pictures Corporation knew the facts, it is in no better position than if it had manufactured the amplifiers itself without a license. It is liable because it has used the invention without license to do so.

We have consequently no occasion to consider what the rights of the parties would have been if the amplifier had been manufactured "under the patent" and "had passed into the hands of a purchaser in the ordinary channels of trade." Nor have we occasion to consider the effect of a "licensee's notice" which purports to restrict the use of articles lawfully sold.

Justice Black, with Justice Reed, dissented on the basis that the exhaustion doctrine controlled.[51] Under *General Talking Pictures,* a sale of a patented article does not necessarily free the buyer from infringement liability. *General Talking Pictures* makes clear that a patent owner may limit a licensee's right to sell to sales for particular purposes or uses.

The exhaustion rule does not preclude all restrictions and conditions on purchasers of patented articles. This was confirmed by the Supreme Court decision in *Brulotte v. Thys* in 1964 that a patent owner may sell the patented product and separately license its use.[52] A patented

---

[51] 305 U.S. at 128, 133.
[52] *Brulotte v. Thys Co.,* 379 U.S. 29 (1964).

6.9 THE MODERN EXHAUSTION DOCTRINE

hop-picking machine was sold by the patent owner for a flat sum with a license to use it for a continuing royalty. The Supreme Court apparently assumed that the provision for a royalty on the machines after their sale by the patent owner was legal so long as a patent continued in force. The Court merely held that the royalty became unenforceable when all of the relevant patents had expired.

General Talking Pictures and *Brulotte* made clear that not all sales of patented products insulate all purchasers and users from infringement liability. Assertions about a purchaser carrying a machine outside the scope of the rights or about sales exhausting the rights are not and never were analytical devices. They were only conclusions. *General Talking Pictures* clearly stands for the view that they are not decisive.

These decisions leave considerable uncertainty about the basis for deciding the extent to which a sale does limit infringement liability. *General Talking Pictures* hints that the question is entirely one of determining what activities the patent owner authorized and those he did not. The Supreme Court on rehearing determined the purchaser's liability based on whether or not he was "licensed." The Court said that it was not considering the presumably different issues that might be raised if the purchaser bought in the "ordinary channels of trade" or without knowing that the seller was not licensed to sell it to him. This remark implies that there may be situations in which the law creates a "license" even though the patent owner did not intend to create one. However, the *General Talking Pictures* decision does not explain when this might occur.

The Court asked whether the sale of the product was within the scope of the license granted by the patent owner, whether the restrictions in the license to the seller were lawful, and whether the purchaser knew that the product was not sold within the scope of the license. If the sale of the product was not within the scope, the restriction put on the seller was lawful, and the purchaser knew of that limit in the license, any use or sale by that licensee beyond its scope constitutes infringement.

The *General Talking Pictures* questions have much to recommend them. The exclusive rights granted by a patent are designed to permit the patent owner to capture the social value from use of its invention during the patent's term. Anyone who uses or sells a patented product without the owner's authorization or "license" captures part of that value.

There are many situations in which a patent owner will sell a patented product and seek to reserve some of its patent rights from the purchaser. If the law precludes the patent owner from doing so, the law simply limits the efficiency by which the patent owner goes about capturing the value of its invention. If that is the only effect of a rule, the rule would be inconsistent with the basic policy of the patent law.

Contrary to what the Supreme Court sometimes asserted, a patent owner is not always indifferent to all uses and sales of patented products after the first. The law should not necessarily adopt an assumption that a patent owner intended to grant unlimited authority to purchasers of products from it or its licensees. Rather, the inquiry the Court seemed to make in *General Talking Pictures* seems logical; namely, did the patent owner in fact grant a license of a scope that permits the purchaser to engage in the activities alleged to be infringing? If it did, there is no infringement. If it did not, there is.

Focusing the inquiry on the existence and scope of a "license" does not require that analysis be confined to written or verbal statements by patent owners expressly granting authority. Rather, law could logically develop a set of rules to fill in the gaps when the patent owner has said nothing or too little. If the patent owner and the purchaser agree as to the scope of the purchaser's authority, the law should enforce that scope of authority unless the particular agreement should be illegal for some independent reason.

It is costly for patent owners and purchasers to negotiate, write, and even discuss the nature of the purchaser's authority in every sale of a patented product. Where the parties do not do so, the law may sensibly fill in the gaps by attempting to discover what the patent owner and purchaser would have agreed, if they could have costlessly addressed the scope of authority. The law may assume that they would have agreed to a scope of authority that would have maximized their joint benefits from the sale and subsequent use and sale of the product, net of their joint costs. By pursuing that inquiry, the law could sensibly serve the policy of patent law.

Under that type of analysis, *General Talking Pictures* presents a relatively straightforward situation. The patented amplifiers were useful in a variety of different types of equipment. The patent owner decided it would be most profitable to exploit different uses for the amplifier in different ways. It granted an exclusive license to its subsidiary to make and sell amplifiers for use in talking picture equipment. It

6.9 THE MODERN EXHAUSTION DOCTRINE

granted at least one license to another company to sell amplifiers for use in radio reception. The value of an amplifier in a radio set may have been much less than the value of the same amplifier in a motion picture projector.

The patent owner may well have been attempting to maximize the amount of those different values that it was going to capture. It is perfectly logical to expect an owner of a patented machine to attempt to charge those who have a higher value more than those who have a lower value. The patent owner may also have been faced with a situation in which use of the amplifiers in talking picture equipment required someone to invest in development of methods to integrate the amplifier with talking picture machines and in marketing the idea to talking picture machine manufacturers. The patent owner may have needed to exploit that use through an exclusive license to induce the licensee to make those investments. Prohibiting amplifiers for which it is paid at the radio reception rate from being used in the motion picture use may have been vital to the success of its attempt to exploit those uses separately. Moreover, the language used in the license expressly said that sales were to be made only for certain uses.

The result in *General Talking Pictures* should not depend on the fact that the seller was a licensee rather than the patent owner. If the patent owner wished to produce and sell for use in radio reception and, for whatever reason, sell for theater equipment, the owner should be able to limit the purchaser's rights. It is the scope of the purchaser's authority that is ultimately important. The seller's authority is secondary. If the law would permit a patent owner to limit the rights of a purchaser only by limiting the rights of the supplier, the law would force patent owners to grant uneconomical licenses to others to produce and sell simply to be able to effectively limit the purchaser's rights. The patent owner should be able to limit a purchaser's rights even though the patent owner, as seller, had unlimited rights to use for any purpose.

A large uncertainty remaining after *General Talking Pictures* is whether the decision applies to other types of limitations, such as those to particular territories. A patent owner may grant licenses to different companies to make, use, and sell in different areas of the country to achieve exactly the same type of benefits the patent owner in *General Talking Pictures* may have been trying to achieve. The territorial limits may assist in achieving economic discrimination, if the invention is more valuable to users in one area than another. Limitation to exclusive territories may also be useful to induce necessary investment in development and marketing. If the purposes of the patent owners in *Adams, Hobbie,* and *Keeler* were precisely the same as those of the patent owner in *General Talking Pictures,* there would seem to be nothing in the logic of *General Talking Pictures* to suggest that the same result would not follow. However, there is also nothing in language of the decision saying it has broader applicability. If *General Talking Pictures* does apply to territorial restrictions, then the only thing the patent owners in *Adams, Hobbie,* and *Keeler* failed to do was use the right language. They should have granted only the rights to sell in the territory only for use in the territory. They failed to apply the right "restriction" or "condition."

If the *General Talking Pictures* analysis leads to the conclusion that the patent owner and the purchaser would have agreed that the purchaser's authority was limited, *General Talking Pictures* then inquires as to whether the limitation and restriction is "lawful." Those limits were discussed earlier (section 5.5(f)).

(c) *Mallinckrodt*

In 1992, the Court of Appeals for the Federal Circuit in *Mallinckrodt v. Medipart* confirmed that, under *General Talking Pictures,* a purchaser of a patented product infringes the patent, when it uses the product in violation of a lawful restriction or condition on use specified by the seller at the time of the sale.[53] The Court also found that the purchaser infringed even though the seller was the patent owner. The facts were described in Chapter 1 and in section 2.7(b). The district court said there could be no infringement because the exhaustion doctrine rendered ineffective all restrictions or conditions on use by a purchaser of a product from a patent owner. The Court of Appeals for the Federal Circuit reversed.

Judge Newman's opinion summarized the conclusions as follows:[54]

---

[53] *Mallinckrodt, Inc. v. Medipart, Inc.,* 976 F.2d 700, 701 (Fed. Cir. 1992). That court also discussed the exhaustion doctrine in *Intel Corp. v. ULSI System Technology, Inc.,* 995 F.2d 1566, 1568–1569, 1571–1576 (Fed. Cir. 1993).
[54] Id. at 701.

6.9 THE MODERN EXHAUSTION DOCTRINE

The district court held that violation of the "single use only" notice cannot be remedied by suit for patent infringement, and granted summary judgment of non-infringement. . . .

* * *

Instead, the district court held that no restriction whatsoever could be imposed under the patent law, whether or not through restriction was enforceable under some other law, and whether or not this was a first sale to a purchaser with notice. This ruling is incorrect, for if Mallinckrodt's restriction was a valid condition of sale, then in accordance with *General Talking Pictures Corp. v. Western Electric Co.,* 304 U.S. 175, *aff'd on reh'g,* 305 U.S. 124 (1938), it was not excluded from enforcement under the patent law.

On review of these issues in the posture in which the case reaches us:

1. Movant Medipart did not dispute actual notice of their restriction. Thus we do not decide whether the form of the restriction met the legal requirements of notice or sufficed as a "label license," as Mallinckrodt calls it, for those questions were not presented on this motion for summary judgment. . . .

* * *

3. We also conclude that the district court misapplied precedent in holding that there can be no restriction on use imposed as a matter of law, even on the first purchaser. The restriction here at issue does not *per se* violate the doctrine of patent misuse or the antitrust law. Use in violation of a valid restriction may be remedied under the patent law, provided that no other law prevents enforcement of the patent.

Judge Newman's opinion primarily focused on the second part of the *General Taking Pictures* analysis, namely whether the restriction on the purchaser was lawful. However, the court first expressly rejected the notion that the *General Talking Pictures* rule is limited to sales by licensees and that patent owners as manufacturers and sellers may not restrict the use by purchasers. The court noted correctly that to limit *General Talking Pictures* in that way would be to make a "formalistic

LICENSES DEEMED TO ARISE FROM SALE OF A PRODUCT

distinction of no economic consequence."[55] The court then considered and rejected the district court's view that the restriction was unenforceable. The court accurately described the history of the development of the exhaustion doctrine and, importantly, it recognized that decisions such as *Mitchell, Adams,* and *Keeler* simply affirm the principle that an "unconditional sale of a patented device exhausts the patentee's rights to control the purchaser's use of the device," and also establish that "the sale of patented goods, like other goods, can be conditioned." The court said:[56]

> Viewing the entire group of these early cases, it appears that the Court simply applied, to a variety of factual situations, the rule of contract law that sale may be conditioned [footnotes omitted]. *Adams v. Burke* and its kindred cases do not stand for the proposition that no restriction or condition may be placed upon the sale of a patented article. It was error for the district court to derive that proposition from the precedent. Unless the condition violates some other law or policy (in the patent field, notably the misuse or antitrust law, *e.g., The United States v. Univis Lens Co.,* 316 U.S. 241 (1942)), private parties retain the freedom to contract concerning conditions of sale. As we have discussed, the district court cited the price-fixing and tying cases as reflecting what the court deemed to be correct policy, *viz.,* that no condition may be placed on the sale of patented goods, for any reason. However, this is not a price-fixing or tying case, and the *per se* antitrust and misuse violations found in the *Bauer* trilogy and *Motion Picture Patents* are not here present. The appropriate criterion is whether Mallinckrodt's restriction is reasonably within the patent grant, or whether the patentee has ventured beyond the patent grant and into behavior having an anticompetitive effect not justifiable under the rule of reason.

---

[55]Id. at 705.
[56]Id. at 708.

7

The Limits on Licensing Under The Doctrine of Federal Preemption

7.1	Federal Preemption and the State Law of Licensing	377
7.2	Patent Invalidity as a Defense to Royalty Obligations	378
7.3	A Licensee May Show Patent Invalidity if Part of an Antitrust Defense to Royalty Obligations	379
7.4	A Licensee May Defend an Action for Royalties by Proving on Patent Invalidity—*Lear*	383
7.5	The Enforceability of Trade Secret and Know-how Licenses—*Kewanee*	403
7.6	The Enforceability of Royalty Obligations in Patent and Know-how Licenses—*Aronson*	407
7.7	The Enforceability of Royalty Obligations in Licenses Made in the Context of Litigation—Consent Judgments and Settlement Agreements	410
7.8	The Enforcement of Patents Against Parties to Assignments and Exclusive Licenses	413

7.1 FEDERAL PREEMPTION AND THE STATE LAW OF LICENSING

The courts interpret the federal patent laws to limit the terms of licenses. Patent Act does not say the courts are to limit licensing options. Based on the statute, the states are free to apply their contract laws to inventions and patents. Owners of inventions and patents also appear free to make any agreements relating to inventions and patents that they find profitable. However, the courts have not been as silent as Congress on whether patent law implies that the states cannot enforce certain state laws and people may not enforce certain kinds of agreements.

The Constitution established a federal government. The states gave up certain powers to the federal government. The states ostensibly retained all other law-making powers. The courts have said the Constitution implies that a federal law within the federal powers may not be rendered ineffective by a state law. The general preemption principle is that state laws are unenforceable if they interfere with a federal law achieving its purposes. State law that directly decreased or increased the private value of a patent would be preempted. Federal law would preempt a California law saying that activities in California do not constitute patent infringement. This law would reduce the private value of patents. A state law that provided remedies against use of patented inventions for five years after the patent expired would be preempted. That law would increase the private value of the patent beyond that fixed by Congress.

However, preemption does not mean that all state laws that might affect in some way the private value or costs of producing inventions are precluded. The courts have had difficulty drawing the line. For purpose of licensing, the important decisions relate to state contract law and trade secret laws. Contract law provides rules about making, interpreting, and enforcing agreements. Invention producers and invention users may agree about production and use of inventions. Those agreements may involve inventions that could have been patented, but were not. They may involve inventions that are unpatented for some time and patented at other times. Trade secret law provides rights to inventions in a variety of situations.

7.2 PATENT INVALIDITY AS A DEFENSE TO ROYALTY OBLIGATIONS

By the 1940s, there was a well-established state contract rule saying that a patent licensee could not defend an action for royalties by proving the patent was invalid.[1] A similar "estoppel" against proving invalidity arose against the former owner of a patent who had assigned it.[2] These rules applied where the agreement was silent about whether the seller or licensee could attempt to show the patent was invalid.[3] Sometimes the parties expressly addressed the subject. Where a licensee agreed not to contest validity, the agreement would be enforced.[4] Royalties were due regardless of validity. The parties were free to agree that the owner guarantee validity, and royalties were due only if the patent was valid.

These "licensee estoppel" rules had two limits. First, the rule applied only to an action for royalties. If the license was terminated or repudiated by the licensee, the former licensee was free to assert invalidity as a defense to an infringement action.[5] Second, the rule generally

---

[1] *Lear v. Adkins,* 395 U.S. 653, 663 n.11, 668, 670 (1969); *Automatic Radio Mfg. Co. v. Hazeltine Research,* 176 F.2d 799, 806 (1st Cir. 1949), *aff'd* 339 U.S. 827 (1950), *overruled in pertinent part,* 395 U.S. 653 (1969). Congress did not change the rule when it enacted a major revision of the Patent Act two years after *Automatic Radio.*

[2] *Scott Paper Co. v. Marcalus Mfg. Co.,* 326 U.S. 249 (1945); *Westinghouse Electric & Mfg. Co. v. Formica Insulation Co.,* 266 U.S. 342 (1924).

[3] For example, *Universal Rim Co. v. Scott,* 21 F.2d 346, 348 (N.D. Ohio 1922).

[4] *Steiner Sales Co. v. Schwartz Co.,* 98 F.2d 999, 1009–1010 (10th Cir. 1938).

[5] *Bucky v. Sebo,* 208 F.2d 304, 305–306 (2d Cir. 1953) (termination); *Eskimo Pie Corporation v. National Ice Cream Co.,* 26 F.2d 901, 902 (6th Cir. 1928) (termination); *Universal Rim Co. v. Scott,* 21 F.2d 346, 348–349 (N.D. Ohio 1922) (repudiation).

permitted an exclusive licensee to defend an action for royalties on the basis that the patent had been found invalid in a suit against a third party.[6] Therefore, while that licensee could not challenge validity (unless it bargained for the right), it could take advantage of a finding of invalidity. Invalidity eliminated the royalty obligation. The courts explained that rule by saying an exclusive licensee was evicted from its exclusive position. Therefore it would not be compelled to continue to pay at the agreed rate. This eviction rule did not apply to a nonexclusive licensee.[7]

In the 1940s, the courts started to limit the operation of state law and private agreements for inventions. For purposes of licensing, the highlight (or lowlight) was a 1969 decision about a state contract rule that provided an implied term to a license agreement. The implied term was that a patent licensee could not defend an action for royalties by proving the invalidity of the patent. The Supreme Court said preemption principles required that a licensee must be permitted to challenge validity. The state contract rule was nullified.

7.3 A LICENSEE MAY SHOW PATENT INVALIDITY IF PART OF AN ANTITRUST DEFENSE TO ROYALTY OBLIGATIONS

The history of modern patent preemption rules is tied to the history of the development of antitrust and misuse doctrines. By the early 1940s, the courts had asserted their power to declare patents unenforceable based on the patent owner's method of exploiting the rights (Chapter 2). The courts also frequently interpreted the antitrust limitations on methods of exploitation.

---

[6] *Drackett Chemical Co. v. Chamberlain Co.,* 63 F.2d 853, 854–855 (6th Cir. 1933) (exclusive licensee is evicted as of the date of unappealed decision of invalidity and notice to patent owner that it would no longer pay); *Ross v. Fuller & Warren Co.,* 105 F. 510, 512 (N.D.N.Y. 1900) (an exclusive licensee may defend action for royalties on ground of eviction).

[7] *Automatic Radio Mfg. Co. v. Hazeltine Research,* 176 F.2d 799, 807–808 (1st Cir. 1949), *aff'd* 339 U.S. 823 (1950), *overruled on other grounds,* 395 U.S. 653 (1969).

THE LIMITS ON LICENSING

In the 1940s, the Supreme Court created a third, broader limit to the licensee estoppel rule. In 1942, in *Sola Electric,* a patent owner brought an action against a licensee for royalties and for an order requiring it to perform its obligations under the license. One provision required the licensee to sell at prices no less than those of the patent owner or its other licensees.[8] The licensee alleged that royalties were not payable because the license was illegal under the Sherman Act. Part of the basis for the alleged antitrust violation was that the licensed patents were invalid. The allegation was that, because the patents were invalid, the provision fixing the price of the licensee's sales violated the Sherman Act. The Court of Appeals said the licensee could not defend the action for royalties on the basis of invalidity. The Court of Appeals said that the price clause was lawful because the patents were presumed valid.

The Supreme Court said the licensee could defend the action for royalties by proving a Sherman Act violation. The Sherman Act violation presumably rendered the agreement, and the royalty obligation, unenforceable. The Court also said that, if the licensee proved the patent was invalid, the price clause violated the Sherman Act. The Court said that the Sherman Act preempted the state estoppel rule.

In 1947 in the *Katzinger* and *MacGregor* decisions, the Court again limited the estoppel rules. In both of those cases, the license required the licensee to sell at prices set from time to time by the patent owner. In both, the licensee had complied with the pricing provisions. The patent owner was not seeking in either case to require performance of the pricing provision.

In *Katzinger,* the licensee also agreed that it would not assert invalidity and would be deemed an infringer if it elected to terminate the contract without also ceasing to manufacture the patented product.[9] The licensee terminated the license. The patent owner sued for unpaid royalties prior to termination and an accounting for damages after. The Court of Appeals enforced the agreement. The Supreme Court changed the result. The Court said that invalidity would be a defense both to royalties and to infringement liability.

---

[8] *Sola Elec. Co. v. Jefferson Elec. Co.,* 317 U.S. 173 (1942).
[9] *Katzinger Co. v. Chicago Metallic Mfg. Co.,* 329 U.S. 394 (1947).

7.3 A LICENSEE MAY SHOW PATENT INVALIDITY

In *MacGregor,* the patent owner brought only an action to collect the royalties.[10] In *MacGregor,* the licensee counterclaimed saying a violation of the antitrust laws based on the price-fixing agreement rendered the agreement unenforceable. The lower court awarded the patent owner royalties. Again, the Supreme Court disagreed. The Supreme Court said that invalidity could be proved to defeat the action for royalties.

Justices Frankfurter, Reed, Jackson, and Burton dissented in both cases. Justice Frankfurter said that the *Sola Electric* decision said nothing about a licensee's royalty obligation. Frankfurter said *Sola Electric* simply decided that a patent owner could not enforce a price-fixing clause if the licensee could show that the patent on which it was based was invalid. Because enforcement of the price-fixing clause was not one of the remedies sought by the patent owner in these actions, Frankfurter said these cases required consideration of the licensee estoppel doctrine or, as Frankfurter put it, "whether we shall allow the licensee to repudiate an agreement for the payment of money made in an arms length transaction."[11]

Frankfurter identified the benefits of an estoppel rule this way:[12]

> But whether an inventor has a valid patent is a matter of increasing uncertainty. Hitherto, under the estoppel doctrine a patentee could be assured that he would not have to litigate the validity of his patent with those to whom he grants license rights under it. Under the present decision, he cannot have this assurance of freedom from litigation if, under reasonable belief that he has a valid patent, he inserts a price-fixing clause in the license, even though afterwards he merely asks for royalties.

Frankfurter perceived no relation between the price-fixing clause and the new permission for the licensee to escape royalty payments based upon invalidity. He said the decision would create great uncertainty among patent owners about whether the estoppel rule could still be re-

---

[10] *MacGregor v. Westinghouse Elec. & Mfg. Co.,* 329 U.S. 402 (1947).
[11] Id. at 413.
[12] Id. at 413–414.

lied on. Frankfurter probably would have been surprised that the issue was not resolved until twenty-three years later, in 1969, and that one argument for abolishing the rule was that the decisions in *Sola, Katzinger,* and *MacGregor* had effectively destroyed the rule.

These decisions said that, in essence, a licensee could challenge validity because the pricing agreement was illegal if the patents were invalid. Each action involved an agreement fixing the prices at which the licensee sold. Price fixing in a license agreement was not always illegal. Prior to these decisions, the Court had never said that antitrust legality depended on the validity of the underlying patents.

By the 1940s, the courts had recognized that patents could be used as a vehicle for a cartel. These decisions did not involve allegations of a patent "cartel." However, assume that cartels are more likely to use patents of questionable validity as covers for price-fixing agreements. If that is true and the parties knew that the licensed patents were invalid, evidence of that knowledge would be evidence of the existence of an illegal cartel. Proof that the parties thought that the patents were valid or were uncertain about their validity would tend to show that no cartel existed. Actual validity as determined by a court would seem to prove little. The primary purpose of the agreement (namely, to exploit the rights or to operate a cartel) is not proved by what the courts say later about the validity of the patents. So why create an exception to the licensee estoppel rule?

There are three potential reasons. The first is that the Court was simply unhappy with the rule that price fixing in a license was lawful. The Court made such agreements less profitable in order to deter them. Permitting the licensee to litigate validity raises risks and costs. If that is what the Court was doing, it certainly did not say so. Let us assume that the Court was not doing that.

Second, the Court may have created a rule that would make it more difficult to use a frivolous patent license to run a cartel. The rule permits a licensee that wants to cheat on the real agreement to destroy the patent that provides the cover. This would make such cartels less stable. If that is what the Court was doing, it did not say so. One must assume that the Court was not doing that.

Third, even if the Court was content with its rule that price fixing was lawful, it may have been unhappy with the estoppel rule and was trying to get rid of it. Frankfurter's dissent suggested that this was the Court's concern and that it should simply have said so. The Court declined to do so.

7.4 A LICENSEE MAY DEFEND AN ACTION FOR ROYALTIES BY PROVING ON PATENT INVALIDITY—*LEAR*

In 1969, the Supreme Court in *Lear v. Adkins*[13] held that the "public interest" required that the contract doctrine of licensee estoppel "give way."

In *Lear,* an inventor of several gyroscope designs licensed its patents to a company. The license said nothing about whether the licensee could defend an action for the royalties based on the invalidity of the patents.[14] The license said the licensee could not terminate the license unless it stopped using the designs described in the patents. The licensee stopped paying royalties. The licensee attempted to terminate the agreement, but the state courts said termination was ineffective because the licensee was continuing to use the designs and had no other right to terminate. The patent owner sued to collect the royalties. The licensee asserted invalidity. The California courts said that under the licensee estoppel doctrine, invalidity was no defense.

The Supreme Court disagreed. The Supreme Court said that the licensee estoppel rule was preempted by the Patent Act.

(a) The Doctrinal Basis for *Lear*

There is room for debate about the legal basis for *Lear.* The decision could have been the result of three different kinds of legal analyses.

First, the decision most probably was based on federal preemption of state law. The principle of preemption is that, because the Constitution makes federal law the supreme law of the land, any state law which conflicts with federal law is unconstitutional.[15] The *Lear* deci-

---

[13] *Lear v. Adkins,* 395 U.S. 653, 670–671 (1969).
[14] *Lear v. Adkins,* 67 Cal. 2d 882 (1967) and 52 Cal. Rptr. 795 (Ct. App. 1966).
[15] *Kewanee Oil Co. v. Bicron Corp.,* 416 U.S. 470, 479–480 (1974).

sion has two parts, the first relating to licensee estoppel[16] and the second part relating to royalty obligations if the patent is invalid.[17] On the second issue, the Court said it was applying preemption principles when it said that "the decisive question is whether overriding federal policies would be significantly frustrated if licensees could be required to continue to pay royalties during the time they are challenging patent validity in the courts."[18] The reference in the first part of its opinion to "the competing demands of the common law of contracts and the federal law of patents" suggests that its decision was premised on preemption. *Lear* was also premised on the *Sears* and *Compco* cases, and those were preemption decisions.[19]

Second, the Court might have been saying that patent agreements are subject to federal contract law. If licensee estoppel was federal common law, the Supreme Court could change it.[20] However, the Court said that licensee estoppel was state law.[21] Therefore, the Court's power to change it must rest on something else.

Third, *Lear* might be an exercise of that Court's power to refuse to enforce patent license agreements or patents under the doctrine of unclean hands.[22] However, the Court seemed to recognize that it was striking down a rule which arose from state contract law and not from any provision of the agreement made by the licensor.[23] Since the licensor's conduct did not create the alleged injury to public policy, the licensor could not be guilty of unclean hands. Moreover, the Court in *Lear* did not find the patent unenforceable. The Court said that the licensee would have to show invalidity on remand, not that the licensor would have to show purge. Hence, *Lear* seems to be a preemption decision.

---

[16] 395 U.S. at 661–671.
[17] 395 U.S. at 671–678.
[18] 395 U.S. at 673.
[19] *Sears, Roebuck v. Stiffel,* 376 U.S. 225, 231 (1965); *Compco v. Day-Brite Lighting,* 376 U.S. 234, 237–238 (1965).
[20] Cf. 395 U.S. at 671.
[21] 395 U.S. at 673, 663 n.11.
[22] *Morton Salt Co. v. G.S. Suppiger Co.,* 314 U.S. 488, 492–494 (1942); *B.B. Chemical Co. v. Ellis,* 314 U.S. 497–498 (1942).
[23] 395 U.S. at 668, 670.

7.4 A LICENSEE MAY DEFEND AN ACTION

(b) The Decision on Licensee Estoppel

The decision in *Lear* proceeds by saying that patents grant "monopoly power."[24] The Court says that patents constitute "a limited exception to the general federal policy favoring free competition."[25] The Court then begins discussing the "equities" of the parties. The Court says that a patent licensee gets only two benefits from the license: (1) that it "avoided the necessity of defending an expensive infringement action"; and (2) that the existence of the patent may deter others from competing with it. That makes sense only if it is assumed all patents are invalid. If a patent might be valid, a licensee also avoids liability for damages and injunction. That is, of course, the reason most people pay for a license.

The Court also suggested that ordinary contract principles do not apply to patents, but rather that patent license agreements are tested by some "standard of good-faith commercial dealing."[26] The Court said that, in deciding whether to enforce a license agreement, without considering validity, it considered the licensor's "equities" and balanced them against "the important public interest in permitting full and free competition in the use of ideas which are in reality a part of the public domain."[27] The Court did reveal how to balance "the equities" of an inventor against the "public interest."

The Court said that licensees "may often" be the only individuals with "enough economic incentive" to challenge patentability. Therefore, "muzzling" them might lead to fewer patents being found invalid by a court. Licensee estoppel was, therefore, theoretically inconsistent with free use of unpatentable inventions.[28] The Court in *Lear* made no effort to evaluate whether there were economically desirable benefits flowing from the licensee estoppel doctrine, which might justify injury to any purpose of patent law. *Lear* says not one word about whether licensee estoppel is inconsistent with providing incentives to make in-

---

[24] Id. at 663.
[25] Id. at 663.
[26] Id. at 669.
[27] Id. at 670.
[28] Id. at 670.

THE LIMITS ON LICENSING

ventions or to utilize the patent system or about the benefits from licensing.

The patent owner argued that licensee estoppel might properly apply where the license there was entered prior to the patent issuing. The Court rejected that distinction because it said such a rule would permit inventors to enter "all important licenses" prior to issue and disable "all those who have the strongest incentive to show that a patent is worthless."[29] If a patent is worthless, a user might accept a license under it, but only at a royalty of zero. If all users obtain licenses at zero royalty, then the public obtains the benefits of free use of the invention without the cost of litigation to show worthlessness and without taking any risk.

The owner also argued that the licensee should be required to pay regardless of validity, because the company had obtained a disclosure of the invention prior to issuance of the patent and that disclosure justified a continuing obligation to pay regardless of validity. The Court said that the core issue there was "whether federal patent policy bars a state from enforcing a contract regulating access to an unpatented secret idea."[30] The Court remanded rather than deciding that issue. Five years later in *Kewanee* the Court said that federal policy did not bar a state from enforcing such a contract.

If the *Lear* preemption analysis is correct, the legality of state enforcement of a license depends solely upon the impact of that license on providing the maximum incentives for challenges to patent validity. If that is true, all patent license agreements made prior to a judgment of validity are suspect. A patent license agreement, by its very existence, deters the licensee at least temporarily from challenging validity. An actual or potential infringer, who is denied a license, must then decide either (1) not to continue or enter that business or (2) to risk litigation. The license permits it to delay that decision. If *Lear* stands for the view that licensees must always have economic incentives to challenge validity, then royalty-free or paid-up patent licenses are also suspect. No court has ever found that *Lear* goes that far.

---

[29] Id. at 672.
[30] Id. at 672.

7.4 A LICENSEE MAY DEFEND AN ACTION

(c) The "Decision" on the Enforceability of Payment Terms of Patent Licenses

The patent owner in *Lear* argued that the licensee, even though not estopped to prove invalidity, must pay the $800,000 judgment based upon its activities prior to 1960, when the patent issued, and from 1960 to 1963, the cutoff date for the damage award. There were two arguments. The first was that the Lear company had obtained access to Dr. Adkins' ideas prior to their disclosure in the patent and was required to pay royalties both before and during the patent term without regard to validity as consideration for that access. The second was that the parties had expressly agreed that royalties would be paid until the patent was held invalid and no court had done so.[31]

The Court refused to affirm the judgment on either of those bases and remanded the case to the state courts to determine whether and how much Lear was liable for.

The Court's discussion of why it rejected both those arguments is confusing. The Court said that, if the patent is about to become technically obsolete, the licensee has "little incentive" to litigate "unless he is freed from liability at least from the time he refuses to pay the contractual royalties."[32] That is the first of the three different conclusions on when royalty liability ceases for patents later held invalid. The second is that *"Lear* must be permitted to avoid the payment of all royalties accruing after Adkins' 1960 patent issued if Lear can prove invalidity."[33] That is what Justice White separately said the Court was holding.[34] The third was that licensees could not be "required to continue to pay royalties during the time they are challenging patent validity in the Courts."[35] The Court did not say which of its three rules was the guiding one.

The facts do not help much to decipher what the Court was saying because the licensee in *Lear* stopped payments prior to the issuance of the patent. The action in which the licensee challenged validity, a state

---

[31] Id. at 672 and 673.
[32] Id. at 674.
[33] Id. at 674.
[34] Id. at 682 n.2.
[35] Id. at 673.

court action to enforce the agreement, was commenced shortly after the patent issued and the licensee presumably promptly pleaded invalidity in that action. All we know is that the Court vacated the judgment in its entirety, including the part of the judgment calling for royalties paid during the first three years of the patent's term. The Court did not say that the inventions involved in the case were about to become technically obsolete. It merely posed that as one possible scenario. If an invention is about to become technically obsolete, it is true that licensees as well as anyone else have little incentive to litigate validity.

The Court did say the parties' agreement did not control. The Court found that a contract permitting a challenge to validity, but requiring the licensee to comply with its terms and "continue to pay royalties until its claim is finally vindicated in the courts," is "inconsistent with the aims of federal patent policy."[36] Without so much as a nod toward policies of encouraging invention, disclosure of inventions through use of the patent system, or efficient use of inventions through licensing, the Court concluded that "enforcing this contractual provision would undermine the strong federal policy favoring the full and free use of ideas in the public domain."[37]

The Court was correct to recognize that if it was going to go into the business of regulating state law about whether a licensee could challenge validity, it was also going to be dragged into the business of regulating the impact of validity challenge on royalty obligations.

(d) The Effects of Licensee Estoppel and a Licensee's Agreement to Pay Regardless of Validity

The estoppel rule said that, when the parties say nothing about whether the licensee may end the royalty obligation by proving invalidity, the law implies a term saying the licensee may not. Is there any reason to assume the parties would have agreed to that term if they expressly addressed the subject?

Assume it is difficult to predict with much certainty the outcome of litigation on patent validity. Assume also that litigation is expensive.

---

[36] Id. at 673.
[37] Id. at 674.

7.4 A LICENSEE MAY DEFEND AN ACTION

In this situation, the parties to a license are likely to negotiate a price that reflects those costs and that uncertainty. In other words, the estoppel rule could assume that the parties would typically negotiate a price to the license discounted based on legal uncertainty and based on the assumption that the licensee would give up the option of litigating in exchange for this reduced price. If the parties say nothing, the law assumes that they would have elected to reduce uncertainty and litigation costs rather than to preserve uncertainty and the option to litigate. The licensee estoppel rule would not operate if the parties expressly addressed those issues. However, the rule put the burden on them to adjust things differently.

Chapter 1 described the effects of transaction costs, legal uncertainty, and infringement litigation costs on the price for a license (section 1.8); a license was treated as a substitute for infringement litigation and remedies. The procedure described in Chapter 1 can be employed to illustrate the effect of licensee estoppel and *Lear* (section 1.8). The same symbols will be used. However, rather than identifying values and costs on a per-unit basis, aggragate or total numbers will be used.

The Patent Owner, *PO*, owns a patent on a product that it cannot make and sell. The per-unit value of the patent to *PO* is $0. A group of Potential Licensee companies, *Lee*, are more efficient. The value of the patent in each *Lee*'s hands would be $110,000 (or $110t). The symbol "t" means "thousand."

$EVnl, owner < EP < EVl, licee$

·////////////////////·————
$0   110t

There are many *Lee*-type companies that could to pay the $110t per unit and make a profit, and they compete for licenses.

One essential condition for licensing is:

$EVnl, owner + TC < EP < EVl, licee - TC$

The owner and potential licensee evaluate the transaction costs of licensing. The owner proposes to reduce transaction costs by permitting enforcement of the royalty obligation without litigating validity issues. If the potential licensee agrees to forgo the option of litigating validity,

THE LIMITS ON LICENSING

the owner and licensee each anticipate transaction costs of $10t$. Assume the owner and licensee believe the patent is 100 percent certain to be found valid. The licensee losses nothing by giving up that option. The minimum the owner will accept is $10t$ and the maximum the licensee will pay is $100t$.

```
——·////////////////·————
$0  10t              100t
```

The owner and licensee as a business proposition had a payment range (given those transaction costs) between $10t$ and $100t$ within which a license would be mutually advantageous.

The other condition for licensing is:

$$EVlit, owner - LC < EP < EClit, licee + LC$$

By licensing, the owner gives up the option of receiving infringement remedies during the term of the license. Assume the remedies for successful patent owners permit the owner to capture a potential licensee's total value from use of the information. Assume an infringement action in which validity was contested will cost each party $50t$ in fees and other costs.

By licensing, the owner gives up the right to receive $110t$ by litigation and pay litigation costs of $50t$. The potential licensee avoids expected costs (i.e., a possible injunction and damages) from litigation of $110t$ and litigation costs of $50t$.

$$\begin{array}{llll} EVlit, owner - LC < & EP & < EVlit, licee + LC \\ 110 \quad\quad -50 & & 110 \quad\quad +50 \end{array}$$

```
————————————·////////////////·————
$0              60           160
```

There is a potential for a license, but at a price between $60t$ (the minimum the owner will accept) and $160t$ (the maximum the potential licensee will pay). The business range overlaps.

7.4 A LICENSEE MAY DEFEND AN ACTION

$$EVnl, owner + TC < EP < EVl, licee - TC$$

```
————————————·////////////////·————————
$0                10               100
```

Given competition for licenses among licensees, the license will be granted for $100t$.

Assume the owner and licensee believe that the patent is 50 percent likely to be found invalid in litigation. The owner proposes again to reduce transaction costs by permitting enforcement of the royalty obligation regardless of validity. The litigation option that the licensee forgoes reduces the value of the license. The third condition for licensing becomes:

$$Pw \times Vw - LC < EP < Pl \times Cl + LC$$
$$.5 \times 110 - 50 \qquad .5 \times 110 + 50$$
$$55 \quad -50 \qquad 55 \quad +50$$

$$EVlit, owner - LC < EP < EVlit, licee + LC$$
$$55 \quad -50 \qquad 55 \quad +50$$

```
·————————————————————/////////////////·————————
$0                        5                 105
```

Litigation is now a viable option for the potential licensee. Assume the owner and potential licensee agree to license and have the licensee forgo the litigation option. The payment is reduced to $55t$ to reflect the option the licensee gave up, and each party will avoid $50t$ in litigation costs. Under licensee estoppel, the parties are deemed to have reduced the price to reflect the probability of invalidity and to avoid the validity litigation costs.

Prior to *Lear*, the licensee must make that $55t$ payment so long as the license continues. If the licensee did not pay the entire $55t$, it could be required to pay without validity litigation. Under the licensee estoppel rule, if the agreement said nothing on the subject and the licensee did not pay, the payment obligation would be enforceable without litigating validity.

After *Lear*, the parties are not assumed to have made this agreement. However, what if the parties expressly addressed the subject? The lower courts said *Lear* also meant that an express agreement by the licensee to pay the royalties regardless of validity was unenforceable. The

THE LIMITS ON LICENSING

situation changes again. The owner is permitted to waive its litigation option. The licensee is not. The licensee is required to keep the option of litigating validity. The licensee may receive the benefits of the license and the option to avoid its cost.

Under this situation, the owner will no longer agree to the $55t$ rate. If the owner licenses, the owner's expected payment from the license declines and the costs of litigation to receive the payment increase. Even if the owner agrees to the $55t$ rate, the licensee retains the option to litigate. The expected payment is no longer certain and could be expensive to collect. From the licensee's perspective, the license is anti-injunction and damage insurance that continues so long as premiums are paid.

The expected payment from the licensee to the owner, $EP,$ is the agreed payment, AP ($55), times the probability that it will win a validity challenge minus its cost from validity litigation. The expected payment from the licensees' perspective is the agreed payment times its assessment of the probability that it will lose plus the cost of validity litigation. The decision to license becomes:

$$EVnl, owner + TC < AP \times Pw - LC < AP \times Pl + LC < EVlic, licee - TC$$
$$0 \quad +10 < 55 \times .5 \quad -50 < 55 \times .5 + 50 \quad < 110 \quad -10$$
$$10 \quad < -22.5 \quad < 77.5 \quad < \quad 100$$

Given the licensees' litigation option (and assuming the licensee will take that option), the expected payment from licensing is $27.5 and (after litigation costs) is a loss of $22.5. Licensing is no longer profitable for the owner. The increased risk of licensing pushes the owner's expected loss even further south (section 1.8(g)). As discussed earlier, if an owner is risk averse, the utility of an uncertain payment is less than its expected value. A risk-averse owner may well prefer a certain royalty of $17.5 to an uncertain royalty with an expected value of $27.5.

Another way to think about *Lear* is to ask whether owners and licensees are likely to regard litigation or private agreements as more efficient mechanisms for reducing the uncertainty about the validity of a patent. The Patent Act permits an invention user to defend an action for infringement based on invalidity. That litigation will reduce uncertainty about validity. If it is found valid, the private value of that patent is measured by the value of the invention to users. The patent's value is de-

7.4 A LICENSEE MAY DEFEND AN ACTION

creased by the ability of the user to substitute litigation for permission from the owner. If the patent is held invalid, the patent is worth zero. That information is beneficial to the parties. However, it is costly to achieve that level of certainty.

If each invention owner and each user had to litigate all patents of uncertain validity, the private and transaction costs of using the patent system for many inventions would rise dramatically and, in many cases, exceed the private value of the invention and the patent.

However, Congress implicitly left open another avenue of reducing uncertainty. It permitted a patent owner to authorize an otherwise infringing activity and waive the remedies provided in the Act. No court had ever seriously questioned that the owner could charge a market-clearing price for that waiver. If a patent is 100 percent certain to be valid, then that price is equal to the value of the invention. If a patent is 100 percent certain to be invalid, the price for that license will be zero. If validity is uncertain, the price will be discounted to reflect it.

Under that system, the private value of inventions exceed what they would be if litigation was the only option, because licensing permits more efficient users access to the invention and permits inventions to be combined with complementary resources in the most efficient way. The transaction costs of licenses at prices discounted to reflect uncertainty are likely to be less costly than litigation. Risk is reduced equally by both methods, but at far lower cost by the licensing method.

The issue posed by *Lear* was whether the state law may make the license method the presumptively chosen means of reducing uncertainty between particular parties. In other words, to what extent may state law infer that the parties would normally choose to limit resort to litigation to reduce that uncertainty? The Supreme Court in *Lear* said the states may not presume the parties would choose that result.

(e) When Do Royalty Obligations End under *Lear?*

Confusion reigned after the Court's separate pronouncement on royalties. The lower courts struggled with this part of *Lear* because it was unclear whether the Court wanted to give a licensee maximum incentives to litigate validity, to reduce the licensor's incentives to delay judgment, or to do something else.

If the rule is intended to reduce incentives to delay judgment, it is unclear which of the three rules would achieve it. The Court suggested that requiring the licensee to pay until the judgment would give the licensor too great incentive to delay. The Court ignored that any rule which gives the licensor incentive to delay gives the licensee an equal and opposite incentive to hurry. There is no reason to believe that licensors are more efficient delayers than licensees are hurriers. It is the judgment, not the lawsuit, which theoretically benefits the public, so it is the judgment which licensees should be encouraged to obtain. If the policy goal is the earliest possible judgment, then a rule under which the licensee must pay until it obtains a judgment maximizes its incentive to obtain it promptly. A rule that the licensee has no royalty liability from the date of suit reduces a licensee's incentives to hurry to judgment. The incentives of the licensor are the opposite.

The Court also seemed to say the issue must be decided based on giving the licensee incentives to litigate. If the goal is to maximize the licensee's incentives to litigate, the obvious answer is to award the licensee everything that it paid to the licensor at any time. This maximizes the value of a finding of invalidity to the licensee and would lead to the maximum number of challenges by licensees. It would also lead to a smaller number of licenses. The effect on total challenges is anyone's guess.

Shortly after *Lear,* one District Court in *Troxel* held that the licensee could require the owner to pay back all the royalties.[38] In that situation, the patent had been held invalid in an action involving a third party. The Court of Appeals for the Sixth Circuit reversed.[39] The Court of Appeals compelled the licensee to pay under the license until the patent was found invalid in a final unappealable judgment in the third-party action. This eviction rule applied in some circumstances prior to *Lear.*[40]

The Court of Appeals said three things. First, the licensee benefited

---

[38] *Troxel Manufacturing Co. v. Schwinn Bicycle Co.,* 465 F.2d 1253 (6th Cir. 1972).
[39] Id. at 1257–1258; *Troxel Manufacturing Co. v. Schwinn Bicycle Co.,* 489 F.2d 968, 972–973 (6th Cir. 1973).
[40] *Dracket Chemical Co. v. Chamberlain Co.,* 63 F.2d 853 (6th Cir. 1933) (as noted by *Lear,* 395 U.S. at 667); *Troxel Mfg. Co. v. Schwinn Bicycle Co.,* 465 F.2d at 1255 (6th Cir. 1972) ("It has been an established rule in this Circuit for nearly 40 years that a final adjudication of invalidity of a licensed patent operates as an eviction from the license, terminating the licensee's obligation to continue making royalty payments after that date, but giving no right to recoup royalties already paid.").

7.4 A LICENSEE MAY DEFEND AN ACTION

from the license prior to its termination. Second, the District Court rule would be inconsistent with encouraging use of the patent system and encouraging licensing of patents.

If one adopts the Court of Appeals' view that one should consider the benefits of the license to the licensee and the impact of the rule on incentives to license (that is, the mutual benefits of the license to the licensor and licensee), the payment rule seems simply to follow. Royalties must be paid until the parties have provided that they cease or, if there is no provision, the patent ceases by a final and unappealable judgment of invalidity. The obvious problem with that rule is that it is not on the *Lear* list and *Lear* says the parties' perception of their interests does not necessarily control. The courts have, by and large, rejected that rule. In the 1980s, one district court did rule that a licensee must continue to pay royalties until a judgment of invalidity.

Most courts have attempted to define some rule that ignores the benefits to the licensee and ignores the corresponding effect of the rule on incentives to use the patent system and to license. Once you do that, it is difficult to conceive of any line other than one that maximizes the size of the carrot for the challenging licensee.

The court in *Troxel,* in *dicta,* tried to find one by saying, third, that *Lear* was designed to achieve an "early" test of validity, not simply to create the maximum incentives for the maximum number of tests. The Court of Appeals said that if the licensee could recover everything paid in the past, it would have little incentive to litigate until the patent had expired. The court rejected the idea that *Lear* required that the size of the carrot, that is, the total economic gain from successful challenge, be maximized. It replaced that idea with an effort to create incentives for as early a challenge to validity as possible.

The *Troxel* Court of Appeals said that if an early test is the goal, a licensee must pay until it initiates the test.[41] However, that rule has little to commend itself over a rule which would say that the licensee must pay until the parties have agreed it may stop or the day of judgment. There is no reason to suppose that a licensee would file suit earlier if the royalty obligation ceases as of that date than if its royalty obligations

---

[41] *Accord, Transition Electronic Corp. v. Hughes Aircraft Co.,* 649 F.2d 871, 874–875 (1st Cir. 1981) (absent fraudulent inducement, a licensee may not recover royalties paid prior to bringing suit).

THE LIMITS ON LICENSING

ceased on the date of judgment. To obtain an early judgment, the licensee must file an early suit. And it is the judgment, not the suit, that places the invention in the public domain. Any rule which does not create incentives to obtain an early judgment seems to miss the point.

The Court of Appeals is correct that licensees who could recover all past royalty payments would have little incentive to litigate until the patents had expired. What should have been equally important was that such a rule would require the patent owner to charge a royalty equal to the value of the invention if the patent was 100 percent to be held valid, and hold that money in trust for payment of its potential liability to the licensee. Such a rule would preclude licenses that had discounted prices based on uncertainty of validity. The number of licenses granted under that rule would decline. Net challenges by licensees are difficult to predict.

Taking their lead from the *Troxel* decision, many courts have attempted to draw a line based on whether the licensee had done something which would prompt a lawsuit. If the licensee does something which would prompt a lawsuit, then the courts generally say that it is freed from the royalty obligation from the date of that act, *if* the patent is ultimately shown to be invalid. The "logic" is simply that *Lear* attempts to create rules which encourage challenges to validity, and, if the licensee "challenges" validity, it is doing what *Lear* wants it to do. *Lear* does not compel such a rule because the licensee in *Lear* had both withheld royalties and had challenged validity in a pending suit. One court said that "the obligation to pay royalties on an invalid patent ceases when a licensee takes affirmative steps aimed at adjudication of the patent's invalidity."[42] The Sixth Circuit formulated the rule as follows:[43]

---

[42] *Chromalloy American Corp. v. Fischmann,* 716 F.2d 683, 685 (9th Cir. 1983). In *Chromalloy,* the Chromalloy Company acquired a patent license, know-how, and the business assets of Fischmann in 1968, stopped paying royalties in January 1975, and repudiated the agreement and commenced an action for a declaratory judgment that the agreement was void because of invalidity in 1976. The Court held that the patent was invalid, but that Chromalloy was obligated to pay royalties up until the date on which it had stopped payment, repudiated, and sued.
[43] *PPG Industries, Inc. v. Westwood Chemical, Inc.,* 530 F.2d 700, 708 (6th Cir. 1976).

7.4 A LICENSEE MAY DEFEND AN ACTION

Under *Lear*, liability for royalties ordinarily is terminated on one of two dates (*i.e.*, if *before* eviction), whichever first occurs: (1) on the date the licensee ceases the payment of royalties for the purpose of prompting an early adjudication of invalidity, or (2) on the date the licensee files suit (or counterclaim) attacking the validity of the patent. It is only when the licensee continues to pay royalties, and does not file suit until after the patent has been adjudicated invalid, that the cutoff date for liability is the date of eviction of the patent.

Simply ceasing to pay royalties was not sufficient action to prompt an early adjudication of validity.[44]

By a rule that liability ceases on the date the licensee files suit or a counterclaim attacking validity, or the date it ceases payment for purposes of prompting adjudication, whichever occurs earlier, the courts adopted a modified version of one of the rules stated in *Lear*. The courts have been reluctant to find that any nonpayment of royalties is sufficient to end ultimate royalty liability. The licensee may fail to pay royalties for a number of reasons, such as: (1) It does not believe it is doing anything that requires payment, or (2) it cannot afford to pay. The courts have generally insisted that the licensee stop paying royalties and notify the licensor that it is not paying because of invalidity.

(f) The Enforceability of a Licensee's Express Agreement Not to Challenge Validity

On its facts, *Lear* could have been a relatively insignificant decision. *Lear* merely precluded state law from supplying the estoppel provision. The decision presumably left the parties free to expressly adopt the provision if they wished, and made mutually beneficial royalty adjustments.

---

[44] Id. at 706. *Accord, Rite-Nail Packaging Corp. v. Berryfast, Inc.*, 706 F.2d 933, 936 (9th Cir. 1983) (licensee must pay royalties until it notified the licensor that the payments were being stopped because the patent was believed to be invalid); *Hull v. Brunswick Corp.*, 704 F.2d 1195, 1202–1203 (10th Cir. 1983) (the licensee "must notify the licensor that they are suspending payment because they question validity . . ."); *Bristol Locknut Co. v. SPS Technologies, Inc.*, 177 F.2d 1277, 1283 (9th Cir. 1982).

THE LIMITS ON LICENSING

Shortly after *Lear,* the lower courts closed the door on that option. Within five or six years after *Lear,* they said that an implication of *Lear* was that agreements not to challenge validity were unenforceable.[45]

This rule has not been applied to other types of intellectual property. Copyright and trademark owners are free to agree that the licensee will not attempt to have the rights declared invalid.[46] In *Saturday Evening Post Co. v. Rumbleseat Press,* Judge Posner explained why.[47]

> Rumbleseat's appeal raises a variety of jurisdictional and procedural issues, of which the most important are whether the validity of a copyright is arbitrable and whether a provision in a copyright license that forbids the licensee to challenge the validity of the copyright is enforceable. Both are novel issues.
>
> * * *
>
> Paragraph 9 of the license agreement provides that Rumbleseat "shall not, during the Original Term [of the agreement] or any time thereafter dispute or contest, directly or indirectly, . . . the validity of any of the copyrights . . . which [the Post] may have obtained." This is the no-contest clause.
>
> * * *
>
> Last, we must decide whether a clause in a copyright licensing agreement forbidding the licensee to contest the validity of the copyright he has licensed is against public policy, as expressed in

---

[45] *Panther Pumps & Equip. Co. v. Hydrocraft,* 468 F.2d 225, 230–232 (7th Cir. 1972); *Massillon-Cleveland-Adron v. Golden State Advertising Co.,* 444 F.2d 425 (9th Cir. 1971); *Wallace Clark & Co. v. Acheson Industries, Inc.,* 401 F.Supp. 637, 639 (S.D.N.Y. 1975), *aff'd* 532 F.2d 846 (2d Cir. 1976); *Congoleum Industries, Inc. v. Armstrong Cork Co.,* 360 F.Supp. 220, 232–234 (E.D. Pa. 1973), *aff'd,* 510 F.2d 334 (3rd Cir. 1975); *Blohm-Voss A.G. v. Prudential-Grace Lines, Inc.,* 346 F.Supp. 1116 (D. Md. 1972), *rev'd on other grounds,* 489 F.2d 231 (4th Cir. 1973).

[46] *Saturday Evening Post Co. v. Rumbleseat Press, Inc.,* 816 F.2d 1191, 1199–1200 (7th Cir. 1987) (copyright); *Windsurfing Intn. Inc. v. AMF, Inc.,* 782 F.2d 995, 1001–1002 (Fed. Cir. 1986) (trademark).

[47] *Saturday Evening Post Co. v. Rumbleseat Press, Inc.,* 816 F.2d 1191, 1199–1200 (7 Cir. 1987).

7.4 A LICENSEE MAY DEFEND AN ACTION

the Copyright Act or other possible sources of federal common law, and is therefore unenforceable. (Rumbleseat's argument that it is barred by state law requires no extended discussion. The argument is based on restrictive-covenant cases; they are too remote to be illuminating.) This is another open question, see *Herbert Rosenthal Jewelry Corp. v. Kalpakian,* 446 F.2d 738, 739–40 (9th Cir. 1971), and again the concern is with copyright monopolies. Suppose the Rockwell illustrations really were in the public domain and both the Post and Rumbleseat knew it, but, also knowing that both would be better off without competition, they agreed to give Rumbleseat an exclusive license with a no-contest clause, hoping that no other potential competitor would discover the invalidity of the copyrights and challenge (or defy) them. Somewhat analogous practices involving patents have been alleged. See George L. Priest, *Cartels and Patent License Agreements,* 20 J. Law & Econ. 309, 340–49 (1977). The danger of this kind of cozy deal would be less if the law forbade the Post to enforce the no-contest clause, so that Rumbleseat, if it changed its mind about the advantages of mutual forbearance, could go into competition with the Post notwithstanding the license.

We cannot call this danger nonexistent, although we suspect it is slight given our earlier remarks about the unlikelihood that a copyright (especially one that by hypothesis is invalid!) would confer an economically significant monopoly, one that would raise the price of the monopolized good well above, and depress its output well below, the competitive level. The danger is not so great, however, as to justify a rule of federal common law outlawing no-contest clauses without evidence of any monopolistic danger or effect. Such a clause serves a useful purpose in most cases. Without it the licensee always has a club over the licensor's head: the threat that if there is a dispute the licensee will challenge the copyright's validity. The threat would discourage copyright licensing and might therefore retard rather than promote the diffusion of copyrighted works. Also, a no-contest clause might actually accelerate rather than retard challenges to invalid copyrights, by making the would-be licensee think hard about validity before rather than after he signed the licensing agreement. Rumbleseat had, in fact, used its expressed doubts of the validity of the Post's copyrights to obtain a lower royalty rate in the negotiations for the license.

What is needed is a balancing of the pros and cons of the clause in each case. That balancing is best done under antitrust law. Section 1 of the Sherman Act, 15 U.S.C. § 1, forbids contracts that restrain trade. If Rumbleseat had wanted, it could have attacked the no-contest clause under that statute. It did not do so. We decline to create a federal common law rule that would justle uncomfortably with the Sherman Act. Noting the convergence of patent-misuse principles with antitrust principles, we said in *USM Corp. v. SPS Technologies, Inc.,* 694 F.2d 505, 512 (7th Cir. 1982): "If misuse claims are not tested by conventional antitrust principles, by what principles shall they be tested? Our law is not rich in alternative concepts of monopolistic abuse; and it is rather late in the date to try to develop one without in the process subjecting the rights of patent holders to debilitating uncertainty." This point applies with even greater force to copyright misuse, where the danger of monopoly is less. We hold that a no-contest clause in a copyright licensing agreement is valid unless shown to violate antitrust law.

This holding is not barred by *Lear v. Adkins,* 395 U.S. 653, 89 S.Ct. 1902, 23 L.Ed.2d 610 (1969), which held that federal law forbids a state court to hold that a patent licensee is, by virtue of having been licensed, estopped to challenge the patent's validity. Our case involves a negotiated clause rather than a doctrine that in effect reads a no-contest clause into every licensing agreement. The doctrine is apt to have a broader effect. We made a similar distinction in *American Equipment Corp. v. Wikomi Mfg. Co.,* 630 F.2d 544, 549 (7th Cir. 1980). Furthermore, the logic of *Lear* does not extend to copyright licenses. The opinion is narrowly written. It emphasizes

> the important public interest in permitting full and free competition in the use of ideas which are in reality a part of the public domain. Licensees may often be the only individuals with enough economic incentive to challenge the patentability of an

7.4 A LICENSEE MAY DEFEND AN ACTION

inventor's discovery. If they are muzzled, the public may continually be required to pay tribute to would-be monopolists without need or justification.

Id. 395 U.S. at 670, 89 S.Ct. at 1911. A patent empowers its owner to prevent anyone else from making or using his invention; a copyright just empowers its owner to prevent others from copying the particular verbal or pictorial or aural pattern in which he chooses to express himself. The economic power conferred is much smaller. There is no need for a rule that would automatically invalidate every no-contest clause. If a particular clause is used to confer monopoly power beyond the small amount that the copyright laws authorize, the clause can be attacked under section 1 of the Sherman Act as a contract in restraint of trade. Rumbleseat does not argue that the clause here restrained trade in that sense. The fact that we can find no antitrust case—or for that matter any other reported case—that deals with a no-contest clause in a copyright license is evidence that these clauses are not such a source of significant restraints on freedom to compete as might warrant a per se rule of illegality.

Several of these points are discussed earlier in this chapter.

(g) Antitrust and Misuse Implications of Agreements Not to Assert Invalidity

The lower courts said that a license provision barring a patent licensee from contesting validity was unenforceable. The former licensee or licensees in those actions frequently said that the provision should constitute patent misuse rendering the patent unenforceable. The courts generally rejected that argument saying that unenforceability was enough.[48] One court said that an agreement not to contest a patent during and after

---

[48] *Panther Pumps & Equip. Co. v. Hydrocraft, Inc.*, 468 F.2d 225, 232 (7th Cir. 1972); *Wallace Clark & Co. v. Acheson Industries, Inc.*, 401 F.Supp. 637, 639 (S.D.N.Y. 1975), *aff'd* 532 F.2d 846 (2d Cir. 1976); *Congoleum Industries, Inc. v. Armstrong Cork Co.*, 366 F.Supp. 220, 233 (E.D. Pa. 1973), *aff'd*, 510 F.2d 334 (3rd Cir.), *cert. denied*, 421 U.S. 988 (1975).

termination of the license constituted misuse but not a violation of the Sherman Act.[49]

If no-contest clauses were found to constitute patent misuse or antitrust violations because they deter challenges to validity, all patent licenses would constitute misuse and an antitrust violation. All license agreements have that effect. That is not the law. In *United States v. Studiengesellschaft Kohle, m.b.H.*,[50] an antitrust action, one Court of Appeals said:

> A patent license might also restrict competition by undermining incentives to attack the validity of the patent or to invent around it.

The court's main authority was *United States v. Masonite*,[51] a decision holding that agency agreements for the resale of a patent product at fixed prices, which became effective only when all competing resellers agreed to identical contracts, violated the Sherman Act. No patent license was involved in *Masonite* and the Supreme Court said nothing of the kind. The Court of Appeals said that the exclusive license to sell unpatented products of a patent process may have undermined incentives to challenge. The court said that provision was not unlawful on that basis because other licensees had incentives to challenge and, perhaps more importantly, all exclusive licenses do the same thing and they are not illegal.

Judge Posner's discussion of this issue is included in the preceeding section.[52]

(h) The Enforceability of Termination Provisions

Lear said nothing about whether a patent owner could terminate if the licensee stopped paying royalties. All the *Lear* Court said about termination was that state law governed. Indeed, the Supreme Court said that the

---

[49] *Bendix Corp. v. Balax, Inc.*, 471 F.2d 149, 158–159 (7th Cir. 1972), *cert. denied*, 414 U.S. 819 (1973), *rev'ing* 321 F.Supp. 1095 (E.D. Wisc. 1971).
[50] *United States v. Studiengesellschaft Kohle, m.b.H.*, 670 F.2d 1122, 1136 (D.C. Cir. 1981).
[51] *United States v. Masonite*, 316 U.S. 265, 278–281 (1942).
[52] *Saturday Evening Post Co. v. Rumbleseat Press, Inc.*, 816 F.2d 1191, 1199–1200 (7th Cir. 1987).

7.5 THE ENFORCEABILITY OF TRADE SECRET AND KNOW-HOW

California rule was enforceable. That rule permitted the parties to prohibit a licensee from terminating without first ceasing use of the invention.

However, in the 1970s some courts said that *Lear* meant that a licensee could continue to pay royalties, deprive the patent owner of the option of terminating, and litigate validity. Those courts ordered that licensees deposit royalties in escrow and enjoined patent owners from terminating licenses based on nonpayment.[53] Most courts have refused to issue such orders, usually noting the licensor's solvency.[54]

In the mid-1980s, the Court of Appeals for the Federal Circuit stopped this development in its tracks and announced that there was nothing in *Lear* that precluded a patent owner from terminating a license based on nonpayment of royalties.[55]

7.5 THE ENFORCEABILITY OF TRADE SECRET AND KNOW-HOW LICENSES—*KEWANEE*

In 1974, the Supreme Court in *Kewanee Oil v. Bicron*,[56] considered whether state enforcement of a contract to keep trade secrets confidential was inconsistent with the purpose of patent law. If the owner of trade secrets may not enforce a licensee's agreement to keep the technology confidential, licensing such rights is virtually impossible. It is remarkable that this fundamental question could arise almost two hundred years after Congress enacted the patent laws. However, *Lear* cast a new and

---

[53] *Precision Shooting Equipment Co. v. Allen*, 646 F.2d 313, 319–321 (7th Cir. 1981) (licensee would have no adequate remedy at law to recover postsuit royalties; and denying licensor those payments results in "safekeeping" them and minimizing "financial risk" for both parties); *Atlas Chemical Industries, Inc. v. Moraine Products*, 509 F.2d (6th Cir. 1974) (in licensee's declaratory judgment action, royalties ordered paid into escrow to "preserve the status quo.").

[54] *Nebraska Engineering Corp. v. Shivvers*, 557 F.2d 1257 (8th Cir. 1977) (reversing grant of preliminary injunction, noting that payment into escrow is not the same as payment to the licensor); *Warner-Jenkinson v. Allied Chemical Corp.*, 567 F.2d 184 (2d Cir. 1977); *USM v. Standard Press Steel Co.*, 524 F.2d 1097, 1098–1100 (7th Cir. 1975) (ultimate entitlement to royalties accruing during action does not depend on possession and licensee failed to show irreparable injury).

[55] *C.R. Bard, Inc. v. Schwartz*, 716 F.2d 874, 880 (Fed. Cir. 1983).

[56] *Kewanee Oil v. Bicron*, 416 U.S. 470 (1974).

fuzzy shadow on the law. *Kewanee* said states may enforce confidentiality obligations. *Kewanee* also defined patent preemption differently than the Court had in *Lear*.

First, the *Kewanee* Court said the constitutional power of Congress to adopt a patent system did not prohibit states from encouraging inventing.[57] The Court said that state enforcement of contracts to keep trade secrets confidential did not offend the policy of patent law to encourage invention because it provided another form of incentive for invention. The Court said that "in this respect, the two systems are not and never would be in conflict."[58]

In *Lear,* the Court said nothing about the impact of its decision on incentives for invention. Rather, the Court said that federal policy requires free use of all inventions not protected by a valid patent. It relied on the so-called "federal policy favoring free competition and ideas which do not merit patent protection." The Court also said, "federal law requires that all ideas in general circulation be dedicated to the common good unless they are protected by a valid patent."[59] Those policies first appeared in the patent law in 1965 in Justice Black's opinions in *Sears* and *Compco.*[60] Those policies sound like policies that preclude use of the contract and contract with trade secret systems for ideas that are not patented and are somehow "in general circulation."

Kewanee made clear that state law may limit free use of ideas for which a valid patent could not issue. If that was the broad premise of *Lear, Kewanee* abolished it. That is what Justice Douglas thought *Kewanee* meant. He dissented in *Kewanee* because the decision was "at war with the philosophy" of *Sears* and *Compco,* which he said were the first decisions based on the premise that "every article not covered by a valid patent is in the public domain."[61]

Second, the Court in *Kewanee* made clear that before preempting state law, the Court must consider the harms or benefits of that law on incentives to invent and incentives to use the patent system, as well as

---

[57] 416 U.S. at 478–479; *accord, Goldstein v. California,* 412 U.S. 546 (1973).
[58] 416 U.S. at 484.
[59] 395 U.S. at 656 and 668 (emphasis added).
[60] *Sears, Roebuck v. Stiffel,* 376 U.S. 225 (1965); *Compco v. Day Brite Lighting,* 376 U.S. 234 (1965).
[61] 416 U.S. at 495.

7.5 THE ENFORCEABILITY OF TRADE SECRET AND KNOW-HOW

on leaving public domain information in the public domain. The Court in *Kewanee* noted that the Constitution establishes a single "objective" for Congress's power, and that is to "promote the Progress of Science and Useful Art."[62] The Patent Act, by its terms, promoted that progress in two ways, (1) by giving a right of exclusion for a limited period as an incentive to inventors to risk the cost of time, research, and development, leading to an increased level of new products and processes in the economy, and (2) by requiring disclosure of the invention to stimulate the development of further advances and to facilitate use after the term of the patent expires.[63] This second purpose is the illusive *quid pro quo* idea. The first is the public good purpose.

The Court in *Kewanee* also noted that the Court itself had "articulated another policy of the patent law: that which is in the public domain cannot be removed therefrom by action of the states."[64] It is impossible to find any support for that policy in the Patent Act, if it means anything other than that, after a patent expires, subsequent activities are not infringement. Justice Burger did not suggest that he found it there. The Court in *Kewanee* did not, as it could have, discard the third purpose. Rather, *Kewanee* redefined it to be more limited than the *Lear* definition. The Court in *Kewanee* did not say that everything which is not properly patented must be available for free use or "competition." It said that things in the public domain cannot be removed from the public domain.

Unlike the Court in *Lear,* the Court in *Kewanee* was very clear that "the public domain" is not defined exclusively by the standards for granting a patent in the patent act. The *Kewanee* Court said that trade secret law did not interfere with that policy because "by definition, a trade secret has not been placed in the public domain."[65] Public domain status was determined by the state law of trade secrecy, not by patent law.[66] Therefore, ideas could be protected by state law even though they did not merit patent protection.

In other words, there are not two states of affairs for information, namely, public domain information and patented information. There is

---
[62] Id. at 480.
[63] Id. at 480–481.
[64] Id. at 481.
[65] Id. at 484 (footnote omitted).
[66] Id. at 484 n.13.

a third possibility, namely, information that state law declares is not public domain information. *Kewanee* suggests that, if the states elect to treat ideas protected by a presumptively valid patent as outside the public domain as a matter of state law, there is nothing in the patent act which says that is wrong.

The more important point is that the Court in *Kewanee* recognized that preemption requires evaluating the impact of state law and incentives for invention and incentives for use of the patent system. The Court in *Lear* made no reference whatever to those purposes. *Lear,* like *Sears* and *Compco,* simply referred to the third purpose and did not ask whether pursuing that purpose harmed the other two. Under *Kewanee* tests, those other effects must be considered.

Third, the Court in *Kewanee* found that any theoretical possibility of injury to one of the patent system's purposes is not sufficient to justify preemption. It found that for certain types of ideas the existence of trade secret law might deter inventors from using the patent system and might, therefore, lead to less disclosure of inventions.[67] However, that harm to one of the patent system's purposes was not sufficient to condemn the state law. Under *Lear* analysis, any theoretical injury to one patent purpose condemns the state law.

Fourth, the Court in *Kewanee* said that in determining how much injury is enough, one must also ask whether there are economic benefits served by maintaining the state law.[68]

The *Kewanee* Court noted the significant economic benefits of trade secret law. Among those were that trade secret protection permitted licensing to achieve more efficient use of inventions. It expressly found that "the detrimental misallocation of resources in economic waste that would thus take place if trade secret protection were abolished with respect to employees or licensees cannot be justified by reference to any policy that federal patent law seeks to advance." The waste the Court referred to was the fact that licensing others permitted most efficient use of the inventions by permitting the invention to be put in the hands of more efficient users without jeopardizing its economic value. It said, in part:[69]

---

[67] Id. at 484–489.
[68] Id. at 487.
[69] Id. at 486–487.

Instead, then, of licensing others to use his invention and making the most efficient use of existing manufacturing and marketing structures within the industry, the trade secret holder would tend either to limit his utilization of the invention, thereby depriving the public of the maximum benefit of its use, or engage in the time-consuming and economically wasteful enterprise of constructing duplicative manufacturing and marketing mechanisms for the exploitation of the invention. The detrimental misallocation of resources and economic waste that would thus take place if trade secret protection were abolished with respect to employees or licensees cannot be justified by reference to any policy that the federal patent law seeks to advance.

The Court in *Lear* made no effort to ask whether the licensee estoppel rule had any economic benefits. If it had asked that question, it would have recognized that reducing litigation costs and reducing uncertainty increased the amount of licensing, increased returns to inventions, and permitted inventions to be placed in the hands of more efficient users. Rather, the Court in *Lear* said that licensees may be the only people with enough economic incentive to challenge validity, therefore, "muzzling" them might lead to fear of patents being held invalid. The existence of those patents might deter use by third parties, and the payments being made to the patent owner decrease licensee output, therefore it was enough in *Lear* that licensee estoppel was theoretically inconsistent with free use of inventions that should not be patented.[70]

7.6 THE ENFORCEABILITY OF ROYALTY OBLIGATIONS IN PATENT AND KNOW-HOW LICENSES—*ARONSON*

One response to *Lear* is to make royalties payable in a lump sum concurrently with the execution of the license. Since the lower courts rejected the notion that the licensee may get back all royalty payments, an owner could require payment before the licensee could start a declaratory judgment action or complain about validity.

---
[70] 395 U.S. at 670.

A second response is to license patents in exchange for something other than royalties. Money becomes a less-favored form of consideration. Barter becomes more profitable. In the patent setting, it became more profitable to license patents in exchange for a cross-license or grantback of future rights.

A third response was to sell a package or bundle of things, including the license, to attempt to shift the price from the patent to payments for other things, such as know-how or personal property. Any time government artificially decreases the price of a good, it creates an opportunity for the seller to try to evade the regulation by shifting the price it cannot collect directly to some other form.

One form of this strategy might be to license an invention that is nonexistent, exists as a trade secret, or exists as a trade secret embodied in a patent application filed but not issued. One might then charge a price and call the entire price consideration for disclosure of the trade secret. That price would be discounted for uncertainty about validity of any patents that might issue and, indeed, be discounted further because they might not issue at all.

In 1979 in *Aronson,* the Supreme Court decided that an obligation to pay was enforceable when (1) a secret product design had been disclosed and licensed, (2) the licensee agreed to pay for the use of that know-how whether or not it continued to be secret, (3) the royalty rate declined if no patent issued within five years of the agreement, and (4) no patent issued.[71] The decision permitted payments for use of information to continue after the information entered the *public domain*—a trade secret that had become public.

It is possible to read *Aronson* more broadly. *Aronson* may stand for the proposition that, if an inventor with the pending patent application licenses someone to use the know-how disclosed in the application and the rights of any patent that might issue, in exchange for some agreeable royalty arrangement, the agreement is enforceable where the invention subsequently enters the public domain by being disclosed to the public and no patent issuing. Under that view the only significance of the royalty rate reduction in the *Aronson* agreement was to establish that the licensee recognize that royalties were justified in its view even though no patent issued. In other words, royalties had been appropriately discounted based on uncertainty.

---

[71] *Aronson v. Quick Point Pencil Co.,* 440 U.S. 257 (1979).

7.6 THE ENFORCEABILITY OF ROYALTY OBLIGATIONS

Aronson could also mean that, in this situation, payments may continue even though a patent issues and is later held invalid or expires. The Court did not say that royalties must stop if the patent issued and expired or had been held invalid. The prospective value of the bundle of rights to the licensee is the same in either event.

However, most Courts of Appeals have ruled that, when both patents and know-how relating to the same subject matter are licensed, and the licensee agrees to pay at a single rate based on use of patents and know-how, those royalties may not be collected at that rate after the licensed patents are held invalid or expire.[72] A District Court adopted a different rule when the agreement was made before a patent application was filed. The agreement was made at a time when no patent application had been filed, and called for royalties for the longer of the life of any patent or twenty-five years. The District Court said the agreement was enforceable beyond the term of the patent.[73] The Sixth Circuit reversed.[74]

When a prospective patent owner has bundled the license with tangible property, the courts have been more reticent to tamper with the price. In one instance, a District Court held that, when a person sold a pending patent application, an experimental model of a machine, drawings, tools used in development, and other tools, in exchange for an agreement to pay "royalties" for seventeen years on products that made use of a machine "covered by the said patent application," the buyer was obligated to pay the royalties regardless of validity of a patent that issued.[75] It distinguished *Lear* on the basis that no license or licensee relationship was involved and the payments were "installment payments for sale."

---

[72] *Chromalloy American Corp. v. Fischmann*, 716 F.2d 683, 685 (9th Cir. 1983); *Pitney-Bowes, Inc. v. Mestre*, 701 F.2d 1365 (11th Cir. 1983) *dismissing in part and aff'ing in pertinent part* 517 F.Supp. 52 (S.D. Fla. 1981) (in a "hybrid" know-how or trade secret and patent license, which does not differentiate between the know-how and patent rights and does not allocate or divide royalties between them, the expiration of all patents makes unenforceable the obligation to pay at the preexpiration rate); *Span-Deck, Inc. v. Fab-Con, Inc.*, 677 F.2d 1237 (8th Cir. 1982); *St. Regis Paper Co. v. Royal Industries*, 552 F.2d 309 (9th Cir. 1977); *Timely Products, Inc. v. Costanzo*, 465 F.Supp. 91 (D. Conn. 1979).
[73] *Boggild v. Kenner Products Div. of General Mills Fund Group*, 576 F.Supp. 533 (S.D. Ohio 1983).
[74] *Boggild v. Kenner Products*, 776 F.2d 1315, 1317–1321 (6th Cir. 1985).
[75] *Heltra, Inc. v. Richen-Gemco, Inc.*, 395 F.Supp. 346, 348, 351–351 (D.S.C. 1975), *rev'd on other grounds*, 540 F.2d 1285 (4th Cir. 1976).

7.7 THE ENFORCEABILITY OF ROYALTY OBLIGATIONS IN LICENSES MADE IN THE CONTEXT OF LITIGATION—CONSENT JUDGMENTS AND SETTLEMENT AGREEMENTS

The lower federal courts did not take kindly to the Supreme Court's idea that every patent should be litigated to the death. As the Sixth Circuit said, "if every patent infringement case filed had to be tried, the courts would be clogged." The lower courts, therefore, took a number of steps to limit *Lear.*

Within four years of *Lear,* it had been fairly well settled that, once infringement litigation has commenced, the parties may settle the action by a stipulated judgment that the patent is valid and infringed. That judgment is binding in any subsequent proceedings between the parties over validity of the patent.[76] Therefore, while a license signed before a complaint is filed cannot be binding on the subject of validity, an agreement signed after a complaint is filed is binding if signed by a judge.

The reasons the courts gave for according finality to consent decrees were, for the most part, the same reasons it would be efficient to enforce a provision in the license that the licensee not challenge validity.

First, the courts said that refusal to accord *res judicata* effect to a consent judgment would lead to "expensive and time consuming litigation."[77] Second, the courts said the finality of consent judgments encourages the user to litigate validity rather than postpone litigation until a time better suiting its ability or interests.[78] One court said finality "encourages earlier and more vigorous challenge. . . ." Third, the courts said

---

[76] *Foster v. Hallco Mfg. Co.,* 947 F.2d 469, 475 (Fed. Cir. 1991); *USM Corp. v. SPS Technologies, Inc.,* 694 F.2d 505 (7th Cir. 1982); *American Equipment Corp. v. Wikomi Mfg. Co.,* 630 F.2d 544 (7th Cir. 1980); *Wallace Clark & Co., Inc. v. Acheson Indus., Inc.,* 532 F.2d 846, 849 (2d Cir. 1976); *Schlegel Mfg. Co. v. USM Corp.,* 525 F.2d 775, 780–781, 783 (6th Cir. 1975); *Broadview Chemical Corp. v. Loctite Corp.,* 474 F.2d 1391 (2d Cir. 1973).

[77] *Carter-Wallace & Co., Inc.,* 532 F.2d at 849; *Schlegel Mfg. Co. v. USM Corp.,* 525 F.2d at 783 ("[I]f every patent-infringement case filed had to be tried, the Courts would be clogged.").

[78] *Schlegel Mfg. Co. v. USM Corp.,* 525 F.2d 775, 780–781 (6th Cir. 1975) ("When a consent decree is to be given res judicata effect, litigants are encouraged to litigate the issue of validity rather than foreclosing themselves by consent decree. . . . By giving

7.7 THE ENFORCEABILITY OF ROYALTY OBLIGATIONS

that consent decrees bind only the parties and those in privity with them, leaving others unrestrained in their ability to challenge.[79] The same is true of a license agreement.

The only other reason found in the cases for enforcement of consent decrees of validity and infringement is that they are judicial decrees and, hence, were entered after an action had been filed and the defendant had an opportunity to litigate.[80] A license entered prior to litigation does not have that feature. However, if the patent has issued, the licensee is producing an allegedly infringing product, and the licensee had reasonable apprehension that it would be sued, the doors of the court were open for a filing fee. A licensee who did not take advantage of that opportunity was in no different position than one who did.

Finally, when people have argued that public interest in challenging validity created in *Lear* precludes court orders from being followed, the courts have responded that any other rule would make an order "a futile, meaningless gesture which will discourage such settlements in the future."[81] The Second Circuit has said that "absent evidence of collision, judicial decrees disposing of issues in active litigation cannot be treated as idle ceremonies without denigrating the judicial process."[82] The decision in *Lear* had a similar effect for licensing patents.

Some courts have found that *Lear* also does not apply to licenses entered to settle litigation. In *Aro* in 1976, the Sixth Circuit found that an infringement action settled by a dismissal of all claims without prej-

---

res judicata effect to consent decrees, this Court protects the public interest in that an alleged infringer is deprived of a judicial device which can be used to postpone and delay a final adjudication of validity."); *American Equipment Corp. v. Wikomi Mfg. Co.*, 630 F.2d 544, 548 (7th Cir. 1980) (according *res judicata* "encourages earlier and more vigorous challenge. . . .").

[79] *American Equipment Corp. v. Wikomi Mfg. Co.*, 630 F.2d 544, 548 (7th Cir. 1980); *Schlegel Mfg. Co. v. USM Corp.*, 525 F.2d 775, 781 (6th Cir. 1975) ("By giving res judicata effect to consent decrees, we do not close the doors of the Courts to litigation on the issue of patent validity, except as to parties or their privities, and only after they have had the opportunity to litigate the issue fully. Third parties are not affected by the consent decree. . . .").

[80] *Wallace-Clark & Co., Inc. v. Acheson Industries, Inc.*, 532 F.2d 846, 849 (2d Cir. 1976).

[81] *Schlegel Mfg. Co.*, 525 F.2d at 783.

[82] *Wallace-Clark & Co., Inc.*, 532 F.2d at 849.

THE LIMITS ON LICENSING

udice and a license for a remaining three years of the patent precluded the licensee from avoiding royalty payments based on alleged invalidity.[83] The court said *Lear* was inapplicable because there was a public interest in settlement of litigation that must be balanced against the interest in invalidating patents. The court also noted that there was competition between the patent owner, the licensee, and other licensees, there was no evidence that the patent gave anyone an economic monopoly, and the royalty was small in comparison to the licensee's profits. The court also noted that other licensees were in a position to challenge validity. The court said that balancing these policies on the facts of each case, the policy in favor of settlement must prevail over the policy relied on in *Lear* unless the patent represents a real economic monopoly and the defendant is the only challenger.

Aro is not the first or only decision to find that the policy in favor of settlement prevails over the desirability of challenging validity.[84] If there is an overriding policy in favor of settling litigation once it is commenced, it would seem efficient that there be an equally strong, if not stronger, policy in favor of settling infringement disputes before litigation begins.

There is another interesting thing about stipulated consent judgments and settlement agreements. In both of those contexts, the parties expressly agreed the patent was valid. In *Lear,* there was no such agreement. The doctrine of licensee estoppel was invoked to supply it. Where

---

[83] *Aro Corp. v. Allied Witan Corp.,* 531 F.2d 1368 (6th Cir. 1976).

[84] *International Telemeter v. Teleprompter Corp.,* 592 F.2d 49, 57 (2d Cir. 1979) (a settlement agreement calling for a lump sum payment as liquidated damages for past infringement is enforceable without respect to validity); *Rausburg Electro-Coating Corp. v. Spiller & Spiller, Inc.,* 489 F.2d 974, 977 (7th Cir. 1973) (same); *Automatic Radio Mfg. Co. v. Hazeltine Research,* 176 F.2d 799, 806 (1st Cir. 1949) (the license agreements were made in settlement of litigation and "[i]t is not apparent to us that the public interest would be served by rendering such common-sense business settlement migratory, which would be the result of a ruling that the licensee could reopen the issue of validity when sued for the stipulated royalty."), *aff'd* 339 U.S. 827 (1950), *overruled* 395 U.S. 653 (1969). In *Wells Cargo, Inc. v. Wells Cargo, Inc.,* 606 F.2d 961, 965 (C.C.P.A. 1979), the court said that the policy in favor of settlement of disputes always prevails over *Lear:*

> Appellant ignores the competing policy favoring voluntary settlement of actual disputes. The latter has been viewed as overriding the policy of encouraging challenges to patent validity promulgated in *Lear.* . . .

the parties expressly focus on this subject and make that provision, a licensee or user electing to be estopped must have agreed to that in exchange for royalty or other concessions which were more valuable than the cost of being estopped. Because a licensee's interest in challenging validity is the same as a consumer's interest, consumers are better off if licensees make such agreements. If the concession is lower royalties, consumers benefit from lower prices.

7.8 THE ENFORCEMENT OF PATENTS AGAINST PARTIES TO ASSIGNMENTS AND EXCLUSIVE LICENSEES

In *Scott Paper* in 1945, a patent owner brought an action for infringement against a company formed by the person who had assigned the patent to the owner "for a valuable consideration."[85] The estoppel rule applied to assignors of a patent. The law implied an agreement by the seller of a patent not to attempt to destroy what it had sold. The Court acknowledged that rule, but said it did not apply. The former owner claimed that it was using an invention disclosed and claimed in a prior art patent that had expired. Therefore, the patent it sold could not properly preclude it from using old techniques.

The Court said that the estoppel rule could not apply in that situation, because it would be inconsistent with the "goal" of patent law to make all inventions disclosed in expired patents freely available to the public. The Court's description of the *quid pro quo* concept of patent law ran as follows:[86]

> By the patent laws Congress has given to the inventor opportunity to secure the material rewards for his invention for a limited time, on condition that he make full disclosure for the benefit of the public of the manner of making and using the invention, and that upon the expiration of the patent the public be left free to use the invention. As has been many times pointed out, the means adopted by Congress of promoting the progress of science and the arts is the

---

[85] *Scott Paper Co. v. Marcalus Mfg. Co.*, 326 U.S. 249 (1945).
[86] Id. at 255–256.

limited grant of the patent monopoly in return for the full disclosure of the patented invention and its dedication to the public on the expiration of the patent.

The aim of the patent laws is not only that members of the public shall be free to manufacture the product or employ the process disclosed by the expired patent, but also that the consuming public at large shall receive the benefits of the unrestricted exploitation, by others, of its disclosures. If a manufacturer or user could restrict himself, by contract, or by any action which would give rise to an "estoppel," from using the invention of an expired patent, he would deprive himself and the consuming public of the advantage to be derived from his free use of the disclosures. The public has invested in such free use by the grant of a monopoly to the patentee for a limited time. Hence, any attempted reservation or continuation in the patentee or those claiming under him of the monopoly, after the patent expires, whatever the legal device employed, runs counter to the policy and purpose of the patent laws. And for the same reason a stranger, such as respondent Marcalus, cannot, by securing and assigning a patent on the invention of the expired Inman patent confer on petitioner any right to deprive the public of the benefits of the free use of the invention for which the public has paid by the grant of a limited monopoly.

The Court said "the patent laws preclude us from saying that the patent assignment, which they authorize, operates to estop the assignor from asserting that which the patent laws prescribe, namely, that the invention of an expired patent is dedicated to the public, of which the assignor is a member."

Justice Frankfurter dissented. Frankfurter saw a valuable purpose in a rule that prevented the seller of anything from receiving payment for it and later taking actions to destroy (and presumably limit) its value. He did not identify precisely why that rule was efficient.[87] He simply as-

---

[87] Such a rule could allocate to the party best able to obtain information bearing on the value of a patent the burden to bring that information to the attention of the buyer. If it does not, and sells the patent for the higher price that the patent would have commanded if the information were available, the seller will be prevented from relying on that information in the future.

7.8 THE ENFORCEMENT OF PATENTS

serted that any other state of affairs would permit unfairness and overreaching in business transactions. For example, Frankfurter said:[88]

> When by a free and fair bargain a man sells something to another, it hardly lies in his mouth to say, "I have sold you nothing." It certainly offends the rudimentary sense of justice for courts to support one who purports to sell something to another in saying "what I have sold you is worthless," even though he did not expressly promise that what he sold had worth. The obvious implications of fair dealing in commercial transactions have been part of our law for at least a hundred years. And it would be surprising indeed if the law made a difference whether what was purported to be sold was a diamond, or a secret process for manufacturing a commodity, or a patented machine.

Frankfurter said there was nothing inconsistent about the rule and the patent law. He said the rule restricts only one person and leaves the rest of the world free to assail the validity (or scope) of the patent. Frankfurter could find nothing in the Patent Act to compel a different rule. He said the disability that the assignor acquired resulted from his dealings with the buyer. Because he has engaged in a transaction relating to the patent, he is no longer a part of the general public. Frankfurter noted that the rest of the public is entirely free to use the patent that had expired. Removing one potential user was likely to have very little effect. Frankfurter also noted that, if the harm that the Court was trying to avoid was the removal of the seller from the ranks of actual or potential manufacturers, that was a harm that arose in every case in which assignors were barred from questioning validity. Hence, the whole rule must be thrown out. Moreover, Frankfurter said the loss of that one possible manufacturer had to be balanced against the policy of "fair dealing between man and man."

In 1978, the Seventh Circuit in *Roberts v. Sears* said that the assignee of a patent could not defend an action for fraud, breach of confidential relationship, and negligent misrepresentation based upon invalidity.[89] While the court could have distinguished *Lear* on the ground that the action was not an infringement action, it did not do so. Rather, it said

---

[88] Id. at 258.
[89] *Roberts v. Sears, Roebuck & Co.*, 573 F.2d 976 (7th Cir. 1978).

Lear did not preclude damages against the assignee regardless of validity because the agreement was an assignment. The court said that this agreement was an assignment, "thus, the primary evil that the Court in *Lear* sought to end—that the public might have to pay tribute to a 'would-be monopolist'—is completely irrelevant to this case. . . . The public's interest would not be injured by our decision to bar Sears from attacking this patent at this time."[90]

Lear said the licensee received only two benefits from the license, avoiding litigation when it could not afford it and possible deterrence of competition by others. An assignee not only receives those benefits and the ability to market the product without damage liability or the possibility of an injunction (a benefit all licensees also receive) but typically receives the ability to enforce the patent against others, including the former owner. After the agreement, an assignee is the "would-be monopolist," not the former owner.

The court also recounted the *Lear* Court's discussion about the spirit of contract law which "seeks to balance the claim of promisor and promisee in accordance with the requirements of good faith" and said that good faith and balancing equities of the parties was a necessary predicate to finding no estoppel. It found that "only after satisfied that the equities were balanced on each side did it [the Supreme Court] consider public policy."[91] The court also said that, because the assignee's actions in taking the assignment had violated good faith by misrepresentations allegedly made, the contract did not have a balance of equities and *Lear* did not apply.

In 1988 in *Diamond Scientific,* the Federal Circuit Court of Appeals found that an assignor of a patent was estopped to challenge validity.[92] The court said *Lear* was limited to estoppel against licensees. The Federal Circuit followed Justice Frankfurter's dissenting opinion in *Scott Paper.* Judge Newman's concurring opinion said the assignor estoppel doctrine should apply for the same reason that sellers of all other types of property are not to render worthless the products they sell.

---

[90] Id. at 982.
[91] Id. at 982.
[92] *Diamond Scientific Co. v. Ambico, Inc.,* 848 F.2d 1220, 1224 (Fed. Cir. 1988).

Index

Index is cross-referenced according to section numbers.

A
Acquisition of rights, 3.1
Antitrust
  economics, 2.10
  law, 2.6, 2.9, 2.10(a)
  licensing limits based on, 1.11, 2.5, 2.12
  remedies, 2.5
  standards, 2.6, 2.12(a)–(e)
Aronson rule, 7.6
Assets
  hold-up problem, 1.9(a)
  specific to intellectual property rights, 1.9(a), 1.10(d)
  technology as, 1.2, 1.4–1.5
Assignee estoppel, 7.8
Assignment of rights, 5.1

B
Bargaining
  costs, *See* Transaction costs.
  limits on payments, 1.8(b)
  options, 1.8, 2.11
  small numbers of buyers, 1.8(b), 1.10(f)
  strategy, 1.10, 2.12
Baxter, William F.
  antitrust standards and, 2.6, 2.9(a)
  effects of discriminatory royalties, 3.6(e)
Bilateral monopoly, licensing and, 1.9(a), 1.10(e)–(f)
Brulotte rule, royalty payments and, 3.5
Business decision. *See also* Strategy.
  time horizon for, 1.7(a)
  to license, 1.4–1.8
  to vertically integrate, 1.6

C
Capital, return to and royalties, 1.4, 1.5, 1.7(d)

INDEX

Cartels
  law and, 1.6(a), 2.12(a)–(b), 5.1–5.9
  license restrictions and, 5.1–5.9
  licensing and, 1.10(m), 1.11, 2.11(b), 2.12, 3.3
  royalties and, 3.3, 3.6
Challenge to patent validity
  agreement not to challenge, 7.4(f)–(g)
  by licensee, 7.4, 7.7–7.8
Clayton Act, 2.9(a)
Commercial value of intellectual property rights, 1.1, 1.4, 2.11, 2.12
  derived demand, 1.5, 1.6
  different uses and, 3.6
  rivalry and, 2.11(a)
Commercial value of technology, 1.1, 1.2
Competition, 1.11, 2.10, *See also* Markets.
  behavior and, 2.10(a)–(f)
  cartels and, 5.6(b)
  competitive effects of agreements and conduct, 1.10, 1.11, 2.10, 2.11, 2.12
  cross licensing and, 5.9
  dealing in substitutes, 5.3
  definition, 2.10(a)
  discriminatory royalties and, 3.6(c)
  economic effects, 2.10(b), 2.12
  extension of rights, 1.11, 2.5, 2.6, 2.11(c), 2.12(c)–(e)
  field of use and, 5.4(b), 5.4(c)
  grantbacks and, 3.10(c)
  intellectual property and, 2.10
  limits on grant of licenses and, 5.9
  market structure and, 2.10(a)–(d)
  package licensing and, 4.6(d)
  price restrictions and, 5.5(a)
  profits and, 1.10, 1.11
  quantity restrictions and, 5.6(b)
  refusal to license and, 3.2
  royalties and, 3.3
  royalty base and, 3.4
  royalty term and, 3.5
  technical information and, 2.10, (c)
  territorial restrictions and, 5.7
  time horizon, 2.12(e)
  tying and, 4.4
Complementary products
  licensing and, 1.10(i)–(j), 4.4(a)–(i)
Complementary technology, 1.10(j)
Consent judgments, 7.7
Contracts to develop intellectual property, 1.3(b)
Cooperation
  among intellectual property owners, 1.10(a)
  among suppliers of substitutes, 1.10(a), 2.11(b), 2.12(a)–(b)
Copyright, 1.3(e), 2.2(b)
Costs
  declining, 1.9(a), 1.10(g)

INDEX

effect on demand for rights, 1.10(g)
information. *See* Transaction costs.
of technology, 1.2
production cost and demand for rights, 1.4–1.6
risk, 1.8(g)
sunk, 1.4(b)
transaction, 1.8(b)
Cross-license, 5.9
Customer restrictions, 5.8

D

Damages for infringement
Royalties and, 1.8(f)–(g)
Dead-weight loss of monopoly, 2.10
Demand for intellectual property rights, 1.4, 1.5, 1.6, 1.8, 1.9(a). *See also* License.
competition for licenses and, 1.8(b)
different demands of different users, 1.9(a), 1.10(b)
expected value and cost, 1.8(a)
for processes, 1.8(d)
for products, 1.5, 1.8(d)
licensee investments and, 1.10(c)–(e)
productive efficiency and, 1.10(g)–(j)
royalties and, 1.7
substitute technologies and, 1.8(c)–(d)
transaction costs and, 1.8(a)

Discriminatory royalties, 1.9(a), 3.6
Baxter, W.F., 3.6(e)
competitive effects, 3.6(c)
economics and, 3.6(e)
tying to achieve, 4.4(c)–(e)
USM rule and, 3.6(b)

E

Economic discrimination, 1.9(a), 1.10(b), 3.5(d), 3.6, 3.8, 4.6, 5.4, 6.10
tying and 4.4(c)–(e)
Economics
competition, 2.10(a)
legal limits and, 1.9, 2.10
licensing, 1.4–1.9, 1.6(a)–(b), 2.12(d)
markets, 2.10(a)
of intellectual property law, 2.3, 2.10(e)
technology and, 1.2
Efficiency
of owner and value of rights, 1.4–1.8
of licensee and value of rights, 1.4–1.9
vertical integration and, 1.6(a)–(b), 4.4
Exclusive dealing, 2.9(d)
Exclusive license
law, 5.2, 5.9, 7.8
nature of, 2.4
reasons to grant, 1.9(a), 1.10(c)–(d)
Exhaustion doctrine
Adams rule, 6.7

INDEX

Exhaustion doctrine *(continued)*
  antitrust and misuse limits to, 6.8
  authorized sales and, 6.6, 6.9
  General Talking Pictures rule, 6.9(b)
  law, 6.5–6.9
  legal theory, 6.4
  Mallinckrodt rule, 6.9(c)
  Mitchell rule, 6.6
  Motion Picture Patents, 6.8
  origins of, 6.5, 6.6, 6.7
  unconditional sales and, 6.6, 6.9
  Univis Lens rule, 6.9(a)
Extension of scope, 1.11, 2.5, 2.6, 2.11(c), 2.12(c)–(e)
  exclusive dealing and, 2.9(d)
  package licensing and, 4.6(b)
  royalties and, 3.4
  theory of, 2.6, 2.7
  tying and, 4.3, 4.4(j)
Externalities
  intellectual property law and, 1.3
  licensee investment and, 1.10(c)–(e)
  network, 1.10(c)–(d)
  technology production and, 1.3, 2.3(a)

F
Federal preemption
  estoppel and, 7.2, 7.4, 7.7, 7.8
  licensing law and, 7.1
  litigation and, 7.4, 7.7
  royalties and, 7.2, 7.4, 7.6, 7.7

Field of use restrictions, 5.4
  competitive effects, 5.4(b)–(e)
  General Talking Pictures rule, 5.4(a), 5.4(c)
  process rights and, 5.4(e)
  resale and, 5.4(c)–(d)
Foreclosure. *See* Extension of scope.
Free riding
  among licensees, 1.9(a), 1.10(c)
  among technology users, 1.3

G
General Electric rule, 2.6
General Talking Pictures rule, 5.4(a)
Grantbacks, 1.7(i), 1.10(g), 3.10
  competitive effects, 3.10(c)
  law, 3.10(a)–(b)

H
Historical development
  exclusive dealing, 2.9(d)
  legal limits, 2.9
  misuse defense, 2.7, 2.9
  package licensing, 2.9(e)
  resale restrictions, 2.9(g)
  royalties, 2.9(f)
  tying, 2.9(c)

I
Implied license, 6.2, 6.3
  law, 6.1–6.3
  legal theory, 6.4
  sale of product and, 6.1
Industry output

INDEX

licensing and, 1.7(b)–(c)
pricing and, 1.7(b)
royalties and, 1.7(b)–(c)
Information
   technology as, 1.2, 1.3
Infringement
   actions and licensing, 1.8(f)–(g), 7.2–7.4
   damages and royalties, 1.8(f)–(g)
Input proportions
   licensee costs and, 1.10(g)
Intellectual property
   as monopoly, 2.10(f)
   commercial options, 2.11, 2.12
   contracts, 1.3(b)
   copyrights, 1.3(e), 2.2(b)
   legal theory, 2.10(f)
   licensing, 1.3(f)
   market performance and, 1.1–1.3
   patents, 1.3(d), 2.2(a), 2.3(a)–(d)
   self-help, 1.3(a)
   technology production and, 1.2, 1.3
   trade secrets, 1.3(c), 2.2(c)
Intellectual property law
   copyright, 2.2(b)
   fundamental concepts, 2.4
   introduction, 2.2
   legal theories, 2.3
   markets and competition and, 2.10(d)
   patent, 2.2(a)
   trade secret, 2.29(c)

Intellectual property litigation, negotiations and, 1.8
Intellectual property rights, 1.3
   commercial value, 1.1, 1.4
   demand for, 1.4, 1.5
   divisibility of, 2.4
   economics of, 2.10(d)–(e)
   market effects of, 2.10(d)–(e)
   refusal to use, 3.2
Investments
   by licensee, 1.6, 1.9(a), 1.10(c), (e), (g)
   free riding and, 1.9(a)
   in R&D, 1.2
   in specific assets, 1.10 (d)–(e)

K

Kewanee, 7.5
Know how license
   enforceability of, 7.5
   royalties under, 7.6

L

Lear, 7.4
Legal limits on licensing
   antitrust, 2.5, 2.6
   economics of, 2.10
   history of, 2.9
   legal principles, 2.4
   legislation, 2.9(a)
   misuse, 2.5, 2.7
   overview, 1.11, 2.1–2.8
   public policy, 2.5, 2.8
Legal theory of intellectual property
   intellectual property law, 1.3, 2.3

Legal theory of intellectual
property *(continued)*
  monopoly rights, 2.3(b)
  natural monopoly rights, 2.3(c)
  property rights, 2.3(a)
  public contract, 2.3(d)

License
  arising from the sale of a product, 6.1
  definition of, 1.3(f), 2.4
  exclusive, 2.4, 5.2
  expected cost of, 1.8(a)
  expected value of, 1.8(a)
  express, 2.4, 6.2
  implied, 2.4, 6.2
  law, general, 2.4
  legal limits on, 2.5
  options, 2.11–2.12
  profits from, 1.1, 1.4–1.9
  refusal to, 3.2
  right to grant, 1.10(a)
  risk and, 1.8(g)
  strategy, 1.1, 1.9
  supply of, 1.10(a)
  time horizon, 1.7(a)

Licensee
  alternatives, negotiations and, 1.8
  efficiency, 1.5, 1.10(g)–(j)
  estoppel, 7.4, 7.8
  incentives, 1.10
  intellectual property rights, 1.7(i)
  investments, terms to Induce, 1.10(c), (e)
  restrictions on output by, 1.10(e)
  royalties and, 1.4, 1.5, 1.7, 1.8
  sharing royalties with, 3.9

License terms and
  capturing demand for rights, 1.4, 1.8, 1.9(a)
  litigation, 1.8(f)–(g), 1.9(g)
  maximizing demand for rights, 1.9(a)
  process demand, 1.8(d)
  product demand, 1.8(a), 1.9(a)
  risk, 1.8(f)–(g), 1.9(c)
  substitute rights, 1.8(c)–(d), 1.9(d)
  transaction costs, 1.8(e), 1.9(b)

Litigation
  effect on licensing, 1.8(f)–(g)

Lump sum payments, as royalty base, 1.7(h)

M

Mallinckrodt, 2.7(b)

Markets
  competition and, 2.10(a)–(c)
  economics, 2.10(a)
  intellectual property and, 1.1, 1.3, 2.10(c)–(e)
  technical information and, 2.10(c)

Misuse defense, 2.5
  creation, 2.7(a)
  law, 2.6
  licensing limits from, 1.11
  patent act, 2.7(c)
  standards, 2.7(b), 2.7(c), 2.12(a)–(e)

Monopoly
  economics of, 2.3(b), 2.10(a)–(e)

INDEX

intellectual property as, 2.3(b), 2.10(f)
Monopsony, 1.10(f)
Morton Salt, 2.7(a)

N

Natural monopoly rights, 2.3(c)
Negotiations
  bargaining problems and, 1.8
  intellectual property litigation and, 1.8
  licensee alternatives and, 1.8
  risk and, 1.8
  transaction costs and, 1.8
  with a single licensee, 1.10(f)

O

Output restriction
  by licensee, 1.10(e)
  terms to limit, 1.10(e)
Ownership
  acquisition of intellectual property rights, 3.1
  competitive effects, 4.6(d)
  law, 4.6(a)
  legal theory, 4.6(b)
  package licensing, 2.9(e), 4.6
  royalties and, 1.10(a), 4.6(c)
  technology, 1.1, 1.2

P

Package license, 4.6
  competitive effects, 4.6(d)
  law, 4.6(a)
  legal theory, 4.6(b)
  royalties and conditioning, 4.6(c)

Patent invalidity, royalties and, 7.2, 7.4
Patent law
  introduction, 1.3, 1.3(d), 2.2(a), 2.3
  misuse defense and, 2.7(c), 2.9(a)
  tying and, 4.5(i), 4.5(k)
Patents, 1.3(d), 2.2(a), 2.3(a)–(d)
Patent term, royalty payments and, 3.5
Per se rules, 2.6
Preemption and licensing, 7.1–7.8
Price discrimination. *See* Economic discrimination.
Price of licenses. *See* Royalties.
Price restrictions, 5.5(a)–(d), 5.6(a)–(b)
  cartel and, 5.5(f)
  competitive effects, 5.5(a)
  cross-licensed patents and, 5.5(c)
  General Electric rule, 5.5(b)
  Line Material rule, 5.5(c)
  resale price, 5.5(e)
Pricing. *See also* Royalties.
  demand elasticity and, 1.6
  economic discrimination, 1.10(b), 4.4(d)
  economics of, 1.5, 1.6
  industry output and price, 1.7(b)
  limit pricing, 1.7(b)
  low cost proportions and, 4.4(g)
  metering use, 4.4(e)

Pricing *(continued)*
  of licenses, 1.10(a)–(b)
  profits and, 1.7(b)
  royalties and, 1.7(b)–(c)
Product demand
  license provisions to increase, 1.6, 1.9(a)
Products and intellectual property rights, 3.8
  compatibility and quality, 4.4(h)
  demand for intellectual property rights, 1.4(b)
  output, 1.4, 1.7, 1.10
  price, 1.5, 1.7(b)–(c), 1.10(c)–(e), (h)
  restrictions on those made by a patented process, 5.4(e)
  sales creating a license, 6.1
  tying arrangements and, 4.1, 4.4
Profits
  as royalty base, 1.7.7
  definition, 1.7(d)
  discriminatory royalties and, 1.10(b), 3.6(d)
  licensing and, 1.1, 1.4–1.8
  royalties and term of rights, 3.5(c)
  royalty base and, 3.4
  royalty rates and licensee, 1.7(c)–(h)
  short-run and long run, 1.7(a)
  strategy and, 1.7, 1.9–1.10, 2.11
  time horizon, 1.7(a)
  vertical integration and, 1.6

Property rights, intellectual property as, 2.3(a)
Public goods, 2.3(a)
Public policy limits, 1.11, 2.5
  legal standard, 2.8

Q

Quantity restrictions, 5.6
  competitive effects, 5.6(b)
  law, 5.6(a)

R

R&D
  cost of, 1.2
Refusing to license, 3.2
Restrictions in licenses, 1.9, 1.10, 2.11, 2.12, 4.1–6.9
  against dealing in substitute products, 5.3
  customer, 5.8
  economic discrimination and, 1.10(b)
  field of use, 5.4
  on purchasers from a licensee, 5.4(c), 5.4(d)
  price, 5.5, 5.5(b), 5.5(c), 5.5(d)
  resale, 2.9(g), 5.4(c)–(d), 5.5(e)
  resale price, 5.5(e)
  territory, 5.7
  tying, 4.1–4.5
Returns to scale
  licensing and, 1.10(d), (g)
Risk
  aversion, 1.8(f)–(g)
  license payments and, 1.8(f)–(g), 1.9(c)

INDEX

litigation and, 1.8(f)–(g)
negotiations and, 1.8
of R&D, technology and, 1.2
royalties and, 1.7
Rivalry
  limiting, 2.11(b)–(c), 2.12(a)
  substitutes and, 2.11(a), 2.11(b)
Royalties
  agreement to pay and validity, 7.4(d), 7.4(f), 7.4.7
  amount as legal issue, 3.3
  antitrust defense to, 7.3
  Brulotte rule and, 3.5(a)
  by licensed buyers, 3.8
  competitive effects of, 3.3, 3.4(b)–(c), 3.5(b)–(c)
  consent judgments and, 7.7
  discriminatory, 3.6, 3.8
  industry output and price, 1.7(b)
  litigation and, 7.2, 7.4, 7.6, 7.7, 7.8
  negotiation of, 1.8
  on use of machine, 3.7
  package licensing and, 4.6(c)
  patent and know-how licenses, enforceability, 7.6
  patent invalidity as defense, 7.2
  patent term and, 3.5
  payments by sellers and buyers, 1.7(c)
  rate, 1.5, 1.7
  scope of patent and, 3.4
  settlement agreements and, 7.7
  sharing with licensees, 3.9
  small number of buyers and, 1.8(b)
  structure, 1.7(c)
  substitute technologies, 1.8(c), 1.8(d)
  use of patented machine and, 3.7
  validity of rights and, 7.2, 7.4, 7.6–7.8
  value in different uses, 3.6
Royalty base
  effects of, 3.4(c)
  lump sum payments, 1.7.8
  profits as, 1.7.7
  sales revenue as, 1.7(f)
  scope of patent and, 3.4(c)
  unit sales as, 1.7(e)
Royalty rates. *See* Royalties.
Rule of reason, 2.6

S

Sales revenue, as royalty base, 1.7(f)
Scale economies
  terms and, 1.9(a), 1.10(g)
Settlement agreements, 7.7
Sharing royalties with licensees, 3.9
Sherman Act, 2.6
Shrimp Peeler Rule, royalty payments and, 3.6(a)
Strategy
  control supply of licenses, 1.10(a), 5.2, 5.9
  extend scope of rights, 1.11
  general licensing, 1.9, 2.11
  increase supply of

INDEX

Strategy *(continued)*
  complements, 1.9(a), 1.10(i), (j)
  inducing asset specific investments, 1.9(a), 1.10(d)
  inducing licensee investments, 1.10(c)
  inducing proper scale of production, 1.10(g)
  inducing use of inputs in efficient proportions, 1.9(a), 1.10(h)
  legal regulation of, 1.11
  limit free riding among licensees, 1.9(a)
  limit licensee output restriction by licensees, 1.9(a), 1.10(e), 2.11(b)
  limit litigation risk, 1.10(1)
  limit supply of substitute rights, 1.9(d), 1.10(m)
  price to capture value in different uses, 1.9(a), 1.10(b)
  profit maximizing, 1.6–1.9
  reduce risk, 1.9(c)
  reduce transaction costs and, 1.9(b), 1.10(k)
Sublicensing, 2.4, 2.9
Substitute products, restrictions against dealing in, 5.3
Substitute rights
  license provisions and, 1.9(d)
  rivalry and, 2.11(a), 2.11(b), 2.12(a), 2.11(b)
  supply of, 1.10(m)
Substitute technologies, and royalties, 1.8(c), 1.8(d)
Successive monopoly, licensing and, 1.10(e)–(f)
Sunk costs, and demand for intellectual property rights, 1.4(b)
Supply of licenses, 1.10(a)

T

Technology
  commercial value of, 1.2
  contracts to produce, 1.3(b)
  copyrights and, 1.3(e)
  cost of, 1.2
  licensing and, 1.1
  markets and competition, 2.10(c)
  patents and, 1.3(d)
  risk of, 1.2
  trade secrets and, 1.3(c)
Termination provisions, 7.4(h)
Territorial restrictions, 5.7
Trade secret license, enforceability of, 7.5
Trade secrets, 1.3(c), 2.2(c)
Transaction costs, 1.8(e), 1.10(k)
  license provisions and, 1.9(b)
  licensing and, 1.8(e)
  negotiations and, 1.8
  products and, 4.4.9
Transparent Wrap rule, 3.10(a), 3.10(b)
Tying, 2.9(c), 4.1
  acquire market power by, 4.4

INDEX

B.B. Chemical, 4.5(f)
Carbice, 4.5(d)
competitive effects of, 4.4
Dawson, 4.5(j)
economic discrimination and, 4.4(c)–(e)
efficient product use and, 4.4(g)
Heaton-Peninsular Button-Fastener, 4.5(a)
Henry v. A.B. Dick, 4.5(b)
law, 4.2
leading decisions and statutes, 4.5
legal theory, 4.3
Leitch, 4.5(e)
Mercoid cases, 4.5(g)
meter pricing and, 4.4(e)
Morton Salt, 4.5(f)
Motion Picture Patents, 4.5(c)
Patent Act and, 4.5(i), (k)
product compatibility and, 4.4(h)
quality assurance and, 4.4(h)
reasons for, 4.4(b)–4.4(j)
Special Equipment, 4.4(h)
supplying components, 4.4(a)
transaction costs and, 4.4(i)

U

Uncertainty. *See* Risk.
Unit sales, as royalty base, 1.7(e)
Use of patented machine, royalty payments and, 3.7
USM rule, royalty payments and, 2.7(b), 3.6(b)

V

Value
   of intellectual property rights, 1.4, 1.5, 1.8
   of license, 1.4, 1.5, 1.8
Vertical integration
   exploitation of intellectual property rights by, 1.6, 4.4
   licensing and, 1.6, 4.4
   supply complementary products and, 4.4(a), (f)–(j)
   supply protected product, 4.4(b)–(g), (j)

W

Windsurfing rule, 2.7(b)

Z

Zenith rule, royalty payments and, 3.4(a), 3.4(d)